# RESEARCH IN BEHAVIOR MODIFICATION

# Contributors

ALBERT BANDURA, Department of Psychology, Stanford University

SIDNEY W. BIJOU, Developmental Psychology Laboratory, University of Washington

KENNETH MARK COLBY, Department of Computer Science, Stanford University

JUDITH E. COWAN, Biometrics Research, New York State Department of Mental Hygiene and Columbia University

RICHARD S. FELDMAN, Biometrics Research, New York State Department of Mental Hygiene and Columbia University

CHARLES B. FERSTER, Institute for Behavioral Research, Silver Spring, Maryland

ISRAEL GOLDIAMOND, Institute for Behavioral Research, Silver Spring, Maryland

ALBERT H. HASTORF, Department of Psychology, Stanford University

FREDERICK H. KANFER, Department of Medical Psychology, University of Oregon Medical School

LEONARD KRASNER, Department of Psychology, State University of New York at Stony Brook

JOSEPH D. MATARAZZO, Department of Medical Psychology, University of Oregon Medical School

GERALD PATTERSON, Department of Psychology, University of Oregon

KURT SALZINGER, Biometrics Research, New York State Department of Mental Hygiene and Polytechnic Institute of Brooklyn

SUZANNE SALZINGER, Biometrics Research, New York State Department of Mental Hygiene

THEODORE R. SARBIN, Department of Psychology, University of California, Berkeley

IRWIN G. SARASON, Department of Psychology, University of Washington

GEORGE SASLOW, Department of Psychiatry, University of Oregon Medical School

ARTHUR W. STAATS, Department of Educational Psychology, University of Wisconsin

LEONARD P. ULLMANN, Department of Psychology, University of Illinois

ARTHUR N. WIENS, Department of Medical Psychology, University of Oregon Medical School

# RESEARCH IN BEHAVIOR MODIFICATION

## New Developments and Implications

*Edited and Introduced by*

LEONARD KRASNER
State University of New York at Stony Brook

LEONARD P. ULLMANN
University of Illinois

HOLT, RINEHART AND WINSTON,

New York    Chicago    San Francisco    Toronto    London

03-050220-9
Copyright © 1965 by Holt, Rinehart and Winston, Inc.
All rights reserved
Library of Congress Catalog Card Number: 65-12804

Printed in the United States of America

90123   22   9876

THIS book grew out of a series of research lectures given within the context of the psychology training program at the VA Hospital, Palo Alto, California. The three major interests of the contributors to this volume, research, training, and social application, were represented in the very inception and locale of the presentations. The purpose of the series was to bring together the current experimental work on behavior modification which underlies newer clinical techniques. We called upon the experts who were in large measure responsible for these advances. To facilitate the integration necessary for the successful completion of this kind of undertaking, we used a number of subsidiary techniques. The first involved the selection of the authors themselves, all of whom had made major research contributions and were familiar with and had used each other's work. Second, all were interested in the social implications of their work and had made various far-ranging applications in clinical settings. In addition, wherever possible, the authors attended each other's presentations, and when they couldn't, listened to tape recordings or read transcripts of prior lectures. All participants were encouraged to discuss the implications of their work with a freedom not always possible in technical journals. Finally, in the introductions to each of the papers, we made use of the question and discussion periods which followed each presentation, and tried to point out the relationships among the papers and other relevant research and clinical literature.

Many people made this book possible. We wish to thank the individual contributors for their cooperation in all the obsessive and seemingly endless tasks involved in bringing this work to completion. The reader will note that many of the authors mention the financial support of various granting agencies. In addition, we wish to acknowledge our debt to Public Health Research Grant M-6191 from the National Institute of Mental Health for general support of our research program and for assistance in the various stages which led to the present volume. Completion of this book was greatly facilitated by the senior editor's tenure as USPHS Visiting Scholar at Educational Testing Service, Princeton, New Jersey. We also wish to thank Dr. Thomas W. Kennelly, Direc-

tor, Psychology Services, VA Hospital, Palo Alto, for his helpful cooperation. Miss Elizabeth Rae Larson, Dr. David Pomeranz, Mrs. Alice Koenig,
Mrs. Dorothy Levit, Mrs. Marguerite Sommers, and Mrs. Marian Barry
were of great assistance in the preparation of the manuscript. Throughout this effort we have been motivated by Miriam, Wendy, David,
Charles, and Stefanie Krasner, and by Rina, Michael, and Nancy Ullmann.

L.K.

L.P.U.

*Princeton, New Jersey*
*Urbana, Illinois*
**February 1965**

# CONTENTS

# RESEARCH IN BEHAVIOR MODIFICATION

# 1

## An Introduction to Research in
## Behavior Modification

THERE have been many attempts to *translate* clinical phenomena into terminology acceptable to experimental psychologists (Dollard & Miller, 1950; Shoben, 1949), but the recent procedures that have led to effective behavior modification are *direct* applications of laboratory data and principles (Wolpe, 1954, 1958; Eysenck, 1959, 1960; Franks, 1964; Ullmann & Krasner, 1965). The present volume brings together a series of papers and viewpoints central to this trend. The principles and technology of behavior modification were first developed and validated in a laboratory setting and then applied to the clinical situation. The implications arising from these developments will be discussed in detail in this introductory chapter.

### ORGANIZATION OF THIS VOLUME

First, however, we wish to point out the organization of this volume. This book is neither a random collection of papers nor an attempt to deal with the entire range of laboratory work underlying clinical psychology. Bachrach (1962) and Eysenck (1960) have furnished collections of material covering a wide range of experimental and empirical approaches to the total field. While psychological treatment of clinical problems is a matter of social influence, it is but one small aspect of such influence. Other books, by Biderman and Zimmer (1961), Berg and Bass (1961), Frank (1961), and Krasner and Ullmann (in press), present material that deal with the total field of behavior influence. The present volume focuses on the clinical segment of this general area and aims to demonstrate the uniformities involved in the application of social reinforcement concepts to increasingly complex behavior.

This area is germane and useful to the practicing clinical psychologist. If a single label had to be given to this subject it would be *behavior modification*. We have found it convenient to use the term *behavior influence* as the generic term to include various investigations of the ways in which human behavior is modified, changed, or influenced. It includes research on operant conditioning, psychotherapy, placebo, attitude change, hypnosis, sensory deprivation, brainwashing, drugs, modeling, and education. We conceive of a broad psychology of behavior influence that concerns itself with the basic variables determining the alteration of human behavior in both laboratory and "real life" situations. On the other hand, the term *behavior modification* refers to a very specific type of *behavior influence*. The best description of behavior modification is given by Watson (1962): "In a broader sense, the topic of behavior modification is related to the whole field of learning. Studies of behavior modification are studies of learning, with a particular intent—*the clinical goal of treatment*." Within this category Watson places such situations as structured interviews, verbal conditioning, experimental neuroses, and patient-doctor relationships. Thus, techniques and research that are relevant for the treatment of deviant behavior are included under *behavior modification*. Our goal as editors is to provide a framework within which each of the chapters makes its contribution in the area of the author's particular competence.

The chapters progress from those dealing with restricted units of behavior to those involving larger units of behavior. Ferster's chapter offers a general orientation relevant to the subsequent presentations. While the next three chapters (Staats, Bijou, Salzinger *et al.*) also provide theoretical material, they illustrate the application of these approaches to research with children in the development of the very basic skills necessary for an eventual wide range of social competence. Goldiamond's chapter reviews a clinical-research program, dealing with verbal fluency, based on the principles presented by the previous authors. Patterson's chapter is pivotal because it introduces verbal conditioning and investigates the dispenser of the reinforcement. The manipulation of single variables in clinical situations is exemplified by Matarazzo *et al's* description of their work on the interview. Further investigation of the reinforcing variables in an interview situation is provided by Krasner, who contrasts verbal conditioning and psychotherapeutic interviewing. Sarason provides further data on the role of the interviewer-therapist-reinforcer by his research on verbal conditioning. Kanfer extends the investigation of social influence techniques to vicarious reinforcement, and Hastorf introduces the use of *groups* of subjects and intragroup reinforcement. Saslow demonstrates behavior modification techniques in an institutional setting. The next three chapters (Colby, Bandura, and Sarbin) illustrate the application of the social reinforcement viewpoint to highly complex human behavior. These chapters, dealing with computers, modeling, and hypnosis, demonstrate the breadth of topics that may be subsumed under the present approach. A summary chapter reviews the fifteen presentations and brings together their implications for clinical psychology. Both the individual introductions and the over-all summary mention investigators who might well have contributed to this volume, but who, for lack of space and other circumstances, have not. Investigators such as Orne, Barber, Lindsley, Ayllon, Eysenck, Rosenthal, Franks, Goldstein, Wolpe, and Frank have made important and relevant contributions that will be referred to in specific chapter introductions.

## AREAS OF AGREEMENT

There are a number of basic common themes running through the volume that define the subject matter of this book and unify the material to be presented. Although all the contributors might not be in complete agreement on all points, some general principles characterize the presentations.

A first commonality is the role identification of the investigators themselves. While all of them are interested in basic research they see socially important applications for their work. They conceive of themselves as behavioral scientists investigating the processes of changing human behavior.

Second, they investigate clinical phenomena through operationally defined and experimentally manipulated variables.

Third, all the investigators emphasize the effect of environmental stimulation in directing the individual's behavior. They virtually eliminate hypothetical concepts such as the unconscious, ego, and internal dynamics. For purposes of their present researches, even such concepts as heredity and maturation are de-emphasized.

A fourth commonality is the approach to maladaptive behavior through a psychological rather than a medical model. Behavior modification deals directly with behavior rather than with "underlying" or disease factors that "cause" symptoms. This point is further discussed in the next chapter.

The psychological model used is that of social reinforcement. In the present volume the term *social reinforcement* is used to emphasize the fact that other human beings are a source of meaningful stimuli that alter, direct, or maintain the individual's behavior.

One of the dimensions of any investigation is the range of material that may be included within its framework. Within behavior modification we are presenting research reports and viewpoints related to a wide variety of areas. In addition to a broad view of the social influence process itself, we can cover specific topics, such as operant conditioning, psychotherapy, interview transactions, leadership and group behavior, man-machine relationships, role-playing, modeling, and institutional behavior. The range of clinical applications includes speech and reading difficulties, mental deficiency, schizophrenia, hypnosis, and ward behavior. While specific tactics or techniques vary, the strategy or general principles remain constant throughout the presentations.

## BEHAVIOR MODIFICATION

Behavior modification deals with changing human behavior. This is the common purpose of all forms of psychotherapy. Any technique that provides "leverage" should be welcomed by the clinician. The clinician's day-to-day practice should be based on laboratory-tested procedures, and he should readily incorporate new techniques as they are developed. In addition to the methods that are explicitly discussed in this book, such as modeling, vicarious reinforcement, use of peer groups, and programing of parents, we will also refer to other techniques such as placebos and programed instruction. These techniques offer great promise as new tools for the clinician.

## LABORATORY AND CLINIC ROLES

While our emphasis has been on the contributions of the laboratory to the clinic, it is equally important to note that the clinic provides many opportunities for the experimental psychologist. First, there is the personal satisfaction to be derived from dealing with socially meaningful problems. Second, the clinic represents an opportunity for obtaining an increased range of criteria to test the effectiveness of experimental procedures. Third, individuals seeking help or hospitalized because of maladaptive behavior permit experimental analysis over relatively long periods of time in a wide range of social situations in which considerable environmental control can be obtained. Behavior modification in the clinic is a procedure that society sanctions and that is "real" and involves the individual in a way that an "experiment" does not. In short, the clinic permits the psychologist to make far greater use of his training as a research investigator and influencer of behavior. Finally, if the application of principles is found to be effective in the clinical setting, the strength of a general theory is vastly increased. Just as learning principles are best validated when replicated with different species, so replication with different types of maladaptive behavior offers increased and vital support for a particular theory.

Of special importance in the merging of experimental and clinical research is the emphasis on the individual. Clinicians have repeatedly insisted that their major focus is on the individual patient and his idiosyncratic behavior. Experimental investigators such as Bijou, Goldiamond, and Ferster center attention on the individual organism and, as Staats points out, may use own-control procedures in very sophisticated designs.

As the title of this volume indicates, we are presenting theoretical viewpoints and laboratory findings dealing with the clinician's major problem—how to effect socially useful changes in individual behavior. We have defined behavior modification and noted certain commonalities. Finally, we have pointed out the potential benefits of this work to both clinicians and research workers.

# 2

## Classification of Behavioral Pathology
### CHARLES B. FERSTER

Ferster's "Classification of Behavioral Pathology" has been chosen as the introductory chapter for a number of reasons. In many ways, Ferster's own progression as a psychologist has been prototypical of the development of the social reinforcement viewpoint illustrated throughout this volume. Ferster has moved from a close association with Skinner (Ferster & Skinner, 1957) and basic research on operant conditioning with infrahumans to work with autistic children (Ferster & DeMyer, 1961, 1962) and the development of self-control in eating problems (Ferster, Nurnberger, & Levitt, 1962). In this chapter Ferster delineates an approach to abnormal behavior that is expressed and elaborated by many of the authors who follow.

Ferster's formulation of behavior pathology is markedly different from the typical medical model that currently dominates American abnormal psychology (for example, Hutt & Gibby, 1957, pp. 78-79; Cameron, 1963, p. 452; Coleman, 1964, p. 56). Ferster argues that environmental stimuli, rather than underlying "illness" or intrapsychic conflict, determine and maintain what is labeled as deviant, maladaptive, inappropriate, disadvantageous, or disruptive behavior. The "abnormality" is not a problem within the individual that must be rationalized by recourse to concepts such as repression, displacement, or symbolization, but rather is the result of the person's interaction with his social environment and represents an understandable outcome of the individual's history of reinforcement.

A continuing difficulty is the development of a definition of adjustive behavior or "mental health." Scott (1958) reviewed the various attempts to arrive at an operational definition of mental health. Such a definition is a necessary first step for any scientific attack on the problem. Scott pointed out the limitations of each approach proposed up to the time of his review and the lack of consistency among these approaches. If, however, we note (as did Szasz, 1961b) the sociological foundations of concepts of mental illness, and if we follow Ferster's reasoning, we see that much of this effort presupposes a disease—health dichotomy which in fact may not exist. Ferster postulates that maladjustive behavior is the result of differential reinforcement. The society in which an individual lives determines both the content of behavior and the persons who "shape" the subject's behavior. Maladjustive behavior may be defined in terms of the behavior that important people in the individual's environment (his social reinforcers) wish to increase, decrease, or change. The dichotomy of "sick" and "healthy" behavior is avoided, and thus makes possible the kinds of researches described in this book which study the mutually reinforcing behavior of influencer and influencee. This conceptual step permits the utilization of the experimental data on behavior influence collected during the last decade (for example, Kanfer, Sarason, Hastorf, Krasner) and bears fruit in the treatment of autistic children (Bijou), retardates (Bijou, Salzinger et al.), speech difficulties (Goldiamond), reading (Staats), child problems (Patterson), and adult social difficulties (Saslow), within a broader range of behavior problems (Ullmann & Krasner, 1965).

In order to appreciate fully the viewpoints expressed by Ferster and the applications described in later chapters, particularly in those by Bijou, Patterson, Staats, and Salzinger et al., we wish to cite briefly Ferster's work with autistic children. The following excerpt from Ferster and DeMyer introduces their approach and results.

A prominent feature of the autistic child's repertoire is a narrow range of activity and a small amount of behavior controlled by its effect on the environment. Whatever the causes or antecedent conditions of the narrow range of the autistic child's activities, it might be possible to deal with them experimentally by building a new behavioral repertoire beginning with activities already in the child's repertoire, finding a method of sustaining them, and then gradually widening their range. . . . The general framework of the experiment is that of operant reinforcement (Ferster, 1958; Skinner, 1953). The focus of the experimental method is on the consequence of the behavior as the factor which maintains it. Reinforcement is the major concept and refers to a technique for increasing the frequency of an activity by following it with a special consequence. The organism acts and the subsequent frequency of this activity increases because of the past effect on the environment. In this experiment simple performances of the autistic children are experimentally developed and maintained because of the specific effects they have on the child's environment. As a result, the behavior being studied is, at least potentially, under close and manipulative control by the experimenter. These methods have been in wide use in the study of animal behavior, where they have provided a behavioral technology in respect to phylogenetically general behavioral processes. Experiments using the technique of operant reinforcement with normal and feebleminded and psychotic children have already demonstrated the feasibility of the technical application and the generality of some behavioral processes (Azrin & Lindsley, 1956; Bijou, 1958a, 1958b; Lindsley, 1954; Long, Hammack, May, & Campbell, 1958). In general, the paradigm of these experiments has been to select a simple response such as pressing an electrical switch (key) and sustaining it by arranging some consequence relevant to the particular organism's repertoire and its current level of deprivation. The reinforcers used have included trinkets with nursery school children (Bijou); pennies with grade school children (Azrin); and candy with feebleminded and psychotic children (Lindsley, Azrin). In many of these experiments, the authors report large satiation effects, inability to sustain the performance of every subject, necessity of using brief experimental sessions and frequently weak performances, all presumably arising from a reinforcer that is not sufficiently durable. (Ferster & DeMyer, 1962, pp. 89-90)

The early results of this experiment, using the techniques of operant reinforcement to sustain and widen the repertoire of autistic children, show that it is possible to bring the behavior of these children under the close control of an artificial environment by means of a conditioned reinforcer possibly generalized. After sustaining simple performances it was possible to widen the behavioral patterns of the child by the normal processes by which behavior is sustained and altered in normal humans and in other species. While the behavioral repertoires developed in these children are still not nearly as complex as those involved in a normal social repertoire, they indicate at least the existence of normal processes at a very basic level. To date the results of these techniques do not suggest any basic deficit except in the rate at which these children acquire new types of behavioral control. Failures to develop normal performances as we get to more complex procedures will be difficult to interpret, however, because such failures might be due either to a basic deficit or to our inadequate development of behavioral techniques for affecting the children. It is difficult to equate the complexity of the various procedures to which the children are exposed, however.

We do not consider these techniques as attempts at rehabilitation but rather as experimental analyses of the actual and potential repertoires of these children. Perhaps these analyses can serve as guides for attempts to use the same processes of developing behavior in social situations where the performances sustained and altered would be activities in respect to other persons (social) and where the important consequences sustaining the activities would be the social effects of these performances. If it proves possible to develop and widen behavioral repertoires significantly in the experimental room, then this would seem to indicate the possibility that the same potential for behavioral change would exist in the social milieu if the proper conditions could be generated. In the same vein, systematic deficits in particular areas may indicate deficient areas of control which may be of use in determining techniques for handling these children. (Ferster & DeMyer, 1962, pp. 97-98)

Hingtgen, Sanders, and DeMyer (1965) reported a successful extension of this technique with autistic children in two-person situations. Bijou (Chapter 4) summarizes still another instance of this approach.

In a later paper on the "Control of Eating" (Ferster et al., 1962) Ferster opened another important area to behavior modification. This paper described a pilot program with a group of overweight women. It reported the development of specific techniques for weight control based on behavioral principles. The authors detailed the application of elementary principles of reinforcement theory to the analysis of the behavior of the human eater. Self-control in eating behavior was defined as performances that would lower the disposition to emit the behavior to be controlled. This involved the manipulation of the conditions likely to elicit the target behavior. The analysis and development of self-control in eating involves four steps: (a) Determination of the variables that influence eating. (b) Determining how these variables can be manipulated. (c) Identifying the unwanted effects of overeating. (d) Arranging a method of developing required self-control.

This program translates into specific usable suggestions a functional analysis of behavior based on the general principles of reinforcement theory. The advantages to the individual of such a program is the demonstration that he can control his own environment by the procedures outlined for him. In effect, this is self-programing based on the concept that all behavior is affected by the consequences of reacting to stimuli, and once the person has mastered these principles he can utilize them in arranging his own stimulus environment.

Similarly, Mertens (1964a, 1964b) used this stimulus-response analysis of self-control to develop a program for the control of alcoholic behavior. In his manuals, Mertens explained in simple terms for the alcoholic, as Ferster did for the overeater, the technical aspects of behavior modification developed in the laboratory and labeled as shaping, chaining, deprivation-satiation, incompatible responses, aversive control, and extinction. Sulzer (1965) and Narrol (1963) also have used this technique of patient self-programing.

Given this background, it becomes clear why Ferster is so suitable a choice to lead off this volume on behavior modification.

L.K.-L.P.U.

To CLASSIFY BEHAVIOR, WE must take into account both static and dynamic factors or, in other terms, a topographic and functional analysis. A static or topographic analysis essentially describes what occurred, as in a movie or speech record. Such a record may be as objective and as reproducible as any other datum in biology. It lacks, however, the functional or dynamic relation of the behavior to the controlling environment. The simple identification of the performance, as it may be recorded, without references to its antecedent conditions or current relations to the environment, omits much important information. Whether a man who moves and acts slowly is "depressed" or merely moving slowly is not easily or reliably determined by observing his behavior alone. The relation of his behavior to events in the past or present environment is a critical element in the description. Very strong behavior can be emitted at a low rate if its successful outcome depends on such a low rate. A complete moving picture record of "a man running down a corridor" provides enough data for only a minimal classification of the behavior. The man could be running because someone is chasing him. The man could be running because the train will leave in ten minutes from a distant station. The man could be running because he has just won a sweepstake prize. All these behaviors are closely similar to each other topographically, yet they are examples of extremely diverse kinds of behavioral control. In the first instance it may be termed avoidance behavior because it increases the distance from an aversive stimulus. We could describe the second as a limited-hold schedule of reinforcement because the fixed schedule of departure of the train increases the rate of running. In the third example, the sweepstake winner is running because of an emotional state. A child's crying is an example of almost identical topographical patterns under even more diverse behavioral control. Crying could occur as a reflex effect of a loud noise, a temperature extreme, or food deprivation; or it could result from a parental reaction providing consequences to the child, which, in turn, increase the frequency of the crying. The relation of the child's cry to the controlling environment is very different in the two cases. If the crying is a reflex, caused by a low temperature or food deprivation, the crying may be controlled by raising the temperature or by feeding the child. If the crying occurs because of the parental reaction, then its control is through changes in the parental reaction to the child. In the case of operant crying, the schedules of reinforcement by the parent, the stimuli present whenever the child and parent interact, and the consequences supplied by the parent will all profoundly determine the frequency, magnitude, and form of the child's cry.

We ordinarily describe an operant response by noting its form. We say that the child raised its arm, or the rat pressed a bar. Yet, the description of the behavior lies in large part in the reinforcing agency that generates it. In the typical lever-pressing experiment, we do not reinforce an exact form of bar-pressing. Rather, we arrange an electromechanical environment that reacts differentially to different forms of behavior. Such an environment generates a class of performances having the common property of activating the food-dispensing mechanism. It is not necessary to teach the rat step by step to raise the forefeet to 2 cm. over the bar, lower the feet while contact is made with the bar, grasp the bar, and then press with a force of 15 grams. All the essential properties of the behavior are already determined by the electromechanical properties of the system.

The essential form of this argument was made by Skinner (1938) in his discussion of the generic nature of the stimulus and response in *The Behavior of Organisms*. The parental reaction to the child's crying similarly determines the actual form of the child's crying. Each parent generates crying behavior in her child with the exact topographic features that affect her most adversely, because the likelihood of the parent terminating the crying by providing a reinforcing consequence is higher for the forms of crying that are most aversive. The form of the child's crying will depend upon the reactivity of the parent, just as the form of the rat's bar-pressing response was determined by the electromagnetic properties of the lever. In both cases, we have described a major part of the behavior when we have described the related part of the environment that changes differentially only when the required form of behavior occurs.

Such a functional analysis of behavior is in contrast to the traditional inner causes we speak of in casual descriptions of behavior; when we say that the rat presses a bar because he has a need for food or because he wants food; or when we say the child cries because it needs its parent. What we actually observe is that the delivery of food or the appearance of the parent will increase the frequency of the behaviors they follow. The specific characteristics of the environment (the electromagnetic system for the rat and the parent for the child) therefore determine the actual form of the behavior reinforced. Such a functional analysis of behavior has the advantage that it specifies the causes of behavior in the form of explicit environmental events that can be objectively identified and that are potentially manipulable. Given an individual for whom money, social approval, control of other individuals, and various forms of social contact are reinforcing events, the environment available to this individual has a vast potential for selectively reinforcing those performances that would be effective in producing the reinforcing consequences.

We may describe a man's behavior in the normal ecology by a functional analysis of the type described. An individual's behavior may alter the physical and social environment in many ways, but only certain kinds of changes will successfully maintain the frequency of critical kinds of behavior. The milieu may be described as a set of those practices that are contingencies applied to particular forms of behavior. Verbal behavior, mores and morals, laws and customs are best considered as a set of contingencies applied by the various members of the community to the relevant performances of the individual. Conversely, if the performances of the individual are considered as being caused by the way they change the environment, the contingencies of reinforcement applied by the culture actually determine the practices of the individuals. The customary behaviors of an individual occur because of consistent reinforcement and nonreinforcement by the community. For example, some of the reasons for the custom of wearing shoes or a tie may be found when we examine what happens when we do not wear them. Wearing a tie and coat is so strongly established that we do not ordinarily consider what might happen if a stockbroker, for example, went to his office without them. The English language is similarly a set of customs maintained by explicit contingencies applied by a community of individuals, all of whom will react only to particular stimuli. Skinner has already presented the outlines of such an analysis of "culture" in Science and Human Be-

*havior* (1953) for the behavioral practices involved in religion, government, law, economics, and psychotherapy, and for verbal behavior in general, in *Verbal Behavior* (1957).

Just as the potential reactivity of the lever and the parent defined the kind of behavior that might be generated in the rat and the child in the previous examples, the milieu specifies the behaviors potentially available to an individual in contact with it. An individual's environment might be thought of as an infinite variety of response keys, all of which are set to produce a reinforcer or avoid an aversive stimulus if—and only if—the individual's repertoire contains the required behavioral items. A low disposition to read in a college teacher and a salesman represent very different relationship to their respective milieus, but a low frequency of reading in the college teacher may be a result of an identical relationship to his environment as a low disposition to tell funny stories or persuade customers bears to the salesman's environment. We may compare the repertoires of two individuals from different cultures both by enumerating the practices (contingencies) that define the potential behavior in a culture; and by comparing the existing repertoires of an individual with those performances that can be potentially supported by the environment. From the point of view of a functional analysis of behavior, the enumeration of the practices of the milieu is essentially an anthropological investigation. After the actual practices of the environment have been established, it becomes possible to classify an individual's behavioral repertoire by comparing it with the behavioral potential of the milieu.

The use of the milieu as a standard of reference provides a classification system that is cross-culturally general, because it does not refer to specific items of behavior or a specific environmental practice. Two entirely different repertoires from two entirely different cultures might, for example, have in common that all the performances in the repertoires are maintained by positive reinforcement, and that the individual repertoires are the maximum that could be maintained by such environments. Conversely, various items of behavior may be missing from a repertoire, even though the environment is potentially capable of supporting them. For example, a given performance might be absent because of the absence of a history of experiences that were necessary in order to approximate a complex form by slow stages; or because the particular schedule of reinforcement currently maintaining the performance reduced the disposition to engage in the performance. Such an evaluation of the discrepancy between the actual repertoire of an individual and the potential behavior supported by the individual's milieu does not depend upon the particular performance that is evaluated. Two very different performances might be absent from a repertoire for the same reason, or a single performance might be absent from the repertoire of the individuals for different reasons.

The basic processes by which behavior is strengthened, weakened, maintained, extinguished, put under stimulus control, and so forth, can provide a framework for specifying the relation between the individual's existing repertoire and the milieu potentially available to him.

A performance can occur because it produces some environmental change that in turn makes possible some further behavior (positive reinforcement), or it may occur because it postpones or allows escape from some event (negative reinforcement). The relative proportions of a repertoire maintained by positive reinforcers and by aversive stimuli are important dimensions for categorizing the repertoire because the positive reinforcers are probably ultimately responsible for maintaining an individual's behavior. The portion of an individual's repertoire maintained by avoidance and escape constitutes an increase in the intermittency of positive reinforcement. It is likely that aversive stimuli maintain behavior so long as the avoidance of the aversive stimuli makes possible the continuation of positive reinforcement. With greater proportions of the repertoire engaged in postponing and avoiding aversive stimuli, the over-all ratio of positive reinforcement gained to behavior emitted gets small, and it is problematical whether a repertoire consisting entirely of escape and avoidance behavior can be maintained.

The major process responsible for the development of the progressively more complex forms of behavior that emerge during the growth and development of an individual is the shaping of behavior by reinforcement of successive approximations of a final complex repertoire. This shaping of behavior implies a complex history of reinforcement in which the individual's behavior is maintained by conditions of reinforcement that make contact with his existing repertoire, and by a gradual shift to more and more complex forms. The growth and development of the child is a specification of such a shaping procedure by which its immediate environment reinforces its existing behavior and gradually shifts the contingencies of reinforcement toward more complex forms as the child grows older. The history of reinforcement conditions required for the successive approximation of the complex performances needed to deal with the adult milieu is a potential source of discrepancy between the behavior of the adult and the reinforcing practices of the adult milieu. Some of the discrepancies between the current behavior of an individual and the potential reinforcers in the environment may be due simply to the absence of a history of reinforcement that would have developed the required performances. Slack (1960), for example, observed that many delinquents do not know how to use money. They cannot save it or find services or goods that in turn would support effective behavior and maintain the reinforcing effects of the money. If money is to maintain the occupational behavior of the adolescent, it must be an effective reinforcer because of the behavior it in turn makes possible. An individual who does not have an effective repertoire with money will be insensitive to one of the major reinforcers of the community.

The development of self-control is another example of a complex behavioral development that requires very specific histories of reinforcement contingencies and a particular order of magnitudes of time and behavior for its initial development. The behaviors that are required before an individual can manipulate his own behavior so as not to spend money as soon as he receives it, but to retain it to avoid later aversive consequences, form a complex repertoire that can be generated only under a specified range of conditions. Reinforcers that require long chains of responses will maintain the required behavior only if very special developmental histories are present. The technical analysis of the development of these long chains of behavior reveals that they must be established progressively. The individual's behavior must first be maintained on short chains, and the order of magnitudes must be very gradually increased as the individual's behavior is well sustained at each value. The accidents of the environment may provide histories of reinforcement by which the contingencies of reinforcement in the milieu potentially available to the individual may not make contact with his available repertoire.

The control of behavior by the environment because of the differential reinforcement of a response on a specific occasion and its nonreinforcement on other occasions specifies another type of behavioral control that may potentially weaken the behavior of an individual and introduce a discrepancy between his current repertoire and the reinforcing practices of the milieu. The process is seen most clearly in a pigeon that pecks differentially at a red and green light, because pecking produces food when the light is green and goes unreinforced when the light is red. The process is one of essentially weakening the bird's behavior by extinction on all occasions except during the presentation of the green light. With such an animal, it becomes possible to weaken the repertoire instantly simply by changing the color from green to red. Similarly, many aspects of human behavior are under narrow control of particular aspects of the environment. An extreme case is the classical description of the psychotic depression that results from the death of one of two spinster sisters who have lived together in complete seclusion. The death of the sister is functionally analogous to changing the color of the light from green to red, virtually denuding her repertoire of behavior because of the very narrow control of the behavior of one sister by the other. Child-rearing practices are frequently a balance between the necessity of restricting the child's behavior by permitting behavior only on certain occasions, and the over-all effect of weakening the child's behavior, as too much behavior goes nonreinforced because of the large number of restrictions. It is paradoxical that the parent who is most attentive to the child and deals with him constantly may be the one who most seriously weakens the behavior of the child. It is quite possible that some cases of childhood schizophrenia stem from parental practices specifying so carefully the conditions under which the child may behave that a sufficiently large amount of behavior goes unreinforced for the over-all ability of the child to deal with environments other than the specific parental one to be seriously impaired.

## CLASSIFICATION OF AVERSIVE STIMULI

A description of an individual's repertoire would include a classification of the kinds of aversive stimuli controlling his behavior and the relation of the aversive stimuli to his positively reinforced repertoire. The aversive qualities of stimuli may be derived from their relations to the positively reinforced repertoire or from their reinforcing phylogenetic effects, as with loud sounds, extremes of temperature, or physical insult to the body, such as physical trauma or infection. The nociceptive stimuli may be classified as those so closely tied to the characteristics of the physical environment that their reinforcement is inevitable, such as withdrawing the hand from a hot surface, or avoiding a fall from a high place or bumping into an object while walking. Or these aversive stimuli may be applied by another person, as in corporal punishment, in which the aversive stimulus occurs not as a result of the physical environment, but is related to behavioral processes in other individuals who apply the aversive stimulus. Aversive stimuli, such as criticism, fines, ostracism, incarceration, or anger, possess aversive properties because they are the occasions upon which there is a discontinuation of normally positively reinforced behavior. In practice, it is difficult to differentiate functionally between direct aversive stimuli (nociceptive stimuli) applied by persons and the withdrawal of positive reinforcement, because both may occur simultaneously. For example, a parent who spanks a child is also less likely at this time to apply positive reinforcement. In most cases it is difficult to determine how much of the effects of the spanking come from the physical trauma and how much from the withdrawal of positive reinforcement. Conversely, even corporal punishment may serve as a positive reinforcer, if a spanking becomes an occasion upon which other behaviors are reinforced. Such a state of affairs would occur when a parent gives a child gifts *only* after a spanking, to escape the guilt countercontrol by the child. As in almost every case, the classification of the aversive stimulus depends upon a functional analysis of the contingencies associated with it, rather than upon a topographic description.

With stimuli that are aversive because they are the occasion upon which the reinforcement of other behaviors may be discontinued or reduced, a description is closely tied to a description of the positive repertoire in general and, in particular, the specific behaviors that are interfered with. For example, the functional significance of a change in facial expression from a smile to a frown depends upon the practices of the smiler and the frowner. In most parts of the American culture, frowning is a potentially aversive event because it is associated with a low probability of reinforcement upon that occasion, and an evaluaton of the functional significance of a frown will largely depend upon an enumeration of those behaviors whose reinforcement is discontinued upon the occasion of a frown. The correlation is by no means perfect, however, as it is with spanking. A particular individual's "bark" may be "worse than his bite," so that a frown may have no aversive consequences, except insofar as there is generalization from similar individuals who would be disposed to punish when frowning. It is possible to consider an entire culture in which the contingencies associated with frowning and smiling were completely reversed. Those individuals who are disposed to punish may smile because they, in general, attenuate the effect of their punishment on those individuals who are disposed to reinforce frowning. A gambling situation is likely to have this state of affairs, with the loser frowning as he gives the money to the winner. An adviser engaging in behavior for the benefit of an advisee might frown as he attempts to solve a difficult problem.

Finally, a stimulus that is aversive because of its correlation with loss of positive reinforcement may be classified in terms of the amount of positively reinforced behavior that is discontinued, as well as the relative proportion of the repertoire that is interfered with as a result of the aversive control. Criticism of speech is an aversive event to the extent that it implies that the listener will not attend to speech of the form criticized. In many cases, such criticism will have minor consequences, but for the public speaker or actor, such criticism might represent the withdrawal of reinforcers maintaining a major part of the repertoire.

The stimuli that characteristically precede the occurrence of an aversive stimulus may often have a larger order of magnitude of effect than the aversive stimulus itself in disrupting or otherwise weakening behavior that would normally occur because of its positive reinforcement in the milieu. The preaversive stimulus is arbitrary, and its relation to the aversive stimulus determines its effect on the ongoing behavior. The preaversive stimuli may be in the external environment as, for example, an audience, a dentist's office, a group of people at a formal party, which may serve as preaversive stimuli because these are the *occasions* that may precede criticism, pain, or a loss of further invitations. Or the preaversive stimuli may be in the indivdual's own behavor, as when aversive consequences follow from particular kinds of behaviors, and the incipient tendencies to engage in these behaviors constitute an *event* preceding an aversive stimulus. In both cases, the process may be responsible for a discrepancy between the existing behavior repertoire of the individual and the behavior repertoire the milieu can potentially support. Since suppression of ongoing behavior by a preaversive stimulus implies a repertoire that is concurrently supported by positive reinforcement, its suppression or disturbance by the preaversive stimulus may be as much a function of its inadequate maintenance by positive reinforcement as of its interruption by the preaversive stimulus. In evaluating the significance of behaviors missing from a repertoire, it is necessary to take into account simultaneously the general strength of the behavior that is a result of the reinforcer maintaining it and the disruption of the behavior by the aversive stimulus. Easily suppressed behavior is probably weak to begin with. With well-maintained behavior, punishment needs to be virtually continuous for each instance of the behavior to be affected (Ferster, 1961; Azrin, Holz, & Hake, 1963). A case in point is the difficulty of suppressing speeding and other traffic violations.

The kinds of aversive stimuli that follow the disruption by a preaversive stimulus, and the particular operant repertoire that is disrupted, may differ from individual to individual and from culture to culture, but the discrepancies from the behavioral potential of the milieu may be very similar.

Preaversive stimuli may sometimes increase the rate of the ongoing operant repertoire, rather than suppress it, when the ongoing behavior is predominantly avoidance- and escape-responding. While the major result is superficially different in the two cases (an increased rate of responding in the presence of the preaversive stimulus in the case of the negatively reinforced ongoing repertoire), the major effect upon the total repertoire is similar. The high rate of the avoidance behavior pre-empts other behavior that might have been supported by positive reinforcement, just as the suppression or distortion of positively reinforced behavior prevents its reinforcement. The classification of the effects of preaversive stimuli, therefore, is based also on the nature of the reinforcers maintaining the ongoing repertoire.

While aversive stimuli in the environment normally lead to avoidance and escape behaviors since they reinforce any performances that terminate or avoid them, the most natural course of affairs is a low frequency of aversive stimuli affecting an individual's repertoire. Some aversive stimuli, however, are closely tied to particular performances which are maintained independently by positive reinforcement, and it is in these cases that the issue of punishment arises. A given performance may have two simultaneous consequences in the environment: a) it may lead to strong positive reinforcers, as, for example, the race-car driver racing for a large monetary prize, or the hungry child reaching for the cookie jar; b) the same performance may have an aversive consequence, as with the possibility of accident and death in racing as a result of the natural relation between the reinforced behavior and the physical environment, or the intervention by the parent, because the child's positively reinforced behavior has aversive consequences for the parent.

## CLASSIFICATION OF PUNISHMENT

The classification of the kinds of punishment that occur in an individual's repertoire will depend therefore both on classifying how the performance is maintained by positive or negative reinforcement, and the kind and degree of the aversive consequence produced by the behavior and its schedule of appearance.

In the case of punishment, the kinds of performances which are required before the aversive control will not occur are more complex than in escape and avoidance, where the only condition that the performance must meet is that it terminates or postpones the aversive stimulus. In the case of punishment, however, not only must the performance avoid or escape the aversive stimulus, but it also must retain enough of its essential form for it to continue to be maintained by the positive consequences in the environment. In the former case, the race-car driver simply quits racing, or the child leaves the room where the cookies are. If the operant consequences of racing or reaching for the cookies, however, have already generated a strong disposition to engage in these performances, then the only possibilities of avoiding aversive control is a shift in the form of behavior so that it is simultaneously effective in achieving the positive reinforcer and in avoiding the aversive stimulus. Thus, the race-car driver learns techniques of driving that allow great speed yet maximize safety. The child develops performances that are effective in obtaining cookies yet will not be punished. The very nature of some performances guarantee that their punishment is inevitable, as, for example, some parental environments where the cookie jar is kept under close surveillance and where the practices of punishment are very strictly adhered to. In these cases, the operant performance may occur from time to time, in spite of its aversive consequences. The effect of punishment will depend critically upon its schedule of application, the kind of aversive stimulus applied and its relation to the individual's repertoire, and the strength of the positively reinforced behavior. It is imposisble to determine in advance and without a detailed analysis of the exact performances whether the aversive consequences of an operant response will totally suppress it if there is no alternative response that can achieve its operant reinforcement without the aversive stimulus.

Even after an operant response is in an individual's repertoire and has been consistently maintained by the environment, its relation to dynamic variables, such as schedules of reinforcement, delay in reinforcement, or the length of response chains may have a large magnitude of effect on whether the behavior will continue.

## REINFORCEMENT

The schedule of reinforcement of a performance is one of the major factors that may seriously weaken behavior, even though it has been reliably occurring in the repertoire for a long time. Fixed-ratio schedules, in particular, where a relatively fixed amount of behavior is required per unit of effect upon the environment, may lead to very low dispositions to engage in the behavior, as, for example, the very low disposition of a novelist to begin another book, the student's disinclination to study immediately following an examination, or the procrastination of the scientist in beginning a new project. In all of these cases, the classification of the dynamic state of the repertoire cannot be made from observations of a limited sample of the behavior, but must depend upon measurements of the frequency of the behavior in relation to its schedule of reinforcement. Simply observing the frequency of some performance does not give us enough information to classify its functional relation to the environment, since a wide variety of factors such as those described above may weaken behavior by diverse processes. Apparently identical repertoires may be caused by very different relations to the controlling environment. Conversely, apparently identical performances may be maintained under very different conditions. For example, the repertoire of the salesman who has to make many calls, engage in persuasion, and entertain his customers can be compared with the salesman who simply makes calls and takes orders. While both salesmen may carry out their activities in a sustained way, with apparently no major discrepancies between the behavior and its controlling environment, the properties of the two repertoires will be extremely different. A larger amount of selling for each sale by the first individual will result in a repertoire more prone to disruption and more likely to disappear because of fixed-ratio strain than in the second individual, whose behavior is, by and large, reinforced continuously. On the other hand, the performance of the intermittently reinforced salesman will persist much longer in the face of a sudden change in environmental contingencies (extinction).

The history of conditions of reinforcement that are required to achieve stable performances on large values of fixed or variable ratio reinforcement is also a critical variable that will determine whether the performance is maintained. In general, a progressive change in schedules of reinforcement is required, in which the amount of behavior leading to the maintaining effect of the environment is increased slowly as the individual's behavior is maintained at lower values. Sudden changes in the environment, in which the amount of behavior required for reinforcement is suddenly increased may produce deficiencies that would not occur if the conditions of reinforcement were adjusted more gradually. A common example of the loss of behavior because of sudden shifts in conditions of reinforcement occurs in some classroom situations, particularly those in mathematics. Very frequently the student fails in mathematics when he encounters a problem whose solution requires sustained applications for a longer period of time than he has successfully applied in the past. The period of adolescence is a time when the community requires new amounts of behavior from the maturing individual, and the particular history by which the youngster is successful in affecting his environment with intermediate amounts of behavior may critically determine whether he can continue to maintain his performance in the new environment.

Factors such as delay in reinforcement will also determine whether or not a given environmental consequence will, in fact, maintain behavior. Money, for example, may be a reinforcer in many cultures, but the schedule of reinforcement may be such as to limit the maintenance of the behavior to very special conditions. Many primitive cultures, such as those in Africa, do not require behavior maintained by delays in reinforcement. For example, dock workers are paid by "the bag" for loading ships; these individuals perhaps could not sustain the performance if they were paid even daily. Even in the American culture, there are some social groups whose employment is limited to those situations in which they are paid daily.

Another class of behaviors, in some parts similar to chains of responses, occurs because it clarifies the environment rather than produces a reinforcer directly.

The experimental analogue of this process has been studied in animals by a procedure in which a pigeon is reinforced on some highly intermittent schedule. The bird can clarify the situation by pecking at another key, which has the effect of producing stimuli correlated with the reinforcement or nonreinforcement of a response on the food key. The behavior of reading a map is an example from the normal ecology. The basic repertoire being considered is moving to another location, and the behaviors of reading the map are maintained because they elicit stimuli that provide discriminative control such that the traveling behavior will have a higher likelihood of reinforcement. These observing behaviors have an important function in almost any milieu and are a basic part of the process by which the behavior of an individual comes under the control of the relevant discriminative stimuli in the environment. For example, moving one's head and eyes, rearranging the environment, and making charts, blueprints, and diagrams are ways of providing additional control of behavior. Included in this category are those behaviors that are essentially descriptions of behavior. There is, first of all, the behavior of the individual occurring as a function of the contingencies supplied by his milieu. Second, there is a verbal repertoire by which the individual may describe his own behavior in respect to the controlling variables in the milieu. The child-rearing practices of many cultures develop these performances very explicitly, as, for example, when the parent continually asks the child, "Where are you going?", "What did you do?", "Why did you do it?" The essential importance of these repertoires lies in their clarification of how the major reinforcers supporting the individual's repertoire are maintaining his behavior. Once the individual is under discriminative control of the critical variables of which his behavior is a function (that is, he can describe the variables controlling his behavior), he is in a position to alter his environment so as to bring his behavior under the control of one feature of the environment rather than another.

## SELF-CONTROL

Another class of behaviors that have indirect effects on the environment are those that alter the individual's own behavior in such a way as to make its reinforcement in the milieu more nearly optimal. Traditionally, the area of self-control is concerned with those behaviors that lead to some ultimate aversive consequence, such as obesity from overeating. The self-control behaviors are those performances that alter the relation between the individual's behavior and his controlling environment, so as to reduce the frequency of eating. The existence of these self-control performances depends upon contingencies in the milieu, just as with any other performance in the individual's repertoire. The existence of behaviors by which an individual may control his own eating depends, for example, upon the ultimate aversive consequences in the individual's milieu of being overweight. If, in fact, there are no aversive consequences for the individual as a consequence of being overweight, then no contingency exists by which the self-control behaviors may be maintained.

Another form of self-control more closely related to the observing behavior described above is those performances that alter one's own behavior to increase its effectiveness in the milieu. When an individual takes a course of instruction, practices the piano, or rehearses the pronunciation of a foreign language, he is essentially engaging in performances that make possible a later reinforcement of behaviors that would not otherwise be available. These performances bear some relationship to chains of responses, but they differ because the early members of the chain lead to the maintaining reinforcer only after considerable behavior has been emitted, and a complex repertoire has been developed. An example of self-control consists of those practices that keep the individual engaged in educational activities whose reinforcement is considerably delayed, as against behaviors that might be more immediately reinforced, such as eating, going to the movies, or social conversation.

Another form of self-control involves a process parallel to the one described above in which the individual alters the physical environment rather than his own behavior. Thus, instead of altering his own behavior so as to make it conform to the reinforcing practices of the existing milieu, the individual alters the milieu; for example, he moves to a new community so that it can maintain his existing repertoire. Such would be the case with an unemployed worker who moves to a new city where employment relative to his skills is available.

It should be noted that none of the performance classifications defined above involve terms such as "abnormal," "deviant," or "pathological," but rather express a degree of a deviation or discrepancy from the practices of the community. The current clinical classifications of behavior as "abnormal" or "pathological" lead to some discrepancies when applied to a functional analysis of behavior along the lines of the classification system described above. Some very gross discrepancies between an individual's behavior and the potential of the milieu go by essentially unnoticed; examples are provided by a chronically unemployed person who in other ways does not cause the community any difficulty, or the quiet child in the rear of the classroom, whose behavior does not cause the parent or teacher any difficulties, yet who is barely functioning in the educational system.

### ABNORMAL BEHAVIOR

We may better understand our present classification system by making a functional analysis of the behavioral practices of those individuals or agencies who designate people as being "abnormal" in the course of attempting to alter their behavior. The behavior of those individuals or agencies engaged in the practices of altering the behaviors of the "deviant" individuals are themselves a function of consequences in the milieu in much the same way as the behavior of the deviant individual. Moreover, the specific conditions and practices that dispose the community to label a given individual as "deviant" or "abnormal" provide a useful definition of abnormality by a specification of the particular practices that are involved. The conditions (consequences, reinforcers) that maintain the behavior of individuals or groups of individuals who attempt to alter the behavior of particular persons in the community involve diverse kinds of behavioral control.

The individual himself may define his behavior as abnormal by engaging in practices whose main effect is to alter his own behavior, for example, psychotherapy or education. In such a case, other members of the community may or may not be disposed to alter this individual's behavior, depending upon whether the factors listed below are operating.

Individuals in the community may attempt to alter the behavior of a person when the expanded or altered repertoire that is attempted is a reinforcer for the individual or agency concerned. The teacher in the educational system, for example, is disposed to alter the behavior of the student because an enlarged repertoire of the kind specified by the educational system is the occasion upon which the teacher is successful and may, on his own part, benefit. The employer may attempt to alter the behavior of an alcoholic employee because the alcoholism is interfering with the performances he requires in the conduct of his business. A government agency may attempt to retrain the unemployed or find the conditions responsible for absenteeism because increasing the economic potential of the community makes possible other reinforcers for the individuals in the agency.

Individuals or agencies may attempt to alter the behavior of an individual in the community when that individual's behavior leads to aversive consequences for those around him. The person with paranoid delusions or a high uncontrolled rate of verbalization interferes with the ability of the people in his immediate environment to communicate with each other. An incontinent person requires someone to clean up after him. The failure of an individual to contribute to his own maintenance leads to a loss of money in his immediate and larger family. Criminal behavior leading to loss of other persons' reinforcers, or a direct assault, also constitutes an aversive stimulus. Lying, hallucinations, paranoid delusions will, under a wide variety of conditions, lessen the ability of the community around the person to function properly. Some of these conditions have been discussed by Goffman (1964). The general effect of all of these behaviors is that they prevent or reduce the reinforcement of behaviors of members of the community and hence function as aversive stimuli that can potentially maintain escape and avoidance behavior.

It is impossible, however, to make a general statement about the aversive consequences of any particular kind of behavior. The effects of identical discrepancies between the behavior of the individual and the performances which are potentially maintained by the environment may be very different in two different communities. The disrupting effects of particular kinds of behavioral discrepancies, such as hallucinations or profound behavioral deficits, depend upon a concurrent analysis of the community in which the person lives and the specific performances interfered with. A person who is a "patient" in an urban family may be a functional member of the family on a farm. A retarded person, for example, will fit more easily into a rural than an urban community because the rural milieu demands less complex behavior and provides reinforcers for routine, monotonous labor of a simple sort. Conversely, behavior that may seriously disrupt a family during the confined living in a winter farmhouse might have less serious consequences in an urban environment, where the members of the family spend less time in the house. The Skid Row section of a community is an example of an environment in which individuals who would markedly interfere with other environments and be labeled as "abnormal" can exist without extreme disruption of their environments.

## TECHNIQUES OF BEHAVIOR CONTROL

When a particular individual or agency in the community is disposed to alter the behavior of an individual, a wide range of techniques of control are available. These include procedures for restricting the behavior of the individual, as in incarceration, hospitalizaton, or ostracization; restrictions in particular activities, such as denying a driver's license or employment; or procedures for altering the behavior of the individual, as in educational practices in schools, driver education classes, outpatient treatment, or psychotherapy. These practices by the community, in respect to behaviors of the individuals whose behavior is to be altered, are by and large avoidance responses maintained by terminating an aversive state of affairs.

Clinical descriptions, partly because they are topographic descriptions and partly because they are based on other kinds of theoretical analyses, classify behaviors functionally related to the environment in very different ways. All the behavioral processes discussed above can contribute to a reduced frequency of emission of positively reinforced behavior of an individual, which is the essential characteristic of a depressed person.

The schedule of reinforcement of a response can weaken it very markedly, particularly by the fixed-ratio schedules discussed earlier. Here, the form of behavior and its effects on the environment are intact, but the consistent amount of behavior required from reinforcement to reinforcement weakens the behavior severely, particularly just after reinforcement. The dynamic properties of fixed-ratio reinforcement may also contribute to reduced frequencies of behavior when the environment supporting the repertoire changes *suddenly* in a direction requiring large amounts of behavior per reinforcement.

Some clinical depressions might be, in part, a result of sudden changes in the environment, as, for example, the death of a close relative or the sudden disappearance of one individual or a group of individuals who maintained the major part of the behavior of the person. As with schedules of reinforcement, the effect of a sudden change in the stimulus environment is a lowering of the frequency of behavior that had been maintained by its effect on this environment.

Punishment and aversive control provide an entirely different set of conditions, which lead to the same result as sudden alterations in the milieu and unfavorable schedules of reinforcement. When the aversive stimulus is the withdrawal of positive reinforcement, the resulting non-reinforcement of enough items in the individual's repertoire weakens behavior sufficiently for a "depression" to be observed. When a large number of performances in themselves come to function as preaversive stimuli because they have been systematically followed by aversive consequences, the conditioned aversive stimulus (anxiety) generated by any incipient tendency to engage in these behaviors will both disrupt and suppress the ongoing repertoire and support any avoidance behavior that prevents the emission of the punished responses. All these effects of a preaversive stimulus lead to reduced frequencies of major portions of a repertoire and reduce the amount of behavior that is emitted, just as do unfavorable schedules of reinforcement and radical stimulus changes discussed above.

Sudden shifts in the contingencies of reinforcement of the milieu, such as those occurring during adolescence, may also contribute to a depression of the repertoire if the new contingencies are so different from those supporting the existing repertoire that extinction occurs because there is no opportunity for successive approximation of the required behavior. Adolescence is such a period, when the environment and social milieu rapidly shift their reinforcement practices so that there is the possibility that the continuous development of the new complex form does not keep pace with the environment. Many of the kinds of disabilities ordinarily diagnosed as schizophrenia could be largely a result of this kind of dynamic interaction with the environment. The major result is very similar to depression, despite other concomitant behaviors, since the important property of the repertoire is the low frequency of behaviors that affect the environment productively. A parental environment based almost entirely on avoidance and escape of aversive stimuli is another way in which the shift from the intrafamily of preadolescence to extrafamily environment of the adult may seriously weaken the behavior of the individual. A sudden change to a new environment in which aversive events are no longer applied might produce a child completely devoid of behavior. Employment situations in which the nature of the employee's activities is left unspecified, except that the eventual outcome of the work is indicated (as, for example, a novelist or basic research worker) may be intolerable (not support any behavior) for an individual whose repertoire consists entirely of escape- and avoidance-responding.

In some cases, the depression in a repertoire may be functional rather than topographic; that is, the total amount of activity the individual engages in is very large, but most of it consists of specific responses to aversive stimuli, rather than of positive effects on the environment. The agitated performances that occur in some kinds of depressions, phobias, obsessions, and compulsions are examples of performances that occur with very high frequency, so that the individual shows an over-all high level of activity that is essentially a depression in terms of the functional relation of any significant behaviors to positive effects in the milieu.

Many current classifications of behavioral pathology, although containing elements of a functional analysis in the sense of describing antecedent environmental histories, consist of topographic descriptions (schizoid personality, rigid, repressed) that frequently prove to be useful in indicating preferred methods of treatments because of the therapist's past experience. Current practices of pathology classification are also useful because the classification system is maintained in terms of consequences important to those segments of the community who are disposed to alter behavior insofar as the existing techniques allow. An alternative classificational system based on the functional relation between the individual's current repertoire and the existing and potential contingencies in the milieu has the advantages of a system of description applicable across the wide cultural differences found even within any one community and across divergent cultures. Such a classification of behavior has the advantage that it is a *direct* description of specific performances and the related aspects of the controlling environment. A description of such specific events may be made in terms of the basic processes that describe, in the most general terms, the conditions determining the frequency of emission of behavior. Such a formulation has the advantage that it specifies specific performances and explicit effects of those performances on the environment, which make possible the application of principles of behavioral control derived from an experimental, natural scientific account of behavior formulated in the same terms as any other datum in biology. To the extent that we understand some of the general processes by which new behavior is created in a repertoire, strengthened, weakened, and so forth, such a formulation leads us closer to procedures by which deficient behavioral repertoires may be altered by manipulating the relevant causes in the environment.

# 3

## A Case in and a Strategy for the Extension of Learning Principles to Problems of Human Behavior*

### ARTHUR W. STAATS

Staats has written extensively on the development of complex human behavior, particularly verbal behavior (Staats, 1957a, 1957b, 1961, 1964; Staats & Staats, 1957, 1958, 1959a, 1959b, 1962; Staats, Staats, & Crawford, 1962; Staats, Staats, Finley, & Heard, 1963; Staats, Staats, & Heard, 1959, 1960, 1961; Staats, Staats, Heard, & Finley, 1962; Staats, Staats, Schutz, & Wolf, 1962). His work is summarized in a text on *Complex Human Behavior* (Staats & Staats, 1963).

Speech and reading skills are necessary for the child to function in our complex society. These skills are basic social tools. Staats (Staats & Staats, 1963) has presented data on the formation of the stimulus-response relationships which are necessary for language associations. These data were summarized in nine statements combining classical, operant, and modeling procedures to explain the development and modification of verbal behavior. These nine statements are as follows:

1. Various environmental stimuli come to control certain specific speech responses. 2. Internal drive stimuli come to control certain speech responses. 3. The stimuli produced by one's own responses come to control speech responses. 4. Printed and written verbal stimuli come to control the appropriate speech responses. 5. Verbal stimuli (or speech responses) come to elicit implicit responses through classical conditioning. These implicit responses may be called meaning responses. 6. These meaning responses produce stimulus characteristics that come to elicit speech responses having a similar component of meaning. 7. Word stimuli (or speech responses, through the stimuli they produce) come to elicit other word responses. Sequences of speech responses may be formed in this manner. 8. Verbal stimuli (written, auditory, and those produced by one's own speech responses), as well as the stimuli produced by meaning responses, come to control certain motor behaviors. 9. The child acquires vocal responses that produce sound stimuli that "echo" or "match" those produced by an authority source as well as other types

* The author's research project which is described herein is currently supported by the Office of Naval Research under contract Nonr-2794 (02).

of verbal "matching" responses. The matching stimuli that result become conditioned reinforcers. (Staats & Staats, 1963, p. 183)

He (Staats & Staats, 1963, p. 183) emphasized that "complex variables underlie the language behavior of an individual even at any particular moment."
Stressing the complexity of language behavior does not remove it from scientific
inquiry. Rather, the major variables need to be investigated in relatively simple
situations involving simple manipulations. Once this has been done, it is possible to move on to greater complexity. Staats demonstrates in this chapter on
language development that reading follows the same learning principles as those
in the development of speech.

However, Staats and Staats (1963) have also pointed out important differences between speech and reading development. While both are basically problems of establishing verbal responses to stimuli, there is often a discrepancy between the ability to speak and the ability to read. Although there is no difference
in the stimuli themselves, both being verbal and complex, Staats and Staats
pointed out the factors that account for this difference. They summarized these
differences and their implications as follows:

> First, the onset of an intensive training program in reading is relatively sudden
> and may involve a good deal of aversiveness. In addition, there are only weak
> sources of reinforcement for many children in the training situation. Furthermore,
> the reinforcers that are available are not made immediately contingent upon the
> many reading responses involved. Finally, if adequate reinforcement for the child
> is not available in the reading program, the behaviors that are prerequisites for
> the acquisition of reading may extinguish. If this happens, progress in learning
> to read will cease. (Staats & Staats, 1963, p. 140)

An important implication of Staats' analysis of reading is that it indicates that
the average child has the potential to read earlier and much more effectively
if maximally reinforcing cues are utilized. A good illustration of this is the work
of Moore (1963), who has developed a "programed typewriter" for use with
children as young as two years of age. Given the increased demands of an
industrial society, Staats' and Moore's work with children of "average intelligence" complements Bijou's and Salzinger's applications to retardates. Two additional years of reading could have profound effects in the realization of human potentialities.

As do the other authors in this volume, Staats deals with overt behavior rather
than concepts and offers both precepts and examples of how this is done. He
stresses the role of reinforcement in shaping and maintaining behavior. Staats
elaborates this theme by raising questions related to training individuals over
long periods of time. Research on prolonged training, to which the Goldiamond
chapter also makes important contributions, involves changes in scheduling and
considerations of satiation effects over periods of time. Staats concludes that the
most effective reinforcement system is one involving tokens, in which the individual selects the reward he will receive. This is an answer to problems of satiation,

particularly when the reinforcer is food, and takes into consideration the usefulness of novelty. A good illustration of a token system is Ayllon's use (1964) of a token economy on an adult pyschiatric ward in a state hospital. The reinforcement contingencies are explicitly spelled out to the patients by printed signs, notices, and staff verbalizations. Various desirable behaviors, such as cleanliness, good grooming, attendance at meetings, good work performance, and completion of special assignments are rewarded with tokens dispensed by the staff. These tokens may be used by the patients for any of the "good things in life," such as candy, cigarettes, clothing, cosmetics, passes, and even a bed in a more desirable room. Within such an economy the patient can progressively better his life on the ward and can leave the hospital when he has increased his performance of socially desirable, hence rewarding, behavior. The use of a token economy is anything but unique because it is modeled on life outside the hospital. A token economy within an institution implies that the principles of behavior in the hospital are similar to those in the community which the patient is being trained to enter. Krasner and Atthowe have also recently successfully established a token economy on a chronic psychiatric ward.

Another illustration of the type of therapeutic endeavors Staats calls for is given by Kerr, Meyerson, and Michael (1965). They were confronted with the problem of developing speech in a mute three-year-old girl with a history of serious maternal, social, and sensory deprivation, who was diagnosed as severely retarded, cerebrally palsied, epileptic, and emotionally disturbed. The authors used joggling on the examiner's knee and singing a nursery song as the reinforcer. They were able to shape this mute child's behavior to the point where she responded to the experimenter's vocalizations 60 percent of the time with a vocalization of her own. The chapter by Salzinger et al. provides a detailed description of this kind of experimental-clinical research. These procedures, which deal directly with behavior, highlight the need for new assessment procedures. Assessment must be related to the treatment program, focusing on both the behaviors to be modified and the reinforcing contingencies to be manipulated.

Finally, there is a generally optimistic tone to Staats' chapter that is characteristic of the authors in this book. Accepting the premise that human behavior is modifiable, they work with individuals other therapists have perhaps been too quick to ignore, such as retarded or brain-damaged children, regressed psychotics, and the physically handicapped. Given the appropriate environmental contingencies, human beings have almost unlimited potentialities for growth.

L.K.-L.P.U.

As EXEMPLIFIED IN VARIOUS experimental sciences, a sound strategy to approach the study of any new set of events is to deal with the more simple occurrences first in order to establish basic principles. This is done in the analytical procedures of the laboratory, where the attempt is made to simplify matters by manipulating a very few conditions (independent variables) to observe their effects upon some other condition (dependent variables). Complications are excluded by insuring that other conditions which would act as independent variables do not influence the outcome, even though in everyday life the various independent variables may act simultaneously.

As a science develops to more advanced stages, after the basic, analytic principles have been established by means of laboratory experimentation, more complex constallations of interacting variables may be considered. Ultimately, in a third stage, after having been verified in complex situations, the basic principles and procedures may be applied to the solution of important practical problems.

## PROGRESSION IN BEHAVIORISTIC PSYCHOLOGY

Inspection of the development of behavioristic psychology indicates that it is going through this progression. In recent times, we have seen the extension of the basic principles to more complex cases and the application of these principles to the treatment of practical problems. Although the practical application phase is far from fully developed, there has been progress in such fields as rehabilitation, educational psychology, and clinical psychology.

These applied developments make essential contributions to the advancement of the science from which they spring—in this case learning theory. When the principles of a science are relevant to practical problems of the world, an important criteria for evaluating their worth is available: the extent to which they aid in the solution of problems. Thus, one way of furthering learning theory is to validate its principles and procedures within the context of solving practical problems of behavior.

These extensions involve the following steps: (a) a learning analysis of the given behavior and the circumstances under which it is acquired, (b) a demonstrational-type of experiment to verify the most significant principles in the area under investigation, (c) increasingly systematic exploration of the various principles involved in that area, (d) the final application of the principles and the procedures developed to the solution of practical problems.

It is within this framework that the studies presented in this paper belong, namely, a project extending over a period of several years concerned with the analysis of reading. Experience on this project suggests a general strategy with which to approach the extension of learning principles and procedures to the solution of problems of human behavior. As a starting point the behavioral analysis of the acquisition of a reading repertoire was based upon Skinner's (1957) interpretation of what he labeled "textual" response—operant vocal responses under the discriminated control of a printed or written verbal.

## ROLE OF REINFORCEMENT

In our earlier extension of this view (Staats & Staats, 1962), we considered the acquisition of reading to involve getting the child to emit an appropriate vocal response while looking at a particular verbal symbol and then reinforcing the response. This training should establish the verbal symbol as a discriminative stimulus that controls the vocal response.

As part of the analysis, we compared the way speech is acquired to the way a reading repertoire is established. We concluded that reading training is not as effective. The usual training, unlike what would be recommended from a learning theory viewpoint, is relatively intensive *and* involves poor conditions of reinforcement—cause enough for many failures of training. Thus, as a first step, a learning analysis suggested that there are aspects of training that might be facilitated by a better understanding of reinforcement within the context of reading acquisition.

When both the stimuli and responses are considered the repertoire that must be acquired in learning to read is very complex. For example, it will be found that a child who has come to respond to the stimulus *the* with the response "the" will also respond at first in the same manner to *then, there, this, these, thus, that, those,* and so on. Since the stimuli share stimulus components, stimulus generalization will occur. Bringing different responses under the control of each word stimulus is a difficult task. The same is true of such words as *pat, sat, hat, fat.* A response brought under the control of one of these stimuli will generalize to the others. It is then necessary that unit stimuli come to control unit responses. The *p, s, h,* and *f,* stimuli must each come to control the correct response. This must also occur for the *a* and *t.*

Additional complexities arise because some of the unit stimuli must control different responses depending upon the other stimuli with which they are presented. For example, *a* not only must control the "ay" response when presented with *f* and *t,* as in *fat,* but also must control the "ah" response when presented with *f* and *t,* and also *h, e,* and *r,* as in *father.* In addition, the unit stimuli themselves represent difficulties of discrimination. There is little difference between the lower case *b, h, n, r,* or between

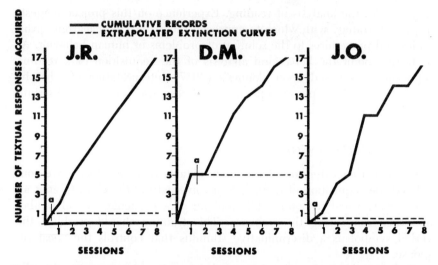

Figure 3-1.   The curves shown here were generated under a beginning period of no "extrinsic" reinforcement. When S would no longer remain in the experimental situation, reinforcement was instated as indicated by the mark on the curve. The dotted line commences at the point S would no longer remain in the experiment, and indicates the curve that would have resulted if reinforcement was not introduced. (Staats, A. W. et al., "The conditioning of textural responses using 'extrinsic' reinforcers," J. exper. Anal. Behav., 1962, 5, 33-40.)

$b$, and $d$, $p$ and $q$. This is but a brief sketch to indicate that the great complexity of a repertoire such as reading may be overlooked until one begins to study it systematically.

The early analysis indicated the importance of reinforcement in learning to read. The next step in the project was a demonstrational study which grossly tested the importance of reinforcement in this type of learning. In addition, this study explored the experimental population and began to develop procedures and apparatus. For this study (Staats, Staats, Schutz, & Wolf, 1962) a small group of words was arranged in a program in which words were presented singly as well as in sentences and in short paragraphs. Each child was prompted to say a word as he looked at it, and was reinforced with small edibles, trinkets, or tokens backed up by small toys. Eight 40-minute training sessions were presented to the children and the number of new words the children learned to read was tested after each training session.

Next, three four-year-old children were introduced to the training and were given only social reinforcers (that is, approval), but no extrinsic reinforcement, as the others had received. This was continued until the child requested discontinuance of the activity. This occurred after only 15 minutes for two of the children and 15 minutes into the second session for the other child. At this point extrinsic reinforcement was

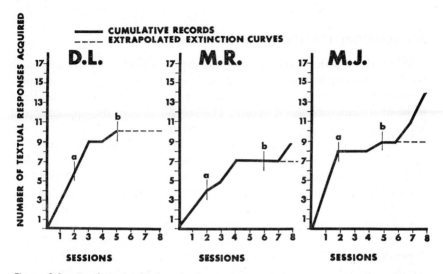

Figure 3-2. For these Ss, the first condition included reinforcement that was discontinued at the point of the first mark on the curve. When S would no longer remain in the experimental situation, reinforcement was reinstated, as the second mark on the curve indicates. The dotted line commences at the point the S would no longer remain in the experiment and depicts the curve that would have resulted if reinforcement was not reinstated. (Staats, A. W. et al., "The conditioning of textural responses using 'extrinsic' reinforcers," J. exper. Anal. Behav., 1962, 5, 33-40.)

reinstated and in each case the child's reading behavior was strengthened and maintained for the remainder of the training. The records of these children are shown in Figure 3-1. These children acquired 16, 17, and 17, respectively, word-reading vocabularies in the eight training sessions.

Three other children were given the opposite treatment. That is, they were started under the reinforcement condition and after two training sessions were switched to no reinforcement. As the figure shows, they learned words readily under reinforcement, but when reinforcement was "cut off," their learning behaviors extinguished. After three or four sessions of no reinforcement each child requested discontinuance, and the condition was changed to reinforcement. In two cases the reading behavior was reconditioned and learning "picked up" again. The records of these children are presented in Figure 3-2.

The results showed that when reading was reinforced, attentional and work habits were strong and new words were learned rapidly, but both types of behavior deteriorated when reinforcement was not forthcoming. Thus, it would appear that under more appropriate conditions of reinforcement, even very young children are capable of sustained work activities and can learn complex verbal skills.

## A LABORATORY FOR THE STUDY OF READING

While the relevance of the basic principles and the general approach received support in this first study, and some of the requirements for a more systematic study were indicated, the experiment can be considered to be of a demonstrational nature. The second step in the application of learning principles appeared to be the construction of a laboratory facility within which to make a systematic assessment of principles important in reading acquisition. For this we needed a good dependent variable, that is, a suitable index of the child's behavior which was sensitive to the manipulation of important experimental conditions. We also needed control of irrelevant conditions and a situation within which the child's behavior could be studied over an adequate length of time.

There were a number of steps in the development of this approach. The dependent variable in the initial study was the number of reading words acquired, as measured after each training session. Qualitative observations of the children's behavior in the learning situation, however, indicated that basic to learning to read are the minute-to-minute attentional and working behaviors of the child. When the child attended to the material and worked at a high rate, he acquired new words rapidly. A record of these actual reading behaviors should result in a much more sensitive tool for testing the effects of different variables upon the learning. Accordingly, an experimental procedure was developed so that each reading response was automatically and cumulatively recorded by a standard operant conditioning apparatus.

As to the control of irrelevant conditions, in the first study the materials were heterogeneous, consisting sometimes of words, sometimes of sentences, and sometimes of paragraphs. With the development of a minute-to-minute recording system it was necessary to have reading materials which themselves would not impose characteristics upon the child's rate of response. Thus, a program was developed consisting of single vowel and consonant-vowel combinations. Although the letters still differed somewhat in stimulus complexity or distinguishability from other letters, response variability was markedly decreased.

In addition, an apparatus for the presentation of the stimuli was required. In the first experiment the stimuli were simply presented by hand, and consequently there was a good deal of variation. The stimulus presentation apparatus which we later developed consists of a panel with four windows, each covered with a piece of plexiglass. One window is centered above the other three, as shown in Figure 3-3. Pressure on any of the plastic covers activates a switch.

The verbal stimuli are presented to the child in a discrimination procedure. The top stimulus is matched by one of the three stimuli in the

Figure 3-3.   The laboratory apparatus for the experimental study of reading behavior. The child is seated before the center panel within easy reach of the various manipulanda that are involved in the reading response sequence. Letter stimuli appear in the small plexiglass windows in front of the child whenever he activates the pushbutton on the table before him. If a correct reading response sequence then occurs, the marble dispenser located at the child's near-right drops a marble into a tray positioned at its base. To the child's left is an open bin in the Universal Feeder cabinet into which are delivered trinkets, edibles, or pennies, whenever the child deposits a marble in the funnel located atop the marble dispenser. A marble may also be "spent" for toys displayed at the child's far right. Whenever the plexiglass tube beneath a toy is filled with marbles the child receives that toy. An intercom speaker at the child's left allows his vocal behavior to be monitored from outside the experimental chamber. The light at the top of the center panel was not used in this study. (Staats, A. W., "A Case in and Strategy for the Extension of Learning Principles to Problems of Human Behavior" in *Human Learning*, A. W. Staats, Ed. New York: Holt, Rinehart, and Winston, Inc., 1964.)

bottom row of windows. The child's task is to select the stimulus which matches the one in the top window. In the procedure, the stimuli are presented, and the experimenter, who is almost entirely hidden from the child, "names" the top stimulus after the stimulus has been presented for 10 seconds. The child must echo the name and press the plastic cover on the window. He must then select the matching stimulus from among the bottom windows, say the stimulus name again and press the plastic cover. When this response occurs correctly, the child is automatically and immediately reinforced. An error at any point in the chain automatically activates the apparatus so that the child must begin the trial over from the beginning. This procedure insures that only correct responses are reinforced. Since the verbal stimuli are periodically repeated, after a time the child's vocal response may come under the control of the stimulus and the child may, without prompting, emit the appropriate sound within the 10-second delay period. In this case the child is immediately reinforced and does not have to go through the whole chain of responses.

While the reinforcement system used in the demonstrational study was adequate for its purposes, the results over the eight training sessions indicated that the effect of the reinforcers was weakening. Repertoires such as speech itself, writing, spelling, and mathematics, etc., as well as reading, are acquired only over a very long period of time, and a great deal of training is necessary. The problem of reinforcement in long-term studies with children has been severe, however, as other investigators have also found (for example, Long, Hammack, May, & Campbell, 1958). Children cannot, of course, as in laboratory studies with animals, be deprived of food for long periods of time and kept at reduced body weight so that research may be conducted. Nor can the withdrawal of aversive stimulation be used as a source of reinforcement. A naturalistic observation, however, is that tokens, like money, become excellent reinforcers for people, even without states of deprivation for primary reinforcers. This occurs because money is paired with, or backed up by, a large number of other reinforcers. Taking this tip from everyday life, a reinforcer system following the same principle was developed. This consisted of tokens backed up by various items which the children had previously selected. The ratio of tokens to back-up reinforcers was dictated by the capacity of the tube in which the tokens were deposited (see Figure 3-3).

## TESTING OF APPARATUS AND PROCEDURE

The next step in the experimental analysis of reading acquisition was to test the combined apparatus and procedure. Each phase of developing the laboratory facility involved pilot work in which it was important to determine certain features such as: whether the entire system would maintain the child's behavior for a long enough period of time to study significant variables in the learning process; whether the stimulus materials and apparatus produced control of attentional responses; the feasibility of cumulative recording; and the sensitivity of the records. The learning curves of two children run for 40 daily 20-minute training sessions under conditions of continuous reinforcement have been presented elsewhere (Staats, Minke, Finley, Wolf, & Brooks 1964). The first child's record is one of great consistency following the preliminary training sessions (see Figure 3-4). For this child the tokens appeared to immediately constitute strong and invariant reinforcers. That is, this child customarily deposited his tokens in the tubes for the larger toys, which meant that several times his behavior was maintained only by tokens for as many as three daily sessions with no back-up reinforcers. The second

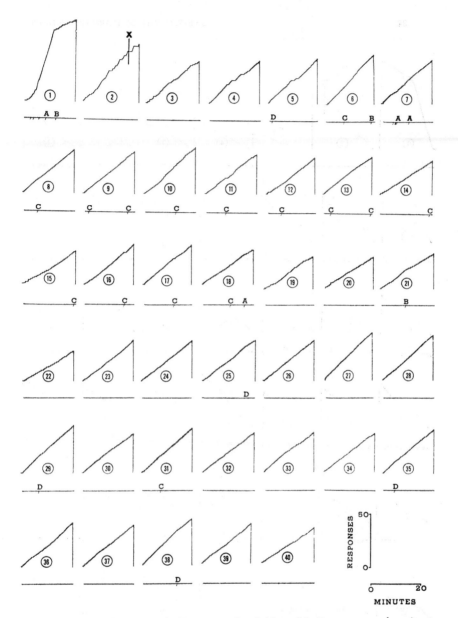

Figure 3-4. Cumulative records by sessions for Subject #1. Responses made prior to point X in Session 2 are those occurring during various pretraining phases. Point X marks the beginning of the actual reading task. The slash marks located on the line below each curve represent the presentation of various back-up reinforcers. A indicates that a $.10 toy was exchanged for 10 marbles; B marks the presentation of a $.35 toy in exchange for 35 marbles; the child's exchange of 80 marbles for a toy is denoted by a C; D marks the exchange of 150 marbles for a toy; unlettered slash marks indicate that the child deposited a marble for some item from the Universal Feeder. (Staats, A. W. et al., "A reinforcer system and experimental procedure for the laboratory study of reading acquisition," Child Development, 1964, 35, 209-231.)

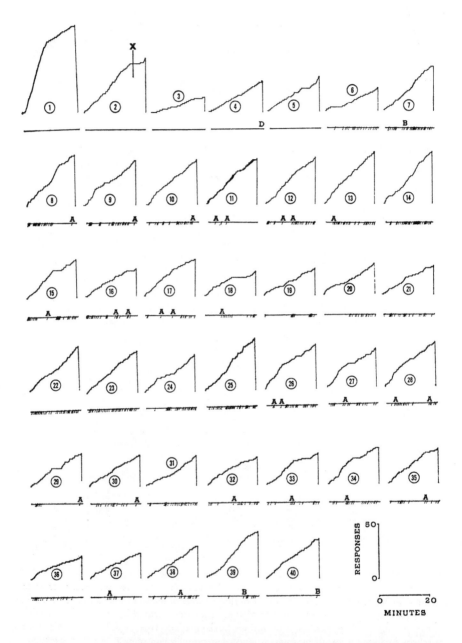

Figure 3-5. The cumulative records by sessions for Subject #2. The sequence of pretraining tasks occurs until point X, at which time the reading program was introduced. The occurrence of back-up reinforcers is indicated below each curve as on the previous subject's records. (Staats, A. W. et al., "A reinforcer system and experimental procedure for the laboratory study of reading acquisition," *Child Development*, 1964, 35, 209-231.)

child's working behavior in the reading training was more variable, including pauses of various intervals (see Figure 3-5).

The results with these children indicate that the various procedural developments were functional in producing a laboratory situation for the study of the complex human learning of a reading repertoire. Long-term studies now appear to be possible since each of these two children emitted about 1500 reading responses in the 40 days of training.

## ASSESSMENT OF VARIABLES

The next step in the systematic analysis was to use the laboratory facility to begin to assess variables important to the acquisition of the behavior. As part of this, also, there was the need to test the extent to which the facility was well enough controlled to be sensitive to the manipulation of important independent variables.

One such variable, needing more systematic study, is the schedule of reinforcement. We know from more basic studies that certain schedules of reinforcement will produce better working behaviors than others. On a practical level of dealing with children's learning, can we improve the rate of response by reinforcement scheduling variables when complex learning is involved? Related to this is also another important goal, the improvement of the reinforcer system. That is, it would be advisable to minimize the delivery of reinforcers to prevent satiation. Thus anything which postpones satiation can be considered to increase the effect of the reinforcer system. Intermittent reinforcement would reduce reinforcer expenditure.

Our next study (Staats, Finley, Minke, & Wolf, 1964), using additional children, was oriented toward these problems. We applied two different schedules of reinforcement to each of our subjects and compared rates of response under each schedule. The procedure was that of discrimination learning: The child was reinforced in one manner under one room-light condition, and in another manner under another room-light condition. These light-reinforcement conditions were alternated during each training session in a manner which has been referred to as a multiple schedule (Ferster & Skinner, 1957; Orlando & Bijou, 1960).

The first child was run under continuous reinforcement for one light condition and under extinction—no reinforcement—for the other light condition. We would expect a discrimination to develop such that the reading behavior would occur under the appropriate light condition to a greater extent than under the other light condition. That is what occurred. The records are shown in Figure 3-6. Each reinforcement condition is depicted as a separate component after which time the recording pen resets to the baseline. By the sixth session the discrimination begins to form and thereafter becomes even more pronounced. We clearly see how

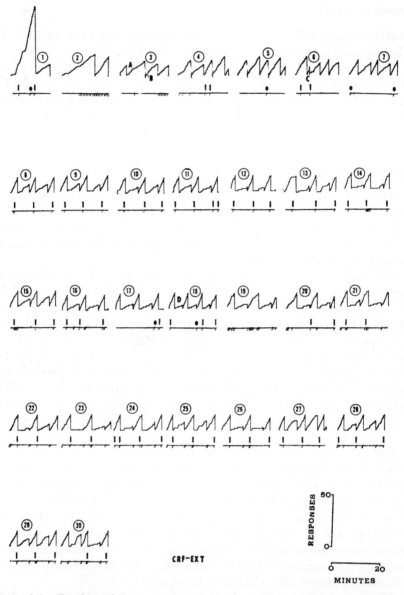

Figure 3-6. The thirty daily session records for the multiple continuous reinforcement-extinction (*mult* CRF-EXT) subject show the reading response rates for the various experimental conditions. Responses prior to point A occurred during the pretraining phases of the study. At this point the reading program was introduced under CRF. Beginning with Session 4 each 20-minute reading session commenced with a CRF component which then alternated with EXT conditions. The event marker on the line below each record indicates the delivery of a back-up reinforcer: *1* notes the exchange of 10 marbles for a $.10 toy, o notes the presentation of a $.35 toy in exchange for 35 marbles, and unlettered event marks indicate the exchange of 1 marble for an item from the Universal Feeder. (Staats, A. W. *et al.*, "Reinforcement variables in the control of unit reading responses," *J. exper. Anal. Behav.*, 1964, 7, 139-149.)

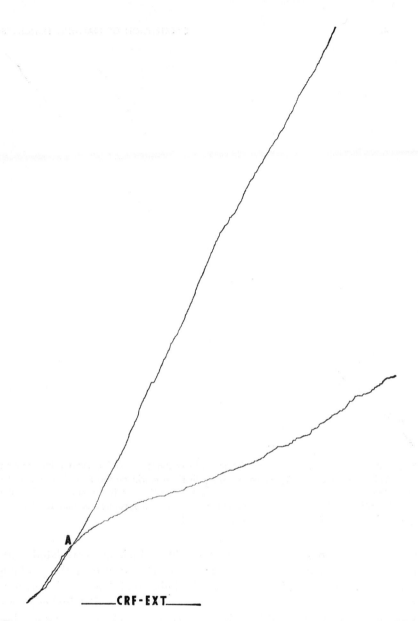

A

——CRF-EXT——

Figure 3-7. Composite record for the mult CRF-EXT subject. In order to make a comparison between an S's response rates for the two experimental conditions the records for reinforcement schedules were separated and recombined to yield an individual curve for each condition according to daily session sequence. All records commence with the introduction of the reading program. The composite records for the four S's are directly comparable; however, the size of each record is determined by S's response rate. Fig. 3-7 shows that for the mult CRF-EXT S the EXT rate was initially the higher rate, but at point A it declined and crossed the CRF curve. The CRF response rate was relatively rapid and stable throughout the experiment. (Staats, A. W. et al., "Reinforcement variables in the control of unit reading responses," J. exper. Anal. Behav., 1964, 7, 139-149.)

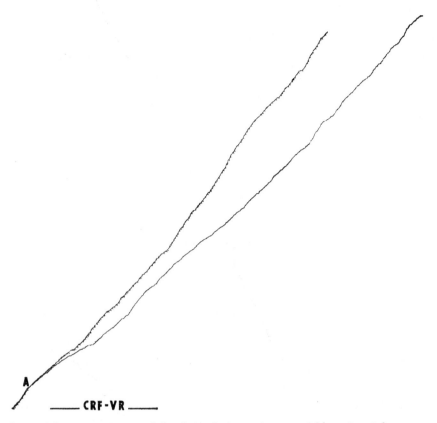

Figure 3-8. Composite record for the multiple continuous-variable ratio reinforcement (*mult* CRF-VR) subject. The VR curve (shown with slash marks on the record) was initially lower than the CRF curve. However, from point A the VR rate is the more rapid of the two. (Staats, A. W. *et al.*, "Reinforcement variables in the control of unit reading responses," *J. exper. Anal. Behav.*, 1964, 7, 139-149.)

stimulus conditions (in this case the light) which are correlated with response-contingent reinforcement can assume control over the working behaviors of the child. That is, when the light condition, which was correlated with reinforcement, came on, the child immediately began responding more rapidly. When the light condition changed, reading behavior deteriorated. The dramatic nature of the discrimination is shown even more clearly in Figure 3-7, where the responses under each reinforcement condition are pieced together so that the two performances can be compared to each other over the 30-session training period. The records of the next three children to be described will also be of this latter type.

The second subject was run in a similar manner under continuous reinforcement and variable-ratio reinforcement—at the end one reinforcer

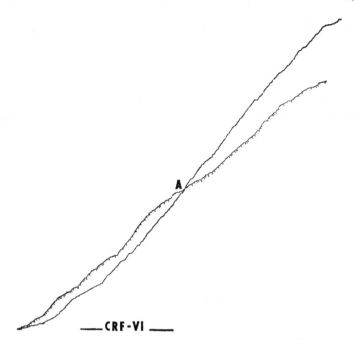

Figure 3-9. Composite record for the multiple continuous-variable ratio reinforcement (*mult* CRF-VI) subject. The VI curve (with slash marks) is depicted above the CRF curve until point A on the record, at which point it becomes the lower of the two curves. (Staats, A. W. *et al.*, "Reinforcement variables in the control of unit reading responses," *J. exper. Anal. Behav.*, 1964, 7, 139-149.)

for an average of five responses. Higher rates of response were produced under the intermittent schedule, using, of course, fewer reinforcers (see Figure 3-8). The third child's results include responding under continuous reinforcement and under a variable-interval reinforcement schedule in which the first response the child made after an average of 2 minutes had passed was reinforced. As would be expected, the child's reading response rate was lower under the variable-interval condition than under continuous reinforcement (see Figure 3-9).

Figure 3-10 shows the record of a child run under the variable-ratio and variable-interval reinforcement conditions. As the results show, no discrimination between the two conditions was exhibited. This seemed to be an artifact of the procedure, however. This child "anticipated" almost none of the letters, waiting 10 seconds until the letter name was given by the experimenter. As a consequence, his rate of response was limited, and both reinforcement schedules had him performing maximally within that limitation.

It thus appears that scheduling variables are important and that the response rate and the efficacy of the reinforcer system may be increased

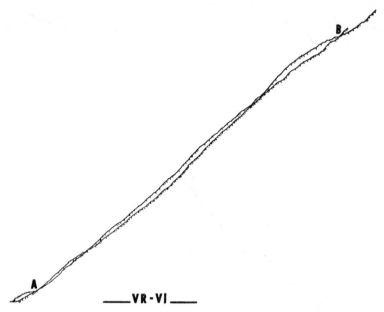

Figure 3-10. Composite record for the multiple variable ratio-variable interval reinforcement (*mult* VR-VI) subject. The VI curve begins lower than the VR curve until point A,
then crosses and remains above the VR curve until point B, at which point the VI rate
declines. (Staats, A. W. *et al.*, "Reinforcement variables in the control of unit reading
responses," *J. exper. Anal. Behav.*, 1964, 7, 139-149.)

by intermittent reinforcement. The results also indicated that the experimental situation was sensitive to the manipulation of experimental variables, producing results generally paralleling those found with subhuman
organisms and with more simple responses.

## PROPOSED RESEARCH

At the present time, on the basis of what has already been found by the
project, the author plans to extend the research in several different directions, some of which are already well underway. One direction concerns
the further investigation of some basic variables whose importance has
been suggested in the progress of the experimental analysis of reading. For
example, our procedure uses a token system. The responses of the child
are reinforced with marbles, which may be exchanged for various back-up
reinforcers. In our early procedure the tokens were backed up by the
reinforcers on a 1-to-24 basis. We noticed at that time that this had an
effect upon the reading behavior of the child which was analogous to a
fixed-ratio pause after the delivery of a reinforcer. Thus, there seem to be
scheduling effects which depend upon the way tokens and back-up reinforcers are related, in addition to the schedules involving the manner in

which tokens (or conditioned reinforcers) are made contingent upon the behavior of the organism. Although this should be but has not been systematically investigated in basic animal studies, it seems that there are two types of schedules that combine to produce effects upon the organism's rate of response. Ultimately, we would like to study the effect on reading performance of the "schedule" by which our tokens are backed up by the other reinforcers.

Another suggestion for basic research emerges from the work on the effects of multiple schedules on the maintenance of the reading behavior. This can be seen easily in Table 3-1. Although these results can be considered as only suggestive because of the number of subjects run as well as some of the control aspects of the procedure, the three continously reinforced children did not respond at the rate exhibited by each of the children under the various multiple schedules. Even the child under the variable-ratio and variable-interval schedule responded at a greater rate than the continuously reinforced children, and with far less reinforcement: one token for 3.72 responses vs. one for each response. In addition, there is considerable variance between the rates of the various children under the several multiple schedules (see Table 3-1), an average of 58.8 for the CRF-EXT child, 53.6 for the CRF-VR child, 44.8 for the CRF-VI child, and 42.4 for the VR-VI child. This suggests that the rates of response per reinforcer produced under different multiple schedules should be systematically studied. Previously, multiple schedules were used as a method for studying individual components, rather than being studied themselves for the over-all rates which they produce. We have begun pilot work to study the relative qualities of different multiple schedules for practical learning situations, that is, the ability of the multiple schedule to maintain vigorous behavior with little reinforcement.

These two avenues of research are cited since it is interesting that these indications for basic study have emerged in the process of studying a complex human behavior.

Another direction of research concerns the implications of our use of experimental designs in long-term studies of children engaged in complex learning. Because of the complexity of the learning, behaviors such as reading cannot be assessed in short-term group studies. Reliable results were obtained over a lengthy period, however, using the multiple schedule design where two conditions were presented to the same child. This design can be applied to the assessment of other independent variables besides those of reinforcement schedules. The different effects of reading materials can also be assessed. That is, using the multiple schedule design we will present the same child with two different types of reading program and record the child's rate of learning under each condition. Thus, as a gross example, whole-word presentation could be compared to phonetic presentation in conditions of good laboratory control. This type of

Table 3-1: Results of Seven Subjects Run in the Laboratory Facility[a]

| Subject | Sessions | | Total responses | Average responses/ session | Average tokens/ session | Average responses/ token | % Responses reinforced | % Total anticipations | % Correct anticipations |
|---|---|---|---|---|---|---|---|---|---|
| | Whole days on reading | Total for computations | | | | | | | |
| CRF #1 | 4-11 | 8 | 294 | 36.7 | 36.7 | 1.00 | 100 | 76.4 | 40.5 |
| CRF #2 | 3-40 | 38 | 1473 | 38.7 | 38.7 | 1.00 | 100 | 2.3 | 2.1 |
| CRF #3 | 3-40 | 38 | 1305 | 34.5 | 34.5 | 1.00 | 100 | 47.4 | 45.3 |
| CRF-EXT | 4-30 less Session 23 | 26 | 1530 | 58.8 | 44.5 | 1.32 | 75.6 | 94.0 | 30.1 |
| CRF-VR | 5-30 | 26 | 1394 | 53.6 | 34.5 | 1.56 | 64.3 | 50.0[b] | 46.9[b] |
| CRF-VI | 4-30 less Sessions 17-19 | 24 | 1075 | 44.8 | 29.3 | 1.53 | 65.4 | 75.7[c] | 25.0[c] |
| VR-VI | 4-30 less Sessions 6-7 | 25 | 1060 | 42.4 | 11.4 | 3.72 | 26.9 | 3.6 | 2.8 |

[a] Subjects CRF #1, #2, and #3 were employed in a procedure comparable to the present study, but were administered only continuous reinforcement conditions (see Staats, Minke, Finley, Wolf, & Brooks, 1964). Computations are based on full-length reading sessions; sessions omitted include pretraining phases, major deviations from normal procedure, or sessions for which complete data were unavailable.
[b] Session 26 omitted.
[c] Sessions 3-16 only.

investigation should yield a deeper understanding of reading acquisition.

Another line of research is the application of these procedures and principles to the study of learning in special populations of children. We are planning experiments with mental retardates. First, we want to determine how the procedures transfer to this new population, and then to establish some of the learning differences between retardates and normals in this significant type of human learning. The methods could also be used with other special children's problems, for example, deaf and autistic children.

Lastly, the research has been extended to the solution of some of the problems involved in actually teaching reading. The detailed results are not yet completed, but one child has been taught the essentials of reading at the age of three years and two months, and additional experiments are underway. The child had a reading repertoire of almost all the lower case and capital letters as well as thirty-two words, which includes variants of one word (for example, *drives* and *drive* are counted as two words). This child (the author's daughter) reads the words alone and in sentences and short paragraphs. The following is a sample paragraph:

> Jenni drives to a zoo.
> Jenni plays at the zoo with a girl.
> Jenni and the girl eat at the zoo.[1]

To summarize the general strategy suggested for the application of learning principles to significant human behaviors, the research project on reading has made the following progress: It began with at least a partial behavioral analysis of reading and of some of the learning factors that contribute to the difficulty of training. Then several demonstrational studies were conducted which showed that the relevant principles of reinforcement and discrimination did indeed apply to the acquisition of reading. Following this, a laboratory procedure and apparatus were constructed within which the systematic study of reading could take place. This facility has been tested in studies which more systematically assess reinforcement variables within the context of reading. This progress has suggested additional plans for continued systematic analysis of reading. In addition, there has been the application of the findings to the actual problem of training children to read. This last development constitutes the final stage of the strategy proposed in the introduction. All of these directions point up the productiveness of this kind of systematic analysis. Based upon the findings so far, it would seem that a procedure and program will eventuate which will make the acquisition of reading possible in young children in a more expeditious way.

---

[1] Since writing this article the author has extended the various procedures and methods to the study of (1) reading learning in other pre-school children, (2) reading learning in retarded children, and (3) remedial reading in delinquent children.

## IMPLICATIONS FOR OTHER BEHAVIORAL PROBLEMS

We can now explore the implications of the reading project for other types of problems of human behavior. To begin with, we might ask where we stand with a behavioristic approach to such problems. We do possess a fine set of principles and procedures established in basic studies, primarily with lower animals. The empirical principles have been well substantiated a number of times. Many of these heavyweight principles have been extended to human behavior in basic studies. The principle of respondent conditioning has been shown to be involved in conditioning fears (Watson & Rayner, 1920), attitudes (Staats & Staats, 1958), and semantic properties of language (Osgood, 1953; Mowrer, 1954b; Cofer & Foley, 1942; Staats, 1961). The principle of reinforcement has been shown to operate with verbal classes (see Krasner, 1958a; Salzinger, 1959), problem solving (Maltzman, 1955; Adamson, 1959), social behavior (Azrin & Lindsley, 1956; Bandura, 1962b), attitudes (Scott, 1957), the learning of mental retardates (Orlando & Bijou, 1960), personality indices (Nuthmann, 1957; Staats, Staats, Heard, & Finley, 1962), and various types of abnormal behaviors as well (Ferster, 1961; Ayllon & Michael, 1959).

Because of the verification of learning principles in these new domains of behavior, we have confidence in the relevance of our principles and procedures and in their eventual ability to solve complex human problems of behavior. But we do not have at this time a large number of analyses of different behavior problems and long-term projects involving systematic and applied studies of that behavior. We do not, consequently, have a complete set of procedures for treatment to transmit to practitioners. For example, several years ago Rheingold, Gewirtz, and Ross (1959) conducted a study in which it was shown that the vocal behavior of 3-month-old infants could be strengthened through response-contingent reinforcement. This was an important demonstrational study, but it also suggested that the original acquisition of speech in infants should be systematically studied. If in a few 30-minute periods the vocal behavior of infants can be strengthened, then systematic application of reinforcers over a long period of time should result in a more rapid acquisition of speech than normally occurs. Study of this process with systematic observation and recording should help us understand the process and lead to procedures that are valuable for producing desirable development of speech behavior. There is no doubt that a primary problem of some children is in their "backward" development of speech. Autistic children are notable in this respect, and it is no doubt the case that many children called mental retardates are victims of poor training histories in this important area.

There are no special obstacles to this type of study. There are many institutionalized children who could only profit from the procedures involved in attempting to shape good verbal behavior in them. Many autistic, brain-damaged, mentally retarded children would serve as fine subjects in procedures which would surely improve the child's adjustment.

As another example, Ayllon and his associates (Ayllon & Haughton, 1962; Ayllon & Michael, 1959) have shown that operant conditioning principles can be applied to behavior problems in psychotics. This research has also indicated that tokens backed up by food can be used as an effective reinforcer in working with psychotics. The next step could be the use of the principles and procedures to shape adjustive behaviors in psychotics. Isaacs, Thomas, and Goldiamond (1960) have shown that mute schizophrenics could be operantly shaped to speak again, using only very lightweight reinforcers and in what constituted a relatively short experimental procedure. With these demonstrations and the use of a reinforcer system like that of Ayllon and Haughton (1962), it should be possible to shape adjustive behavior in psychotics of a much more extensive type. The work behaviors of psychotics should be studied in long-term systematic projects. This should also be applied to actual adjustive social and language behaviors; in fact, to any behavior in which the psychotic is deficient and which could be shaped through the manipulation of reinforcement variables.

Again, the back wards of neuropsychiatric hospitals are full of patients who could only profit from such treatment-research activities. Systematic attempts to shape the behavior through reniforcement should yield a general understanding of the behavior and also general procedures for the treatment of other patients.

Returning again to autistic children, Ferster and DeMyer (1961) have indicated that the behavior of these children is subject to reinforcement principles. This constitutes a demonstrational study in that the behaviors under study were relatively simple, for example, bar-pressing. The behavior problems of children should generally be approached using behavioral methods, as Bijou suggests in the next chapter. Several years ago Williams (1959) showed that temper tantrums could be treated by extinction procedures. More recently this has been extended by Wolf, Risley, and Mees (1964) with a child diagnosed variously as mentally retarded, schizophrenic, and brain-damaged. As Bijou describes in the next chapter, several different behaviors were modified in this child by means of learning treatments, resulting in marked improvement in the child's adjustment.

These studies may be considered to have moved past the demonstrational stage and into the application of learning principles to the solution of behavior problems of some importance. This successful treatment should be extended to a systematic study of various behavior problems in children.

One of the areas in which the application of learning principles is needed is in the field of rehabilitation. Discussions with therapists in this field suggest that much of their work, especially with children, involves training new behaviors under circumstances in which the reinforcers are weak. For example, *prior* to developing skill with a prosthesis, the child secures reinforcement more easily for various already learned substitution movements. Thus, some way must be found at first to supply "extrinsic" reinforcement for the more difficult "prosthetic responses," since in a competitive sense these responses are not themselves "naturally" reinforcing. Research being conducted by our students at Arizona State University has begun to apply reinforcement principles to such problems of training and to many others. For example, two students[2] have been working with a boy whose arm was paralyzed through brain damage and who has not responded to rehabilitation efforts. That is, he continues to use his good arm rather than develop new skills with his paralyzed arm. The plan has been to reinforce the boy for arm movements directed toward a large visual target. When these types of arm movements have been strengthened sufficiently, the target would be reduced in size until the accuracy of the arm movements improved. So far the treatment has met with some success using social reinforcers backed up by toys.

Following this demonstration it has also been possible to achieve startling improvements in motor performance through the use of a token reinforcer system such as has been described herein.[3] When reinforcement was made available for a child who refused to walk alone, the desired behavior was obtained readily. The same was true of a child whom rehabilitation specialists had been trying to train to fall down properly. This immediate improvement coincides with our own previous observations of some remedial reading cases with whom we began work in the process of the experimental analysis of reading. Although they had been diagnosed as "remedial readers" by school tests, when we introduced response-contingent reinforcement, we obtained remarkable improvement, too remarkable to be considered merely as acquisition curves. The conclusion is that many problems appear to be more of a reinforcement problem, called motivational problems in common-sense terms. This means that the development of an appropriate reinforcer system and a method for its application according to learning principles may be the most important step in the solution of the problem. At any rate, we need long-range, systematic studies of sensory-motor training procedures emphasizing the development and application of reinforcement procedures.

Another problem which can be considered similar to those of rehabilitation involves the problems of stuttering as dealt with in a later chapter by Goldiamond. His work in this area may be considered to be a system-

[2] William G. Heard and Karl A. Minke.
[3] Edward M. Hanley and Albert E. Neal.

atic application of certain principles of reinforcement to the study of this type of behavior. In general, the principles seem to hold well and this suggests that the behavior is acquired, at least in part, according to reinforcement principles. The next step is to work with actual problems of stuttering in an attempt to modify the behavior of stuttering and produce procedures and principles that have general applicability.

Thus, at this time we need to multiply the number of investigators who approach a specific type of behavior via the experimental analysis of that behavior in long-term projects. We have the basic principles of learning and a number of experimental procedures for applying the principles to the problems of individuals. But the fact remains that we need many more experimental analyses of behavior problems that are carried as far as they can go in the solution of complex human behavior problems. With reference to these needs, we will describe more fully the general requirements for long-term studies of a specific type of behavior.

To begin the extension of basic learning principles to a complex human behavior, it is necessary to make a learning analysis of the behavior involved. This analysis can be of several types. One way (such as Bijou describes) is to begin with systematic observations of the behavior. This might be elaborated to include observations of the reinforcers which are acting upon the behavior, as well as deprivation and satiation operations which affect the reinforcers, and the way the reinforcers become reinforcing, if conditioned reinforcers are involved. The discriminative stimuli which have come to control the behavior may be important. This may include various types of stimuli—environmental, response-produced, interoceptive, and so on. The behavior in which one is interested may actually be a complex chain itself, not a singular, momentary response. The observations should include reference to competing behaviors. As both Lindsley (1956) and Ferster (1961) have shown, whether or not psychotic episodes occur is a function not only of the strength of the psychotic behavior itself but also of competing behaviors.

But the learning analysis does not have to start with such systematic observations. It may be worthwhile to emphasize, because of misdirected general disdain for theory by some reinforcement "theorists," that the start of the extension of learning principles may be theoretical. It may be done tentatively, on a verbal level, prior to obtaining any further observations. It was interesting to me in reading the chapters of the other authors in this volume that in two cases there were vigorous denials of any interest in theory, yet Skinner's analysis of human behavior, especially verbal behavior, in the absence of any experimental substantiation, was the basis of their own work. It should be pointed out that any extension of a learning principle to a new domain of behavior is theoretical until corroborated, and can quite legitimately be called a hypothesis.

The fact is that this type of "theoretical" analysis is important, and in many cases precedes even systematic, naturalistic observation. It is only a misconception of what constitutes theory in psychology which leads to the general rejection of analysis before experimentation or, as Skinner calls his *Verbal Behavior,* "exercises in interpretation." Tentative guesses concerning the types of learning variables which may have accounted for a behavior are more than empty gestures. They suggest procedures that can, when applied, verify the guess or eliminate it as a possibility. Untestable concepts such as those that abound in dynamic approaches may not offer this advantage, but guesses in terms of empirical principles do suggest empirical applications.

Whether the analysis is based upon systematic observations or theory, the next step in the extension of learning principles frequently involves a "demonstrational" study. This means testing some of the main principles of the analysis in the context of the behavior in which we are interested. For example, is reinforcement important in the acquisition and maintenance of the behavior involved? In demonstrational studies one may choose to use group designs and statistical analyses in short-term experiments. The most expeditious way to verify the basic principles in the new behavior domain may be advisable. In any event, we have found that in these demonstrational studies one begins to learn more about the behavior and subject population involved, and one may get ideas pertinent to more systematic study of the behavior.

The next step is to make a more systematic attempt to explore the principles involved in the acquisition, maintenance, or change in the behavior under study. Additional variables may be tested at this time, such as reinforcement schedules, discriminative stimulus control, etc. The studies of Bijou and associates (Bijou & Oblinger, 1960; Bijou & Orlando, 1961) with the operant conditioning of mental retardates may be considered as an example here. At this stage of the long-term study of a behavior problem, the attempt may be made to achieve better experimental control, perhaps through the development of improved procedures or apparatus. If the behavior under study is complex, as most significant human behaviors are, it can be expected that short-term group studies will not suffice. Procedures will have to be worked out in which the behavior can be studied over a long period of time. We have to distinguish the modification of what are actually relatively simple behaviors, or classes of behavior, from the modification of more complex behaviors. It is stimulating to us, and a momentous step, to extinguish temper tantrums, or shape walking versus crawling, or shape going to bed at night without a fuss, or the striking of a target in a previously useless arm. But we have to realize what the nature of this progress in learning extension is, and the task that lies ahead as well. These are impressive demonstrations of the relevance and applicability of learning principles to the treatment of behavior problems. However, we cannot expect to restore the word salad of the schizophrenic to high-level communication and good language behavior in reasoning through a short-term procedure. There are many behaviors, such as the original acquisition of speech, the acquisition of reading, the development of complex social behaviors, work behaviors, and so-called mental retardation, which are acquired, or are not acquired, only over a period of many years. We must expect that it will take years to change or institute those behaviors even under good training procedures. Nevertheless, we must begin the study of such complex human behaviors, as well as more simple ones. But a belief that the operant shaping of a simple behavior in a short time indicates that all behaviors will fall into place this way is unrealistic. Although it would be expected on the basis of our findings that the principles hold from rat to man, the repertoire to be acquired by man is fantastically complex.

The learning approach appears to be tremendously productive, but there is much to do. This fact brings us to the final step in the extension of learning to the solution of practical problems of behavior. On the basis of our research in the acquisition of reading, it can be concluded that when one works over a period of years with the same problem of training behavior, he learns a great deal about what can be done about some of the problems involved in modifying the behavior in a benign way. With this experience he is better prepared to begin research on actual practical problems. For example, prior to training a child to read, the procedure to be used had been worked out carefully on the basis of past research. For solving actual problems, however, the simple knowledge of basic learning principles will not provide adequate background. Many learning theorists occupied solely with basic problems will confess quite frankly that they would not have the foggiest notion of how to help solve human problems involving learning, for example, how to train a child to read. The preceding steps outlined will, on the other hand, provide knowledge for approaching practical problems of behavior in quest of general solutions.

It is important for investigators to become interested in the systematic and detailed study of a type of behavior and continue with the study over a long period of time, extending their progress as far as they can go toward the solution of the practical problems involved. A great deal of knowledge can be gained in the practical situation in which one attempts to modify behavior, even if the situation does not involve precise laboratory control. This is a point worth stressing, for there are many experimental psychologists of a learning orientation who are really opposed to the applied extension of learning principles. Many are methodological "purists" who feel that if one cannot achieve precise experimental control one should not tackle a problem. There is also in some circles a denigration of applied research when contrasted with basic or "pure" science. Actually, the full status of a science is achieved when it aids in the solution of practical problems and improves on common-sense notions. The application of learning principles and methods to practical problems is an important way of advancing the science of behavior. These applications are one of the most important types of problems in which a behavioral psychologist can be involved.

In this process one can expect that the first efforts will not be accomplished with laboratory precision. To expect this would be to place too difficult a standard on the activity. Successive approximations to precision should be expected. The first development of a procedure may be relatively gross, but these steps must be taken to gain further knowledge on which to make improvements.

This raises some questions about the assessment of one's results. If the training requires long-term procedures, single organism research is implied. What means can be used to assess results? One way is the one we used in the context of reading, in which the same child was put under two experimental conditions and the behaviors produced under each could be compared. In long-term studies it was possible to produce reliable results.

Another way is to consider the patient's previous history of behavior as the baseline, as the controlled period. Then, when learning conditions are instituted, the resulting behavior may be compared to the pretreatment behavior, Wolf, Risley, and Mees, (1964) used this method. They plotted the child's behavior of wearing glasses after instituting reinforcement procedures, when previously the child could not be made to wear glasses. The work of Isaacs, Thomas, and Goldiamond (1960), in which the speech of two long-standing mute schizophrenics was restored by operant procedures, is another example.

It might also be suggested that, at first, assessment may not be crucial. It would seem perfectly appropriate at first to apply learning methods solely as methods of treatment. The psychologist who first works out procedures for behavior modification, even without precise means of assessment, will have performed a service to the science and to the profession. This is especially the case if the procedures can be generally applied.

In conclusion, the methods and principles of learning seem to offer the possibility for dealing with disorders of behavior in a more profound manner than is otherwise currently available. However, it is suggested that great advances still lie ahead in the application of learning methods and principles to behavior problems. In this task, because behavioristic psychotherapy is based upon the manipulation of observable independent and dependent variables, the method should have advantages charcteristic of other applied sciences—one of which is their "self-corrective" nature. That is, when working with observable events, it is evident when something has been accomplished and when it has not, where principles hold and where they do not, where development is still necessary and where it is satisfactory. Since learning approaches to behavior modification are based upon a set of experimentally established principles, a development consistent with that occurring in other applied sciences can be confidently predicted.

# 4

# Experimental Studies of Child Behavior, Normal and Deviant*

## SIDNEY W. BIJOU

As Bijou points out, the research on enhancing the capabilities of children, reported on in this chapter, was made possible by his previous basic research dealing with the effect of reinforcement schedules on performance (Bijou, 1958b; Bijou & Orlando, 1961), discrimination performance (Bijou, 1961), the use of positive reinforcers with children (Bijou & Sturges, 1959), and the differential reinforcing effects of an experimental situation (Bijou & Oblinger, 1960). These studies developed the methodology and techniques for the observation and quantification of children's behavior (Bijou, 1957, 1958a). Bijou's theoretical position has been clearly stated in an excellent and concise review of the operant viewpoint (Bijou & Baer, 1961), which presents "a systematic and empirical theory of human psychological development from the point of view of natural science." In a recent paper, Bijou (1963) outlines a program for research and treatment of mental retardation. He summarizes his formulation as follows:

> Instead of viewing the cause of psychological retardation as being a theoretical construct such as mentality, or as a biological phenomenon such as impairment of the brain, it is suggested that it be conceived as generated by adverse histories or simply as failures of coordinations of stimulus and response functions. This position suggests a search for the specific conditions of which limited repertoires may be a function. The search may be directed, as it would in studying normal and accelerated development, toward analyzing organismic variables—the role of the hereditary process and the environmental events influencing consequent organismic variables—and the life history of the total organism interacting with environmental events from the time of fertilization. A functional analysis suggests a search into interactions conceptualized as intermittent reinforcement and extinction, inadequate reinforcement history, severe punishment, and other factors, such as extreme satiation and deprivations, and emotional operations. (Bijou, 1963, p. 109)

Bijou's chapter reflects a progression from laboratory to field, from theory to

* Many of the investigations reported here have been supported in large measure or entirely from three grants (M-02208, M-02232, and MH-01366) from the National Institute of Mental Health, Public Health Service.

application, and from application to future implications. Bijou has developed a mobile laboratory that can be taken directly to the field. Not only is a traveling laboratory a matter of convenience, it also brings to the field a rigorous experimental framework. In the previous chapter, Staats raises the problem of how to collect information for a functional analysis of behavior. Bijou illustrates how this can be done by describing studies at the nursery school and at the child development clinic. Bijou's method involves observation over long periods of time of the frequency and duration of specific classes of behavior and the stimulus consequences of such behavior. Later chapters by Salzinger et al., Patterson, and Goldiamond further illustrate this approach.

Bijou exemplifies Ferster's earlier comments on categorization and diagnosis. By observing the multiple conditions that operate at any given moment, Bijou demonstrates the clear line from assessment to treatment. This is possible only when behavior is dealt with directly. The point can also be made that the nature of the treatment determines the focal areas of assessment. This is very different from the current popular views in clinical psychology on the relationship between diagnosis and treatment. In one view diagnostic procedures take on a functional autonomy manifested by long, comprehensive, beautifully written evaluations that are completely irrelevant to subsequent therapeutic endeavors. A reaction to such exercises in futility is the opposite view that diagnosis is unnecessary and even contrary to creating a nonevaluative, accepting, therapeutic atmosphere. Further, like Ferster before him, Bijou questions the usefulness of current nosologies and presents evidence for the usefulness of behavioral descriptions and therapies.

Bijou gives specific illustrations of treatment potentialities. The work on the autistic child represents an extension of the earlier research of Ferster and DeMyer (1961), Hingtgen et al. (1965), and Williams (1959). When the behavior of a disturbed child is put within the framework of a functional analysis, retraining and programing of socially desirable behavior becomes feasible. This retraining may involve important figures in the child's life, his parents, his teachers, or the ward staff if he is institutionalized. The adult figures are guided in taking more active and effective roles. Almost paradoxically these roles are often easier for adults to accept than the typical injunction to "be loving and kind." The parent is used to extend the therapeutic situation and to facilitate generalization (Phillips, 1960; Rickard & Mundy, 1965; Patterson, 1965a). This active role is satisfying to parents and to staff workers because they feel that they are making useful contributions to the child.

One of the important implications of Bijou's research is the focus on the development of new repertoires through improved environments rather than a focus on the child's deficiencies. The responsibility devolves upon the therapist to use considerable ingenuity in programing the learning situation. As we have seen in Staats' chapter, reading is not a matter of "reading readiness" so much as it is a question of arranging appropriate environmental stimuli to elicit and shape reading behavior. Other examples of programed learning are given by Dailey

(1963), Holland and Skinner (1961), and Berlin and Wyckoff (1963). These latter two investigators devised a programed course for improving communication in marriage. This course applies behavior modification procedures on a "do it yourself basis." In addition to providing information about communication in a step-by-step "program," the home course requires the husband and wife "students" to set the book aside and discuss specific ideas or to "role play" hypothetical situations. Other illustrations of the usefulness of programing people to modify their own environment to obtain greater control over their own behavior are given by Sulzer (1965), Ferster et al. (1962), and Mertens (1964b).

Bijou's approach leads to functional analysis of other important human behaviors such as concept formation and creativity. Work in this area depends more upon the ingenuity of the examiner than nebulous characteristics within the subject. In a broader fashion, both in formal training programs and in day-to-day child rearing, abilities at problem-solving or creativity may be fostered by reinforcement of selected behaviors and shaping to progressively higher levels. For example, Polya (1954, 1957) offers a series of suggestions on how to approach problems. In a similar fashion, the creative act might be broken down into necessary behaviors and approaches to problems such as question-asking, set-breaking, and implication-seeking. These behaviors can be systematically reinforced to make their application in new situations more likely. Parents may easily apply the concept of shaping in reinforcing "good mistakes" by their children; that is, mistakes that indicate thought, application of previous information, or deductive thinking. While such mistakes involve incorrect answers (frequently through lack of information or mature discrimination), they should be reinforced as responses that progressively approach desirable solutions. The great danger for parents is to reinforce only perfect solutions, in which case the result is extinction.

Finally, Bijou's research with "normal" nursery school children has many implications for preventive measures. Knowledge of the basic principles of social reinforcement would prove extremely valuable for parents in child rearing. More often than not parents "love" their children, but still do not know how to influence them to develop the habits necessary to success in the schoolroom and in later life. Bijou echoes Staats' optimism both in terms of prevention and treatment of deviant behavior, and adds impressive empirical evidence for the effectiveness of behavior modification.

L.K.-L.P.U.

## TREATMENT OF "PROBLEM" PARENT-CHILD RELATIONSHIPS
## IN A CLINICAL SITUATION

MUCH OF A CHILD's deviant behavior is established and maintained by parents, especially by the mother because of her unique relationship with the child. On this assumption, studies have been conducted at the University of Washington to explore the feasibility of treating "problem" parent-child relationships through the training of the mother in a clinical situation. These investigations have been carried out by Wahler and his associates since 1962.

The specific object of the research was to determine whether a child's deviant behavior as initially reported by the mother could be effectively modified by her under the supervision of a clinical investigator. The deviant behavior studied would be considered mild by psychological standards but was serious enough to bring the mothers to the clinic. The children were of preschool age, two 4-year-olds and one 6-year-old. The mothers were well educated and of middle-class socioeconomic status.

### The Research

A résumé will be given of the research with the 6-year-old boy who was described by his mother as overdemanding.

The mother was first oriented to the plans and procedures to be used to gather and analyze data. She was then asked to accompany her child to the playroom and play with him the way she would if she were at home.

Two observers, monitoring the room through microphone and one-way glass, recorded all of the child's behavior, verbal and nonverbal, and all of the mother's verbal and nonverbal behavior occurring immediately following the child's behavior.

Data of the child's behavior collected over two sessions were classified as deviant or normal. Behaviors related to the mother's complaint were considered deviant. In this case, the behavior in point was commanding behavior, defined as any verbal instructions to the mother such as "Now, let's play this!" "You go there and I'll stay here!" "No, that's wrong! Do it this way!"

Behaviors that were incompatible with the deviant behaviors were considered normal; in this case these consisted of the child's playing and behaving in a cooperative manner. They were defined as any verbal or nonverbal behavior clearly directed to the mother which involved requests, statements, or nonverbal activities not imperative or aggressive in content, such as, "Will you help me?" or "This is fun," or bringing a toy to his mother and placing it on her lap.

Data on the mother's behavior following her child's problem behavior or socially acceptable behavior were also classified and analyzed. This information provided clues to the type of social reinforcers the mother habitually used in such situations.

Following the analysis, two more sessions were held in which the mother was again instructed to play with her child in the way she would at home. The observers now recorded only three classes of behavior—two for the child (commanding and cooperative) and one from the mother, following either class of the child's behavior. The recording was done through a checklist in which one mark was made every five seconds for any of the previously classified deviant or socially acceptable behaviors occurring during the five-second intervals. In addition, one check per interval was made for any behavior of the mother's which occurred immediately after the child's two classes of behaviors. *No other classes of behavior were recorded.*

These sessions provided a measure of the frequency of occurrences of the child's commanding and cooperative behaviors and a measure of the frequency with which the mother responded to them. They served as baseline measures.

Data were plotted as two separate cumulative curves. One showed the frequency of commanding behaviors and the mother's complying reactions to them such as "OK, let's do it," "Am I doing it right now?" and "OK, if that's what you think." The other curve showed the frequency of cooperative behaviors and the mother's reactions to them, such as looking, smiling, and saying "That's fun," "Aren't you good," etc. The rate of the commanding curve was, not surprisingly, much greater than the cooperative curve.

In order to determine whether the mother's behavior following the boy's commanding behavior was in fact serving a reinforcing function, the mother was instructed during the next two sessions, 20 minutes each, to ignore her child completely except on signal from the investigator. A flashing red light, arranged so that it was apparent only to the mother, served as her cue. When the light was on she was to do whatever seemed natural to the situation but was to restrict herself to one statement or action. The investigator used the signals so that commanding behavior was not reinforced while cooperative behavior was. The results showed that the rate of commanding behaviors decreased while cooperative behaviors increased over the baseline rates.

In order to test further the functional properties of the mother's behavior consequent to the child's, the experimenter instructed her during the next two 20-minute sessions to behave the way she did during the baseline sessions. She was told also that the signals would be discontinued. The cumulative curves for these sessions showed a marked increase in rate of commanding behavior and a marked decrease in rate of cooperative behavior as compared to the two rates in the two previous sessions.

The last four sessions produced convincing data that the mother's responses, made contingent upon commanding and cooperating behavior, could be said to have reinforcing functioning properties.

The next phase of the research is still in progress. It consists of having the mother revert to ignoring commanding behavior and socially reinforcing cooperative behavior. While this is in progress she is being taught to discriminate between the two classes of behavior with increasing accuracy. The object is to provide her with a program which would increase her perceptual skill in this regard and would at the same time wean her from the investigator.

The program consists of (a) describing and giving examples of commanding and cooperating behaviors, (b) giving instructions on how to react to each class of behaviors, (c) holding sessions in which she decides which form of behaving is being displayed, and having her react accordingly. (If it is commanding, ignore; if it is cooperating, reinforce.) The investigator helps her form her discriminations by flashing the light when her decision is correct. It is assumed that the light flash serves as a reinforcer.

The final stage, if there is a *final* stage to this or any other research, will consist of checking on the generality of the mother's responses in other situations, mainly in the home. This phase of the study, which will use similar observation techniques, is yet to be undertaken.

## Clinical Implications

As is apparent, the procedure described combines some features of child therapy and some features of parent-counseling. It is possible that after they are extended and refined by other investigations, these procedures will be more economical in terms of professional time and more effective in terms of durability and generality than current methods for correcting the same type of problems (Bijou, 1954).

It is more than possible that this procedure could become an effective technique for solving mild parent-child relationship problems in cases where the mother is capable of and interested in participating in this type of learning procedure. While this limitation might restrict its use to a small segment of clinic cases, the procedure applied in a situation where such mild problems usually come into bold relief, for example, kindergarten and the first grade, would undoubtedly prove invaluable as a way of helping mothers help their own children make a better adjustment in school. The entire procedure could be carried out in a pair of adjacent rooms in a school building. Here, indeed, is a method that could go a long way in preventing more serious personal-social problems and academic learning problems.

The approach described here could well be used to bring together the diagnostic and treatment functions in child clinical practice. In addition to or in place of ascertaining mental abilities and personality traits, this approach suggests a way of collecting data on specific behavior in specific problem situations. Clinicians with a knowledge of behavior techniques could combine data of this sort with information from the child's history and current family situation to effectively plan child therapy programs in the clinic.

This research could not have taken place without the members of the Developmental Psychology Laboratory staff first working out a field analysis methodology yielding data on response strength, in terms of frequency of occurrence, and on functional relationships (Harris, Johnston, Kelley, & Wolf, 1964; Hart, Allen, Buell, Harris, & Wolf, 1964; Allen, Hart, Buell, Harris & Wolf, 1964). Once the method was devised, the relationships between mother and child could be viewed in objective terms by the clinic staff and used as an effective aid in training. Summaries of the data could be shown to the mother, helping her to understand the significance of the relationships and showing which specific changes ought to be made. Furthermore, this method of collecting data, along with careful planning, made it possible to carry on provocative research and effective service activities simultaneously.

## GUIDANCE OF PRESCHOOL CHILDREN
## IN A NURSERY SCHOOL SETTING

The objectives of nursery school are given in various forms in the literature. Read (1955), for example, outlines these goals: (a) promote physical health, physical growth, and motor development; (b) promote mental health—increased independence, self-confidence, security, liking for others, understanding of self, acceptance of reality, and constructive handling of emotions; (c) develop skills—self-expression in art, music, rhythm, and language; and (d) increase knowledge—understanding of world, and broaden intellectual horizons through trips, experience with animals and materials, and the like.

The nursery school curriculum also includes a program for parents. The objectives of this phase of the curriculum usually include helping parents to understand their children, other children, themselves, and other adults.

Recommended nursery school practices are usually based on current conceptions of mental hygiene. Here are some samples from a list drawn up by Landreth (1942): (a) The teacher should keep contacts with the children at a minimum and when made they should be based on the children's needs. (b) The teacher should get the child's attention before making requests or giving directions. (c) She should give suggestions in a positive rather than negative form. (d) She should avoid raising issues. (e) She should attempt to redirect a considerable amount of the child's activity in terms of his motive rather than the activity. (f) She should remember that the best help is that which foresees and forestalls trouble rather than that limited to straightening out difficulties. (g) She should do nothing when in doubt, unless a child's physical safety is involved.

The research reported here relates to that aspect of nursery school guidance which aims at improving the child's mental health. The approach involves applications of reinforcement or empirical behavior principles (Bijou & Baer, 1961). Since this is a relatively new theoretical orientation upon which to base nursery school procedures, many of the practices described here will be in contrast with those generally advocated.

## The Research

Since 1962, investigations have been conducted to determine whether disadvantageous social behaviors can be weakened and adjustive behaviors can be strengthened by systematically applying reinforcement procedures involving social stimuli. These studies may be described as field-experimental since they were carried out in the natural setting of a nursery school.

A prerequisite for research of this sort is a method of gathering data in a form suitable for functional analysis. As mentioned in the previous section, such a method was initially worked out in preliminary studies both in the Laboratory Nursery School and the Child Development Clinic of the Developmental Psychology Laboratory and later refined in research dealing with actual behavior modification. The special features of the method used are: (a) observing and recording changes in frequency of occurrence, or frequency and duration of occurrences of one class of behavior (for example, time spent on the climbing equipment), (b) recording the stimulus consequences of behavior usually in terms of changes in the behavior of the teacher (for example, giving attention, praise, or support) and the behavior of other children (for example, running away), and (c) using samples extending over the full school day or the majority of school hours.

These procedures were systematically applied to reinstate walking, running, jumping, etc. in a 3-year-old girl who had regressed to crawling (Harris et al. 1964), to reduce operant crying and strengthen socially acceptable responses in two 4-year-old boys (Hart et al. 1965), and to increase social interaction in a 3-year-old boy and a 4-year-old girl (Allen et al., 1964). The last study will be described in some detail.

The subject, Ann, was of above average intelligence and came from a family in the upper-middle socioeconomic class. After 6 weeks in the nursery school, which is considered the normal period required for adaptation, it was noted that she spent a small part of her time with children. Most of her time was spent with adults or alone, sometimes in constructive occupation, other times just sitting and standing about. Most of her time with adults was devoted to trying to attract the teacher's attention with her collections of rocks, pieces of wood, etc., and talking about her scratches, bumps, and bruises. Her speech was hesitant and low, and at times she showed tic-like behaviors.

Two trained observers recorded Ann's behaviors each morning under the regular and usual conditions of school attendance. With the exception of snack time, time spent with children and time spent with adults was recorded at 10-second intervals over 5 mornings. Data derived provided a baseline and information on the reliability of the raters. Over the 5-day period Ann spent about 10 percent of her time with children and about 40 percent with adults.

On day 6, one of the teachers was assigned to go to Ann immediately and remain with her and her group as long as she was with children. Under these circumstances the teacher watched, commented favorably on Ann's play and especially the play activity of the group. The teacher was also instructed to give Ann minimal or no attention when she was alone or with adults, including the teacher herself. Under these conditions, which were in effect for 6 days (day 6 to day 11), Ann spent about 60 percent of the mornings in play with her peers and less than 20 percent in contact with adults.

On day 12, and the 5 succeeding days, the contingencies were reversed, that is, the baseline conditions were again reinstated. During this period (day 12 to day 16) interactions with children fell to about 20 percent and interactions with adults rose to about 40 percent.

On day 17, and during the succeeding 8 days, the teacher again reinforced Ann for contact and play with peers. Over this time span, play with children stabilized at about 60 percent, and contacts with adults at about 25 percent. Adult attention for interaction with children was gradually made more intermittent, and the schedule of nonreinforcement of adult contacts was gradually relaxed during the last days of this period.

Six days (day 31) after the last day of the study (day 25) the first post-study check was made to see whether the changes persisted. Other checks were made on the thirteenth, fifteenth, and twenty-sixth days after completion of the main study. These data showed that the changes were maintained in that Ann was spending about 54 percent of her mornings with children and about 18 percent with adults.

### Clinical Implications

It seems probable that empirical behavior principles may be applied to achieve other objectives of nursery school guidance—promotion of physical health, development of essential skills, and increase of knowledge. In fact, several investigations along these lines are under way. Saltzman, at Harvard, has been intensively studying, during the past 4 years, the programing of the basic elements of music for children in the Lesley-Ellis school, Cambridge, Massachusetts. In regard to intellectual and preacademic skills, Long, at North Carolina, has been developing programs of deductive reasoning, form perception, analytic and synthetic processes, and the like, and administering them to elementary school children in marginal economic communities. Likewise, Holland, at Harvard, has been concerned with programed instruction in inductive reasoning, and Bijou with form discrimination and concept formation in young normal and retarded children. In reference to motor skills, Harris, Allen, Johnston, Hart, Buell, and Kelley, at the University of Washington, have worked on applying behavior principles to increasing activities and motor skills on outdoor play equipment, especially with reluctant children. In addition, Hart has programed fine motor responses involved in knot-tying. With respect to improving emotional adjustment, these same investigators have systematically applied reinforcement techniques to children with personal-emotional problems in the form of tantrums, sulking, passivity, resistance, and fears of specific situations such as manipulating wet materials.

Research along these lines can lead to effective procedures for preventing mental health problems that generate from: (a) the growth of personal-social problems, and (b) the lack of adequate preacademic and academic experiences. The anticipated effectiveness of the method would stem from the fact that the principles used are applied in a systematic fashion and are continually checked against change in actual behaviors.

Investigations of the sort described here have already resulted in bringing together in an efficient manner (a) the diagnostic and guidance components of nursery school practices, and (b) educational and research activities.

As an example of how diagnostic and guidance functions are integrated in the nursery school, we cite the procedure in the school in which this study was conducted. Here the practice is to make a baseline analysis on any child suspected of needing special attention. If the data substantiate the teachers' impressions, a conference is held with the child's parents to discuss the problem and proposed treatment procedures. With the cooperation of the parents, the problem is again assessed under baseline conditions, reinforcement operations are applied, and follow-up procedures are applied to check on maintenance of the resulting change in behavior.

As can be seen, service functions, in this case, educational, can be readily combined with research functions. The main requirements are personnel trained in the behavioral principles of child development, trained observers, and a zest for problem-oriented research that stands or falls on the basis of unencrusted empirical findings.

Finally, findings from this line of investigation suggest that these same principles and practices may be profitably applied to nursery schools for accelerated, retarded, emotionally disturbed, and physically handicapped children. They are at the present time being applied successfully to young retarded children in a school in the Seattle area. It is believed that these techniques may also be applied to older individuals in other settings appropriate for field-experimental procedures as described above.

## TREATMENT AND REHABILITATION OF SEVERELY DISTURBED YOUNG CHILDREN IN A RESIDENTIAL INSTITUTION

Probably the most difficult group of children to understand and treat are those diagnosed as schizophrenic or autistic. Although many clinicians question the clinical usefulness of classificatory terms for emotionally disturbed children, most agree that these two diagnostic terms designate a mental disorder characterized by (a) loss of interest in the environment, (b) emotional disturbances involving rigidity and lack of personal warmth, (c) symptoms of regression or primitivization of behavior, (d) hyperactivity or extreme immobility with posturing, active negativism, and grimacing, (e) disturbances of language, speech, and thinking (Bradley, 1941). It is apparent that this disturbance is believed to pervade all aspects of development.

Psychotherapies applied to schizophrenia or autism have ranged widely, from classical psychoanalysis to milieu therapy. Some therapies include techniques which establish "distance" between the therapist and child, such as story-telling, to avoid strong dependency relationships, since it is believed that transfer of therapeutic effects from clinician to parents is difficult to achieve. In any event, there is consensus among workers following these treatment procedures that progress is slow, difficult, and irregular, and that the ultimate outcome is uncertain. Defective interpersonal relationships are said to be the main stumbling blocks.

Shock and drugs have also been applied widely. Electroshock, and the use of metrazol, metrazol modified by B-Erythroidin, amphetamine sulfate (benzedrine), sodium amytal, ephedrine sulfate, and other drugs have been attempted. The results have been sporadic and variable.

Recently Ferster and DeMyer described a treatment program which combines milieu and individual therapy (Ferster, 1961; Ferster & DeMyer, 1961, 1962). Milieu therapy was based on psychoanalytic theory. Treatment in the laboratory which was designed to bring the child in contact with the environment in gradual stages was founded on reinforcement principles (Ferster, in press). The outcomes of the program were encouraging and provocative.

The study to be discussed here is an extension and elaboration of the work by Ferster and DeMyer. It was planned and supervised by Wolf, Risley, and Mees, (1964). Since its inception, over a year ago, similar studies have been conducted by these investigators and by Daniel Kelleher, of the Child Treatment and Study Center, Fort Steilacoom, Washington.

### The Research

The object of the Wolf, Risley, and Mees, study was to reduce the severe emotional disturbances of a 3½-year-old child and to train him to wear glasses through the systematic application of behavior principles. To achieve these therapeutic and rehabilitation aims, new techniques had to be forged during the course of the study. This dual task was imposed upon the investigators because there was only limited information available on workable behavioral techniques for young children, and practically no information on behavioral techniques applicable to treatment of children in the natural setting of a hospital.

The subject, Dicky, progressed normally until 9 months of age, at which time it was discovered that he had cataracts in both lenses. At this time he also began to display severe temper tantrums and to have sleeping problems. When he was 2 years old he underwent a series of eye operations designed to remove both of his occluded lenses. Following the surgery, glasses were prescribed. His parents attempted to teach him to wear the glasses without success.

During this period, his problem behavior increased. His numerous tantrums now included head-banging, face-slapping, hair-pulling, and face-scratching. His sleeping pattern was extremely irregular; one or both parents were forced to remain by his bed until he was asleep. His eating behavior was far from that expected of a 3-year-old. Furthermore, his development was grossly retarded, especially in the social and verbal aspects. He was diagnosed by specialists as retarded, brain-damaged, and psychotic.

At the age of 3, he was admitted to the state hospital for children with the diagnosis of childhood schizophrenia. After 3 months there was some improvement in his emotional behavior, but none in his willingness to wear glasses. At this time, Wolf, Risley, and Mees, were appointed as consultants to institute a special treatment and rehabilitation program.

All treatment and record-keeping procedures were carried out by the attendants on the ward and parents in the home under the training and supervision of the consultants.

Tantrum behaviors were treated mainly by withdrawal from the immediate social situation. When a tantrum occurred the attendant took Dicky to his room and closed the door. When the tantrum abated and a short interval had elapsed, the attendant took him from his room and continued the activity previously interrupted. After 2½ months the tissue-damaging aspects of the tantrums (head-banging, hair-pulling, and face-scratching) were practically eliminated, and after 5 months the milder components (face-slapping, whining, and crying) became infrequent, on the ward and on home visits.

Normal sleeping habits were developed by weakening getting-out-of-bed behavior and strengthening remaining-in-bed-after-being-"tucked in" behavior. At bedtime Dicky was bathed, cuddled for a while, put in his bed, and left there with the bedroom door open. If he got out of bed he was told to return or the door would be closed. When it was necessary to close the door it remained closed for a short time. If a tantrum occurred while the door was closed, the door remained closed until after the tantrum subsided. Bedtime routine ceased to be a problem after the sixth night.

At mealtime Dicky snatched food from the other children's plates and threw it around the room. Furthermore, he had not yet learned to eat with a spoon. The corrective procedure was to remove him from the dining room whenever he took food from others or whenever he threw food, and when he ate with his fingers his plate was removed for a few minutes. Both of these contingencies (removing him from the dining room for snatching and throwing food and removing his plate for eating with fingers) were applied only after Dicky failed to respond to a warning. While this was going on he was shown how to use a spoon, and when he did, even in an approximate manner, he was reinforced. It was necessary to warn him and send him away from the dining room or remove his plate only a few times to establish appropriate eating behaviors.

Shaping procedures were used to get Dicky to wear his glasses. The initial step was to place lenseless frames around the room. He was reinforced for picking them up, holding them, and carrying them. He was reinforced for bringing the frames closer to his eyes by successive approximations. It was found necessary to use food as reinforcers and to conduct training sessions prior to meal times, using the meal for training.

It was also found necessary to add mechanical aids to the frame of the glasses to facilitate placement on the nose and over the ears. After the initial phase of getting the glasses on the child's head, a feat that called for great patience and proficiency on the part of the senior investigator, glasses-wearing was extended over an increasing number of hours a day by making glasses-wearing a prior condition for going for a walk, taking automobile rides, playing outdoors, going for snacks, etc. At the time of Dicky's release, 6½ months after admission, he was wearing glasses about 12 hours a day.

Two weeks after he began to wear glasses, he began throwing them. This behavior was treated the same way as other forms of undesirable behavior were treated. Following each throwing episode he was taken to his room for 10 minutes or, if a tantrum developed, until it ceased. After 5 days of such training he stopped throwing his glasses.

After glasses-wearing was established, training was begun to maintain this behavior through reinforcement of visual attending. The same training was also designed to enhance the youngster's verbal development. Initial procedures included the use of pictures and verbal promptings to prime responses and food as reinforcers. By the time Dicky was ready to return home he could initiate requests and make casual comments without prompts from the therapist. The authors point out that the rapid progress made over the 4-month period of training was probably due to the fact that he could, at the beginning of training, mimic phrases and short sentences at least now and then.

Six months after the child's return home the mother reported that "he continues to wear his glasses, does not have tantrums, has no sleeping problems, is becoming increasingly verbal, and is a new source of joy to the members of his family" (Wolf, Risley, & Mees, 1964, p. 312).

*Clinical Implications*

One obvious implication of this study is the need for further explorations of behavior therapy techniques for children. As pointed out, Wolf, Risley, and Mees had little or no information on techniques and therefore had to develop treatment methods while carrying out the therapy. Field-experimental studies are indeed needed which would not only refine the techniques described here but would also develop techniques for dealing with other problems such as toilet training, aggressive behavior, hyperactivity, hypoactivity, and the initiation of language functioning. The work of Lovaas and his colleagues on the treatment of self-destructive behavior and the establishment of social reinforcers in childhood schizophrenia (1964, 1965), and that of Wolf, Birnbrauer, Williams, and Lawler on extinction of vomiting (1965) are examples.

The problem of how to maintain and advance therapeutic gains after treatment is particularly critical in therapy with children since the major portion of children's environments is made up of the behaviors of their parents. Thus far the main procedure for preventing therapeutic "regressions" in children is to administer therapy to one or both parents. It seems from this study that further investigations are needed which would aim at developing techniques for modifying specific parental practices. Parent-training in child-rearing practices might well be programed by the therapist and the consultant in the hospital (after initial therapeutic gains have been made) and in the home. In both settings the guiding principle would be differential reinforcement of successive approximations to the desired practices. Part of the problem would be, of course, to define clearly and explicitly what is meant by "desired practices," and to discover and utilize highly effective reinforcers.

This research also calls attention to the need for re-evaluation of diagnostic procedures for children with respect to (a) terminology, and (b) mode of assessment. In regard to terminology, concepts such as brain injury, mental retardation, and autism need to be evaluated to determine whether they are in fact based on appropriate observable data. For example, if the clinician is considering brain injury as a diagnostic category, he should determine whether the available data are in fact neurological phenomena, not psychological interactions. This is a critical point. It is not advantageous to infer brain injury from psychological behavior. Why? It is axiomatic in a natural science approach that any sample of psychological behavior is the result of many conditions including social, physical, anatomical, or physiological factors, in the subject's past and present (Skinner, 1953, 1959; Kantor, 1959). It is therefore not reasonable to expect a one-to-one correspondence between behavior and any one single class of determining components, whether social, physical, neurological, or any other aspect of biological structure or functioning.

When terms such as mental retardation or autism are employed, the clinician should be aware that they are not merely descriptive terms. For the most part they imply theoretical terms which require evaluation. But even more important, the user should be cognizant of the fact that these labels may carry conceptions and assumptions that generate premature attitudes of futility of treatment. For example, mental retardation in the sense of retarded development, or autism in the sense of predisposition to emotional disturbance, has not been demonstrated to be hereditary. These disturbances, like other forms of psychological behaviors, are undoubtedly determined by multiple conditions—social, physical, and organismic (Bijou, 1963; Ferster, 1965)—and, as such, call for not a dismissing label but a challenge for analysis.

Turning to the second consideration regarding the clinical assessment of children, research efforts are needed to develop diagnostic procedures and concepts based on a functional rather than a correlational analysis. Advances in this direction would lead to an actual continuity between the diagnostic and treatment procedures. Ferster (Chapter 2), among others, has recently made a systematic attempt in this direction.

It has long been apparent that effective psychological treatment must be carried out by hospital attendants, aides, nurses, recreational workers, and others who are in direct daily contact with the patients. Training such personnel poses a problem, particularly when (a) the treatment procedures involve systematic attention to details, and (b) the data to be collected are to be in the form of objective descriptions of behavior occurrences.

What is suggested from this research is renewed interest in the development of effective ways of training and supervising child-care personnel.

## TRAINING OF RETARDED CHILDREN IN READING, WRITING, AND ARITHMETIC IN A SCHOOL FOR THE RETARDED

The long-standing problem of educating the retarded child has come to the forefront in the current wave of concern over the mental health of the nation. What can or cannot be done for the retarded child is still ambiguous, however. Textbooks on the subject suggest that children with IQ's below 50 can be taught self-care, practical skills, and rote understanding of essential words; children with IQ's between 50 and 75 can be taught these skills and the academic tool subjects to about the second- or third-grade level. Academic learning is said to come slowly and with difficulty; therefore curricula for both groups should emphasize motor development. Finally, recommended ways of implementing these objectives vary widely. However, there is consensus on one point: retarded children need lots of repetition and drill in all phases of teaching.

The problems of what retarded children can learn and how they can effectively be taught (whether they do in fact need lots of repetition) present challenges to those interested in applying psychological principles to academic instruction.

As is well known, one group of psychologists who have become interested in applying reinforcement principles to these problems are identified with an approach known as programed instruction or programed learning (for example, Green, 1962). Ever since 1954, when Skinner delivered a paper entitled "The Science of Learning and the Art of Teaching," there has been accelerated activity in resarch and application in this area (see Lumsdaine & Glaser, 1960).

Looking back over the past decade, one sees that the initial efforts were directed toward developing programing machines. This was followed by an increasing interest in the preparation of programs, especially on subjects such as mathematics, which are readily arranged in discrete sequential units. At the present time, one sees the beginnings of three other trends: (a) programing subjects not currently taught in a systematic fashion (for example, deductive thinking), (b) programing preacademic and primarily nonverbal discriminations and skills (for example, nonverbal concept formation), and (c) programing the foundational phases of reading, writing, and arithmetic. Finally, ground is just being broken on the development of programing techniques for children said to require special sequences and contingencies because of their unusual histories or physical disabilities.

The research summarized here is an application of programed instruction to the teaching of reading, writing, arithmetic, and academic behavior to retarded children in a special classroom within a residential institution (Birnbrauer, Bijou, Wolf, Kidder, & Tague, 1964).

### The Research

The study is being conducted at the Rainier School, Buckley, Washington, as a joint project of the University of Washington, the Rainier School, and the White River School District. The specific objective of the research is to produce programs and procedures for instruction in the academic tool subjects.

The pupils are 14 residents of Rainier School and three children from neighboring communities; eight are enrolled for the second year; nine for the first. At the time of first enrollment, their chronological ages ranged from 7-10 to 13-8; their mental ages, from 4-2 to 8-11 on the Peabody Picture Vocabulary Test. IQ's ranged from 44 to 77 with a median of 56.

The subject pupils had attended school prior to the study from 6 months to 5 years. Before special instruction began, California and Metropolitan Achievement tests were administered. Their reading scores ranged from zero to 1.6 grade with a mean .34 grade, and their arithmetic scores from zero to 1.8 grade with a mean .45 grade. Their former teachers described the behavior of some of them as marked by refusals to study, or simply noncompliance with instructions, temper tantrums, pouting, and "wandering attention."

Their clinical diagnoses include mongolism, familial retardation, and retardation associated with brain damage.

The special classroom consists of a large observation room at one end, three individual instructional rooms at the other, and a quiet room off to one side. The classroom proper contains pupils' desks, tables for writing exercises, and general-purpose or work tables for material and equipment storage and for exercises requiring larger working areas. The individual instruction rooms are separated from the classroom by curtains, providing space for observers. Programs requiring the greatest amount of concentration and/or involving auditory stimuli such as reading are presented in these rooms; writing, spelling, and practical exercises are conducted in the classroom proper. The quiet room is for children removed from the classroom because they engage in behavior which interferes with academic work and appropriate school conduct.

Although there are always several pupils in the class at a given time, each child receives instruction on an individual basis, sometimes working alone, sometimes with one of the four assistants, sometimes in the individual instruction booths, sometimes in the classroom proper. The amount of time spent in the room is gradually increased as the child learns to work productively for longer time spans.

The motivation system, which has undergone several major revisions, currently consists of reinforcing correct academic behavior and appropriate classroom conduct with tokens and social reinforcers. The tokens are in the form of "marks" made on one of three sheets of paper in the pupil's booklet. A completed page of marks is redeemable for trinkets, models, pencils, candy, money, or credit toward a larger sum of money and an opportunity to spend it in town. When a pupil makes mistakes in his academic work he is given the correct answer, and in general, systematic procedures are followed to strengthen correct responses and extinguish incorrect responses. When a pupil misbehaves he is given the choice of stopping and returning to his studies or leaving the room. If he does not stop quickly he is placed in the "quiet room" until he remains quiet for a preselected period of time (3-10 minutes). Then assignments continue as before.

At the end of the first year of this research, during which the reading, writing, and arithmetic programs were revised almost on a daily basis, all the programs were completely revised.

The present version of the reading program has three beginnings. The first is instruction in a phonetic alphabet consisting of only short vowels, "hard" consonants, and script letters. The second is instruction in sight vocabulary patterned after the work of Staats, Staats, Schutz, and Wolf (1962). In this program, the pupil selects the printed word, and intermittently reads aloud the same word. The third is a sequence in spelling. The pupil moves printed letters on cards around until he advances far enough in the writing program to write simple words. At first, training in spelling consists of combining letters to match a written word. Then the child is trained to spell from the spoken word or from a textual representation of the word.

Cursive writing is programed by means of an illuminated tracing box. The first stage begins with tracing, because this task provides the pupil with continuous and immediate information about performance as long as the model is clear. The second stage consists of tracing from a model or copying another model located nearby. The third stage involves copying longer items and translating from script models into cursive writing. Writing from dictation, completing sentences to describe pictures, and copying from the child's dictation material follow.

Arithmetic begins in the writing program for the child who cannot write numbers. He then engages in dot-number matching and ordering objects and numbers. Then the concepts of "greater than," "less than," and "equals" are programed with the dot-number approach. From these concepts subtraction and addition facts are begun. As soon as the child can read simple directions, reading, arithmetic, and writing are combined in simple arithmetic reasoning problems and comprehension exercises.

In addition to the basic programs in reading, writing, and arithmetic, there are practical sequences such as telling time, reading the calendar, and the like. These are, of course, integrated with what the child is doing in the tool subjects.

According to the California achievement tests, at the end of the past year, changes in reading skills ranged from −.1 to 1.3 with a median gain of .6 of a grade; and changes in arithmetic, from .3 to 1.4 with a median gain of .8 of a grade. Twelve were using cursive writing in their vocabulary exercises. In addition to their academic achievement they have demonstrated that they can work productively alone up to a half hour or more, and can engage in appropriate school conduct. Judging by their behavior before and after school hours and their easy and pleasant relationships with the teachers it may be said that they have learned to enjoy and be interested in the activities of a class that concentrates entirely on academic subjects.

*Clinical Implications*

What has been described is, of course, a treatment program, since it is geared to teach children academic skills and social behaviors which are bound to improve their adjustment in or out of the institution. Similar procedures could be applied to the treatment of other groups with special or general disabilities. It should be emphasized, however, that the mere programing of academic subjects does not solve the problem of how to instruct exceptional children in the tool subjects. The development of empirically based programs in all the essential detail is only one part of the task. The other parts include the development of a workable motivational system and systematic procedures for the strengthening of precurrent and associated behaviors essential to school work, for example, paying attention, extending work chains, and eliminating personal-social behaviors which compete with academic behaviors. Good programs with ineffective contingency procedures are no more serviceable than poor programs with effective contingency procedures.

Another implication of this study relates to current conceptions or misconceptions of retarded development. Notions about what retarded children can or cannot do are closely tied to an implicit or explicit theory of retarded development. Hence theories that attribute retardation to inherited mentality, or to causes based on medical analogues or on response-inferred hypothetical variables, need to be reviewed, preferably from a natural science point of view.

In addition to offering a positive approach, the natural science view reasserts that when adequate data are not available to reach a conclusion (for example, the limited nature of the attention span of a retarded child), an open-minded attitude should be maintained. It is particularly imperative that caution be exercised in inferring hypothetical variables simply from observed behavior. Such a practice may readily mislead one to believe that he has reached a solution, whereas in reality he has merely given a verbal label to the behavior sequences observed. Examples of this practice include labeling defects in a child's verbal repertoire as alexia or stephosymbolia.

The final implication of this research pertains to the need for further integration in educational diagnosis and treatment procedures. The question of which child can profit from an educational program and how much is still open. In addition to what is now available, techniques based on functional analyses are needed (Ferster, Chapter 2). Such techniques would provide samples of children's actual behavior in relation to academic subject matter and to personal-social emotional situations, under reinforcing conditions and setting events.

## ANALYSIS OF CONCEPTUALIZING BEHAVIOR IN NORMAL AND RETARDED CHILDREN IN A LABORATORY SITUATION

An analysis of concept formation is believed to have considerable promise for the understanding of normal and deviant development, not only because of its complexity but also because of its centrality in much of human behavior. Research on concept formation has been concerned with (a) normative, longitudinal descriptions of verbal and nonverbal concepts, (b) strategies subjects employ in order to arrive at categorizing behavior, (c) differences in performance as diagnostic indicators, especially in suspected organics and schizophrenics, and (d) processes involved in learning. The research to be discussed here—how children learn nonverbal concepts involving left-right orientation—falls into the last category.

How do we define concept formation? Concept formation refers to behavior in which the subject learns to respond to one aspect of the stimulus properties of an object while ignoring (inhibiting responses to) all of the others. It is behavior which shows discrimination to one stimulus dimension of an object and generalization of that dimension to other stimulus objects.

### The Research[1]

The problem was to analyze the stimulus conditions in which young children learn to identify, as similar, geometric forms in the presence of distracting stimuli created by (a) differences in vertical plane rotations, and (b) differences in vertical plane rotations and in right-left orientation. The forms were presented as samples to be matched to one of five forms presented together.

One group of subjects was made up of 100 preschool and primary-grade children from the Lesley-Ellis School, Cambridge, Massachusetts.

[1] This study was conducted during 1961-1962 while the author was on a National Institute of Mental Health Senior Fellowship at Harvard University, working with B. F. Skinner and J. G. Holland.

Intelligence tests were not available; however, according to the usual indications (samples of test scores, reports of teachers, educational and socioeconomic status of parents, father's occupation, etc.), they were probably above average in intelligence.

The other group was composed of 100 retarded children from the Fernald School, Waverly, Massachusetts. They were classified as educable and had mental ages on individual scales of intelligence ranging from 3 to 8.

The stimuli consisted of ten forms cut from 1½-inch squares of red, yellow, green, and blue paper. Each was composed of five ½-inch squares; three formed a vertical column, and two served as appendages protruding from the sides of the column. In some forms the two squares indicating direction were on the same side of the column (for example, L); in others they were on opposite sides (for example, +). Three of the forms (P, ⌐, and ⊢) could be presented in mirror-image orientation when rotated in the horizontal plane (ꟼ, ⅂, and ⊣). Regardless of whether a form had or had not mirror-image possibilities, three-fifths of its total area was oriented north and south, and two-fifths, east and west.

The sample and matches constituting a trial were photographed on 16 mm. color-sensitive film and developed into standard 2 x 2 slides. The slides, also referred to as "frames," were projected on a match-to-sample apparatus, a variation of a device used in infrahuman research. The apparatus was conceived by Skinner and developed by Holland and Long (Holland, 1960, 1963). It consists of a box with a panel of windows to display the stimuli and to register selections, a slide projector, and an event recorder, The child was seated so as to face the two horizontal, translucent plastic windows. The upper window was a single unit, the lower one was divided into five equal parts. The geometric forms were projected on the windows from behind. One form appeared in the center of the large upper window and one in each of the five lower windows. The form in the upper window was the sample; those in the lower windows, the matches. The sample was presented first. The matches appeared only after the child pressed on the sample window. Temporal relationships between the presentations of the sample and choices, the order of slide presentations, and a reinforcing feedback (light and chime) were controlled by automatic programing circuits.

The child indicated which of the five forms matched the sample by pressing on the window in which it appeared. If he made a correct selection a red light glowed momentarily, a chime sounded, the sample and the five choices disappeared, and another sample appeared. The child could then produce the choices by pressing on the sample window and proceed to make the next match. If he made an incorrect choice, the light and chime did not operate but the matches disappeared. (There was also a clearly distinctive thud produced by the mechanism which blacked out the matches.) Pressing on the sample window restored the choices (removed the blackout device) and provided a second opportunity for matching. If the second response was also incorrect, the choices blacked out once more. Pressing again on the upper window restored the matches again. This sequence (press on sample window to display matches; selection of a mismatch; disappearance of matches; press on sample window to display matches, etc.) would be continued until the correct response was made. Making the correct response removed both the sample and the matches and presented another sample. Under this arrangement of contingencies the last response to a problem was always the correct response.

However, when a correct response was preceded by one or more incorrect responses, the next slide presented was the *previous* slide. That is to say, the next slide was a repeat of the slide previously "passed" rather than an advancement to the next slide in the sequence. Thus, a child would not move forward in the program after an error without first reacting a second time to both the preceding slide and the slide just "missed." It was therefore possible for a child to make "new" errors on slides previously passed without error, and to go backward in the program.

Slides were composed with the objective of constructing a sequence of discriminations in which the probability of a correct response to each task would be high; at the same time each would include an increment, as large as possible, of stimulus complexity in the direction of final mirror-image discriminations. In lieu of well-established empirical principles many "first approximation" assumptions were made regarding (a) the selection of the order of samples, its rotational position, and its color, (b) the window location of the correct match, its rotational position, and its color, and (c) the relationships among the samples, correct matches, and incorrect matches with respect to similarities in form, color, degrees of vertical plane rotations, and window locations.

On the basis of a series of studies the slides were graded in order of difficulty and arranged in three sequences: the Elementary Set (25 slides) which enabled children as young as 3 to perform the task and to move smoothly through the initial part of the program; the Intermediate Set (40 slides) which gave experience in matching on the basis of form despite the appearance of figures in any of 12 rotated positions in the vertical plane; the Advanced Set (205 slides) which provided training in discriminating nonmirror-images from mirror-images despite the appearance of figures in any of 12 rotated positions in the vertical plane.

In addition to the Elementary, Intermediate, and Advanced sets, three other sets were prepared with only 20 slides in each. These served to evaluate performance before and after training. One set, designated as the "Original," was made up of 20 duplicates drawn from the Elementary, Intermediate, and Advanced sets. It was designed to test for retention. A second set, the "New Nonsense series," consisted of slides with forms never seen before but resembling those in the training sets in size and color. This set was designed to test for "transfer." The third test, the "Alphabet," was composed of ten letters of the alphabet. The size and color of the letters were the same as the forms in the Original and New Nonsense series. This set was designed to provide information on "transfer of training" to letters.

The problem of teaching the child as young as 3 years of age how to perform the task was solved by the use of special forms—a circle, square, and triangle—and beginning the series with three rather than five choices. The special forms were gradually eliminated and five-choice problems were introduced in easy stages.

The problem of training to discriminate forms solely on the basis of differences in east-west orientation was most difficult. The final solution was the "fading in" of the essential parts of mirror and nonmirror-image forms. After one mirror-image form was discriminated from a nonmirror form, other mirror-images were introduced to strengthen and generalize the acquired discrimination.

The retarded children did not require a special training sequence; that is, they did not need a series with more repetitions or one with more gradual transitions. Like the Lesley-Ellis children, the retarded children made fewer errors on the Original, New Nonsense, and Alphabet tests after training. For both groups, relatively more errors were made on the New Nonsense material. Both groups showed that the location of the sample influenced the selection of the match.

For the retarded group there was a relationship between mental age and extent of progress through the program; the higher the mental age, the greater the probability of completing the sequence. Also, several of the retarded children showed a high frequency of repetitious errors. None of the Lesley-Ellis children did.

### Clinical Implications

This research suggests an approach to the handling of children who come to the clinic because of academic problems which seem to be related to "perceptual" difficulties (including dyslexia). At present the practice is to give tests such as those described by Goldstein and Scheerer (1953), Hanfmann (1953), and Bender (1938) to ascertain the extent of the difficulties, make a diagnosis in terms of abstract and concrete attitudes or level of abstract thinking or perceptual pathology, and evaluate the need for treatment by a specialist.

Perceptual training programs, like the one described here, could be developed for use in the clinic. The end of a program could be administered as a diagnostic test to determine the severity of the difficulty; and then the program would be given, over as many sessions as required, in an attempt to develop the required skills. Of course, care would have to be taken to be sure that the child is properly motivated and reinforced and that the learning achieved "carries over" to materials in reading, writing, and arithmetic.

The approach described in this research could also be used to diagnose and treat perceptual, symbolic, and language disabilities in aphasic children and adults. The objective would not simply be to diagnose the variety and extent of the disablement but also to treat by means of programing techniques. It would also not be designed to pinpoint further the location and extent of neurological damage, but rather to discover what is required by way of arranging and rearranging materials, procedures, and motivational states to recover lost functions.

Finally, this research suggests an approach which could help prevent school failures. It is generally assumed that when children are enrolled in the first grade they have learned the discriminations and skills necessary for the beginning phases of reading, writing, and arithmetic. Those who do not have these behaviors are said not to be "ready." In all probability many of the unprepared children are those who have not had the necessary opportunities with preacademic stimuli to allow them to develop appropriate perceptual, cognitive, abstraction, and concept-formation behaviors. Programs designed to train children in the essential discriminations (for example, size, shape, color, orientation) and processes (for example, deductive and inductive reasoning, analysis, and synthesis) could be constructed for use in the nursery schools, kindergartens, or the early part of the first grade. Such sequences would be similar to Thelma Thurstone's training exercises in primary mental abilities and the nonverbal programs that Long is using in his research at North Carolina.

## SUMMARY AND CONCLUSIONS

This chapter presents a review of some of the investigations with children in progress at the University of Washington viewed in the light of their implications for clinical practice. Since all studies have a common theoretical orientation, often referred to as empirical behavior theory (Skinner, 1953; Kantor, 1959; Bijou & Baer, 1961), the task has been, in large measure, to show how such a behavior theory may make contributions to clinical psychology (Birnbrauer, 1963).

The research discussed included the treatment of "problem" parent-child relationships in a child-clinical situation in which the mother is the recipient of training as therapist; field-experimental studies in the guidance of nursery school children with mild emotional and behavior problems; the psychological treatment and physical rehabilitation of severely disturbed young children in a residential institution; the training of retarded children in reading, writing, arithmetic, and academic behavior in a special classroom in the context of a residential school; and the analysis of conceptualizing behavior in normal and retarded children in a laboratory situation.

The clinical implications of each line of investigation have been given. We may summarize them in terms of their pertinence to clinical work.

1. *Diagnosis.* Many of the currently used diagnostic terms for children might well be re-evaluated with respect to their empirical moorings, and the concept of "symptom" be re-examined in relation to the subject matter of psychology from a natural science point of view, and the meaning of the term in medical practice. It is further suggested that explorations be made in developing a diagnostic approach based on a functional analysis. It is expected that diagnostic procedures based on a functional analysis will eventually replace the normative-correlational analysis now in general use, because it is expected to be more efficient and more effective.

2. *Psychotherapy and rehabilitation.* There is need for systematic investigations to refine and develop treatment techniques based on behavior theory. Such techniques would be designed to be serviceable in the hospital, clinic, school, and home.

3. *Integration of diagnostic and treatment procedures.* Concepts and procedures need to be further developed that would by their very nature make apparent the continuity of diagnostic procedures on the one hand, and treatment, guidance, and rehabilitation procedures on the other. In most instances at present, diagnostic and treatment methods do not stem from a common theory, systematic view, or set of assumptions. Integration of the two functions are "forced" mainly through the instrumentation of the case conference method.

4. *Prevention.* Explorations might well be made into empirically established programs dealing with mild emotional and behavior problems in preschool and elementary-school-age children. Such programs, which could be carried out in the school setting, would be designed to prevent the development of severe problems in the later years. It is also suggested that the principles of learning as applied to programed instruction techniques be explored to provide preacademic experiences for children with disadvantageous economic and social histories.

5. *Training child-care personnel in psychotechnology.* Research reviewed here suggests that effort be devoted to the development of techniques for training personnel who work with children in hospitals, clinics, preschools, and schools. This is an aspect of clinical work that has received considerable attention by the profession but has as yet resulted in only limited action in the university and field situations.

6. *Integration of research and service.* It has been demonstrated in the studies reviewed that service functions in education, remediation, rehabilitation, and therapy may be rendered and that meaningful experi-

mental investigations may be conducted at the same time. Research of the sort described here differs from much of the research currently being carried on in clinical settings in that it is not based on impressions from clinical contacts or on correlational analyses of data collected in the clinical procedures. Experimental research in the clinic would not only lead to practical and theoretic advancements but would also add a new source of stimulation to clinical work.

Although it is not pointed out in the body of the chapter, the research methodologies themselves, the field-experimental and laboratory-experimental procedures described, have implications for clinical psychology. Some of the procedures can be employed without modification; others may have to be changed slightly to take into account conditions in diagnosis, treatment, and prevention not considered in research to date.

# 5

## Operant Conditioning of Verbal Behavior of Two Young Speech-Deficient Boys*

### KURT SALZINGER, RICHARD S. FELDMAN,†

### JUDITH E. COWAN,† AND

### SUZANNE SALZINGER†

The central interest in Salzinger's work has been verbal and vocal behavior, its units (Salzinger, 1962; Salzinger, Feldman, & Portnoy, 1964), and its content (Salzinger, Portnoy, & Feldman, 1962; Salzinger, Portnoy, Zlotogura, & Keisner, 1963). The range of the subjects he has worked with includes dogs (Salzinger & Waller, 1962), normal adults (Salzinger & Pisoni, 1960), schizophrenics (Salzinger & Pisoni, 1958), and, as in the present chapter, children. As called for by Staats and Goldiamond, Salzinger has progressed from the single-meeting experimental sessions typical of academic studies of verbal behavior to the long-term relationships described in this chapter.

The authors of this chapter provide greater detail about the application of operant conditioning procedures than any of the other contributions in this book. The authors illustrate how technical jargon has specific operational meaning in regard to examiner behavior. Like the presentations by Bijou and Saslow, this chapter serves as a useful illustration of specific techniques.

* This research was supported in part by the following grants from the National Institute of Mental Health, United States Public Health Service: M1541, MY2785, MY4758, MH04842, and MH07477.

We are very grateful to the many people at the New York State Psychiatric Institute, whose cooperation made possible our work with these children: Dr. L. C. Kolb, Director; Dr. H. D. Dunton, Director of Children's Service; Dr. S. Bennett, Assistant Director of Children's Service; Dr. J. Sours, Dr. D. Coddington, Dr. D. Hansen, Dr. T. Cassidy, S. Howell, J. Hodge, and J. Schaeffer. We especially thank M. Van Hook, J. Armellino, P. Kleeman, and the many nurses, attendants, and students who helped us in innumerable ways. Dr. S. J. Coen brought the first child discussed here to our attention and participated in the initial stages of the research. V. Schmauder assisted in the analysis of vocalization rate. Finally, we thank Dr. J. Zubin, whose interest and assistance have continued since the very beginning of this work.

† A portion of Richard S. Feldman's participation in this research, and all of Judith E. Cowan's and Suzanne Salzinger's participation, took place during the tenures of Predoctoral Fellowships from the National Institute of Mental Health, United States Public Health Service.

Just as experiments are replicable because the procedures are operationally defined, so too behavior therapy of the type described by Salzinger *et al.* is readily taught. This point is made by Davison (1965), who presents data on training undergraduate students for work with disturbed children.

Salzinger *et al.* broaden the conception of what is a reinforcing situation. For instance, they use behavior which they wish to reduce, such as leaving the experimental room, to reinforce the behavior they wish to increase, such as remaining in the room. This use of one behavior, often an undesirable one, to reinforce another, is also illustrated by Homme *et al.* (1963) with nursery school children, and Schwitzgebel and Kolb (1964) with delinquents. Michael (1963) also illustrates this by using rest periods as a reinforcer in rehabilitation work.

The description of the toilet training procedures given by Salzinger *et al.* is consistent with the reports of a number of other investigators utilizing conditioning procedures to bring the eliminative processes under control. Neale (1963), Peterson and London (1965), and Madsen (1965) present cases illustrating the successful application of operant procedures to toilet training. In these papers the development of the operant response is through positive reinforcement. What is avoided is the usual suggestion of "holding back" so typical in our culture. The desirable behavior is an appropriate response, not the lack of a response. Mowrer and Mowrer (1938) and Lovibond (1963a, 1963b) present similar material on the treatment of enuresis through conditioning procedures.

A major issue touched upon by Salzinger *et al.* is the importance of the human reinforcer. Some investigators, such as Lindsley (1956), tend to deemphasize the role of human beings and strive for greater mechanical control of reinforcement. Eysenck (1959) and Wolpe (1962) also tend to focus more on the procedure than on the personal characteristics of the therapist. However, most of the authors in the present book, particularly Patterson, Sarason, and Krasner, place greater emphasis upon the role of the human being who dispenses social reinforcement (Krasner, 1963a, 1963b). This issue is related to the training of psychological technicians to administer treatment. While this is still a controversial matter, given the present framework it may be resolved through research. For example, Sarason, Patterson, and Bandura all make contributions in this direction by presenting data about the conditions under which a person is reinforcing. Thus, the Salzinger *et al.* chapter has important implications for current professional as well as scientific issues.

L.K.-L.P.U.

ALTHOUGH MANY INVESTIGATORS HAVE applied operant conditioning techniques to the study of verbal behavior (see reviews by Krasner, 1958a; Salzinger, 1959; Greenspoon, 1962), almost all of them have dealt with the modification of various response classes in verbally fluent adults. Outstanding exceptions are a series of studies by Flanagan, Goldiamond, and Azrin (1958, 1959), who produced stuttering in normally fluent subjects and relative fluency in stutterers; a study by Isaacs, Thomas, and Goldiamond (1960), who reinstated speech in two acute schizophrenic patients; and a study by Lindsley (1963a), who worked with vocalizations assumed to constitute hallucinatory behavior and showed them to be independent of external reinforcement contingencies, except by indirect changes caused by reinforcing nonsymptomatic behavior.

As to work with very young children, one study (Salzinger, Salzinger, Portnoy, Eckman, Bacon, Deutsch, & Zubin, 1962) showed that it is possible to condition speech rate of normal 5- and 6-year-old children in much the same way as one can condition behavior in lower organisms. Furthermore, other studies (Long, Hammack, May, & Campbell, 1958) showed the effectiveness of operant conditioning techniques on nonverbal behavior in normal children. Ferster and DeMyer (1961, 1962) demonstrated the efficacy of operant conditioning of nonverbal responses in getting autistic children to interact effectively with their environment.

Our present work stems from an interest in determining how effectively operant conditioning techniques can be employed to instate speech in children who have either none or very little at the beginning of the experiments. The study of such children not only presents the opportunity to evaluate another technique of behavior therapy but also should put us into the position of tracing the process of acquisition of language in children in whom a pathological process has forced the slowdown of the natural acquisition, thus providing the opportunity for more detailed observation. The advantage of studying the speech process of children in pathology has already been demonstrated in a study by Lenneberg (1962). While it is too early for us to comment on whether, for example, children acquire discrete responses and then chain them, as opposed to acquiring a set of rules, it might be well to point out that a topological description of the language learning process will eventually provide the necessary data for evaluating such theories of language acquisition as those espoused by Miller, Galanter, and Pribram (1960), who base their notions largely on Chomsky's (1957) description of syntax, or by Braine (1963a), who has begun to collect data in experimental situations for his theory. In any case, our efforts in this paper will be directed toward the description of some of the procedures we employed to modify the verbal behavior of two young children.

## PROCEDURE

### Subjects

1. The first child (C-1) was born full term to a mother who has been described as emotionally disturbed, perhaps psychotic, but at any rate rejecting, and neither parent wanted C-1 returned home after hospitalization. C-1's younger twin siblings were described as physically sound but emotionally unresponsive.

The parents reported noticing the first symptoms of disturbance when C-1 was 18 months old. These were hyperactivity, lack of speech development, and occasional trembling and convulsions. When C-1 was 3 years and 1 month old he was admitted to an acute-care hospital, where he was treated as physically well but severely hyperactive, although not purposefully destructive, and was either confined to a netted crib or tied in a wheel chair during his 6-month stay there. The psychologist's report gave an IQ of 32 with basic performance at the 11-month level, discounting verbalization. Estimated social maturity was 16 months.

At the age of 3 years and 7 months, he was released directly to the psychiatric hospital at which we saw him. His admitting diagnosis was psychosis due to unknown or hereditary cause but associated with organic change, with other disease of the brain or nervous system. This was subsequently changed to mental deficiency and chronic brain syndrome, without psychosis or mental disorder. Skull films and electroencephalogram were normal. It was noted that he had an awkward gait and sometimes bumped into things, but his physical examination was otherwise negative. His coordination and agility in climbing and other activities seemed normal.

We began our work with C-1 2 months after his admission. At that time he was still hyperactive, but, according to the ward staff, less so than at the time of his admission. He was subject to sudden tantrums or fits, during which times he might scream, hit his head with his hands, beat his head on the wall or floor, or roll on the floor. He resisted being handled at these times and was not distractable. At other times he was easily approachable and seemed to enjoy being held and talked to. He paid little attention to the other children on the ward, all of whom were older than he.

His vocal behavior consisted of a variety of vowel and consonant sounds plus a wide array of whines, screams, grunts, and other sounds that varied enormously in pitch, intensity, and duration. There were no recognizable words and none had ever been reported for him except by his father, who claimed to have heard "cookie" used appropriately at home a few times. Neither did he appear to use any sound consistently in a given situation. He did not imitate, either on demand or spontaneously. He could respond promptly and appropriately to many simple commands, such as to come when called, and to pick something up.

A few final points are that he could partially dress himself, that he could feed himself, and that he had not been bladder- or bowel-trained and would occasionally play with his feces.

We worked with C-1 for a period of 9 months in nearly daily sessions. At the end of this time he was sent to an institution for mental defectives. The psychiatrist's report upon his discharge from the psychiatric hospital noted that organic involvement had been confirmed by observation and by drug reaction, since C-1's hyperactivity had been refractory to or aggravated by a variety of drugs which had been tried for short periods.

2. The parents of the second child (C-2) were born abroad and came to the United States about 2 or 3 years prior to his birth. The pregnancy was planned on the basis of the father's insistence that it would be good for his wife to have a child to care for, although she did not especially want a child. Her pregnancy was medically uncomplicated, but she reported nervousness and attacks of hysteria.

The parents have both been described as exhibiting emotional disturbance and inability to meet C-2's needs and demands for attention. They beat the child and locked him in his room for long periods, frequently from early evening until noon the following day. They do not appear to want him returned home. The case record notes that C-2's lack of speech development and destructive, negativistic behavior seem related to family patterns: his isolation from human contact and the lack of communication between the parents. It should be added that the parents speak German, Hebrew, and English, and may have spoken mostly German at home. The child did have English-speaking baby sitters.

C-2's mother had done reading in the area of mental retardation and was convinced her son was retarded. She felt that speech was extremely important and that it had been unfortunate for her that she herself had been late in developing speech as a child. She appears to have made a great issue of this at home and showed particular concern, for example, over getting C-2 to call her "mama."

The parents eventually consulted a hospital service and at the age of 3 years and 10 months C-2 was referred to the psychiatric hospital at which we have been seeing him. His diagnosis is primary behavior disorder. The outstanding presenting symptom was lack of speech, and some hyperactivity was noted. An electroencephalogram obtained during natural sleep was within normal limits, and his physical examination was negative. His general motor coordination was excellent and his manual dexterity outstanding. The psychologist who saw C-2 shortly before his admission estimated him to be of at least normal intelligence, but this is merely an impression, since adequate testing was not then possible.

We began seeing C-2 about 2 months after his admission. In contrast to

C-1, he was reported to be emotionally responsive, even affectionate with the regular ward personnel, but he appeared only moderately more concerned with the other children on the ward than had C-1. However, in marked contrast to C-1, he showed fear of all strangers, although it was reported to us that at the time of his admission such fear was confined to women only. He would back away and even show panic if strangers attempted to come closer to him than ten feet or so. Thus, considerable conditioning was necessary before it was even possible to get him to the experimental room. He was also subject to occasional very sudden tantrums involving screaming and head-banging on the wall or floor. These often seemed related to his being prevented from doing something. At these times he usually responded quickly to being picked up and talked to.

His verbal behavior was free of the babbling and animal-like sounds typical of C-1 and, when we first saw him, was almost exclusively limited to the word "no," always used appropriately—for example, when we attempted to approach him. Although he then spoke only rarely in our presence, his active vocabulary (as reported by, among others, the social worker who has seen him regularly since his admission) already included other words. The most frequent of these was "key," which he used to request keys to play with or to indicate that he wanted a door opened. His articulation ranged from fairly good to very poor. He could respond promptly and appropriately to a wider variety and greater complexity of commands, such as to go and get an object and bring it back, than could C-1.

Like C-1, he could partially dress himself and could feed himself and had not been bladder- or bowel-trained and would occasionally play with his feces. It should be noted that he reportedly urinated and had bowel movements on the floor while he was locked in his room at home.

C-2 is still hospitalized at the time of this writing, about ten months after his admission, and we are continuing experimentation with him on a nearly daily schedule. He has begun to leave the hospital to attend a nursery school for normal children, although the nurse or attendant who takes him must remain there with him.

Finally, it is interesting that Ferster (1961) has elaborated a hypothetical history very much like C-2's which might be expected to produce a child who has symptoms quite similar to his.

### Procedures for C-1

The work with C-1 can be divided into two broad types of sessions: 195 sessions in which predetermined procedures or strict reinforcement ($S^r$) contingencies were primarily in operation (these will be called experimental sessions, abbreviated EXP), and 61 special sessions in which the experimenter ($E$) used a variety of techniques to introduce words into C-1's repertoire and to attempt to gain stimulus control over various verbal and nonverbal responses, whose emission was then reinforced.

*EXP 1-2.* Establishing *E* as a source of $S^r$ by following C-1's sounds with praise and a variety of edible $S^r$s (candy, peanuts, spoonfuls of soda, etc.).

*EXP 3-82.* Fixed ratio (FR) $S^r$ for sounds. FR increased from 1 to 1 initially to 37 to 1 by EXP 76. The different kinds of $S^r$s (candy, etc.) were varied freely within sessions, although mostly candy was used in later sessions. Beginning with EXP 21, *E* spoke the name of each particular $S^r$ as it was given to the child but did not say anything else, for example, he said "candy" when presenting it.

Certain sounds, such as spitting noises or animal-like screeches, were never reinforced, since we judged that they would have no utility in the eventual production of words, and since they often accompanied wild or otherwise objectionable behavior. C-1 often produced extended continuous vocalizations punctuated by one or more stresses. While we began by reinforcing discrete sounds only, some sessions consisted almost entirely of these extended vocalizations (see Salzinger, 1962, for an extended discussion of the problem of the unit) and therefore, the $S^r$ contingency through EXP 15 was frequently based on number of stresses rather than number of discrete sounds, to maximize the number of $S^r$s which could be given in each session. In subsequent sessions, C-1 began to produce short discrete sounds predominantly.

*EXP 83-104.* FR continued and increased to 50 to 1, with the additional contingency that words or close approximations to words were reinforced with *E*'s repetition and delivery of candy whenever they occurred (FR = 1 to 1).

*EXP 105-113.* $S^r$ (candy and repetition) given only for words or close approximations to words (FR = 1 to 1).

Table 5-1 summarizes the $S^r$ contingencies for EXP 3-113. In general the sessions follow one another on consecutive days, weekends included, the few exceptions being primarily due to occasional physical illness and extreme sleepiness or irritability. The missing entries in the EXP column correspond to sessions in which variations in the basic procedures described above, or quite different procedures, were tried. There is not enough space here to describe them and we will simply say that they were discontinued for a variety of reasons, among them practical difficulties, such as lack of adequate apparatus, or the apparent need to do an enormous amount of pretraining or response-shaping before the particular behavior in question could be adequately dealt with.

The changes in FR were based on *E*'s judgment, which took into account factors other than C-1's vocal behavior per se. If the child was very irritable, for example, or seemed uncomfortable because of a bad cold, *E* would not increase the FR unless these factors were counteracted by a

Table 5-1: Reinforcement Contingencies for Experimental Sessions 3 through 113

| EXP | FR | EXP | FR | EXP | FR |
|---|---|---|---|---|---|
| 3-6 | 1:1 | 43 | 6:1, 7:1, 8:1 | 68 | 24:1, 26:1 |
| 7 | 1:1, 2:1 | 44 | 8:1 | 69 | 26:1, 28:1 |
| 8 | 2:1, 3:1 | 45 | 7:1, 6:1, 8:1 | 70 | 26:1, 28:1 |
| 9 | 3:1, 4:1, 3:1 | 46-47 | 8:1, 9:1, 10:1 | 71 | 28:1 |
| 10-12 | 3:1 | 48 | 8:1, 6:1, 8:1 | 72 | 28:1, 29:1 |
| 15 | 1:1 | 49-55 | 10:1 | 73 | 29:1, 30:1 |
| 16 | 3:1 | 56 | 10:1, 12:1 | 74 | 30:1 |
| 21-24 | 1:1 | 57-58 | 12:1 | 75 | 32:1, 35:1 |
| 25-29 | 3:1 | 59 | 12:1, 13:1 | 76 | 35:1, 37:1 |
| 33 | 3:1, 4:1, 5:1 | 60 | 13:1 | 77-82 | 37:1 |
| 34 | 3:1, 6:1 | 61 | 13:1, 15:1, 16:1, 17:1 | 83-97 | 37:1, + 1:1 for words |
| 35 | 5:1, 8:1 | 62-63 | 17:1 | 98 | 37:1, 40:1, + 1:1 for words |
| 36-38 | 6:1 | 64 | 17:1, 20:1, 22:1 | 99-102 | 40:1, + 1:1 for words |
| 39 | 6:1, 7:1 | 65 | 22:1 | 103 | 42:1, + 1:1 for words |
| 40-41 | 6:1 | 66 | 22:1, 24:1 | 104 | 42:1, 45:1, 50:1, + 1:1 for words |
| 42 | 6:1, 7:1 | 67 | 24:1 | 105-113 | 1:1 for words only |

very high vocalization rate early in the session. However, the decision to decrease the FR was made almost exclusively as a result of very long periods of silence. As Table 5-1 shows, these decreases or reversals were confined to the lower FR values and never occurred after FR = 10 to 1 had been established in EXP 49-55.

The maximum session length for EXP 3-113 was 60 minutes. Most of the sessions were about 40 to 50 minutes long, and those that were much shorter were terminated because of the occurrence of a violent tantrum or some other event requiring immediate attention.

*EXP 114-142.* Discrimination training. A book and several stuffed animals, with which C-1 had frequently played and which were appropriate to the few recognizable words C-1 could by this time utter spontaneously, were selected to become discriminative stimuli ($S^D$s) in the presence of which the words were reinforced and in whose absence ($S^\Delta$ periods) no $S^r$ was given. It should be emphasized that the objects chosen as $S^D$s did not initially exert any discriminative control over the words.

EXP 114-142 always began and ended with an $S^D$ period and consisted of 3 or 5 periods in all, alternating $S^D$ and $S^\Delta$. The initial $S^D$ period was 10 minutes, and subsequent $S^D$ and $S^\Delta$ periods were 5 or 10 minutes at different points in the series of sessions. Thus total session length ranged from 20 to 50 minutes.

*EXP 143-178.* The presence or absence of the $S^D$s was made contingent on C-1's behavior rather than on arbitrary time periods; thus the $S^D$s were also being used as secondary reinforcements. The $S^D$s were first presented with C-1's first word and their duration in the experimental room was timed from zero again for each subsequent word emitted. They were removed from the room if no word was emitted within 3 minutes, in which case they were immediately returned upon the next emission of a word. Thus the minimal requirement for the child's keeping the toys in the experimental room was the emission of one word every 3 minutes. For EXP 170-178 the critical interval was reduced to 2 minutes.

The $S^r$ for EXP 114-178 consisted of candy, repetition of the given word, and handing C-1 the appropriate object if he were not already touching it.

*EXP 179-195.* C-1 was required to pick up one of four toys and bring it to E upon verbal command. The toys were a book, a "big" and a "little" stuffed dog, and a stuffed teddy bear. In the earlier sessions of this procedure, E requested one toy a predetermined number of times (usually five) and then switched immediately to another toy if C-1 did not comply. In later sessions, E insisted on one toy until C-1 brought it, or, if several minutes passed without the child at least attempting to select a toy from the group, E handed him the appropriate one, returned to his place across the room, and asked C-1 to bring it to him. If C-1 had taken a particularly long time to approach the toys or pick one up, and then hesitated again, $E$ reinforced his behavior to that point and added another command with the statement, "That's right. Now bring the ——— over here." If C-1 picked up the wrong toy, $E$ said, "No, that's your ———. I want you to bring me the ———."

When the child finally completed carrying out the instruction, he was praised, given candy, and allowed to play freely for 2 or 3 minutes, at the end of which time $E$ took the toy, replaced it with the others and resumed the procedure by asking C-1 to bring another toy.

Before the special sessions are described, some general comments are in order on the conduct of the experimental sessions.

Although C-1 invariably accompanied us willingly to the experimental room, he was extremely active once we got inside, walking or running around, climbing on the radiator or the few pieces of furniture present, and sometimes trying to leave. The method of dealing with this behavior was begun in the very early sessions and consisted simply in delivering the edible $S^r$s in one part of the room only. The candies or spoonfuls of soda were put into a cup standing on a table in the corner of the room, or, if C-1 had removed the cup, candies were dropped onto the table itself. The child learned to spend increasing amounts of time near the table and often climbed up and sat on it for long periods.

The door of the room was never locked, and C-1 was allowed to open it and leave the room if he persisted in the attempt after $E$ stood in front of the door to block his way. On those occasions when he did not return of his own accord in a minute or two (during which time $E$ remained in the room), $E$ was usually able to bring him back easily with a minimum of talking and handling. It soon became possible to discourage attempts to leave simply by $E$'s putting his hand on the door.

There were two other noteworthy exceptions to the rule that physical contact with the child and talking to him during the experimental sessions were to be rigorously avoided except as they constituted part of the planned $S^r$ contingency. The first exception concerns toilet-training and will be discussed below since it raises a procedural question of some importance. The second exception concerns the occurrence of tantrums, during which it was sometimes necessary to hold the child to prevent his injuring himself and to talk to him in order to calm him down rapidly enough to allow continuation of the session. Such behavior on $E$'s part was kept to a minimum, and C-1's tantrums, as in the case of Ferster and DeMyer's (1961, 1962) autistic children, decreased in frequency and severity, rarely occurring in later sessions except for a temporary increase in frequency when the $S^D$s were removed from the room during the discrimination procedure.

The special sessions were instituted following EXP 93. In EXP 83, as stated above, we introduced the contingency that words or close approximations would be reinforced on FR = 1 to 1, in addition to the higher ratio in effect for other vocalizations. However, C-1's operant level for words was actually zero in some sessions. The special sessions were set up to elicit words by presenting a variety of stimuli and to reinforce imitation whenever possible, and thereby to increase through generalization the frequency of occurrence of words during the experimental sessions.

The procedure involved talking to the child most of the time, using short simple sentences and frequent repetition of the words appropriate to his activity at the moment, and freely encouraging him to repeat the names of the objects to which his attention seemed directed. Three activities were introduced into most of these sessions: drawing with crayons, pointing to pictures in a book, and playing with some stuffed animals (the book and the animals were those later introduced as $S^D$s during discrimination conditioning). The child's attention was gained by a variety of means, most frequently through repeating words (mostly nouns) in short rhythmic sequences while tapping along lightly on C-1's hand. E often held the child in his lap at these times.

Thus C-1 was exposed to a relatively small vocabulary very frequently repeated and associated with a limited range of objects and behaviors. E reinforced, with candy, repetition, praise, and often by hugging the child, any approximation to naming or imitation, even, at first, if no actual vocalization were produced. For example, C-1 would sometimes watch E's lips quite intently and make deliberate lip and mouth movements of his own, often seemingly made with great effort. In later sessions the $S^r$ was made contingent on the production of any vocalization at these times, and, eventually, on the production of a vocalization having some vowel or consonant element in common with either the word E was repeating or the name of an object C-1 pointed to or picked up.

Since no quantitative data from these special sessions will be presented, no further detailed description of procedures will be given. It can be stated as a general principle that, while the particular behavior dealt with was often unspecified in advance of a given session and in some aspects varied greatly among sessions, the $S^r$ contingencies were made increasingly strict in the manner already described for C-1's vocalizations but applied as well to nonvocal behavior (length of time spent at one activity, for example).

The maximum length of the special sessions was about 30 minutes. The 61 special sessions were interspersed at fairly regular intervals with the experimental sessions after EXP 93. One session of each type sometimes occurred on the same day, but never two of the same type.

Finally, a few words about the experimenters. There were five Es in all for the experimental sessions, three of whom were primarily responsible for the early sessions, and two of whom conducted nearly all the experimental sessions after EXP 30 and all but a few of the special sessions.

Two Es were present during nearly all sessions up to EXP 93, with one monitoring the tape recorder but otherwise being a silent observer, except in very early sessions where C-1 required some mild physical restraint to prevent injury to himself or the equipment. With rare exceptions, only one E took part in the special sessions.

Sessions of both types were tape recorded.

### Procedures for C-2

The initial problem with C-2 was getting him to the experimental room without upsetting him to the point where no experimentation would be possible. Unlike C-1, he would back away from approaches by anyone other than regular ward personnel, and would cry and appear fearful simply at mention of the idea that we take him off the ward.

We began by visiting the ward once or twice a day, talking to C-2 but not approaching closer than he appeared willing to tolerate without interrupting his activity. Eventually he would approach us long enough to take a piece of candy, for which he received much praise as well. Gradually, he began to respond to the suggestion of leaving the ward with a verbal "no" but no particular signs of distress, then he would allow us to pick him up for brief periods, then to carry him about if we did not approach the exit from the ward. Each successive stage was reinforced with candy and praise, and the candy was generally accompanied by E's talking about leaving the ward.

The next step was to have one of the regular ward staff accompany us to the experimental room, where pieces of candy had been conspicuously placed. It was soon possible for E alone to get the child to the room by reinforcing every few steps with candy. After this, it was possible for E to carry C-2 to the room, for while the child often cried when this was done, he had ceased to put up physical resistance. He was taken to the room, where he quickly calmed down long enough to eat the candy and was reinforced in addition by being allowed to leave freely and return to the ward. Thus we were able temporarily to use the very behavior we wished to reduce (leaving the experimental room) as a reinforcer for the behavior we wished to strengthen (remaining in the room). By the end of about four weeks, C-2 would stay in the room with E for periods up to an hour in length, climbing immediately onto the table and beginning to play with his toys.

The sessions at this time were basically the same as the special sessions described above for C-1. The major difference concerned the relative ease of establishing a criterion for the reinforcement of words. C-2 already showed verbal, as opposed to merely vocal behavior, although it was emitted very infrequently—that is, his small output consisted almost entirely of words, which were generally recognizable in spite of very poor articulation, and which were clearly under discriminative control. Therefore our first aim was to use reinforcement to increase the frequency of word emission.

The special sessions were terminated after about a month, and the following experimental procedure was then instituted. C-2 was brought into the room and allowed to play freely with a number of toys, books, and miscellaneous objects. E remained silent until C-2 uttered a word, phrase or sentence, at which time E responded with an utterance as close as possible to the length of the original and as exact a repetition as seemed appropriate. Thus, if the child pointed to a book and said "book," E repeated the word, but if the child said "Gimme ice cream," E would say "I can't give you ice cream," "I have no ice cream," or if C-2 persisted, "no ice cream." If C-2's utterance was a request which could reasonably be carried out, E complied as he gave the verbal Sr. Thus, if C-2 dropped an object off the table and asked E to "pick it up," E would do so as he said "I'll pick it up." However, if C-2 attempted to make a game of this by deliberately dropping things, E would respond with, "No, I won't pick it up." Candy was given only when C-2 specifically asked for it, and further requests were denied if he accumulated several pieces without eating them. If E could not understand all or part of any utterance, he made the best guess he could using whatever vocal or nonverbal cues were available. This was generally easy, since C-2's verbalizations typically concerned objects in the immediate environment and were frequently accompanied by responses such as pointing. Such vocalizations as humming or imitations of noises made by various toys were never reinforced. The response had to consist of at least one actual word.

*EXP 1-2.* The 60-minute session was divided into two types of alternating 15-minute periods: one type, as described immediately above, where E's speech served as the Sr by being made contingent on C-2's speech, and the other like that of the special sessions, where E spoke at a fairly constant rate throughout, making remarks relevant to the child's activity at a given moment. E attempted to interest the child in several of the same toys in each period of the second type, so that there would be considerable overlap among these periods in the content of E's speech. EXP 1 began with a 15-minute period of the first (speech contingency) type, EXP 2 began with the other type.

In EXP 1, at the beginning of the first period of the new procedure, C-2 reacted as he did when being punished or reprimanded on the ward, that is, he stopped playing, became very still and appeared to be on the verge of crying. E told him that he was a good boy and that he could go right on playing. The child immediately smiled and resumed play, and no such incident recurred.

*EXP 3-4.* The speech-contingency procedure was in effect for the entire session. After about 40 minutes on each day, C-2 lay down on the table where he was playing, watched E for several minutes, and then appeared about to fall asleep. *E*, without speaking, sat the child up and pushed the toys closer to him. In EXP 3, C-2 lay down again and *E* terminated the session after several more minutes. In EXP 4, however, the child remained awake, and the session continued for the planned 60 minutes.

*EXP 5-13.* The speech-contingency procedure was in effect for the entire 60 minutes.

*EXP 14.* Same as EXP 1-2.

*EXP 15-19.* C-2 was reinforced only for requesting whatever object *E* held in his hand. A sentence, such as "Gimme ————," not simply naming the object, was required. $S^r$ included *E*'s giving the child candy and the object as well as the verbal $S^r$.

*EXP 20-31.* Here the procedure was changed completely and C-2 was reinforced only for imitating *E*'s verbalizations. These were generally names of objects or pictures in a book, and included an article or adjective of size or color in addition to the noun. The $S^r$ was candy and praise and several minutes of free play following completion of a series of imitations (for example, all the pictures on one page, or all the parts of a toy).

*EXP 32-56.* Conditioning of color names and their discriminative control. Briefly, five color names were established in C-2's vocabulary and brought under the control of the appropriate $S^D$s. Various nonverbal responses were also brought under the discriminative control of color stimuli. Since analysis of these data is still in progress, detailed description of the procedure will be reserved for a later paper.

## RESULTS AND DISCUSSION

*Response Unit*

For both children, the unit of measurement of amount of vocal or verbal behavior is the number of seconds of vocalization time per one minute of clock time (for discussion of this unit of measurement, see Salzinger, 1962; Salzinger, Portnoy, and Feldman, 1964; Salzinger, Salzinger, Portnoy, Eckman, Bacon, Deutsch, and Zubin, 1962). Analysis was done from tape recordings. The observer released a switch whenever the child vocalized and depressed it during silences, thereby starting and stopping a chronoscope accurate to .01 seconds. Readings were taken once per minute. Typical interobserver reliability for two well-practiced observers, and intraobserver reliability for one of them, are shown separately over 20 minutes of session time in Figure 5-1.

For C-1 all vocalization was cumulated which was acceptable under the definition of the $S^r$ contingency for EXP 3-104 (see procedure for C-1). For C-2, the definition for purposes of analysis was the same as for C-1, even though the $S^r$ contingency during conditioning had been based on words only.

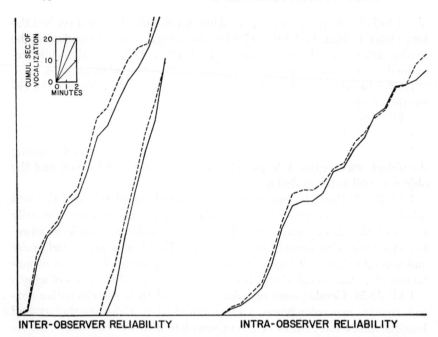

INTER-OBSERVER RELIABILITY              INTRA-OBSERVER RELIABILITY

Figure 5-1.    Reliability for timing of vocalization from tape recordings. Left part of figure shows typical agreement between 2 well-practiced observers, for cumulative vocalization in the first 20 minutes of EXP 61 with C-1. Right shows typical intra-observer reliability for one of the observers for the first 20 minutes of EXP 6 with C-2.

*Results for C-1*

Cumulative seconds of vocalization are presented for the first 20 minutes of EXP 5, 9 and 33 (see Figure 5-2A), 57, 64 and 83 (see Figure 5-2B). These sessions were originally selected for analysis because they are free of such contaminating variables as physical illness or medication and relatively free of interruptions. Subsequent analysis of additional sessions from this FR procedure confirmed the general result: an over-all increase in rate with increasing FR. The long near-plateau in EXP 5 was a feature of very early sessions only.

Thus operant conditioning accomplished our basic aim of increasing a large class of responses to the point where selective reinforcement could be attempted. However, we obtained another result whose implications are at least as important from the point of view of behavior control, and that is the essentially complete elimination of certain objectionable behavior which was not reinforced and which was incompatible with other, reinforced behavior. C-1's miscellaneous animal-like sounds were eliminated outside of the experimental sessions as well as within them because we never reinforced them and they were incompatible with behavior whose emission was reinforced. Similarly, his hyperactivity was controlled

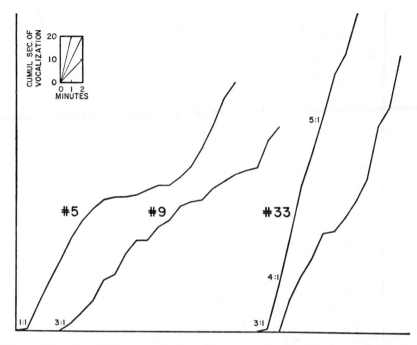

Figure 5-2A. Cumulative seconds of vocalization for the first 20 minutes of EXP 5, 9, and 33 for C-1. Fixed-ratio reinforcement schedules are indicated at the points where they went into effect.

simply by making $S^r$s available in only a restricted area of the experimental room. As Ferster and DeMyer (1961) comment with regard to the decrease of tantrums and atavistic behavior in their conditioning sessions, such decreases suggest that the behavior may have been at least partly socially maintained and may be displaced through establishing the prepotency of other behavior.

In EXP 83-104, the relatively high, steady vocalization rate continued to be maintained, but the additional contingency of FR = 1 to 1 for words produced no clear evidence for conditioning. The rate of word emission remained extremely low, with only a few very small temporary increases in some sessions. In EXP 105-113, $S^r$ only for word emission again failed to produce conditioning in the sense of a regular and substantial increase within sessions or across successive sessions. However, while the rate of word emission remained generally low, it was higher than formerly, with all sessions in this group containing at least a few words. This may be a generalized effect from the special sessions, where we had been reinforcing imitation of words and where praise and physical contact with the child, in addition to candy, may have constituted a more effective reinforcer for word emission than simply repeating the

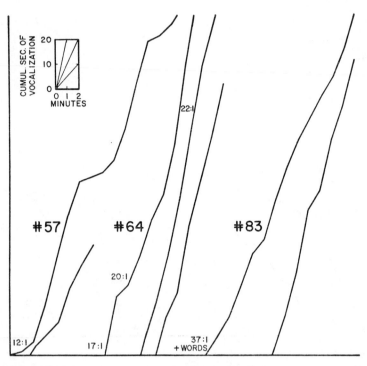

Figure 5-2B.   Cumulative seconds of vocalization for the first 20 minutes of EXP 57, 64, and 83 for C-1. Fixed-ratio reinforcement schedules are indicated at the points where they went into effect.

word and giving candy as we did in EXP 83-113. An analysis, now in progress, of the phoneme distributions of C-1's vocalizations is expected to give us a more precise picture of the results of selective reinforcement of approximations to words.

The discrimination training in its several variations in EXP 114-178 was unsuccessful, the only notable consequence of the procedure being a temporary increase in emotional behavior when the $S^D$s were removed.

The procedure in EXP 179-195 was successful in the sense that C-1 was soon making only very rare errors in selecting the correct toy. The problem was in getting him to respond at all, with only two or three complete responses executed in some sessions. Thus, while he had learned to respond correctly to the verbal $S^D$s, such $S^D$s remained weak in their power simply to increase amount of responding. It may be that the $S^r$ was not sufficiently powerful to increase and sustain discrimination behavior, while at the same time the aversive consequences of responding incorrectly (this prolonged the task by requiring correction and thus also postponed the free play interval) combined with the mild effectiveness of the positive $S^r$ to permit the conditioning of occasional correct responses.

*Results for C-2*

One observation made during the special sessions with C-2 was that social reinforcers ($E$'s talking and smiling, etc.) appeared to have become very powerful, whereas the candy was often treated as just another toy and often remained uneaten at the end of the session. This suggested that $E$'s speech alone could be used as a reinforcer and furthermore that the "value" of each $S^r$ might be made contingent on C-2's behavior simply by having the amount of speech in each $S^r$ correspond to the amount of speech in the response. In EXP 1-2, the effectiveness of this $S^r$ was confirmed by direct comparison of contrasting 15-minute periods (see procedure for C-2). The four speech-contingency periods (two each in EXP 1 and 2) show a continuous increase in percentage of time C-2 spent vocalizing (6.7, 10.8, 15.5, and 17.5 percent), while vocalization in the alternate periods where $E$'s speech was not contingent on C-2's speech, does not increase regularly nor reach as high a rate (9.7, 7.9, 9.7, and 15.4 percent). In the alternate periods, which were conducted like the special sessions, a check on the timing of $E$'s speech showed a very steady rate in all four periods and about 35 percent of each period was occupied by his speech; thus about 50 percent of each of these periods was silence, and it cannot be argued that C-2's speech would have increased more in these periods if $E$ had not monopolized the speaking time.

Cumulative seconds of vocalization are presented for the first 20 minutes of EXP 3, 5, and 6 (see Figure 5-3A), and 7, 11, and 13 (see Figure 5-3B). Except for EXP 3, which began at a relatively high rate but concluded with the child nearly asleep (as explained under procedure), the trend is for an increase in rate.

The percentages of time spent in vocalization for the 20-minute periods shown are 16.2, 4.9, 9.5, 17.5, 18.6 and 14.6. The corresponding numbers of $S^r$s are 56, 64, 78, 114, 80 and 67. It is necessary to remember that the number of $S^r$s is contingent not on total vocalization or on number of words, but on number of utterances comprised of words. Thus, there was an increase in such utterances from EXP 3 to EXP 5 in spite of the drop in total vocalization. At the same time, the decrease in number of $S^r$s from a maximum (for the sessions analyzed so far) of 114 may well have been accompanied by an increase in the length of each utterance if, in fact, longer $S^r$s were really more powerful $S^r$s as hypothesized. A detailed analysis, including word counts and study of the lengths of response units, is now in progress to clarify these relationships.

As for the remaining sessions there is no doubt that C-2 learned both the asking and the imitation responses very quickly. In EXP 32-56, while the errors have not been examined in detail, we can state that long after C-2 could respond correctly to the color names as $S^D$s and could use the names spontaneously without error, he still made many errors in naming colors on demand, and did not reach the criterion of two successive error-

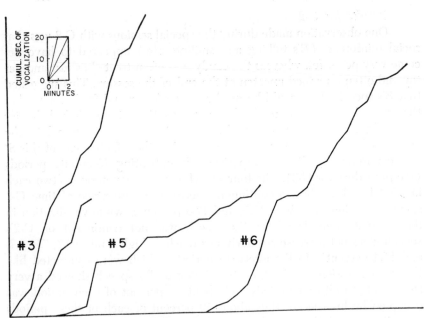

Figure 5-3A.   Cumulative seconds of vocalization for the first 20 minutes of EXP 3, 5, and 6 for C-2.

less series on the naming task until the last session of the group. We plan further experimentation to determine whether this represents a general deficit in this child's language ability.

One of the striking features of C-2's language development has been the broadening of its range along lines not required by our specific $S^r$ contingencies. We said earlier that we hoped this study would allow us to observe the acquisition of language in "slow motion." The detailed observation performed by Braine (1963b) on very young children's speech can, in fact, be done under more controlled conditions in a hospital setting. One of the interesting phenomena we have been able to observe is the acquisition of the very complicated series of intraresponse relations which are commonly referred to as grammar. How does a child learn, as C-2 has learned, from having uttered and being reinforced for saying "gimme car" that one can also say "gimme tape"? C-2 has even generalized farther along the same line, in a perfectly logical, albeit grammatically unacceptable, extension of the "gimme ———" frame, to such utterances as "gimme pick it up" (where someone else is to perform the action). This is in extreme contrast to the behavior of C-1, who generalized only to the extent of emitting outside the experimental situation the responses conditioned within it. He never acquired a single word other than those we conditioned by reinforcing successive approximations; these

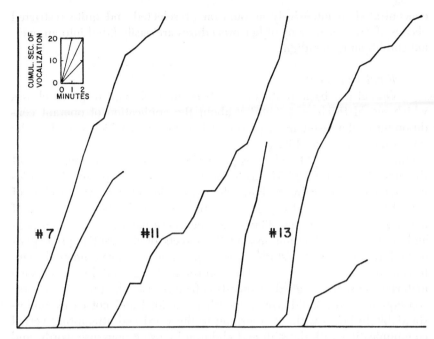

Figure 5-3B. Cumulative seconds of vocalization for the first 20 minutes of EXP 7, 11, and 13 for C-2.

numbered only about 25, among which all but 4 or 5 remained very infrequent and difficult to understand.

It is interesting that in Ferster and DeMyer's (1961) study, the autistic child with less speech and a generally narrower range of behavior also responded far less quickly to attempts at gaining stimulus control over his behavior, and in general food and candy reinforcements maintained his experimental performance; the child with more speech responded quickly to the $S^D$s, and nonfood $S^r$s proved very effective. These differences parallel those between C-1 (who had at one time been diagnosed as autistic) and C-2 in our study, in spite of differences in age, diagnosis, the responses involved, etc. There may prove to be a very general relevance for Ferster and DeMyer's comment that, "The differences between the two children are closely related to the amount of speech present, probably because the verbal repertoire, by itself, represents a large potential of control by the environment" (1961, p. 342).

Also, we must strongly emphasize that while our work with C-1 represents the only sustained and systematic attempt at changing his behavior during his hospitalization, except for his care on the ward, the same is not at all true for C-2. In particular, a social worker has been seeing him on a nearly daily basis since his admission. While her work has generally not concentrated so intensively as ours on preselected and quite restricted classes of responses, many of her procedures are easily fitted into an operant conditioning paradigm.

### Final Comments

One of our basic problems has been to work with response classes which would teach us something about the application of operant conditioning to the instatement of verbal behavior and which would at the same time benefit the children.

One example should make this point clear. With C-2, the major aim of the procedure in EXP 32-54 was to locate and examine specific difficulties in language learning by studying the acquisition of a restricted class of verbal responses. Usual experimental practice would dictate the use of materials such as nonsense figures and nonsense names, rather than pegs and color names, thus minimizing the effects of differential pre-experimental reinforcement histories and concurrent extraexperimental reinforcement contingencies. But the control to be gained by using such materials must be weighed against two factors: (a) the possible adverse consequences to a child whose speech is minimal and not easily understandable to begin with, of returning to the ward and attempting verbal communication with the staff and children by using nonsense words, and (b) the loss of the opportunity, in the case of a child who may learn slowly or who is available for a limited time, to condition responses which might also be reinforced outside of the experimental situation and which could generalize to other members of the response class which could themselves be reinforced.

In fact, since C-2 was as a matter of course continually surrounded by stimuli appropriate to the use of color names, generalization quickly took place, and he not only used the conditioned responses outside the experimental situation but learned other color names in addition. As well as we could determine, he had nearly ceased to make errors in color-naming on the ward at the same time he achieved the criterion of two successive errorless series in the experimental situation.

Another general problem concerns the extent to which we interrupted the planned procedure to deal with the occurrence of behavior secondary to our purpose but of great importance for the child. The principal example of this involves toilet training of C-1. Close observation often made it possible to predict from his behavior that he needed to be taken to the bathroom. Since these behavioral signals (all nonverbal, for example, pulling at his pants) were not obvious enough to be effective routinely on the ward, we decided to deal with them specifically by strengthening them through reinforcement.

Thus, during a session, we responded to such behavior by interrupting the procedure, taking the child to the bathroom, and reinforcing him by praising and hugging him if he went to the toilet or returning to the experimental room with as little talking and handling as possible if he did not. If C-1 wet or soiled himself during a session, we continued the procedure without interruption unless he became very upset. Since the child invariably showed some degree of distress if he became wet or soiled, a response which resulted in his being taken to the bathroom at the appropriate time was effectively an avoidance response as well as one leading to direct positive $S^r$.

This program—in conjunction with the cooperation of the ward personnel, who took C-2 to the bathroom at regular intervals, showed great approval if he used the toilet, and minimized the positive reinforcing events (talking, playing, etc.) connected with changing his wet or soiled clothes—resulted in great improvement. He even began occasionally to demand the attention of a nurse or attendant when he needed to be taken. The original response never became simply a means of escape from the experimental situation, mainly because we rarely permitted more than one such interruption in a session and therefore far more $S^r$ was available by remaining in the situation. In fact, such interruptions became less frequent in later sessions because the child had learned to use the toilet more frequently at other times.

Briefly, we can mention another use of the same technique, although involving very different behavior, with C-2. This child, if he became very insistent about wanting a particular toy or object which could be quickly obtained, and if he expressed this desire by a clear verbal response, was sometimes permitted to leave with E and bring it back to the room. Rather than using this more and more frequently as a means of escaping the experiment, the child learned to make such requests before the session began and his demands for such interruptions eventually ceased almost completely. At the same time, this procedure contributed to the fact that C-2 has learned to request objects rather than simply name objects present in the immediate environment.

A third general issue to be discussed here concerns the relationship of our work to other relatively long-term applications of operant conditioning. Ferster and DeMyer (1961, 1962), working with autistic children in an automatically controlled environment in which simple free operant motor responses produced machine-delivered $S^r$, showed that reinforcement could be used to develop and sustain various aspects of these children's behavioral repertoires. While they make clear that their work was not aimed at therapy or rehabilitation, they add that rehabilitation "would have to be carried out through the manipulation of social contingencies and the development of performances with which the child would interact with other individuals" (Ferster and DeMyer, 1961, p. 344). In fact, DeMyer and Ferster (1964) report successful use of social reinforcers to teach new social behavior to autistic and symbiotic children, and while they did not treat these results quantitatively, their techniques appear to have proved effective with a wide range of behaviors, including verbal behavior. Our work in the special sessions was in many ways similar to the work they describe.

We would point out in this regard that, no matter how simple the response in question, the mere fact that positive reinforcement is delivered by another person rather than by a machine may be of great importance in the case of a child for whom other individuals have become $S^D$s primarily for socially unacceptable responses or for whom they have never in any significant way become $S^D$s at all. In our work, C-2 presents the example of a child whose history prior to hospitalization provided relatively little opportunity for the establishment of other individuals as $S^D$s for speech. Nevertheless, by pairing $E$'s speech with stimuli already possessing positive reinforcement properties (candy, toys, etc.), $E$'s speech itself was made to acquire strong, secondary reinforcement properties for C-2's behavior, and at the same time other individuals have clearly become $S^D$s for the emission of the conditioned verbal responses. If the fundamental distinguishing characteristic of verbal behavior is its reinforcement through the mediation of another person (Skinner, 1957), the particular relevance of another person is emphasized as the source of positive reinforcement in conditioning speech in children who have lost it or never attained it.

Verbal behavior—because it is subject to the kind of basic behavioral analyses Ferster and DeMyer (1961) present for nonverbal behavior and in addition plays such a crucial role in the development of social control (Ferster, 1961)—would seem to provide a valuable opportunity for studying the ways in which the experimental manipulation of relatively simple responses is related to the therapeutic manipulation of more complex behavior by the same techniques. The grouping of children in terms of their performance in the strictly controlled experimental environment might even provide a means of evaluating the effects of such therapy. It would at least provide a basis for comparisons now meaningless because of inexactness of diagnostic labels. Such basic data might ultimately prove far more valuable than the current diagnostic categories in deciding how best to apply the techniques of operant conditioning to the treatment of a given individual.

## SUMMARY

Operant conditioning techniques were applied to the vocal and verbal behavior of two young hospitalized boys, one having no speech and the other very little. With the first child, it was possible to condition vocalization rate and to shape a small vocabulary by reinforcing successive approximations to words, but not to gain discriminative control over word

emission. With the second child, it was possible to use a social reinforcer to condition speech and to gain discriminative control over a
variety of responses.

We discussed some uses of reinforcement to control broad aspects
of these children's behavior concurrent with the experimental manipulation of the responses with which we were primarily concerned. We
considered issues related to the generalization of conditioned behavior
from the experimental to the extraexperimental environment. Our results were discussed with particular reference to Ferster and DeMyer's
behavioral studies of autistic children. The parallels between their findings and ours, evident in spite of large differences in the responses and
the children involved, suggest that the techniques for controlling operant
behavior may cut across present diagnostic categories and play a valuable part in the assessment and treatment of many types of children.

NOTE ON C-2.   We continued to work with C-2 almost daily until his
discharge from the hospital to a foster home, 22 months after admission
and about 20 months after we began work with him. His social worker
also continued daily sessions throughout this period. At the time of discharge, he was speaking almost entirely in sentences and employing a
variety of grammatical structures, and was markedly improved in many
aspects of his social behavior, particularly his response to strangers. A
detailed analysis of his acquisition of speech over the 20-month period is
planned for a later paper.

# 6

## Stuttering and Fluency as Manipulatable Operant Response Classes[*]

### ISRAEL GOLDIAMOND[†]

G oldiamond has applied behavioral analysis to many topics including perception (Goldiamond, 1962b), treatment of mute schizophrenics (Isaacs, Thomas, & Goldiamond, 1960), and marriage counseling (Goldiamond, 1963). In marriage counseling, Goldiamond overtly instructs his clients in how to be more effective in manipulating their environment by use of a functional analysis of behavior in everyday life.

In the present chapter, speech is approached as an ongoing operant behavior maintained by its consequences. Goldiamond delineates the aspects of the environment which reinforce stuttering. He then demonstrates that stuttering may be developed and modified in the same manner as any other behavior. Thus his treatment, like that of most behavior therapists, is ahistorical, in that the "originating circumstances" are of no consequence. One particularly good example of this is the treatment (Bachrach et al., 1965) of an anorexic patient in which the focus was on increasing the behavior of *eating* rather than the *causes* of not eating.

As Ferster and Bijou have pointed out in earlier chapters, a behavior modification approach changes the evaluation of the classic clinical problems of the nature of symptoms and the phenomenon of symptom substitution. Goldiamond discusses these problems in relation to stuttering behavior. If, as the medical model contends, stuttering is symptomatic of an underlying cause, then in cases where stuttering is dealt with directly, the real cause remains unchanged and is likely to "erupt" again into more stuttering or into another undesirable symptom. The evidence for the phenomenon of symptom substitution is slight (Yates, 1958; Eysenck, 1959; Rachman, 1963). Ullmann and Krasner (1965) discuss

[*] Written under contract between the Office of the Surgeon General, U. S. Army Medical Research and Development Command, and the Washington School of Psychiatry, DA-49-193-MD-2448, entitled "Study of Interviews (Therapeutic and Interrogative) by Operant Conditioning Methods." Supported by Grant Ns G-450, NASA.

[†] Research Career Development Award, NIMH, administered by the Institute for Behavioral Research.

the theoretical difficulties and alternative explanations which make a formulation of symptom substitution highly untenable.

If it is not the result of an underlying cause then how does maladaptive behavior come about? Goldiamond discusses the development and experimental production of stuttering behavior. Other instances of deliberate induction of maladaptive behavior have been provided by Watson and Rayner (1920) and Haughton and Ayllon (1965).

We see clearly from Goldiamond's presentation that in a learning approach the therapist's repertoire is limited only by his ingenuity in finding ways to modify behavior. Other techniques of modifying stuttering within a learning framework illustrate this point. Among these are: the use of negative practice (Dunlap, 1932; Case, 1960), increased drive through prior deprivation (Case, 1960), desensitization of the stimuli likely to lead to maladaptive behavior (Walton & Black, 1958), interference with the reinforcing sequence maintaining stuttering (Sheehan, 1951), distraction from perceptual feedback (Cherry & Sayers, 1956), direct use of positive reinforcement with additional training of parents as therapists to facilitate generalization (Rickard & Mundy, 1965). The common factor in all this work is the *direct* manipulation of the stimulus situation. Stuttering is a particularly attractive behavior for learning approaches in that it can be objectively evaluated and its consequences on other people can be readily observed.

The goal of learning approaches is to develop a new, more responsible role for the patient-stutterer. This is attained by direct explanations of the stuttering situation so that the patient can develop self-control. The patient comes to realize that he can have a major influence on his own environment. As Goldiamond points out, "tender loving care" in the very nature of supporting the patient maintains his stuttering behavior by rewarding it. The behavior therapist's purpose is to assist the patient to greater responsibility and less dependency on the therapist. Thus there is a genuine partnership with the patient and respect for his ability to control his environment. In this sense, behavior therapy is far from being a mechanical and cold process, as some authors have asserted (May, 1963). Rather, from the patient's point of view, therapy changes from a vague, often inexplicable process, with a superior all-knowing therapist, to an understandable process between equals.

Another important point which Goldiamond emphasizes in the retraining of an individual for a more effective social role is the effect of audience feedback. It is from the significant others in his life that an individual receives feedback as to the consequences of his behavior. In the chapters immediately following, Patterson will discuss programing the feedback of parents and peers, and Matarazzo will discuss some of the *formal* characteristics of that feedback. The importance of the audience, per se, is discussed by Sarbin (Chapter 16).

Finally, Goldiamond provides another important link between the laboratory and psychotherapy by emphasizing the effects of prolonged experimentation.

In the laboratory, for example, he notes the adaptation effects of delayed auditory feedback. Research utilizing the paradigm of a single subject seen repeatedly has also been described by Salzinger *et al.*, Bijou, and Staats, and closely approximates the present social definition of psychotherapy.

L.K.-L.P.U.

THE PRESENT PAPER REPORTS a systematic series of experimental investigations of fluent speech and stuttering, and the derivation of a procedure which, when applied to chronic stutterers, has virtually eliminated stuttering and has replaced it by a fluent verbal pattern within the laboratory, with some carry-over to speech outside. Procedures for extending the behavior outside the laboratory are also being investigated. The experiments are part of a program of basic research in variables governing the establishment, maintenance, and alteration of patterns of verbal behavior, and in the experimental analysis and utilization of verbal interactions under specified conditions to alter referent behaviors outside.

The working assumption which initiated the series was the consideration of verbal behavior as operant behavior, that is, it was assumed that verbal behavior could profitably be studied using analytic procedures developed in operant laboratories. Such research has produced a body of basic knowledge in the form of functional relations between specified behaviors and conditions which has been obtained by carefully altering conditions and observing their effects on the rate or form of ongoing behavior. This research has also produced a set of generally applicable procedures which can be used to alter specified response patterns, or establish, or maintain them. Among the response patterns which we shall consider are those of fluent speech and stuttering.

Operant behavior manipulates its environment; it may be defined as behavior whose rate or form is governed by its consequences. The rate and form of much verbal behavior is so governed (as, for example, the slowed speech of dictation, or the altered forms of translation). Stuttering may be defined by a high rate of certain forms of speech. These include repetitions, breaks, pauses, arhythmias, and other blockages. They occur in normally fluent speech, but at a rate so low as not to define a communicative problem. The experimental question arose as to whether the rates and forms differentiating stuttering from fluent speech could be altered by using operant procedures, both within the laboratory and outside it.

In operant research, different consequences are systematically programed to different response classes. The peck of a pigeon at a disc, for example, immediately activates a food dispenser or a shock device. If this response does not occur, the device will not act. Such systematic relations between consequences and behavior exemplify *differential reinforcement*, which may be used to alter the rate and form of behavior, as well as its relationship to many features of the environment.

Where response pattern is maintained when such an event is provided, the stimulus is termed a *reinforcing stimulus* (food, in the example just cited). Where the pattern is attenuated, the event is termed an *aversive stimulus* (shock, in the case cited). The experimental procedures are defined as *reinforcement* and *punishment*, respectively. Similarly, the response may temporarily *eliminate* an ongoing stimulus (which would not be eliminated otherwise). The stimulus eliminated may be an aversive stimulus (continual shock) or a reinforcing stimulus (ongoing music). These experimental procedures are defined as *negative reinforcement* and *punishment*, respectively. Where differential reinforcement is no longer provided, the procedure is defined as *extinction*.

Differential reinforcement may also alter the *form* of the response. If the pigeon is reinforced when he raises his head, but not when he lowers it, he may respond with an outstretched neck. The process is called *shaping*, or *response differentiation*. Differential reinforcement may also define what will be responded to. If reinforcement is provided for responding when the light is green, but not when red, a green light may occasion responding which stops when it turns red. This defines *stimulus control* or *stimulus discrimination*. These simple cases may be extended to highly complex relations between the environment and behavior. Novel relations hitherto not in the organism's repertoire may be established. Precise laboratory research has often made evident or established a relationship which would otherwise be unobservable, seem capricious, or seem unobtainable.

Consideration of stuttering and fluency as behaviors maintained by differential reinforcement in complex, but systematic, relation to the environment suggested some interesting possibilities for analysis and treatment. Stuttering has often been regarded as an emotional response,[1] or as

[1] Emotional behavior may also be operant. Where stuttering is regarded as emotional behavior, it has more typically been considered respondent, rather than operant. Respondent behavior is governed by stimuli which elicit it (the salivation of Pavlov's dog elicited by a tone *preceding* it), whereas operant behavior is governed by the stimuli which are *contingent* upon it. Whether the emotional behavior is respondent or operant depends upon the stimuli maintaining it. If a tantrum is maintained by the attention and upset it provokes under certain conditions, it is operant. If it is maintained by conditions whose control derives from their being paired with unconditioned stimuli which elicit tantrums, it is respondent. To assess which form of behavior it is, one could manipulate the differentiating stimuli involved, and observe which

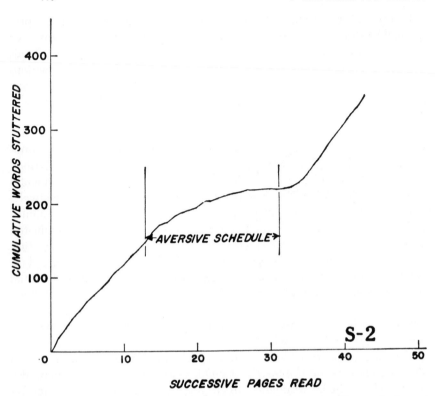

Figure 6-1. Attenuation of stuttering in a chronic stutterer upon punishment. Each word stuttered produced a 1-sec. blast of noise during the aversive period.

an emotionally induced breakdown, governed by the conditions which produce such upset, rather than by the way in which it (as opposed to fluency) differentially manipulates its environment. Such consideration has dictated a different approach toward its analysis and treatment.

## CONTROLLED ALTERATION AND INSTATEMENT OF NONFLUENCY [2]

In the first experiment in this series (Flanagan, Goldiamond, & Azrin, 1958), three stutterers read aloud from printed pages; E pressed a micro-

---

altered the behavior. At the present, many treatments are based upon the implicit assumption that stuttering is respondent. The degree of acceptance of this assumption as exclusive is not matched by supporting evidence. Nothing in this paper should be interpreted to imply that stuttering may not have respondent properties. Whether stuttering is respondent or operant or some combination, or whether different types of stuttering exist, defined in this manner, is not a matter of competing ideologies, but an empirical matter of the maintaining stimuli.

[2] This research was supported by a grant from the Mental Health Fund of the State of Illinois, administered by the Illinois Psychiatric Training and Research Authority.

switch for each word blocked, and recorded each page read. There were two 90-minute sessions for each S. In the *aversive* session, following about 30 minutes of recording of stuttering, each blockage definition now produced a 1-second blast of 105 decibels white noise into S's earphones. After about 30 minutes of such punishment, the noise was turned off and reading continued for another 30 minutes. The results for one S are shown in Figure 6-1; the stuttering curve is cumulated against pages read. Stuttering was almost completely eliminated toward the end of the aversive period; S read almost ten pages without stuttering. Stuttering by the other two Ss was also attenuated during this period.

In the *escape* session, following 30 minutes of recording alone, a 30-minute period was introduced during which each definition turned off ongoing noise for 5 seconds, defining negative reinforcement. Stuttering rate rose during this period, dropping when it was no longer negatively reinforced. This experiment suggested that stuttering rate could be affected by its consequences, dropping when they were aversive, and rising when negatively reinforced.

In the next experiment (Flanagan, Goldiamond, & Azrin, 1959), nonfluencies were increased in a *normally* fluent S (cf. Bilger & Speaks, 1959, who report similar results). He read aloud as before. After a stabilization period, a continual electrical shock was introduced via the electrodes he was wearing. Each blockage definition shut off the shock for 10 seconds; a response made during this period recycled the timer, so that by blocking at appropriate intervals, S could avert shock. Results are presented in Figure 6-2. Blockage rate rose dramatically during the escape period. When the shock was turned off, blockage continued for a while at its high rate: absence of shock was maintaining blockages; accordingly, turning the shock off continued to maintain it. Such persistence of avoidance behavior in the absence of its maintaining conditions is one of the characteristics of avoidance behavior which has been noted clinically. Two days later, S was run again. His blockages were now at so high a rate that he received only two brief shocks during the escape period. Elimination of the new pattern during extinction was considerably prolonged.

At the end of the second session, E interviewed S, who repeatedly attributed his nonfluencies to his anxiety and his anxiety to his nonfluencies.[3] He then attributed his nonfluencies to the slowness of his reading (which had obviously been caused by the nonfluencies). He was finally asked if a shock might have been contributory. "Oh, no," he said. "On the first day, you had a short somewhere, and your equipment leaked so badly that I meant to tell you about it. You had it fixed by the second session. Shocks had nothing to do with my stuttering. I stuttered worse to-

---

[3] Circular reasoning that is not restricted to this S. Where anxiety and stuttering are defined independently, it is not always clear which is causal. Among the consequences that stuttering may produce are stimuli eliciting emotional reactions.

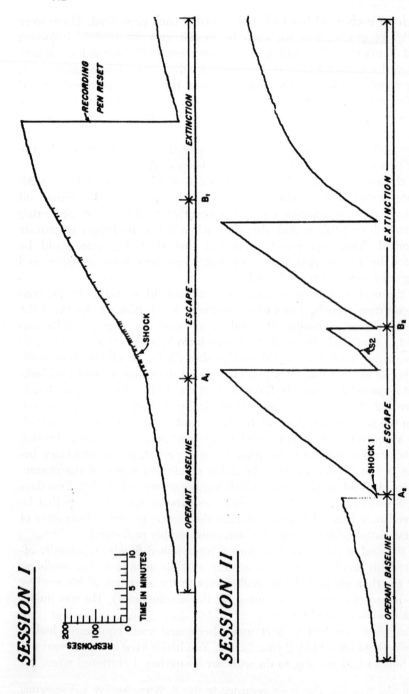

Figure 6-2. Instatement of a high nonfluency rate in a normally fluent S through presenting continual shock (during escape period), with each word blocked eliminating shock for a fixed period of time.

day, but there were no shocks at all today," which was almost true, but it was S's behavior that produced this condition of no shock. So much for S's explanation of his own behavior. It should be noted that elimination of the shock served to maintain the nonfluencies which eliminated it, just as elimination of noise did with regard to stuttering. If presenting noise during the experiment had produced anxiety, then anxiety was responsible for both the *increase* in stuttering (during negative reinforcement) and the *decrease* in stuttering (during punishment). Its explanatory value as a cause of stuttering is questionable in this case, at least.

## AN EXPERIMENTAL ANALYSIS OF STUTTERING [4]

Since nonfluencies could be treated as operant response classes, we undertook a long-term experimental analysis of stuttering. In the next study (Goldiamond, 1960, 1962a), chronic stutterers were run daily, 5 days a week, two for as long as 9 months. They read aloud from printed material for 90 minutes a day. To get material which was uniform in style, and which was not likely to have been read before, Tolstoy's *War and Peace* was chosen; when this was completed, it was followed by *Anna Karenina*, then *The Short Novels of Tolstoy*, and a collection of short stories. Stuttering was monitored as before, with E reading another copy of the book along with S in another room; at approximately every hundredth word, a slash appeared in E's copy, and E pressed another microswitch, thereby defining ongoing reading rate.

Obtaining generalizable data from a few S's run for extended periods of time under carefully controlled conditions is, needless to say, a time-honored procedure in many areas of natural science. This point needs reiteration these days when research design is often exclusively equated with groups of Ss, run for short and equal periods, and differentiated on the basis of some variable. Obtained differences between groups are assessed statistically to evaluate their relation to the variable studied, to other variables, or to chance. While such methods are important, much of our knowledge about nerves, for example, has been obtained from single nerve fibers, stimulated over extended periods of time. The branch of psychology known as psychophysics has been characterized by controlled research (hence, the appellation "brass instrument psychology") with single organisms. In operant research, S may be run until a steady state pattern of behavior ensues, at which point a variable may be introduced. If response rate is, say attenuated, the variable may be reintro-

[4] Research performed under contracts with the Operational Applications Laboratory, Air Force Cambridge Research Center, contract No. AF 19(604)-6127, 1960, and with the Operational Applications Office, Electronic Systems Division, U.S.A. FCCDD, 1961, 1962. The author wishes to express his appreciation to Mr. Bruce Flanagan, then a graduate student in speech correction, who was research assistant under the former contract.

duced with a negative value to see if the original rate is now increased. A functional relation between dependent and independent variables may be established, and its generality to other organisms may be assessed by running them (cf. Sidman, 1960). This was the procedure applied in this case, and it posed several problems that had to be settled first.

### The Adaptation Effect

Extended investigation is called for. Consultation of literature and investigators in the field immediately brought up the "adaptation" effect. This may be related to consideration of stuttering as the product of an emotional state. A characteristic of some emotional states is that in familiar surroundings their effects are progressively lessened, and "adaptation" occurs.[5] The experimental *phenomenon* described is a decrease in stuttering rate as a session progresses. The consistency of this phenomenon poses problems for long-term research of the type described, since it may lead to disappearance of the behavior being studied. Long-term experimental analysis of stuttering of the extent used here had not been assayed before, and accordingly, Ss were first run for extended periods of time, reading aloud from the books, to see what would happen. Results for the four Ss run are indicated in Figures 6-3, 6-4, 6-5, and 6-6. As can be seen in each case, *there is an adaptation effect within each session,* that is, the terminal stuttering rate is lower than the initial stuttering rate, as evidenced by the slopes of the curves.[6] However, the stuttering of all four Ss *did not* adapt over the long run. Stability did ensue, with the steady state rate depicted at the bottom of each figure. It will be noted that two Ss, Z and K, stabilized at a *higher* rate of stuttering than their initial sessions; one, L, stabilized at a *lower* rate; and one, S, maintained the *same* rate. Apparently, the change in rate *during* a session may be independent of the change in rate *between* sessions. Adaptation between sessions has often been obtained with repetitious readings of the same passage, which is not the case here. The data also indicate that a

---

[5] Relatable (a) to respondent extinction: repeated presentation of the new situation without previously paired emotionally eliciting stimuli extinguishes emotional disruption; (b) to operant stimulus change: behavior disrupted by novel stimuli is re-established if old contingencies are unchanged.

[6] A word about reading the curves. These are cumulative curves, that is, the response pen goes up at each response, and stays up, going further upward at the next response. The paper, in the meantime, moves at a fixed speed to the left, producing a record which moves to the right. If there is no responding, the pen will drag, and the result will be a straight line with a slope of 0. The more rapidly it moves, the steeper the line.

The recording pen resets after 500 responses, returning to the bottom to start up again. Accordingly, a second way to compare rates is by the number of resets of the pen, since each session is constant in time.

Reading rate is indicated by closeness of slashes on the bottom line of each session. Each slash represents 100 words read.

Number of words blocked (WB), and words read (WR) per session are summarized in the upper left hand corner of each session.

NO CONTINGENCIES
OBSERVER DEFINITION

**Z**

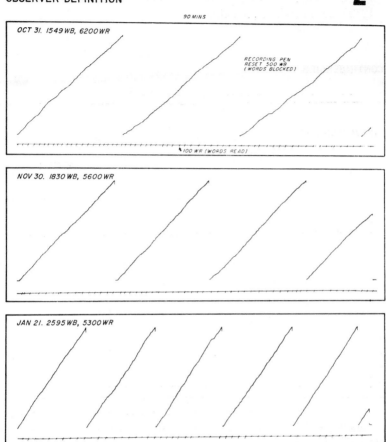

Figure 6-3. Temporal course of stuttering in a chronic stutterer reading aloud 90 min. daily. Note that stuttering rate rises over time between sessions, but decreases within sessions.

long-term analysis may produce results different from short sessions. That transient and steady states may differ would seem to be of special concern to those dealing with long-term effects, for example, the clinician.

*Immediacy of Reinforcement*

For reinforcement to be maximally effective, it must be presented concurrently with the response. Where it is not immediate, special laboratory procedures are used to make the contingency effective. If differential consequences are applied by a monitor, there may be a slight delay before he defines a pause as a blockage, since pauses also occur as normal parts of fluent speech. It was presumed that the stutterer is better informed in this matter, and, accordingly, it would be desirable to attach consequences to his definitions. Would this affect the data (Wingate, 1959) and introduce an artifact?

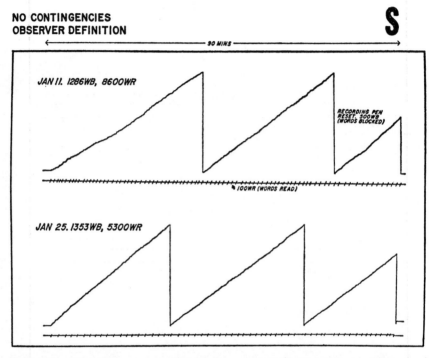

Figure 6-4. Temporal course of stuttering in a second chronic stutterer reading aloud daily. Note that stuttering rate remains fairly constant over time between sessions, but decreases within sessions.

Stuttering rates before, during, and after self-definition are presented in Figures 6-7 and 6-8. The rates are those defined by the listening monitor.[7] It will be noted that for Z, there are no differences in rate during these three periods. For S, only the last day prior to self-definition and the first day of self-definition are presented. There was no difference. For K, there were fluctuations, but within the rate ranges for each category. For L, self-definition resulted in a drop in stuttering rate, from 769 to 481 words. Within 2 days, however, the rate during self-definition had returned to its baseline prior to self-definition. Self-definition produced either no discernible effect or a transient change. Accordingly, when contingencies were attached, they were attached to S's definition.

[7] To save space, spaces between the curves have been collapsed. Slope has not been altered. Each day represents a 90-minute session.

NO CONTINGENCIES
OBSERVER DEFINITION

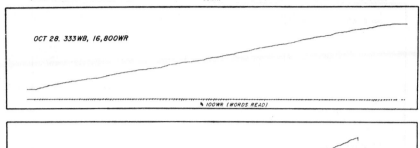

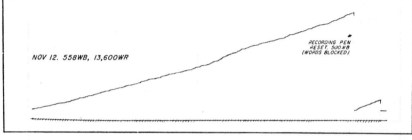

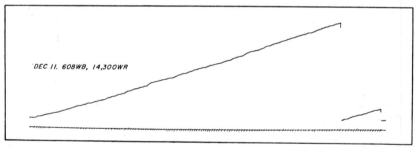

Figure 6-5. Temporal course of stuttering in a third chronic stutterer reading aloud daily. Note that stuttering rate increases over time between sessions, but tends to decrease within the session.

### Reliability of Definition

Two observers defining the same phenomenon raises the problem of reliability. (An independent third definition was included from tape recordings.) Let us assume that one observer defines 1000 responses and a second 800. A depressant variable is now introduced; the two definitions are 500 and 400. The variable is now withdrawn, and the definitions are 1500 and 1200. Similar functional relations obtain between them. They may be considered reliable, although different criteria are being used. This definition of reliability through cofunctional relations was used in this investigation, and will be illustrated in the curves shown.

### Choice of Consequence

In the preceding investigations, noise and electric shock were used. Both are contraindicated as clinical procedures. Instead, we used delayed

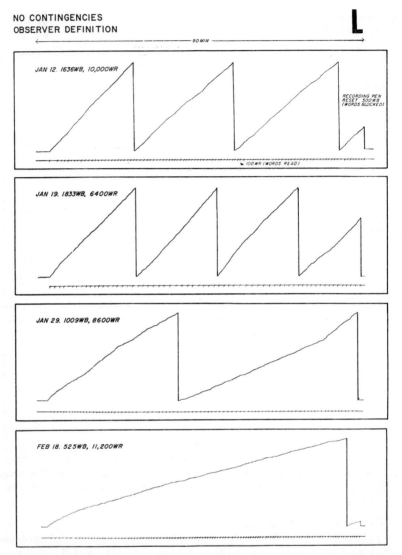

Figure 6-6. Temporal course of stuttering in a fourth chronic stutterer reading aloud daily. Note that stuttering rate decreases over time between sessions, and also within sessions.

auditory feedback of S's own voice as a consequence. It was related systematically to the response classes studied: (a) it was made contingent on stuttering, (b) its elimination was a consequence, (c) it was presented continually without relation to behavior, (d) it was continually absent. Procedures c and d involve no differential reinforcement. If delayed feedback is an aversive stimulus, procedure a defines punishment of stuttering, and procedure b defines its negative reinforcement. When

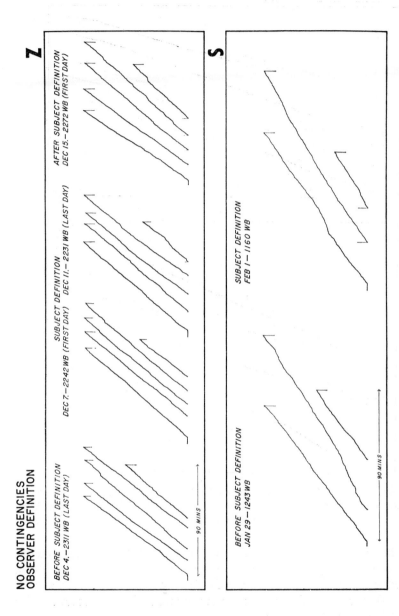

Figure 6-7.  Effects upon stuttering of having S define his own moments of stuttering. Definition is by a monitor. There are no changes in rate.

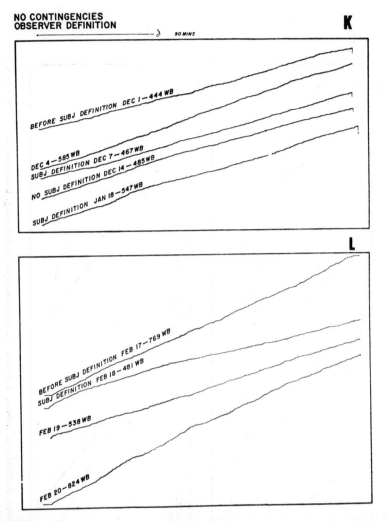

NO CONTINGENCIES
OBSERVER DEFINITION

K

→ ⟩ 90 MINS

BEFORE SUBJ DEFINITION DEC 1—444 WB

DEC 4—585 WB
SUBJ DEFINITION DEC 7—467 WB
NO SUBJ DEFINITION DEC 14—485 WB
SUBJ DEFINITION JAN 18—547 WB

L

BEFORE SUBJ DEFINITION FEB 17—769 WB
SUBJ DEFINITION FEB 18—481 WB
FEB 19—538 WB
FEB 20—824 WB

Figure 6-8.    Effects upon stuttering of having S define his own moments of stuttering. For K, changes are within range without self-definition. For L, self-definition was accompanied by considerable attenuation of stuttering, which returned to baseline conditions by the third day.

the switch defining a *word* stuttered was depressed, it activated a cumulative recorder. During procedure *a*, the switch also shunted speech to a delayed feedback device for 5 seconds. During procedure *b*, the recording was shunted *from* that device to normal feedback for 10 seconds. The input delay was 250 ms from output.

*General Procedure*

The S sat in a small booth and was instructed to read aloud from printed pages at as rapid a rate as was consistent with comfort. His

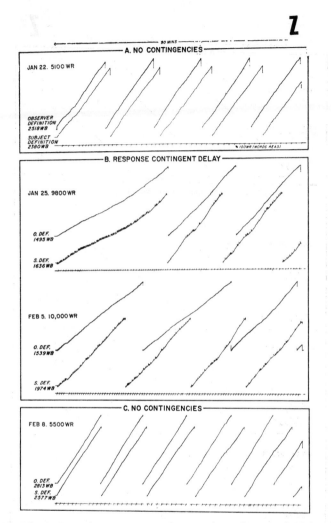

Figure 6-9. Effects of punishment upon stuttering: each word stuttered produced a 5-sec. period of delayed feedback. Note return of previous pattern of behavior when conditions prevailing prior to contingencies were reintroduced.

voice was presented to him through earphones, with masking noise in the booth as well as through the earphones to mask bone conduction. Each S read 90 minutes a day, and was paid. Other details will be presented with the results.

## RESULTS

The effects of making a fixed period of delayed feedback contingent upon a stuttering response (hereafter referred to as *punishment*) are

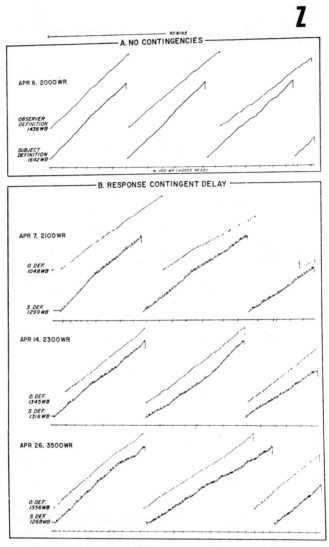

Figure 6-10. Effects of delayed feedback as punishment for stuttering upon slowed reading. Stuttering rate is somewhat lowered, but reading rate (and words read fluently per stuttered word) almost doubles.

presented for Subject Z in Figure 6-9. The upper curve of each pair is the monitor's definition; the lower is S's. The definitions are quite similar, and accord with the cofunctional reliability defined earlier. On Friday, January 22, S read 5100 words and blocked on about 2500 of them. When, on Monday, January 25, punishment of stuttering was introduced, stuttering dropped to about 1500 words, while reading rate almost doubled.

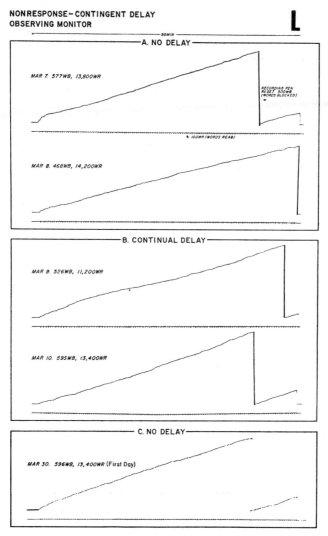

NONRESPONSE-CONTINGENT DELAY
OBSERVING MONITOR

**L**

A. NO DELAY

MAR 7. 577WB, 13,800WR

RECORDING PEN
RESET 500WB
(WORDS BLOCKED)

100WR (WORDS READ)

MAR 8. 468WB, 14,200WR

B. CONTINUAL DELAY

MAR 9. 526WB, 11,200WR

MAR 10. 595WB, 13,400WR

C. NO DELAY

MAR 30. 596WB, 13,400WR (First Day)

Figure 6-11. Effects of delayed feedback presented continually during both fluencies and nonfluencies. Note initial drop in reading rate, with recovery thereafter.

The adaptation effect noted in previous sessions was reversed, with stuttering rate higher at the *end* of the session than at the beginning. This reading rate and attenuated stuttering continued for the 2 weeks of this procedure. On Monday, February 8, the baseline condition was reintroduced, and the verbal patterns prior to punishment reappeared.

Delayed feedback functioned as noise had in the first experiment; it was aversive, and its depressant effects were specific to the stuttering behavior upon which it was contingent. Attenuation of the blockages, pre-

RESPONSE CONTINGENT DELAY

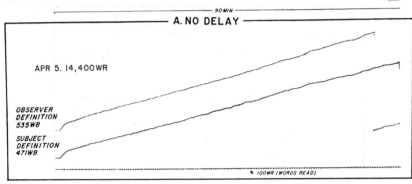

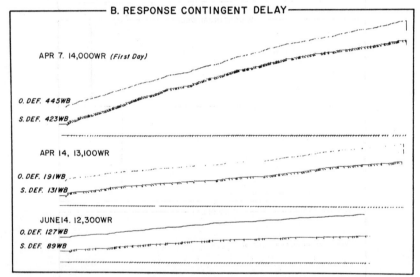

Figure 6-12. Effects of making delayed feedback contingent upon stuttering in S for whom continual delay had produced only transient changes. Note attenuation of stuttering.

sumably hindrances to communication, almost doubled the flow of fluent verbal behavior.

The S was run without contingencies for 2 more months. There was a slowing of reading rate (no contingencies were attached to rapid reading) to 2000 words, with 1500 of them stuttered; this was an absolute drop from the 2500 words stuttered during the previous baseline. Punishment was then reinstated; the new baseline and results are shown in Figure 6-10. The immediate effect was to decrease the rate of the punished response, which remained at a new low level, as reading rate in general gradually rose.

RESPONSE CONTINGENT ELIMINATION                                   **S**

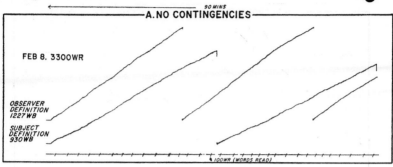

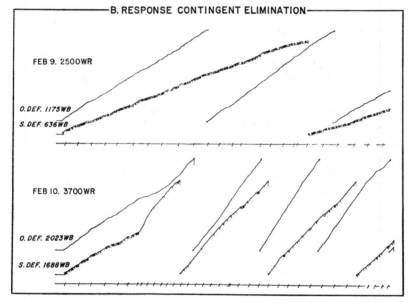

Figure 6-13.   Effects of presenting delayed feedback continually, with each word stuttered eliminating it for 10 sec. Note rise in stuttering on second day.

Did delayed feedback have to be response-contingent for its effects? Continual delay was presented for Subject L; results are shown in Figure 6-11. The immediate effect of continual (nonresponse-contingent) delay was to reduce reading rate; stuttering was not markedly affected. By the next day, reading rate had recovered, and both it and stuttering rate were similar to baseline data.

Since this S might have been insensitive to delayed feedback, *punishment* was introduced. Results are presented in Figure 6-12. The effects are similar to the preceding S: stuttering was considerably attenuated, dropping to about 100 words after 2 months of such treatment. The

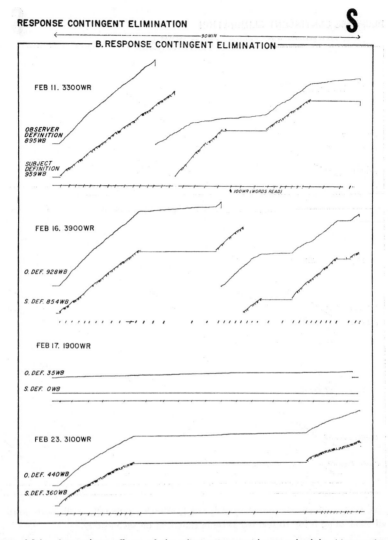

Figure 6-14. Anomalous effects of the elimination-avoidance schedule. Note existence of two competing patterns: one with high stuttering rate and high reading rate, and one with low (or null) stuttering rate and low reading rate.

reading rate, however, also dropped, but the ratio of words read to words stuttered rose from about 30 to 1 during baseline to about 100 to 1 when aversive consequences were applied. These changes contrast to those produced by noncontingent presentation of delayed feedback. It was apparently the contingency which produced the attenuation.

For Subject S, avoidance-conditioning was instituted after stabilization. Delayed feedback was presented continually, with each nonfluency

RESPONSE CONTINGENT ELIMINATION

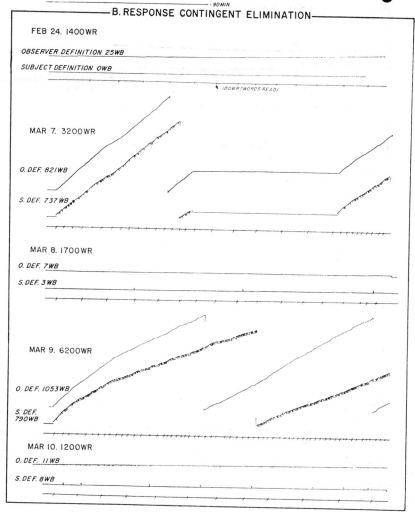

Figure 6-15. Continuation of competing patterns under elimination-avoidance schedule. Response pattern of Mar. 10 typified behavior thereafter.

restoring normal feedback for 10 seconds. Results are presented in Figure 6-13. There was an immediate drop in both reading and stuttering rates. On the second day, however, both rose, with stuttering almost double the baseline rate. Delayed feedback again seemed to be functioning like shock and noise in that its elimination increased the rate of the response that eliminated it.

The hypothesis that delayed feedback is aversive appeared confirmed

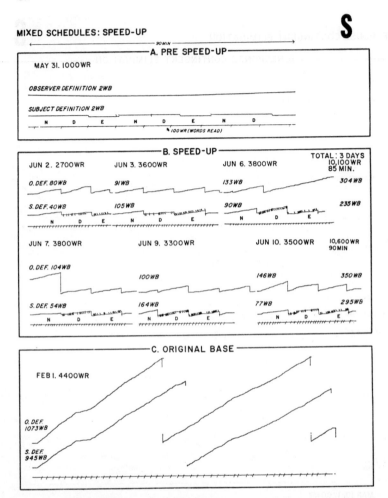

**Fig. 6-16.** Effects of speeding up reading of S who emerged with a pattern of prolonged vocalization that persisted beyond elimination-avoidance procedure under which it was instated. Note that, compared with baseline, S is reading over twice as rapidly, with one third as many stutters, during comparable periods of time.

and, had the experiment terminated here, little new would have been learned other than such confirmation. During the next few days, however, S taught E something else. Curves from these days are presented in Figures 6-14 and 6-15. Two response patterns seemed to be competing. These were most evident on February 23. One involved both a high reading and high stuttering rate, and the other a low reading rate with almost no stuttering. The latter eventually won out, and by March 10 the reading rate was about 13 words a minute. Two days later, negative reinforcement was eliminated, and baseline conditions of no delay were rein-

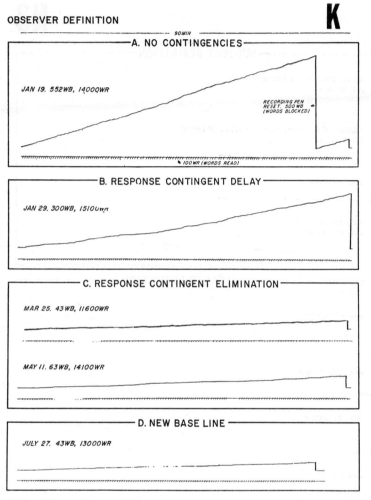

OBSERVER DEFINITION                                           **K**

Figure 6-17.   Effects of three different procedures upon stuttering. The last session was obtained after a six-week hiatus. Note persistence of pattern.

stated. The prolonged speech continued, without stuttering. The S was reading thus: "A-a-a-a-and whe-e-e-e-en A-a-a-a-an-na-a-a-a-a ca-a-a-a-a-a-ame . . ." Fearful that we had substituted for one undesirable speech pattern (stuttering), something worse, we tried a variety of conditions to disrupt this behavior, but it perseverated. On June 2, an attempt was made to increase the reading rate: the number of pages S had been reading was tripled, and he was told he could leave as soon as he had read them; the total pay would be the same. He read this tripled amount in one third the time; results are shown in Figure 6-16. (The N, D, E refer to different schedules, which had no differential effect.) Comparison of three

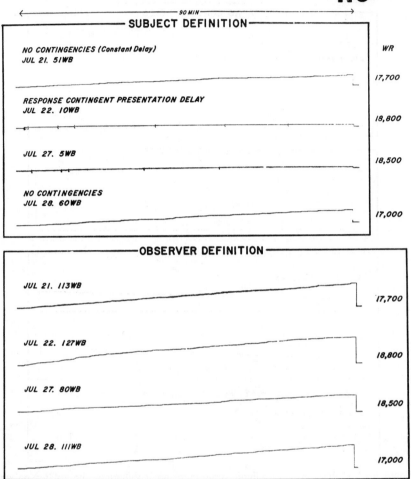

Figure 6-18.    Delayed feedback as punishment of button pressing, rather than the nonfluencies supposedly indicated, in a normally fluent S.

sessions of the speed-up (which total about 90 minutes) with the baseline session indicates that reading rate increased from 4400 words to 10,600, while stuttering dropped from about 1000 words to about 300. There was an eightfold increase in the ratio of fluency to nonfluency.

A summary presentation of procedures used for Subject K is presented in Figure 6-17. Punishment resulted in an attenuation of stuttering rate; the attenuation remained after the punishment was withdrawn. When elimination of delay was made contingent upon stuttering, nonfluencies were almost completely eliminated, falling within the rate of normally fluent Ss. Six weeks after the termination of the experiment, S was asked to read again under conditions of no delay. The booth maintained its stimulus control of the new pattern of rapid stutterless reading developed during the avoidance procedure.

## FEEDBACK AS A RESPONSE SPECIFIC REINFORCER

If delayed feedback is an aversive stimulus (as the punishment data indicated), its elimination should have increased response rate, which it did not. Further, one of the Ss stabilized under delay. We accordingly investigated delayed feedback further. Like stuttering, it has typically been studied for short periods using groups of Ss. Eight normally fluent Ss were run for extended periods, under conditions similar to those described for the stutterers.

That the delay contingency was indeed aversive is suggested by Figure 6-18. Button presses defining nonfluency dropped from 51 to 10 when this contingency was introduced, and remained at a low level, rising to 60 when withdrawn. However, the *monitor's* corresponding definitions of nonfluency (lower half of figure) indicated no such effects upon nonfluency. The S's button-pressing response was being affected in exactly the same manner that bar pressing is affected by shock. These results, corroborated with other Ss, suggested that delayed feedback was aversive; its anomalous effects on speech during avoidance suggested the possible intrusion of additional variables during speech.

Verbal behavior produces auditory and proprioceptive stimuli, which ensemble will not be produced unless verbal behavior occurs: these stimuli are *contingent* upon verbal behavior. Since withholding them may disrupt the behavior, their presentation also serves to *maintain* the behavior. These two properties of a stimulus, contingency upon behavior and maintenance of the behavior, define a reinforcing stimulus, and the feedback produced by speech may be among its reinforcing stimuli. Other consequences include those controlled by the audience. The feedback reinforcing stimuli are specific to speech, and may have different properties when made contingent on a button press. When this reinforcement, normally immediate, is withdrawn, behavior may be disrupted. However, audience-controlled contingencies may require continuation of speech. One method of maintaining the behavior under such conditions of deferred reinforcement is to prolong the behavior so that the immediate overlap is reinstated. Figure 6-19 illustrates this explanation of the prolonged speech noted in Subject S. During normal speech, the verbal outputs (responses) from "then came John" become immediate inputs (stimuli). Under delay, there is an asynchrony, and response and stim-

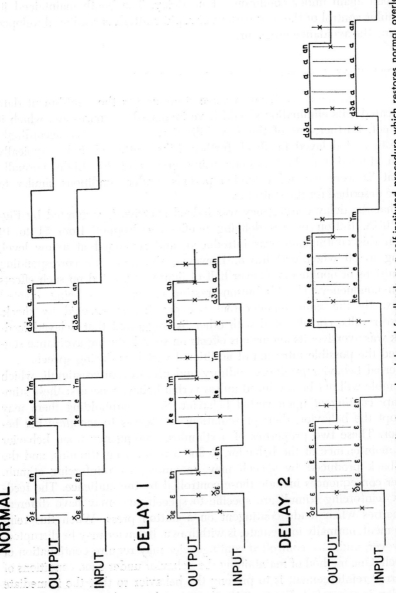

Figure 6-19. Prolonged vocalization under delayed feedback as a self-instituted procedure which restores normal overlap between speech and its auditory consequences.

ulus do not overlap. By prolonging the medial units as indicated in Delay 2, the "e" output overlaps the "e" input. Asynchrony is restricted to terminal-initial units, whose relative contribution is decreased as speech is prolonged.

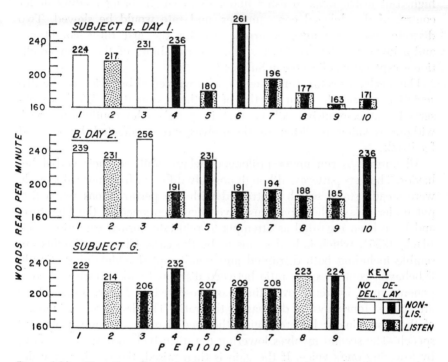

Figure 6-20. Disruptive effects of delayed auditory feedback upon reading rate when the auditory stimulus controls the response, as opposed to effects when it does not. Reading rate under delayed vs. immediate feedback, with instructions to listen and not to listen.

The maintaining stimuli are proprioceptive as well as auditory. Since temporal disruption characterizes auditory but not proprioceptive inputs, another method of reinstating immediacy of reinforcement is by switching maintenance of behavior from auditory to proprioceptive inputs. Results from two Ss whose reading rate had stabilized at a high rate under delay are presented in Figure 6-20 (Goldiamond, Atkinson, & Bilger, 1962). The Ss were given 10-minute reading periods. Each period was either under delayed or normal feedback. Prior to each period, S was either instructed to listen or not to listen to what he was reading. The experimental design, indicated in the key, is that of a 2-by-2 table, with the interaction of delay-listen predicted to be significant.[8] Without delay, S's speech would be controlled by the usual undisturbed auditory component, whether told to listen or not, and reading rate would be high. Under delay, with instructions not to listen, reading rate might be controlled by the undisturbed nonauditory components, and would also be high. But instructions to listen under delay might bring reading under control of the delayed consequences, and rate would be slowed. Two discrete response ranges occurred: one for the first three conditions, and a lower one for the fourth. The low variability of the latter condition is especially noticeable in Subject G.

The mechanisms for "tuning out" one's own verbal behavior, or the dissociation of speech, seem worthy of further exploration. We have observed that compulsive talkers, that is, people who continually speak without seeming to listen to themselves, are unaffected by delayed feedback.

All normal Ss run under prolonged delay stabilized their verbal behavior. The new patterns, although possibly different from normal speech, were steady states which contrasted with the perturbations when first put under delay. These patterns have been mentioned in the literature, and have been regarded as attempts to reinstate normal conditions (cf. Black, 1955), which indeed seems to be the case. Given a stimulus ensemble including both disrupted and nondisrupted maintaining stimuli, if behavior continues, the ratio between disrupted and undisrupted components must decrease over time, as presented in Figure 6-21. There are at least four ways of decreasing this ratio. The first involves increase of the denominator by prolonging the medial units, through prolonged speech. The second involves lowering the disturbed auditory numerator, by lowering one's voice. If the gain is then raised, the speaker may decrease the ratio by increasing the denominator through accentuating muscular movements; a tenseness is often reported in the throat. The fourth procedure is the tune-out procedure, in which whatever stimuli are involved in auditory-attentive control are decreased, while others are either increased or constant.

Outside the bounds of this set is another method for overcoming delay. This simply involves not speaking, or withdrawal: S may take off the earphones, leave the booth, etc. Our Ss, however, were paid to read; in order to read, they had to return that behavior to the control of the specific stimuli maintaining what may be called its *microstructure*. This suggests that there are at least two concurrent sets of stimuli maintaining verbal (and probably other) behaviors. Both are generated by the response and occasion its further occurrence. Verbal responses (or pigeon

---

[8] Such a 2-by-2 design, with interaction predicted as significant, is normally designed using analysis of variance. The results demonstrate that this type of interaction can also be analyzed using an *experimental* analysis of behavior.

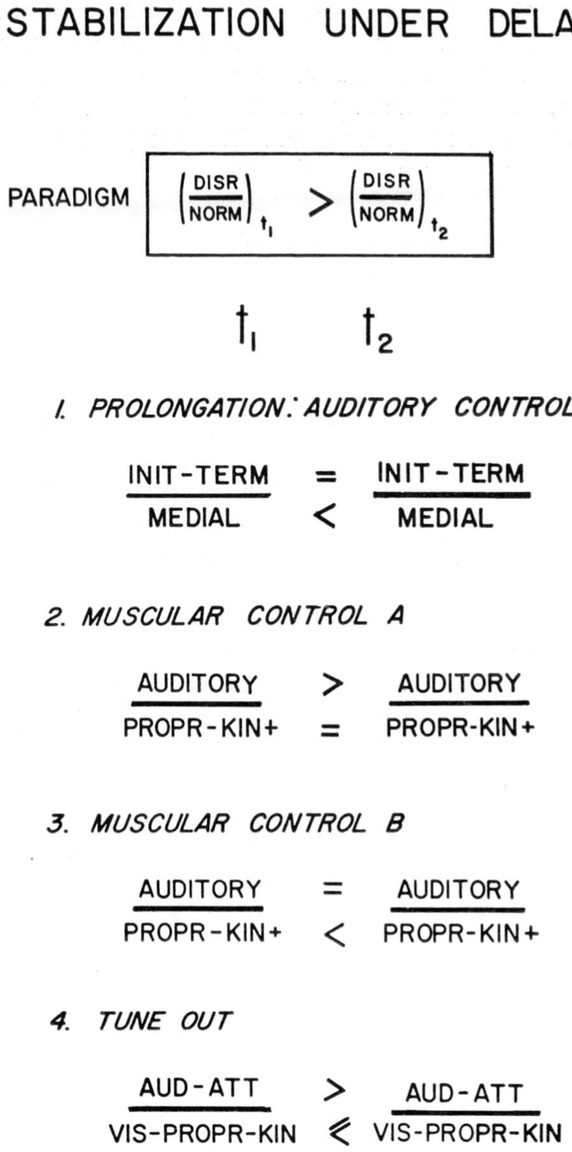

# STABILIZATION UNDER DELAY

PARADIGM $\left(\dfrac{DISR}{NORM}\right)_{t_1} > \left(\dfrac{DISR}{NORM}\right)_{t_2}$

$$t_1 \qquad t_2$$

*I. PROLONGATION: AUDITORY CONTROL*

$$\dfrac{INIT-TERM}{MEDIAL} \;\; \overset{=}{<} \;\; \dfrac{INIT-TERM}{MEDIAL}$$

*2. MUSCULAR CONTROL A*

$$\dfrac{AUDITORY}{PROPR-KIN+} \;\; \overset{>}{=} \;\; \dfrac{AUDITORY}{PROPR-KIN+}$$

*3. MUSCULAR CONTROL B*

$$\dfrac{AUDITORY}{PROPR-KIN+} \;\; \overset{=}{<} \;\; \dfrac{AUDITORY}{PROPR-KIN+}$$

*4. TUNE OUT*

$$\dfrac{AUD-ATT}{VIS-PROPR-KIN} \;\; \overset{>}{\lessdot} \;\; \dfrac{AUD-ATT}{VIS-PROPR-KIN}$$

Figure 6-21. Mechanisms for stabilizing verbal behavior under delayed auditory feedback, involving decreasing the ratio between disrupted input under delay, and normal input not effected by delay.

pecks) produce both auditory feedback (or proprioceptive feedback), on the one hand, and money-attention (or grain), on the other. Presentation of these stimuli provide the occasion for the next response, as well, producing a chain (Skinner, 1938). The difference between the two sets of stimuli does not lie entirely in their part-whole relation to the response units involved. A response unit is the response between the stimulus which occasions it (the discriminative stimulus) and the reinforcing stimulus (which maintains it) contingent upon it. Thus, the 32 words of the Pledge of Allegiance are a response unit. Each word, however, is contingent upon the preceding word and occasions the next, also defining a *word* as a response unit. We can go further into progressively decreasing constituent units, and come to those bounded by the occasioning and reinforcing properties of the auditory and proprioceptive feedback units of the microstructure, which do not necessarily end the regression. The original environmental discriminative stimulus ("Recite the pledge") may occasion a 32-word unit, which long chain is maintained by all the submacrostructural reinforcers and discriminative stimuli on the way, culminated by the final macrostructural reinforcer.[9] Since there are varying units and subunits, the part-whole relationship is not sufficient to distinguish between the two sets of stimuli (exemplified by grain and feedback) we have been discussing. The necessary difference between the two sets of stimuli may lie not so much in their part-whole relation or in their contingency upon behavior, but in the *agency that schedules the contingency*. In the one case, the agency may be the physiological and natural ecology of the response (nerves, ambient air, and bone conductors); in the other case, the agency may be the grosser environmental ecology (the experimenter, the apparatus, society, the habitat). Both sets of stimuli may control and direct the behavior and also serve as constant stimuli (Goldiamond, 1962b), and their relationship to each other is a fruitful field for research. For verbal behavior, there are thus at least two audiences (or agencies of reinforcement) when the person speaks: himself and the social audience. The former stimuli can evidently be conditioned reinforcers to the latter (Kelleher & Gollub, 1962) when, for example, a child consoles himself after a scare by saying aloud to himself, "There, there, don't cry," which input was previously produced by his mother along with other stimuli which were effective in producing comfort. These considerations suggest that the class of stimulus changes represented by delayed feedback (which can be called response-specific-reinforcers) have interesting properties meriting their further consideration in psychological research.

There is at least one other property of delayed feedback that merits its experimental interest. This concerns the logical relation between responses and stimuli. The former are the dependent and the latter are the independent variables in most psychological research. Where the

---

[9] Guthrie (1952) makes a distinction between an act and the movements it comprises. The foregoing discussion suggests that an analysis in terms of operant chains, derived from consideration of acts, may be fruitful in the analysis of the movements Guthrie regarded as critical.

reinforcing *agency* is outside the organism, the agency can program the stimuli in a variety of ways, and observe the functional relations between the independent variables he manipulates and the dependent variable of behavior. Where the reinforcing *agency*, however, is not of this kind, that is, in the case of response-produced stimuli of the microecology, the dependent and independent variables become behaviorally contaminated, that is, the independent variable (the stimulus) becomes dependent upon the dependent variable (the response) rather than being controlled by *E*, whose control and analysis become devious, within a behavioral framework. By using delayed feedback, *E* withholds the stimulus produced by the response and can manipulate it, thereby making it an independent variable, analogous to the other situation, in which he controls this variable.

For these reasons, and others related to the effects of delay upon the microstructure of speech, we decided to utilize it to attempt to develop a rapid way of alleviating stuttering as a personal problem.

## NEW RESPONSE PATTERNS AND THE ATTENUATION OF STUTTERING

At least two alternative behavioral procedures are theoretically available to alleviate stuttering as a personal problem. One of these may be considered as *correcting* the speech pattern in which stuttering is embedded. An alternative approach involves *substituting* for this pattern some other pattern which does not contain stuttering.

With regard to correction, given some undesirable behavior, there are a variety of means to alter it to a more desirable form. These include attenuating stuttering through extinction or punishment, changing stimulus control, establishing incompatible responses, or any of the at least one dozen methods whose parameters are being investigated in operant laboratories, where modification of behavior is a tool used in the analysis of behavior. Where the undesirable behavior is embedded in more desirable behavior, the proportion of the desirable fluent components may be increased. Again, there are a variety of available procedures. In certain cases, one type of modification procedure may be contraindicated or indicated on a priori grounds, in other cases, a considerable amount of time may have to be spent in behavioral analysis and modification of the behavior to ascertain which is to be used or avoided.

On the other hand, development of entirely new patterns may not require such extensive analysis, and a procedure for the development of a pattern devoid of stuttering was the elimination-avoidance of delay procedure found to be effective in the present investigations. The fact that this pattern had unusual components, such as prolongation, does not necessarily contraindicate its use, since procedures exist which can eliminate such undesirable features.

Consideration of stuttering as an operant means that it must be considered as being under stimulus control.[10] Stated otherwise, the new patterns developed may be specific only to the laboratory, with S stuttering in his old haunts. It may also be added, however, that corrective procedures may also produce a speech pattern which is also under stimulus control, and is confined to the clinic. Accordingly, additional procedures may be required in either case to extend the behavior from the conditions in which it was established to the more general conditions outside the laboratory or clinic. It may also be, in both cases, that the establishment of speech without blockages may generate new consequences and conditions on the outside which serve to maintain it there. Interestingly, stutterers on their own often develop both procedures, developing glides and other methods of overcoming blockages, or substituting in conversation words on which they do not block for words on which they do.

Both corrective and substitutive procedures require analysis of the variables maintaining the behavior outside the clinic or laboratory, but *within* these settings, the corrective procedure requires an additional analysis which the substitutive procedure may circumvent. Accordingly, we decided to establish an entirely new verbal pattern for the stutterers, and to proceed from there. The program adhered to is presented in the following outline; the specific experimental procedures and their rationale are combined thereafter under headings paralleling the program outline.

1. ESTABLISHMENT OF A NEW RESPONSE PATTERN. A new pattern

---

[10] Stimulus control rather than genetics may be involved in the observation that stuttering sometimes runs in families. At our home, the children often yell for their father. An ordinary conversation call of "Daddy" may initially have occasioned no response. The call was made continually louder until he responded. Their mother, who had answered immediately, is not yelled for. The yelling is under stimulus control, that is, it occurs under one set of conditions and not another, because of differences in systematically scheduled consequences under these different conditions. We may envisage another case, where the call of "D-d-daddy" has no immediate answer forthcoming, and so on, until a full fledged "D-d-d-d-daddy" provides attention. Such shaping of nonfluencies may typically not be systematic; that is, on the following day, it may be extinguished, and other behavioral patterns may be reinforced. Where, however, there is a relative who stutters, or familial circumstances exist which focus attention upon nonfluencies, differential attention may be applied to fluency–nonfluency, thereby establishing these as response classes. In this case, defining stuttering as a problem, made more probable by the existence of relatives who stutter, may actually produce the problem. Other social consequences of stuttering will be discussed in this report.

The behavior may not only be under the stimulus control of different social audiences, but also of the audience which is the speaker himself; that is, the different stimuli produced by one's own voice when one speaks in different ways. This may underlie the reports of stutterers who do not stutter when they sing or declaim on the stage (the audience, as well as the voice, may differ here), or speak to their dog (who does not apply differential consequences to fluency–nonfluency), or in a foreign language, and so on (cf. Bloodstein, 1950).

of verbal behavior would be established, in which stuttering had not been differentially reinforced. Optimally, such a pattern should be strikingly different from the normal pattern.

2. ALTERING THE STIMULUS CONTROL OF THE NEW PATTERN. Since behavior is under stimulus control, and the stimuli that produced this pattern are not in the general environment, the ratio of special conditions (which established the behavior) to more general conditions would be decreased in a systematically programed manner, derived from experimental research.

3. SHAPING THE RESPONSE PATTERN TO NORMAL SPEECH. This pattern, being an odd one, would then be gradually shaped to a pattern which has the formal characteristics of standard speech.

4. SELF-CONTROL PROCEDURES. Procedures would then be programed to have this speech carried out of the laboratory and used wherever the previous patterns had been used. The regular reinforcers that maintain normally fluent speech might then maintain and strengthen this new pattern, just as they do normally fluent speech. Thus, although S returns to his old haunts, it is a different environment by virtue of its alteration by an altered operant.

The program was implemented by the following specific procedures, the experimental rationale or evidence for which is given in each case:

### Establishment of a New Speech Pattern

PROLONGATION. The new speech pattern should be one whose direction E can control, so that he can shape it into standard speech, in accord with the requirements of Step 3 in the program. Of the four possible novel patterns which may emerge under delay (prolongation, voice lowering, proprioceptive increase, tuning out), prolongation lends itself most readily to shaping, since control equipment and response definition are currently superior in this case than with the other patterns. Nevertheless, since alternative response patterns are available to S under delay, special procedures are required to produce a specified one. At least the following procedures are available:

Running S until prolongation occurs: Where prolongation occurred in the experimental analysis reported, its establishment took a great deal of time. Since other competing patterns may also be maintained by the delay, letting delay take its own course is contraindicated.

Instructing S to prolong: This depends on the degree to which S is under the control of instructions. Since instructions are discriminative stimuli, their control is governed by differential consequences attached to obedience-disobedience. Under appropriate conditions, instructions are a very rapid and efficient way to control behavior. They are both utilized and omitted in the course of this investigation.

Pacing the discriminative stimuli: Various devices exist for presenting

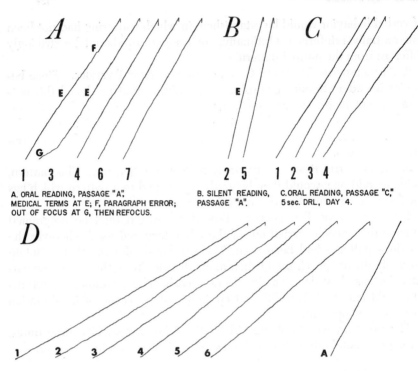

A. ORAL READING, PASSAGE "A",
MEDICAL TERMS AT E; F, PARAGRAPH ERROR;
OUT OF FOCUS AT G, THEN REFOCUS.

B. SILENT READING,
PASSAGE "A".

C.ORAL READING, PASSAGE "C",
5 sec. DRL, DAY 4.

D. REPEATED ORAL READING, PASSAGE "D"; 1-6, 9 YEAR OLD GIRL; A, COLLEGE GIRL, SAME PASSAGE.

Figure 6-22. Cumulative curves of ongoing oral (A, C, D) and silent (B) reading rates obtained through procedures discussed in text.

reading material at different rates. Such rates may be compared with rates when S reads at his own pace. The author (Goldiamond, 1962c) has put pulses of the PerceptoScope, which present successive displays of reading material, under the control of S's button. The cumulative recorder activated presents an ongoing record of oral and silent reading rate. Figure 6-22 presents such data. Sessions at B are of silent reading of the same material read aloud at A; other variations are depicted in the illustration. These procedures were used in the present research. Other recording devices for the same purpose, to be assayed, are voice-operated relays and pause or duration analyzers. In contrast to the other procedures, pace itself can be manipulated.

Dynamic control over prolongation: The foregoing equipment may also be used to activate devices that supply differential reinforcement for different rates and forms. Curve 4 at C in Figure 6-22 depicts the effects of differential reinforcement for low rates. Such control may take considerable time to establish. Neither this procedure nor aversive control was utilized here.

DELAYED FEEDBACK IN THE ESTABLISHMENT OF NOVEL PATTERNS. Delayed feedback has certain properties (Fairbanks, 1955) which suggest its use in the development of novel speech. It interferes with the microstructure of speech and forces a new pattern. Among the nonprolongation patterns it establishes are those involving greater muscular control, which may be utilized to improve articulation. Finally, in terms of Step 2 of the program presented, it can gradually be faded out.

It will be recalled that prolonged and stutter-free speech was produced under the procedure involving elimination-avoidance of delay. Assuming that prolongation has been established, the following three possible consequences may be systematically related to verbal patterns under the elimination-avoidance procedure:

1. Normally fluent speech————➤ delayed feedback, disruption
2. Normal stuttering speech————➤ normal feedback of stuttering
3. Prolonged novel fluent speech———➤ delayed feedback, no disruption

It will be noted that possibility 3, prolonged novel fluent speech, is the aim of the program presented in the preceding section. Regarding patterns 1 and 2, it is presumed that the depicted consequences of both patterns of speech normally available to the stutterer, fluency and nonfluency, are aversive, describing a classical avoidance–avoidance conflict. If, however, the speech patterns is prolonged, the delay is not disruptive, and this pattern is thereby established and maintained. Being a novel pattern in which stuttering was never differentially reinforced, it is free of stuttering. In effect, this pattern produces continual delay, since there are no blockages to turn off the delay. It remains to be seen if continual delay alone (without the contingency) has the same effect. Given such a novel pattern, whatever blockages occur may extinguish if no differential consequences are attached to them. The course of extinction of a response differs from its attenuation by punishment (supplying an aversive consequence upon its occurrence, the present case). Holz and Azrin (1963) report more rapid attenuation by the latter procedure—under different circumstances, however.

*Altering the Stimulus Control of the New Pattern*

Once the new pattern is established, the delayed feedback which was involved in its instatement may be gradually faded out, from 250 ms, in gradual steps to no delay. In the early cases to be reported, the delay was initially decreased in daily decrements of 50 ms; in later cases decreases occurred *within* the session. If the new behavior is then sustained without its initiating stimuli, like the grin on the Cheshire cat after the cat had vanished, the verbal behavior is transferred to the control of stimuli closer to those normally present. This procedure is borrowed from programed instruction, which initially borrowed it from animal research on successive approximations. It has been re-extended into animal research (Terrace, 1963) and has been adapted for the errorless establishment of difficult discriminations in children (Moore & Goldiamond, 1964).

### Shaping the Response Pattern to Normal Speech

Where the new prolonged behavior is maintained without the delayed feedback, the reading rate may now be speeded up, by machine control of the presentations, through appropriately programed steps, to normal and supernormal rates.

Should the verbal behavior at any moment deteriorate to its previous patterns, E may retreat, and reinstate the supporting conditions which had been withdrawn.

### Self-Control Procedures

The S may now be instructed to observe his own speech patterns, and use them on the outside, under conditions which will be discussed under a separate heading. Self-control procedures are to be distinguished from generalization procedures, in which other stimuli assumed to be more general may be introduced, or control is transferred from one set of discriminative stimuli to another through stimulus manipulation by E (as in Step 3). In self-control, the S is instructed to analyze the functional relations between his behaviors and the conditions under which they occur, and to change his environment in a manner likely to optimize the desired changes in his behavior. Accordingly, considerable cooperation is required from S. The author has been utilizing this procedure in counseling with regard to a variety of personal problems, such as study behaviors, obesity, and marital problems. The present paper will report their extension to stuttering.

### RESULTS

At the present writing,[11] these procedures have been applied to eight successive Ss, all stutterers with a prolonged history of stuttering, and in all eight cases there has been complete elimination of stuttering within the laboratory, with reading rate far more rapid than previously (in one case, four times as high). The speech is well articulated, and is considered pleasant by listeners, that is, there are no sing-song, delayed, or otherwise unpleasant patterns. This behavior has carried over outside the laboratory in certain of the cases. A more detailed description follows.

### Preliminary Cases

The first Ss on whom the procedures were tried were referrals from the Speech Clinic at Arizona State University;[12] they had a long history of

[11] December, 1963.
[12] The author wishes to express his appreciation to Dr. Robert Albright, professor of speech, and chairman, who made the referrals and whose cooperation in innumerable other ways made this part of the study possible.

differing treatments for a perseverating problem. They sat in a specially constructed booth, their speech was monitored outside it, and from tapes thereafter, using control and recording equipment more precise than in the preceding analysis. They were run during the 1962-1963 academic year, for 3 days a week, for approximately 50 minutes a day. Initially, they read from pages projected at a rate governed by their own ad-lib depressions of the button, which successively exposed about 3.2 words per response. After a stabilization period, they were instructed to depress a second button for each word on which they stuttered. The delayed feedback elimination-avoidance procedure was then introduced. Instructions to slow down were varied. At a later period, the timer was set to pulse the reading material at the new low rate they had established ad lib, and the reading rate button was withdrawn. The delayed feedback was later faded out, and the reading presentation rate was then speeded up. Instructions to extend the speech outside the laboratory were also varied.

Since these two cases were the earliest in which the procedure outlined was applied, many more sessions than later proved necessary were run. About 70 sessions extending over 7 months were run, with a change being made only after the author was assured of stability.

The author did not communicate with the Ss, but affected their conditions through instructions to the monitors after examination of the records.[13]

SUBJECT WD. A summary of the performance and procedures for this S is presented in Figure 6-23. The ordinate is logarithmic. During the initial baseline period, except for 1 day of very rapid reading, the rate was about 110 (words per minute). Stuttering rate during the same period was about 15 wpm, except for the high-reading day, which was accompanied by a high nonfluency rate, as well. At session 22, self-definition of stuttering was introduced; there was an immediate but transient decline in both rates. At session 34, the elimination-avoidance procedure was introduced, with S instructed to slow his reading. Reading rate dropped to about 70 wpm, but stuttering rate plummeted to about 3 wpm, and continued to drop, remaining thereafter at less than 1 wpm, except for 1 day, when the material included difficult medical terms (MED in the illustration). At session 47, timer control of the reading rate was instituted at 78 wpm. Four sessions later, the 250 ms delayed feedback was cut to 200 ms and then in successive days to 150, 100, 50, 50, 20, 20, 20, (the 20 ms series was an unnecessary precaution) and finally it was eliminated completely. Since stuttering was still almost nonexistent, reading rate was speeded up, and then again, to 140 wpm, well above the

[13] The research assistants were Mr. Larry Nims and Mr. Robert Moore, graduate students in the Department of Psychology, to whom the author wishes to express his appreciation. Special equipment was constructed for the project by Mr. Robert Dickie of the Physics Laboratory.

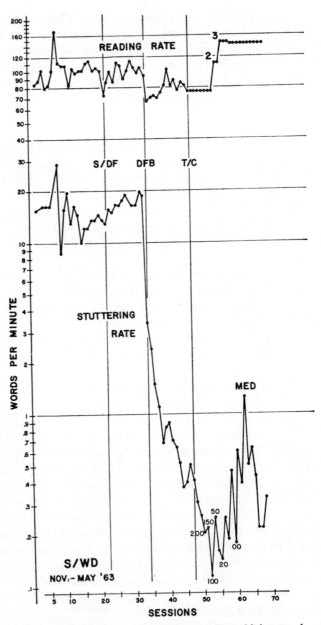

Figure 6-23. The virtual elimination of stuttering and establishment of a better-than normal reading rate in a chronic stutterer, the first S subjected to the applied programed procedures that were derived from the preceding experimental analysis.

previous baseline. Stuttering was not reinstated, but ranged between 0.2 and 0.6 wpm.

The S was informed of his progress, and was instructed to practice his

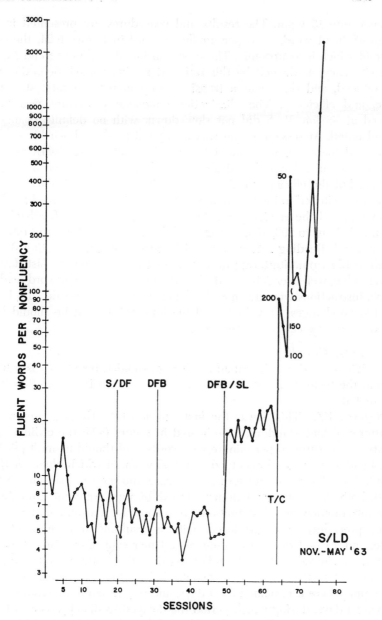

Figure 6-24.   Ratio of fluent to stuttered words in the second S subjected to applied procedures, as a function of programed treatment.

new pattern of speech with his wife, with his friends, and during classes. He delivered an extensive talk in an education class, without nonfluencies, and both he and his wife reported that he was "cured."

SUBJECT LD.   Initial reading rate was about 100 wpm, and nonfluency rate 15 wpm. The results and procedures are presented in the form of fluent words read per nonfluent word in Figure 6-24, the ordinate of which is logarithmic. There was an initial declining trend in verbal efficiency, as defined by this ratio. At session 20, self-definition was introduced, and there was a transient drop in reading rate, stuttering rate, and efficiency. The elimination-avoidance procedure was introduced at session 31; S did not slow down, with no definite change in trend noted. At session 49, he was instructed to slow down his reading rate, and there was an immediate drop in nonfluencies (with rate between 1.5 and 2.5 wpm) and also in reading rate (between 30 and 40 wpm), but the efficiency ratio rose considerably. At session 64, reading rate was switched to the timer, at 34 wpm; nonfluencies dropped to about 0.5 wpm, and the efficiency ratio rose markedly. Delayed feedback was then faded out to 200, 150, 100, 50, and 0 ms; the low stuttering rate was maintained. Reading rate was raised in successive stages lasting 3 days each to 120 wpm. Stuttering rate continued low, and on the last day, he was reading well over 2500 words fluently for each nonfluent word read.

No instructions were given S about behavior on the outside, and he reported no changes; he volunteered the information that he should have tried his new speech pattern outside.

### Later Cases[14]

The procedures described are being extended for other cases being run at the Institute for Behavioral Research. Curves from two Ss will be presented.

SUBJECT EZ. This S was the first run at I.B.R. He is a pronounced stutterer of long standing, as indicated in Figure 6-25; the ordinate presents words stuttered per minute, but words read should be multiplied by 10. Reading rate aloud averaged about 45 wpm, of which *almost half exhibited nonfluencies!* Stuttering rate rose during the baseline period with both stuttering and reading rate exhibiting a transient drop during the introduction of self-definition. At session 14, the elimination-avoidance procedure was introduced, with a resulting drop in nonfluency rate, and a slight drop in reading rate. Timer control of reading presentation was introduced on the following day; the stuttering rate dropped to zero. At session 16, the timer-controlled reading rate was dropped to 20 wpm, where it remained for 4 days, and was raised to 34 wpm the following 4 days, during which period the delayed feedback was also faded out. On session 23, the first day of no delay, three different rates were

[14] The research reported in this section and thereafter, on stuttering and counseling, is being performed under the contract between the Office of the Surgeon General and the Washington School of Psychiatry, mentioned in Footnote °.

Miss Evelyn Wetzler, a speech major who spent the 1963-1964 academic year at I.B.R., served as monitor and research assistant in all phases of this project, and contributed immeasurably to its progress. The author also wishes to express his appreciation to Mr. Peter Edmondo for assistance in the instrumentation.

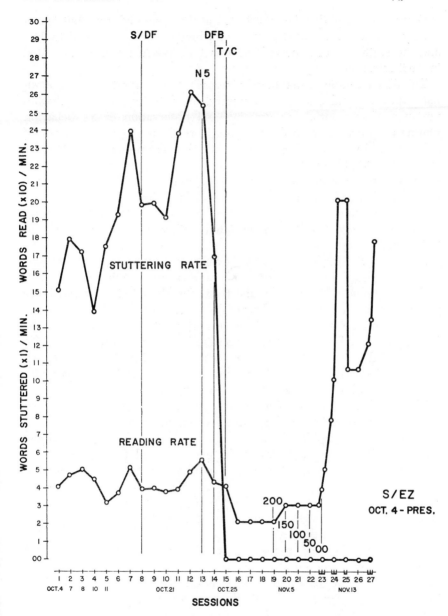

Figure 6-25. Laboratory elimination of stuttering and quadrupling of reading rate in a very severe stutterer, the third S tried.

presented within the same session; S continued not to stutter at 50 wpm, the highest rate. At the next session, he was started at 72 wpm, then raised to 102 wpm, *then to 204 wpm,* a rate he reports never having attained in his life, with no stuttering.

On the following day, he was started at the same high rate, but immediately started stuttering. He was accordingly quickly dropped to 110, and the stuttering disappeared; he was then raised again, as indicated in the illustration.

This S's data indicate that merely increasing reading rate will not attenuate stuttering and can, on the contrary, reinstate it; it suggests the importance of appropriate programing and observation of S's behavior. During one of the slow reading sessions, S read each presented phrase at a fairly rapid rate, and then paused until the next presentation. He was told that if he did this, the forthcoming speedup might merely compress the pause rather than affect his speech, and was told to prolong the phrases so that he filled up all the time available, which he did.

The S's reading in the booth is at a level never attained before, and without stuttering. Articulation and intelligibility are very high. Self control procedures are in progress.

SUBJECT JF.    This S had to leave town in two weeks and, accordingly, condensed procedures were tried; there was one baseline day, 2 days under additional self-definition, and thereafter the elimination-avoidance procedure was introduced. Fading of delay was introduced 3 days thereafter. As can be seen in Figure 6-26, stuttering rate became zero. On the first day of no delay, reading rate was raised twice within the session. On the second day, it was started at a lower rate (the E having learned from the preceding case), and then raised twice, *to a final 256 words per minute*, which was also sustained on the following day.

The S remained in town an extra day, during which E prescribed exercises for him at home. These involved reading very slowly for 1 minute, then reading rapidly, for another minute. His wife was then to join him and ask him questions about the material read (so that the same words might be used), and then switch to other conversation for a total of 5 minutes. During all this time he was to use his booth voice. A metronome was prescribed as a pacer, along with a hand counter for nonfluencies. These morning exercises were to be extended gradually to cover increasing sections of the day.

The S was delayed in getting the equipment, and decided to speed things up on his own (he had taken the I.B.R. course on behavior analysis). He has reported that he now sounds "like John Gielgud, without the accent"—and tapes corroborate this evaluation.

### Standardized Procedure

By now, a fairly standardized procedure has emerged for behavior modification within the booth. It is exemplified by the following 3 Ss.

S-A.    The S is a 40-year-old male, professional, who came in three times a week after work. His schedule (reading words per minute [wpm] and nonfluency words per minute [spm] are in parentheses)

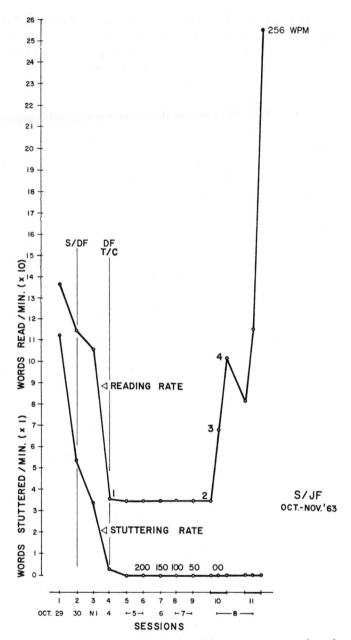

Figure 6-26. Typical results being obtained in laboratory using condensed standardized procedure developed at request of S with only two weeks available for treatment.

was as follows: 3 days Baseline (107 wpm, 6 spm); 3 days Self-definition (112 wpm, 1.3 spm); 3 days Elimination-Avoidance Delay, Reading Rate machine-controlled (30 wpm, 0.2 spm); 5 days Fadeout Delay (30 wpm, 0 spm). On the following days, reading rate was altered within sessions, each cluster representing a day: 30-51; 102-245; 120-245; 30-185. The final rates are above his baseline ad-lib rate. There were no nonfluencies at all. On the last day of the regular sessions, he requested a "reminder" of speech under delay, and he was given a few minutes under 200 ms delay.

The S is now on a schedule of home exercises. For the first week, he read for 2 minutes at both a slow and a normal rate, and engaged in immediate conversation thereafter for 1 minute; during the second week, the conversation was raised to 2 minutes; it is now 5 minutes, with next week's assignment scheduled for persisting in this manner all morning. Nonfluencies are recorded by S and an observer; they have averaged 1, with a range of 0-3. Reading rate per day during the ad-lib part of the first week was 112, 130, 135, 138, 130; during the second week it was 147, 148, 159, 153, 152, 148.

The S turns in his records once a week during which he and E discuss changes in procedures. He reports that his work associates have asked him what happened to his stuttering, and tapes of conversations in the laboratory and with E validate these queries, as does the referral source.

S-B.    The S is a female high school junior, whose father brings her in three times a week after work. Her schedule was as follows: 2 days Baseline (171 wpm, 5.5 spm); 3 days Self-definition (153 wpm, 2.5 spm); 3 days Elimination-Avoidance Delay, Reading Rate machine-controlled (30 wpm, 0 spm); 5 days Fadeout Delay (30 wpm, 0 spm). Reading rate altered within sessions, with each cluster a day: 30-102-204; 121-204; 51-204. Final rates were beyond her baseline, and there was no stuttering at all. The S has been given home assignments.

S-C.    The S is a college junior, majoring in foreign languages, for whom stuttering is a problem, since he also stuttered in these classes. He came daily. He was one of the earlier S's; his baseline was accordingly protracted: 7 days Baseline (151 wpm, 6 spm); 4 days Self-definition (157 wpm, 3 spm); 3 days Elimination-Avoidance Delay, Reading Rate machine-controlled (30 wpm, 0 spm); Fadeout Delay (30 wpm, 0 spm); Reading Rate altered within sessions, 51-64; 102-136-204; 102-143-224; 102-157-204; no nonfluencies within these sessions.

The S reported he was no longer stuttering in his English speaking classes, but was stuttering in his foreign-language classes. He was instructed to bring his French book into the booth, and read from that, averaging 2 spm. Accordingly, he was given the Elimination-Avoidance Delay procedure, with Delay set at 50 ms. There were no nonfluencies at all during this period, nor during the next 4 days when Delay was removed. He was instructed to read from his German book in the booth; there were no nonfluencies. On the following day, he read both German and French, with 50 ms Elimination-Avoidance Delay, and French on the next day without Delay. There were no nonfluencies. Two days of rapid English reading paced by the machine then followed, and when he read French on the third day, his nonfluency rate was 2 spm; he read 10 minutes under 50 ms Elimination-Avoidance Delay, then without it. There were no nonfluencies then, nor have there been any since then. His ad-lib reading rate in French is now 93 wpm. Most recently, he read *Fathers and Sons* at 186 wpm, in a section containing many Russian names. He reported that he was being pushed, felt under tension and strain—but there were no nonfluencies. He has been using his new speech pattern in such readings, in discussions with $E$, and reports using it at school. The new speech pattern is well articulated. He has been given home assignments.

### Summary

Other cases are under way; the information they contain is redundant. There is an almost total elimination of nonfluencies upon introduction of the Elimination-Avoidance Delay procedure, coupled with machine control of Reading Rate (to 34 wpm). The nonfluency rate is maintained when the Delay is faded out. It is also maintained when the reading rate is then speeded up beyond the baseline rate. It has been possible to get $Ss$ to use the speech patterns outside the laboratory, and there have been consistent reports of improvement from referral sources as well as from others. All sessions, including discussions in the office, are taped, and these reveal a similar trend.

### Some Questions Raised

The program mentioned follows the course of much medical research, where an attempt is made to establish and control some phenomenon within the laboratory (often with animals), to develop procedures which alleviate the problem, and then to engage in further analysis to refine and simplify the procedures so that they may be used in practice, and so that practice becomes more of an applied science, and less of an art.

Several questions with regard to the application of the procedure and its refinement for practice may be raised. Among these are: Is prolongation the most advisable new behavior from which to shape the new patterns—could others serve as well? Probably, but shaping conversational speech out of, say, singing, may require considerable skill on the part of the practitioner; in the present procedures, it is the machine which is skilled. If prolongation is used, is delayed feedback necessary in its establishment—could not instructions or other prolongation procedures, alone, or in ensemble, do the job? One consequence of delayed feedback which has already been mentioned is its control of more precise articulation. Metronomes have been used in the past, but these may produce sing-song patterns. Can explicit procedures be developed to avert this? It may very well be that for some cases, the delay is required, and that others may yield to lesser treatment. Is the Elimination-Avoidance procedure necessary or would continual delay, accompanied by instructions, do the job? Should conversation, rather than reading, be programed in the booths? Other applied questions may be raised which can be answered only by further research. Some of the basic research questions generated have been raised during the report. Nevertheless, the current procedures are effective and rapid in their control over the elimination of stuttering, and the development of fluent and rapid verbal behavior. It is our intention during the next months to refine these procedures, along the lines of the questions raised, as well as others.

### SECONDARY GAIN AND SELF-CONTROL

The author has frequently been asked if he has investigated the likelihood that stuttering is supplying secondary gain, that is, that it manipulates the environment favorably some way, and that if this behavioral method of manipulation is removed, S may establish some other undesirable behavior to achieve the same results. Frequently, the question is made in the form of an assertion, namely, that some other undesirable behavior *will* develop. The assertion assumes as fact what is a model, namely, that behavior is like water filling a tightly closed container. Since water is not readily compressible, pushing in a bulge in one place to straighten out the side will only produce another bulge elsewhere. The author would like to see some actuarial data here, for example, in how many cases when stuttering was eliminated without personal therapy did, say, a tic replace it, and in how many cases not? Or, on the other hand, in how many cases did eliminating the stuttering also eliminate shyness and make the person's hold on his environment far more effective? Barring such data, the author's inclination is to view stuttering as a problem which can have considerable consequences, inasmuch as our major means of controlling our environment is through communicating with people. When S requests relief from this problem, and such relief can be rapidly provided, suffice unto the day the good thereof.

The question of secondary gain has some legitimate properties. It assumes that stuttering is an operant, namely, that it is maintained by differential consequences attached to fluency-nonfluency. It also assumes that stuttering may be a symptom. This term is currently in disrepute in behavioral research, inasmuch as it has often been used to suggest some deep, nonbehavioral state underlying the behavior. If, however, we examine the conditions of its usage, it may be a very valuable term.

When, for example, the dermatologist says that a skin rash is a symptom of blood imbalance, he indicates that *rather than primarily treating the distress which brought the patient to the clinic, he will treat something else*, in this case, the blood. By this reasoning, if we state that stuttering is symptomatic, we state that rather than treating only the stuttering behavior which brought S to the clinic, we shall also go about trying to change some other behaviors in the process of treatment. The author would regard this possibility as legitimate, but would insist that it not be an article of faith. In some cases, treatment of the stuttering may make S more effective, and in other cases it may not. The author's working assumption has been that both approaches may be necessary, depending on the case.

Psychotherapy and counseling are classical approaches to behavior modification, and considerable attention has been devoted to operant control of events within the session; the verbal behavior of the patient may be affected by contingencies supplied by the therapist (Krasner, 1958b), and it can probably also be shown that in this reciprocal relation, the therapist himself can come under the control of the patient, a situation which is not unfamiliar to therapists. Unfortunately, very little attention has been devoted to the relation between the fine details of verbal interchanges within the hour, and the fine details of behavioral alterations outside, which is the ultimate test of the effectiveness of psychotherapy and counseling. This question was raised in the present research with reference to elimination of stuttering outside the booths. The practice sessions mentioned in the assignments given to Ss are one procedure for such carry-over.

Another procedure involves self-control. This consists in training S to recognize those behaviors of his which he wants to modify. Rather than telling him to modify them (something which he may have already told himself), he is trained in the experimental analysis of behavior, and also in the variables which maintain it, or which he can recruit to modify it. He gets regular weekly reading assignments in a private tutorial. The S's behavior is the laboratory, demonstration, or focus of discussion, along with the standard experimental animals discussed in the assigned text. The procedure may be summarized in the form of the following question: if a pigeon were exhibiting these behaviors, and you wanted to get rid of them (as in stuttering) or wanted to establish new ones (as in marital or study counseling), how would you go about programing the environment to do so? The weekly therapy sessions then become research conferences, as though between a professor and his research associate on what has to be done next to bring the organism's behavior into line. The S is the acknowledged expert in the content of the field—his own behavior and its ecology—and E brings to bear on the problem his knowledge of procedures and past effects. Eventually, as in a good professorial relation, S may become an independent investigator, capable of tending to things on his own.

The sessions start with a delineation of the problem, and S is then asked: "Under what conditions do you stutter?" He typically has a ready answer—when he is anxious, threatened, or the like. One answer was: "When my thoughts outrace my ability to put them into words." Leaving aside the referents of these answers, one must question their usefulness as research guides or as guides to modification.[15] The question may then be rephrased by E in a form such as: What are the environmental conditions under which you stutter (feel anxious, have thoughts outracing your words, etc.)? Are there (a) any events which occasion these responses, and (b) any particular consequences occurring in the environment as a result of your stuttering which might not occur otherwise? The answers to these questions not only provide a basis for further analysis and modification but are illuminating in their own right.

One S reported that he stuttered when called upon in class for an immediate answer. If he stuttered, the teacher waited patiently, giving him more time to formulate an answer, something he might not get otherwise. The military adviser whose thoughts outraced his words stated that the

---

[15] We are considering stuttering as *behavior* whose modification is an aim of the therapist. It has been argued that anxiety (for example) underlies this behavior, and that the way to eliminate it is to alleviate the anxiety, often by altering the personality structure. Indeed, patients do report seeking help because of *feelings* which disturb them. It can be argued that such disturbance is related to behavioral deficits, which, when remedied, are accompanied by altered feelings. Behaviors are observable, both to E and S, their consequences are observable, and alterations in both are also observable. The S may be trained in more precise observation and in procedures for altering the environment and observing its effects on behavior.

The feelings of S, on the other hand, are unobservable to E and it can also be argued that their definition or validity of observation by S himself raises serious questions. In the perception of color, the term "blue" may be assigned by S to his own experience by virtue of a common referent, a wave length, he shares with the verbal community which differentially reinforces the term "blue" in its presence (cf. Graham, 1959; Skinner, 1957). A communicable definition of color experience is taught. Feelings lack such ready common referents. Communication to E is hazardous, and since E is but a special representative of the verbal community, the referent of the verbal term when S uses it to define it to himself also becomes questionable.

A basic datum becomes S's verbal statement of feeling, which can be observed by others, but if this is considered as being an indicator of perception, or having a perceptual referent (of feeling), the author can only reiterate his previous statement (Goldiamond, 1962b) that credence in the verbal response is among the least valid indicators of perception. The verbal statement, however, is an operant, and may manipulate the environment, including the therapist. Conceivably, as long as such manipulation occurs, the behavioral deficit which is the major problem may remain uncorrected. And correction may require greater effort than the present control.

Focusing on behavior and its consequences may also involve long-term changes equivalent to those involved in altering personality structure. But by dealing directly with observables, their relations, and their alteration, such focus may sidestep the thorny definitional problems raised in the feelings and their alteration. And to the extent that feelings of, say, inadequacy are attributable to behavioral deficits, alteration of behavior may alter the feelings which brought S to the clinic.

stuttering provided the time for him to catch up—an answer identical to the college student's. Stuttering was also reported as serving another avoidance function, in that the stuttering student found himself called on less often. Stuttering had an even more interesting effect: when the college student stuttered and *gave the wrong answer*, he was not corrected. In his own words: "People feel that you stutter because you are nervous, and they're not going to make you any more nervous by telling you you're wrong." The military adviser said he stuttered when he contradicted himself, that is, started out with one set of statements, and wound up with opposing ones. This is under similar control by a sympathetic audience. In another case, S reported stuttering when (a) a verbal response was required, that is, its absence would get aversive consequences, and when (b) the only verbal response immediately available was one which was likely to produce aversive consequences. The stuttering then produced neither aversive consequence from the audience. Our experience has convinced us that the world can be considered as being in a conspiracy to maintain stuttering, out of ingrained decency and respect for others' tribulations. Being "indecent" in these circumstances is no help, since S may go elsewhere, where the consequences will be favorable. One S's report indicated that his stuttering was maintained by positive rather than negative reinforcement: polite attention was commanded during stuttering, and no one left the group or interrupted him while he was stuttering.

That these response patterns can come under increasing environmental control, where they start to take over increasing amounts of verbal behavior, is quite evident to Ss, hence their application for treatment. None of the foregoing should be read to imply that the secondary gain is deliberate: the behavior comes under environmental control because of differential consequences, and may, through intermittent reinforcement (Ferster & Skinner, 1957), occur when the consequences are absent. Where the stuttering is avoidance behavior, it will be maintained by absence of differential consequences, as in the second experiment cited, where the normally fluent S continued his nonfluencies when the shock was turned off. To attenuate such behaviors on the outside may require procedures differing from cases where it is maintained by reinforcement. Other cases, in which S has "learned to live with his stuttering," that is, commands the appropriate reinforcers despite his stuttering, may require yet other behavioral procedures.

It can be argued that in the case of the college student, the stuttering was symptomatic of his insecurity in class. Restated procedurally, to work appropriately with this S one must develop efficient study patterns and procedures for school work—in addition to attenuating his stuttering. This is precisely what is being done, with the cooperation of S, who is also displaying initiative in suggesting further leads. Where the verbal behavior is weak (as it is in children), procedures may be required to strengthen it (through acquiring mastery of the subject matter being discussed, for example). Where S's consequences are aversive for not speaking and aversive for his only available response, the procedures involved may call for making other responses available. Competing responses may also weaken speech.[16]

By this time, it will be gathered that considerable behavioral modification may be involved in treatment of stuttering, and that every step in the self-control procedure is public knowledge to S. The aims, procedures, and rationale are explicitly spelled out to S in advance of the sessions (including those in the booth), and thereafter. This explicit analysis is helpful in the self-control of this behavior, and in personal explorations of ways in which to modify it. As the author has stated elsewhere, Ss involved may have "licked their own problems and have provided their own solutions. . . . Thus, paradoxically, the application of self-control procedures derived from controlled laboratory research can supply the fulfillment of the aims of those clinical psychologists who pride themselves on effecting change through providing greater freedom for the client" (Goldiamond, 1963). Hopefully, such explicit analysis may provide procedures for social explorations of ways to modify stuttering behavior, and other behaviors of clinical import, of which stuttering may be considered but one example.[17]

[16] The maintaining variables cited are not intended to be exhaustive, but are merely those thus far suggested by S's themselves. It should also be pointed out that continual punishment may also maintain behavior—if it is the discriminative stimulus for at least occasional reinforcement (Holz & Azrin, 1961).

[17] Since completion of this chapter, further research has been conducted (under NIH Grant, MH 08876-01, "Operant Properties of verbal fluency and nonfluency") during which some of the questions raised in the discussion have been answered and new ones have been raised. The research has led to the development of a set of explicitly specified procedures, an outgrowth of those mentioned earlier. Our total population of stutters upon whom the procedures have been utilized thus far is 30. In all 30 cases, at a specified 50-minute period in the program there has emerged a fluent pattern of reading which is well-articulated, rapid, and deviod of blockages. The pattern persists for other 50-minute periods thereafter under similar laboratory conditions.

# 7

# Responsiveness to Social Stimuli*

## GERALD R. PATTERSON

atterson's chapter is pivotal in this volume for a number of reasons: he uses response to reinforcement as a dependent variable; he makes use of statistical analyses in contrast to the single case behaviorial analysis of the previous authors; he integrates his work with investigations of personality, social, and child psychology not previously mentioned in this volume.

Patterson's chapter also represents an extension of the social reinforcement viewpoint into an interesting and relatively unexplored area: What are the important natural sources of social reinforcement in the environment? The obvious sources are one's parents and one's peers. The individual's social learning history affects his current susceptibility to social reinforcement. Bandura and Walters (1963) have briefly and succinctly summarized the effect of the relationship between subject, examiner, and situational factors on children's susceptibility to influence.

> Children who have developed strong dependency habits are more influenced by social reinforcers than are children in whom dependency responses have been only weakly established (Baer, 1962a; Cairns, 1961, 1962; Cairns & Lewis, 1962), and imitative behavior is more readily elicited in high-dependent than in low-dependent children (Jakubczak & Walters, 1959; Ross, 1962). Thus, social behavior can be both more easily elicited and more strongly reinforced in children in whom strong dependency habits have been built up. Children who have had a history of failure, including negative reinforcement of independence behavior, are more likely to match the behavior of others and to be influenced by the social reinforcers they dispense (Gelfand, 1962; Lesser & Abelson, 1959). Experiences associated with institutionalization appear also to increase the responsiveness of children to social reinforcers (Stevenson & Cruse, 1961; Stevenson & Fahel, 1961; Zigler, Hodgden, & Stevenson, 1958).
>
> Although there are individual differences in susceptibility to social influence, it

* The series of studies described here were supported by USPH grants M-4063 and M-5429. The writer also gratefully acknowledges the efforts of C. Hinsey and R. Young, who designed and constructed the equipment used in these studies. The general goals and hypotheses reflected in these studies are the result of the continuous cogitations and interactions with a research staff comprised of R. Littman, W. Bricker, R. King, C. Hinsey, D. Anderson, Isabelle Littman, and H. Hawkins.

is usually possible to predict what reinforcers will be effective for most members of a particular group, since group members share many common social experiences. Some sex differences in responsiveness to social reinforcers, dispensed by same-sex and different-sex experimenters, have already been identified (Epstein & Liverant, 1963; Gewirtz, 1954; Gewirtz & Baer, 1958a, 1958b; Hartup, 1961). Differences between sex of model and sex of child also influence the extent to which imitative behavior will be elicited (Bandura, Ross, & Ross, 1961, 1963a; Rosenblith, 1959, 1961), thus channeling social responses in the direction of sex-appropriate behavior. Moreover, reinforcement procedures are more effective when the agent of reward is a high-prestige person than when the reinforcers are dispensed by a person of low prestige (Prince, 1962), while models of high prestige are also more likely to serve as major sources of imitative behavior (Asch, 1948; Lefkowitz, Blake, & Mouton, 1955; Lippitt, Polansky, & Rosen, 1952). A reinforcer is, in addition, more effective if it represents a class of events that is highly valued (or greatly disvalued) in the recipients' reference group (Zigler & Kanzer, 1962).

The effectiveness of a reinforcer in changing the behavior of a given individual may vary from time to time. It may be enhanced if the individual has been deprived, for some time before its introduction, of reinforcers of this class; it may be reduced if reinforcers of the same class have been freely dispensed for some time preceding its presentation (Gewirtz & Baer, 1958a, 1958b). Deprivation may also result in increased initiative behavior (Rosenblith, 1961). Deprivation and satiation effects are readily observed in the case of reinforcers that are related to biological processes in the organism. In the case of social reinforcers, apparent deprivation and satiation effects are probably due to the occurrence of conditioned emotional responses, learned because of past association of physiological discomfort and pain with the absence of nurturant figures (Gerard & Rabbie, 1961; Schachter, 1959; Staples & Walters, 1961) or with prolonged social interaction resulting from fatigue. Evidence is accumulating that the effectiveness of social-influence procedures is greater if the observers or recipients of social reinforcers are emotionally aroused (Walters, 1962; Walters, Marshall, & Shooter, 1960; Walters & Ray, 1960), possibly because a moderate degree of arousal results in a restriction of attention to salient environmental events. One may suspect, however, that an extreme degree of emotional arousal may result in attention to too many irrelevant cues or in failure to attend to a sufficient number of relevant ones, and so disrupt the learning process (Bindra, 1959; Easterbrook, 1959). (Bandura & Walters, 1963, pp. 10-11)

Another important variable in assessing social reinforcement with children is the degree to which the reinforcing stimulus indicates correctness. Some investigators have reported that being "correct" is more reinforcing for middle-class than for lower-class children; Zigler, Hodgden, & Stevenson (1958) found that while verbal reinforcers primarily connoting "praise" improved the performance of lower socioeconomic retarded children, they did not affect the performance of middle-class children. Using groups of lower- and middle-class seven-year-old children and the Gewirtz-Baer procedure of reinforcing one of two holes into which the child could drop marbles, Zigler and Kanzer (1962) found that "praise" ("good," "fine") reinforcers were more effective with lower-than with middle-class children, while "correct" ("right," "correct") reinforcers were more effective with middle- than with lower-class children. This performance may be related to previous differential class learning; that is, for the middle-class child "correctness" has resulted in a more immediate and better pay-off in terms of primary reinforcements than for the lower-class child. Related to those studies are those of Terrell, Durken, and Wiesley (1959) and Zigler and de Labry (1962), who found that "intangible" reinforcers were less effective with lower- than with middle-class children on discrimination learning and concept-switching tasks.

All of these studies point to the importance of the type and schedule of reinforcement used by parents. Patterson (1959) has reasoned that the effectiveness of control is determined, in part, by the characteristics of the person dispensing reinforcement (see also Sarason, Chapter 10). Thus, it follows that there are differences among parents in their effectiveness as reinforcing agents. While two parents may use the same reinforcers, the same schedules, and may attempt to shape the same behavior in their children, they may still differ in the degree of control that they achieve. Based on his earlier investigations, Patterson (1959) concluded that a reinforcement hypotheses by itself oversimplifies the parent's role in controlling the child's behavior. He conceptualized the parent as having the dual role of eliciter and reinforcer. In effect, this treats the parent in the same manner as any other environmental stimulus. To investigate parents as stimuli, Patterson had to develop an adequate dependent measure. As he describes in this chapter, Patterson demanded of responsivity to reinforcement the same stringent measurement characteristics that psychologists demand of any test procedure. Similar uses of response to reinforcement as a dependent variable may be found in the chapters by Kanfer, Sarason, and Matarazzo.

Another interest Patterson shares with Bandura is that of investigating aggressive behavior in children (Patterson, Ludwig, & Sonoda, 1963). Approval, interest, and attention are effective reinforcers for the operant behavior labeled "aggression" (Lerner, 1960). As such, the pay-off for aggressive behavior comes from the environment. Individual differences in aggressive responses, which Patterson calls personality traits, probably reflect differences in previous experience with eliciting discriminative and reinforcing stimuli.

Patterson extends his experimental work to clinical situations. He has called attention to enhancement of the therapist's reinforcing value by his association with rewards (Patterson, 1965a, 1965b). He has published a report (Patterson, 1965a) on the treatment of a school phobic child, in which he programed the mother to reinforce desirable ("brave") behavior by the child and, during play therapy, shaped up the emission of more advantageous behaviors. In another case report, Patterson (1965b) devised a situation to reduce the disruptive classroom behavior of a hyperactive child. For every 10 seconds of appropriate behavior the child received a point. These points were then converted to pennies and candy which were shared with all the child's classmates. This procedure draws on Patterson's research which emphasized that the greater the "value" attached to a behavior by peers (or parents) the more likely that behavior is to elicit reinforcing responses. The use of peers who depended on the child to get their reinforcement both increased the pressure on the child to change his behavior and altered their perception of him. Hingtgen, Sanders, and DeMyer (1965) make use of a similar procedure in their work with severely disturbed children. This principle of interdependence is also utilized in Russian education (Bronfenbrenner, 1962), particularly in Makarenko's (1936) long-range rehabilitation program for delinquents.

If we had to point to one conclusion from Patterson's paper as of prime importance for future research, it would be the continuation of investigations of the behaviorial contingencies in "real life" situations that constantly influence the child's behavior.

L.K.-L.P.U.

In our research, we are applying a stimulus-response theory of learning to investigate the problem of how personality behaviors are acquired in children. We believe that much of what is called personality trait behavior is conditioned in the process of a child's interacting with the adult and the peer members of his social world. Within this interaction, it is the immediate reinforcement by the social agent that determines whether the response being emitted by the child will be strengthened. For example, if the child's temper tantrum is consistently followed by the parents' withdrawal of attention and approval, then this response is likely to be replaced by some other behavior. If, on the other hand, cooperative behaviors typically elicit social reinforcers from the adult and peer groups, it is this class of behaviors that will be strengthened.

This general assumption would imply that the particular payoff schedules provided by the culture are crucial in the acquisition of behaviors. This being the case, it should be possible to observe the effect of positive and negative reinforcers in a natural setting. A preliminary study was carried out to determine the effect of the peer group in modifying or maintaining instrumental aggressive behaviors in nursery school children (Patterson & Anderson, 1964). The data show clearly that the reinforcing contingencies determine the relative frequencies of occurrence of various aggressive responses as well as the choice of target for attack. Those responses most likely to be punished by the peer group occur with the lowest frequency, and the targets most likely to reinforce aggressive responses are most likely to be selected for attack. A second observational study shows that the delinquent peer culture almost invariably reinforces antisocial responses and punishes responses that correspond to middle-class value systems (Patterson, 1963a). Taken together, these two observational studies point to some exciting possibilities for applying an S—R framework to the traditional problems of how aggressive and delinquent behaviors are acquired. Although we plan to continue with this approach, our major research activities have been focused upon another implication drawn from the S—R framework; it is this second approach which will take up the major share of the discussion.

This second approach is based upon the assumption that not all children are equally responsive to social reinforcers or to aversive social stimuli. The fact that some children are more responsive than others would lead to the prediction that they would show different rates in the acquisition of social behaviors. The more responsive the child is to social reinforcers, the more likely he is to display the behaviors that are valued and reinforced by his culture. This assumes that the parent and the peer culture are conditioned to place particular value on certain classes of behaviors in the child. The occurrence of one of these valued responses creates a situation in which the peer or parent is most likely to dispense a social reinforcer. More specifically, our hypothesis would be that the laboratory procedure used in this study to measure responsiveness to social reinforcers would relate to ratings of personality trait behaviors. If we examine the pattern of traits that correlate with the measure of responsiveness, they should correspond to the child behaviors valued by the social agent. For example, responsiveness to the peer group would be correlated with one set of personality traits while the traits correlated with responsiveness to the parent would very likely correlate with a different set of traits.

We will also present data to show the relationships between responsiveness to social disapproval and personality trait behaviors. Although we consider these behaviors to be a kind of avoidance response learned in conjunction with punishment, we have no theoretical framework for specifying in advance how these traits will be patterned.

Another section of data will be concerned with a question rather than a prediction. This is the question of what is the best process for producing a child who is responsive to social approval or disapproval. The kind of data required for an adequate answer would, of course, necessitate a longitudinal study. As the next best thing, we have assessed current parent practices in the home and related this to the child's responsiveness in the laboratory.

Before we can study a topic as complicated as the one outlined here, there are several problems to be faced. The first requirement is that we have an adequate assessment of the child's responsiveness to social approval and social disapproval. In our own case, we constructed a laboratory procedure to provide measures of responsiveness. When we first started this work, we approached it with some type of "halo effect" believing that any procedure, if it were a laboratory procedure, would be sensitive and reliable. Three years of research have more or less removed the halo effect, but the research has also resulted in the development of a sensitive procedure for providing reliable estimates of a child's responsiveness to social reinforcers. The development and description of this procedure will constitute the first section of our discussion.

## THE MEASUREMENT OF RESPONSIVENESS

In the beginning, we assumed that to measure responsiveness to social reinforcers it was necessary only to find some task in which the child would emit some type of behavior at a fairly steady rate. Following a baseline measure of this behavior we would make social reinforcers contingent upon some aspect of his behavior. The magnitude of change from baseline to the reinforcement period would constitute the measure of responsiveness.

The first procedure we constructed was a cylinder about 5 feet tall that looked very much like the leaning tower of Pisa. In front of the tower was a panel with four doors that the child was to open. The parent was to reinforce the child on a fixed-ratio schedule for opening the doors: it was assumed that the increase in frequency of door-opening would provide an estimate of how responsive the child was to the parent. However, we quickly discovered that the "game" was so exciting that the children started out at maximum rates of responding. It was physically impossible to increase rate of response with this apparatus.

We then constructed a less exciting procedure in which the child was to press two telegraph keys. After a baseline period in which the child's preference for one of the keys was established, the parent would reinforce him whenever he pressed the least preferred key. We used this apparatus in one study to show that fathers are more effective than neutral male adults in shaping the preference behavior of boys (Patterson, 1959). However, in a second study we conditioned twelve children with the procedure and then had them return a few days later to be conditioned by the same experimenter on the same apparatus. The correlation between the magnitude of preference change on these two occasions was −.02! This, of course, was very disappointing and led us to search further for a procedure that would provide more reliable estimates of responsiveness.

The procedure we investigated next was an adaptation of the two-holed marble box described by Gewirtz and Baer (1958). The instructions given to the child for playing this game are as follows:

> Would you stand over here behind this box. O.K., now here you see a whole bunch of marbles and up here are two holes. What I want you to

do is drop the marbles into these holes. Pick up just one marble at a time, and drop it into either one of the holes. You may use either hand, but only one hand at a time. Like this. (E demonstrates with one marble.) Now you do it. (If the child hesitates after dropping only one or two marbles, he is encouraged until he has dropped at least five or six marbles.) That's all there is to it. Remember either hand and either hole; but just one marble at a time and one hand at a time.

In this first situation, the experimenter sat a few feet away from the child and counted the frequency with which marbles were dropped in either hole. After two or three minutes, each time the child dropped a marble into the least preferred hole, the experimenter would say one of the following phrases: You're doing fine; mm-hmm; good; very nice; very good; fine; that's good; that's fine.

In our first study with this apparatus, we conditioned seven children with the marble box procedure and then immediately conditioned them with the same experimenter on the telegraph procedure. The correlation between magnitude of change for the two procedures was .74. In a second study of the test-retest stability of the marble box, we conditioned nine children on two trials spaced one week apart. The correlation between magnitude of change on the two trials for the marble box was only .27.

This random schedule of reinforcement and punishment for the experimenters led us to believe at one point that responsiveness to social reinforcers might very well be an ephemeral phenomenon that fluctuates chaotically from one time to another or that the children's preference behavior itself was unstable. If this were true, we would, of course, have to give up this particular approach. However, we decided to make some rather minor changes in the marble-box procedure to see if it were not possible to increase the stability of measurement.

We guessed that the variable responsible for the fluctuations was in part fatigue and in part the extreme position preferences generated by the apparatus. The marble box was redesigned so that the child was required to move the marble a distance of only 11 inches; this was half of what was required in the previous apparatus. To reduce the tendency for extreme position preference, the holes were placed closer together (1 inch apart). The box developed at this point, which was used in all of the studies that followed, was 8 inches high and 18 by 10 inches in length and width. The two holes at the top were ¾ inch in diameter and placed 1 inch apart.

After making the changes in the marble box, we wondered at first if children's position preferences in such a game were stable. If those preferences were ephemeral, we might have to seek some response other than dropping marbles into a box.

In testing for the stability of position preferences with this new apparatus, 26 boys and girls from the third grade were run on two trials 7 days apart. Each child dropped a total of 400 marbles in both trials. They carried this out without the saving grace of a single reinforcement.

The data are presented in Table 7-1 and show that estimates of baseline position preferences are reliable if based upon 100 responses; that is, given the first 100 responses, we can predict the position preference shown in the next 300 responses during the same trial or predict the position preference shown on a trial a week later. Children's preference behavior *is* stable.

The second question involved the same set of data. Even though the subjects as a whole maintained their same ordinal ranks within and between trials, it was possible that the trend for the group would be to show a change in the mean preference split. The data show that this is not the case. A Friedman two-way analysis of variance for the blocks of responses within the trial was not significant.

*Table 7-1:* Characteristics of Baseline Measures of Position Preference

|  |  | Blocks of responses | | | |
|---|---|---|---|---|---|
| Variable | N | 100 | 200 | 300 | 400 |
| Stability of position preference | | | | | |
| Intertrial consistency | 26 | .61 | .67 | .69 | .76 |
| Intratrial consistency | 26 | .64 | .66 | | |
| Proportion of least preferred response | 26 | .333 | .313 | .296 | .283 |

At this point we had established that position preference based upon a sample of 100 responses was stable regarding both mean level and the ordinal rank of the subject. We were in a position to determine whether we could reliably measure the effect of social reinforcers in changing these preferences.

For this experiment, 24 subjects from the third grade were reinforced by the same experimenter on two trials 1 week apart. Following the baseline period, the experimenter reinforced the next 20 least preferred responses on a 1-to-1 schedule and the next 40 responses on a 2-to-1 schedule. The proportion of least preferred responses was calculated for each fifteen-second interval during the trial. The difference between the median of these proportions for the base operant and the conditioning period provides a measure of change in preference.

The test-retest correlation for the change in preference score was .75. The net result of this series of experiments was to show that we had a measure of responsiveness to social reinforcers that was both sensitive to experimental manipulations and provided scores with high enough stability to assume that it would be possible (if the theory were correct) to make predictions from the laboratory to parental practices or personality traits.

It is our assumption that, in many of the studies using fixed-ratio schedules of 1-to-1, awareness variables undoubtedly confound the results. To counteract the effect of this variable we instituted a rather complicated reinforcement: a 1-to-1 schedule for the first 20 appropriate responses and a variable 4-to-11 schedule for the next 20 appropriate responses. In addition to this, we carefully interviewed each child at the end of the conditioning trial. The interview consisted of a series of questions beginning with such general comments as "What kind of a game was this?" and ended with "When you dropped a marble in one of the holes it made your mother talk; guess which of the holes it was that made your mother talk." Each child is rated for his awareness of the contingencies involved in the conditioning trial. In the studies carried out thus far none of the correlations between awareness ratings and preference change scores were significant (Patterson, Littman, & Hinsey, 1963; Patterson & Anderson, 1964; Patterson, 1963b).

Most operant conditioning researchers have been quite willing to assume that they are conditioning an organism that is responding in some random fashion and that it makes no particular difference what sequence of responses are occurring at the moment the reinforcing stimulus is introduced. Our own research shows that neither of these assumptions is correct. During the base operant procedure children adopt highly stable sequences or patterns of responses and, furthermore, some of these patterns are of such a nature as to make it impossible to change a child's behavior with the schedules described above. Children who adopt a 50-to-50 position preference during the base operant are typically using an ABABA . . . type of alternating pattern. If reinforcement is made contingent upon A, for example, this child is receiving a heavy payoff *for continuing to use alternation.* Only 48 percent of these children show *any* change in preference with our schedule of reinforcers. As might be expected, the magnitude of the change scores is very small for this group. The more extreme the position preference shown during the base operant period, the greater the magnitude of change due to social reinforcers. The correlation between base operant position preference and magnitude of preference change varied from $-.47$ to $-.63$ over a series of studies. These data indicate a need for some technique to partial out the effect of original position preference. To meet this problem, data were analyzed from over 200 children who had been subjected to various reinforcement schedules dispensed by a variety of social agents. The frequency distributions of change scores were tabulated for four base operant levels of preference split. The deviation scores for each of these distributions were transformed into $T$ scores (McCall's $T$). With this procedure, there were equivalent scores for a child who began with an extreme position preference and changed moderately and a child who began with a 50-to-50 position preference and changed very slightly. These $T$ scores were used in most of the analysis of variance procedures described below and in all of the correlational analyses. The nonsignificant correlations found in all of the studies between base operant preference and $T$ score values would indicate that most of the confounding has been removed from the change scores.

## PROCEDURE

The same procedure was used in all three of the studies to be described in the next sections. The laboratory was mounted in a 15-foot house trailer that could be taken directly to the home or the school. A soundproof partition separated the subjects from the electronic equipment and from the experimenters. To reduce distracting sounds, most of the electronic recording equipment was mounted inside a portable ice cabinet. In a tray at the base of the marble box previously described were 250 blue glass marbles. The box was located on a level platform adjusted so that the base was approximately at waist level for the subject. The subject faced the reinforcing agent, who sat on a bench 3 feet to the front and right of the subject. The apparatus was automated to the extent that frequency of response to either hole was recorded along a time line on a multiple-channel event recorder. A programer was used to signal the reinforcing agent, who read a statement from a list given to him by the experimenter.

Both the subject and his assigned reinforcing agent were brought to the trailer. While the subject waited outside the trailer, the reinforcing agent was ushered to his bench in the laboratory and shown the earphone. After putting it on, signals were sent until it was clear that he recognized what they sounded like. The instructions were as follows:

> This is an earphone and it fits in your ear like this (demonstrate). O.K.?
> Now what I will be doing is to send you signals over this earphone that
> sound like little clicks. So to familiarize you with the signal, I'll drop some
> marbles into this box and you raise your hand when you hear a signal.
> (Four or five signals were sent until discrimination was perfect.)
> Now on the seat next to you is a sheet of paper with a list of words on
> it. Would you pick that up please? Can you read all those words? Would
> you read them once to me? Now, when you hear a signal, I'd like you to
> read a word on that list, starting at the top and working down one at a
> time. (The reinforcing agent went through entire list at least twice.)
> That's very good. Be sure to say the word as soon as you hear the click,
> and say it nice and clearly as though you really meant it. Will you wait in
> the next room now while I talk to (subject)?

The words on the reinforcing agent's list were printed in very large capital letters; the words were: GOOD, YES, GREAT, OK, FINE, VERY GOOD.

The measure of preference change was obtained by computing $X/(X + Y)$ for each 15-second interval, where $X$ is the frequency of the least preferred response and $Y$ is the frequency of the most preferred response. The median of this relative frequency score was calculated for both the base operant phase and the conditioning phase of the trial. The difference between these two medians provides a measure of the magnitude of shift in preference. As indicated earlier, these raw difference scores are transformed to $T$ scores in all of the analysis that follows.

## SAMPLES

Forty-one pairs of parents and their children participated in a study in which parents dispensed positive reinforcers (Patterson, Littman, & Hinsey, 1964). Sixty pairs participated in the study in which parents dispensed disapproval (Patterson, 1963b). By and large, these were middle-class families, and the children ranged in age from 7 through 10 years. Mothers and fathers were assigned on a random basis to function as social agents for their own children.

In the third study, 33 boys and 32 girls from the second, third, and fourth grades served as subjects. They were reinforced by members of their own peer group. A sociometric technique was used to identify the child's "best friend" and a "neutral peer." Half of the subjects were reinforced by a best friend and half were reinforced by a neutral peer (Patterson & Anderson, 1964).

Children in all of the samples were rated by their teachers on 48 items pertaining to classroom adjustment. The rating schedule was developed by Becker (1960), who selected his items to sample the personality domain as outlined by Cattell (1957). Becker's centroid factor analysis of teachers' ratings of nursery school behavior produced six factors. The items with the highest loadings on Becker's factors were selected for the rating schedule used in the present study

In the parent studies cited above, each of the mothers was given a 20- to 30-minute tape-recorded interview by one of the experimenters.

In the interview, 20 to 30 questions were asked covering a wide range of topics pertaining to child-rearing practices in the home. For each area, questions were asked until the interviewer felt he had enough information to make a rating on a mimeographed scale provided for this purpose. On the following day, a second interviewer listened to the tape recording and made an independent rating. The median correlation between judges for the 30 items was .74. The majority of the scales were drawn from the research of Bandura and Walters (1958) and Sears, Maccoby, and Levin (1957). Scales were selected or constructed which sampled the bipolar factors derived by several researchers from parent interview data (Roff, 1949; Sears, Maccoby, & Levin, 1957; Peterson *et al.*, 1961). The bipolar factors that these items presumably sampled were Warmth vs. Hostility and Permissiveness vs. Strictness.

## RESULTS

In all of the studies, there was a significant change in preference. The mean increase in the least preferred response was .098 when peers functioned as reinforcers, and .070 when parents reinforced their children. There was a mean decrease in the response punished by the parent of .155.

### Effect of Sex of Parent, Sex and Age of Child, Status of Peer

It was hypothesized that, in part, responsiveness would be a function of the sheer number of contacts the child has had with people. Specifically, the older child should be more responsive to reinforcers dispensed both by the parents and by the peer group. The data support this hypothesis. When peers are functioning as reinforcers, the older child is significantly more responsive to the neutral peer than to the friend.

There were no significant differences in responsiveness for boys and girls in any of the three studies. These results are in keeping with the study by Gewirtz and Baer (1958), who found no sex differences when using the neutral adult to reinforce children on the same apparatus.

The research by Kagan and Lemkin (1960), Emmerich (1961), and Hess and Torney (1962) suggest that the father is seen by the child as being more punitive and fear-arousing than is the mother. This provides the basis for predicting that fathers will be more effective than mothers in dispensing social disapproval in the marble-box procedure. In keeping with the prediction, fathers tended to be more effective than mothers in controlling the child's behavior with disapproval. This difference, however, was not significant.

There were no significant differences between mothers and fathers in dispensing social reinforcers. There was, however, a highly significant interaction between sex of the child and sex of the parent. The child was most responsive to the opposite-sexed parent. Part of this interaction effect was also obtained in an earlier pilot study by Patterson and Ludwig (1961). These findings would suggest that the opposite-sexed parent might be of particular importance in shaping appropriate behaviors in the child.

In summary, the variables that relate significantly to the responsiveness of the child to positive social reinforcers are: age of the child, the status of the peer, and the interaction between sex of parent and sex of child. Sex of the parent is a potential variable determining the response of the child to parental disapproval.

*Consequences of Responsiveness to Social Approval and Disapproval*

In the earlier discussion, it was hypothesized that there are certain classes of child behaviors that are more likely to elicit social approval from social agents such as the parent or the peer. Presumably, the behaviors that serve this eliciting function are those behaviors "valued" by the peer group or by the parent. The more responsive the child is to social reinforcers the more likely he is to acquire these valued behaviors. This leads to the prediction that personality trait behaviors that correlate with measures of responsiveness will correspond to the behaviors valued by the social agent functioning as a reinforcer. When parents function as reinforcers, the personality trait ratings that show a significant correlation should correspond to behaviors valued by the parents. When peers are functioning as reinforcers, the pattern of significant personality trait correlations should correspond to child behaviors valued by the peer group.

The data relevant to this prediction are provided by teachers' ratings of classroom adjustment. The teachers rated the children serving as subjects within 6 months following the conditioning trial. The teachers' ratings were correlated with the preference $T$ scores; the data were analyzed separately for boys and for girls. Only those ratings with the Pearson product-moment correlation significant at less than .10 are presented in the tables. The magnitude of the correlation is indicated by the figure in parentheses. Table 7-2 presents the data for boys and girls from the studies in which parents and peers served as reinforcing agents. The significant items are categorized according to the factors that had the highest loading from Becker's investigation.

One feature of the data stands out very clearly: this is the difference between the sexes. For girls, responsiveness to reinforcement by the parent is related to a wide variety of personality traits while responsiveness to the peer group does not correlate with a significant number of personality traits. Just the reverse is true for boys' responsiveness to social reinforcers. In this latter case, most of the variance of personality trait ratings is accounted for by the measure of responsiveness to the peers. Although this difference in findings for boys and girls may relate to the differential importance of parents and peers as social agents, it is also quite possible that combining the data for mothers and fathers or friends and nonfriends may have different confounding effects for the two sexes.

In general, girls who are responsive to social reinforcers from the parent are described by teachers in such a way as almost to fit the adult stereotype of the well-adjusted girl. The responsive girl is described as being low on the Hostile-Withdrawn factor, high on the Relaxed Disposition factor, and low on the Aggression factor. These data are in keeping with the hypothesis that responsiveness to social reinforcers will correlate with personality trait behaviors valued by the social agent. The findings for the

*Table 7-2:* Personality Traits Correlated with Responsiveness to Social Reinforcers

| Girls | | Boys | |
|---|---|---|---|
| *Parents as reinf.* | *Peers as reinf.* | *Parents as reinf.* | *Peers as reinf.* |
| *Schoolroom intelligence factor* | | | |
| | | Intelligent (.44) | Intelligent (.47) |
| | | | Quick (.45) |
| | | | Self-confident (.52) |
| *Hostile-withdrawn factor* | | | |
| Warm (.49) | | | |
| Happy (.44) | | Optimistic (.56) | Responsive (.48) |
| Responsive (.46) | | | |
| Loving (.49) | | | |
| Interesting (.52) | | | |
| Optimistic (.78) | | | |
| *Relaxed disposition factor* | | | |
| Relaxed (.49) | | | |
| Placid (.47) | Tense (.36) | | Nervous (.41) |
| Calm (.48) | | | |
| Stable (.58) | Stable (.41) | | Excitable (.54) |
| Not fearful (.75) | | | |
| *Aggression factor* | | | |
| Not demanding (.42) | | | |
| Not prone to | | | |
| anger (.75) | | | Conceited (.46) |
| Not prone to tan- | | | |
| trums (.62) | | | |
| Patient (.48) | | | Self-centered (.46) |
| Self-critical (.68) | Conceited (.40) | | |
| Outgoing (.62) | | | |
| *Dominance factor* | | | |
| | | | Strong willed (.39) |
| | | | Adventurous (.48) |
| | | | Noisy (.44) |
| *Conduct problems* | | | |
| Irresponsible (.55) | | | |
| Cooperative (−.52) | | | |

relation between girls' responsiveness to the peer group and personality trait behavior valued by the peer group are so meager that they must be considered as a disconfirmation of the hypothesis.

For boys, responsiveness to the parent is correlated with the personality trait behaviors that would elicit approval from the parent. However, the number of significant findings are too limited to accept these data as supporting the hypothesis.

Pope (1953) shows that being a good student is behavior that is valued by the middle-class peer culture. These findings are in agreement with the present data, which show significant correlations between items loading on the School Room Intelligence factor and responsiveness to the peer group. Because these items seemed to show up in all three studies, we thought that the preference change scores might be related to intelligence. As a preliminary check upon this, the preference scores and group intelligence test scores for a sample of fifteen children were correlated. The correlation, close to zero, shows that the laboratory task is not measuring intelligence. Evidently, the present findings reflect reports by other researchers (McDavid, 1959) stressing the relationship between academic achievement and responsiveness to social stimuli.

The research findings of Bonney (1944) and Tuddenham (1952) show that, for boys, it is the friendly, assertive, bold, and active behavior which is valued by the peer group. The correlations in the present study provide a close fit with these descriptions. Boys who are responsive to reinforcers delivered by the peer group are described by teachers as being to a considerable extent rather high on the Aggressive and Dominance factors.

In summary, girls' responsiveness to reinforcers dispensed by the parent is correlated with ratings of behaviors presumably valued by and reinforced by the parent. Boys' responsiveness to the peer group is correlated with behaviors valued by and presumably reinforced by the peer group. These two sets of data offer support for the hypothesis about the relation between responsiveness and the occurrence of behaviors valued by the social agent. The two sets of data, responsiveness of girls to the peer group and responsiveness of boys to parents, do not offer support for the hypothesis.

In Table 7-3, data are presented showing the correlations between responsiveness to social disapproval and the teachers' ratings of personality trait behaviors. As before, only those items with a Pearson product-moment correlation significant at p less than .10 are presented. Because of the somewhat larger sample involved in this study (N = 60), the data are presented separately for boys and girls and sex of parent acting as social agent.

These data suggest quite clearly that responsiveness to social disapproval of the opposite-sexed parent is related to poor adjustment behaviors. Girls responsive to the disapproval of the father are described as rather angry, anxious, and distrustful, while boys responsive to their mothers are described as being difficult to control. These two groups of children seem very similar to problem syndromes which are present in child guidance clinic populations and suggest that responsiveness to social disapproval of the opposite-sexed parent might be of crucial importance in the acquisition of deviant behaviors.

*Table 7-3:* Personality Traits Correlated with Responsiveness to Social Disapproval

| | Girls | | Boys |
|---|---|---|---|
| Mothers | Fathers | Mothers | Fathers |
| | *Hostile-withdrawn* | | |
| Responsive (.43) Extraverted (.51) | Distrusting (.52) | | |
| | *Relaxed disposition* | | |
| | Tense (.47) Anxious (.57) Fearful (.65) | Fluctuating (.61) | |
| | *Lack of aggression* | | |
| | Demanding (.58) Jealous (.48) | | |
| | *Submissive* | | |
| Noisy (.56) | | | Not dominant (.64) |
| | *Schoolroom intelligence* | | |
| | Subject to distrac- tions (.74) | Poor memory (.48) | |
| | *Conduct problems* | | |
| | Disobedient (.52) Irresponsible (.46) Obstructive (.52) Difficult to disci- pline (.64) | | |

*Parental Practices Associated with Responsiveness*

The preliminary data collected so far show that the child's acquisition of a wide range of personality trait behaviors may, in part, be a function of his responsiveness to social stimuli. This being the case, it becomes crucial to identify the conditioning process that determines this responsiveness. As a preliminary step in investigating this problem, we have used the parent interview to obtain data relevant to current parental practices in the home.

The parent interview data is limited in two extremely important respects. In the first place, it seems unlikely that we can use assessments of parents' *current* practices as an index of their earlier techniques of handling the child. Research data show quite clearly that parental practices change as a function of the age of the child (Schaefer & Bayley, 1960). The study by Wenar and Coulter (1962) shows that it is not safe to assume that the parent can accurately recall these earlier child-rearing practices. Because of these restrictions placed upon the interview data, it can only be assumed that the assessment of current parental practices clarifies the nature of parent-child interactions which *maintain* the child's responsiveness to social stimuli. Preliminary findings based upon these data can be used to identify salient areas of interaction, which can then be studied more intensively using observation techniques.

Table 7-4 presents the correlations between parental practices and preference *T* scores for boys on both the study using parents as positive reinforcers and the study using parental punishment. Only those correlations significant at .10 level are reported here.

*Table 7-4:* Boys: Parental Practices Correlated with Changes in Preference

| Agreement between raters | Interview variables | Positive reinforcers Reinforcing agent: Fathers | Mothers | Punishment Reinforcing agent: Fathers | Mothers |
|---|---|---|---|---|---|
| | *Warmth factor* | | | | |
| | Enjoyment of the child | .68 $^b$ | −.73$^b$ | | |
| .81 | Use of praise | | −.60$^b$ | | |
| | *Permissiveness-restrictiveness factor* | | | | |
| .90 | Restrictions outside home | −.69$^b$ | | | .52$^b$ |
| .84 | Restrictions inside home | −.66$^a$ | .70$^a$ | | |
| .85 | Use of physical punishment | | | | .58$^b$ |
| .83 | Use of deprivation of privileges | | −.68$^b$ | −.60$^b$ | |
| .54 | Frequency mother explodes | | | | .64$^b$ |
| .85 | Use of reasoning | | | | .57$^b$ |
| .91 | Interference with child | −.80$^b$ | | | |
| | *Parental role* | | | | |
| .71 | Parent agreement on discipline | .65$^b$ | | | |
| .77 | Agent discipline, mother | | .67$^b$ | | |
| .80 | Identification, mother | | .64$^b$ | | |
| .69 | Identification, father | | −.56$^b$ | | |
| | In case of argument, father takes his side | | | .52$^a$ | |
| | Mother's interaction with interviewer is spontaneous | .76$^b$ | | | |
| .74 | Mother tries to create socially desirable impression | | | | −.61$^b$ |

$^a$ $P$ less than .10
$^b$ $P$ less than .05

In general, a warm permissive home is related to the boy's responsiveness to the father. On the other hand, the restrictive punitive home is related to responsiveness to social approval by the mother. Notice also that in this latter type of home, the boy is strongly identifying with the mother in that he is described as more likely to imitate her gestures, manners, and general temperament.

There are not a significant number of parental practices associated with boys' responsiveness to parental disapproval. Those items which are significant, however, indicate that it is the punitive and restrictive home which is associated with responsiveness to disapproval.

The correlations between parental practices and responsiveness of girls to parental disapproval are presented in Table 7-5.

*Table 7-5:* Girls: Parental Practices Correlated with Changes in Preference

| Agreement between raters | Interview variables | Positive reinforcers Reinforcing agent: Fathers | Mothers | Punishment Reinforcing agent: Fathers | Mothers |
|---|---|---|---|---|---|
| | *Permissiveness-restrictiveness factor* | | | | |
| .84 | Restrictions within the home | .58ᵃ | −.70ᵇ | | |
| .85 | Use of physical punishment | | −.52ᵃ | | .41ᵃ |
| .83 | Deprivation of privileges | .74ᵇ | | | |
| .66 | Scolding and nagging | | −.68ᵇ | −.49ᵃ | |
| .91 | Interference | | −.49ᵃ | | |
| | *Parental role* | | | | |
| .79 | Strictness of father | | −.70ᵇ | | |
| | In argument mother supports child | | | .75ᵇ | |
| .69 | Identification with father | | −.60ᵇ | | |
| | Mother's effect during interview | | −.65ᵇ | | |
| | Defensiveness of parent on MMPI (K) | | | −.57ᵇ | |
| | Anxiety level of parent on MMPI (MAS) | | | | .67ᵇ |

ᵃ P less than .10
ᵇ P less than .05

These data are a replication of the results obtained for boys in that it is the permissive home which is associated with greater responsiveness to the same-sexed parent. Again, it is also the more restrictive home that is associated with greater responsiveness to the approval of the opposite-sexed parent. These consistent findings lead us to predict that future studies will show that in the permissive home the child behaviors are most likely to match those valued by the same-sexed parent. In the case of the restrictive home, the matching will be closer to the behaviors valued by the opposite-sexed parent.

The type of home associated with the greater responsiveness of girls to parental disapproval is again a repetition of the data already obtained for boys. The more restrictive and punitive the home, the more responsive the girl is to parental disapproval.

In summary, then, permissive parental practices are associated with greater responsiveness to social reinforcers delivered by the same-sexed parent. Restrictive parental practices are associated with greater respon siveness to social approval of the opposite-sexed parent and to social disapproval dispensed by either parent.

## DISCUSSION

Two general implications of these kinds of data for clinical psychology can be noted. One relates to its implications for the acquisition of personality trait behaviors and the second has some relevance to the treatment of children's behavior disorders.

A long-term interest in investigating the acquisition of personality trait behaviors has led us to assume that we can best utilize our efforts by focusing upon a single determining variable. We have labeled this variable "Responsiveness to Social Stimuli" and assume that the more responsive the child is to social stimuli the more accelerated he will be in acquiring socially acceptable behaviors. In thinking of personality development in this way, we are forced to assume that to some extent the culture—in this case parents, teachers, and peer group—are programed to respond consistently with approval to certain child behaviors and consistently to punish other behaviors. To the degree that this programing is consistent across parents we will obtain a pattern of correlations holding among personality trait behaviors and our measures of the child's responsiveness to his parent. Similarly, to the degree that the peer culture is programed consistently, we will obtain a pattern of correlations between personality trait behaviors and the laboratory measures of responsiveness to the peer group.

It seems obvious that not all parents are programed in exactly the same way. Some parents, because of their own history of conditioning, would place the greater value upon some child behaviors than would other parents. This difference in parental reinforcement would lead to different schedules of reinforcement and, by implication, different rates of acquisition of these behaviors by the child. Our interest in this contribution of the social agent to the "uniqueness" of some personality trait behaviors has led us to include, in the research now under way, an assessment of the child behaviors valued by each social agent. It is our prediction that, taking into account the behaviors actually "valued" by the parent (or peer) for each child, we can combine this with our laboratory measures of responsiveness to account for an even larger share of the variance in personality trait behaviors as seen by outside observers.

In the discussion, I have rather frequently used the term "measure of responsiveness" in its plural form. I have used the plural form intentionally because we do not believe that assessment of the child's response to

social reinforcers is the only, or even the most important, measure of responsiveness to social stimuli. We see the RSS (responsiveness to social
stimuli) variable as having at least three components: responsiveness to
social approval and disapproval, imitation, and ability to discriminate
among social cues. It is our general assumption that there is some overlap
among all three of these variables but that each of them also contributes
some unique variance in accounting for personality traits. Thus far most
of our efforts have focused upon the development of laboratory techniques for assessing responsiveness to social approval and disapproval.
In the past two years, however, we have carried out a series of six studies
investigating a group of laboratory procedures used to assess the child's
tendency to imitate in social settings (Patterson & Littman, 1963). Without going into the details of these new procedures, it might simply be said
that there is a relation between what may be characterized as responsiveness to approval on the marble-box apparatus and shifts in preference in
an imitation apparatus. This is very encouraging and partially confirms
our predictions about some overlap among these measures. Our next step
will be to determine the unique contribution of imitation procedures used
in conjunction with the operant techniques such as the marble box.

In spite of our enthusiasm for this approach, we are not so overwhelmed
as to believe that our simple conditioning paradigm is going to account for
all of the variance in personality trait behaviors. Inevitably, our single-
minded neglect of cognitive and affective variables will impose limits
upon the amount of variance handled by our procedures. However, it is
our strong conviction that many of the personality traits and problem behaviors that have been ascribed to such determinants as "ego," "latent
anxiety," and "aggressive drive" can more efficiently be accounted for by
a straightforward application of the conditioning paradigm outlined here.

If, in the future, formulations such as the present one are borne out,
some changes in current clinical practice would result. There would tend
to be an increased emphasis upon the determinants of responsiveness to
social stimuli with a particular emphasis upon building these into treatment programs. For example, our own research, and that of Levin and
Simmons (1962), would suggest that emotionally disturbed boys are not
responsive to social approval dispensed by adults. This being the case, it
would seem imperative to generate procedures that can be used in the
clinic setting (or in the home, for that matter) to condition a child to be
responsive to social approval. In doing so we would make it possible to
bring his behavior under the control of a variety of social agents, including
the therapist and the parent, so that the patient could acquire adjusted
behaviors in the usual way. We discovered quite by accident that such
a process for increasing responsiveness is quite feasible and, on the basis
of a sample of three children, very effective.

At the University of Oregon Psychology Clinic, we have been working on developing techniques, based upon learning theories, for treating intense school-phobic and hyperactive behavior reactions in children. In our counterconditioning work with these children, we have emphasized the importance of nonsocial reinforcers in shaping behavior in the clinic. This emphasis is based upon the research mentioned above. During these intensive counterconditioning sessions the therapists were dispensing enormous quantities of candy and pennies in conjunction with praise and approval for better-adjusted behavior. We were pleased to discover that these procedures produced profound changes in the behavior of these children (Patterson, 1965a, 1965b). More interesting, perhaps, was the fact that these children at the end of treatment were significantly more responsive to social reinforcers dispensed by their therapist in the laboratory procedure described earlier in this paper. In effect, the therapist had gained additional status as a reinforcing agent. The kind of data we have at present does not tell us whether this effect was due to the association of the therapist with candy and money or due to the "relationship" formed during the conditioning trials in the clinic. It is believed, however, that, regardless of what we call it, massive pairings of primary reinforcers with the behavior of the therapist will result in his having a greater effect upon the behavior of the disturbed child. Within our framework we would emphasize that the therapist should use this increased status to condition (reinforce) better adaptive behaviors in the child. We would further assume that this increased effectiveness as a reinforcer would generalize to other social agents such as the parent and that this secondary effect would in turn suggest further changes in clinical practice.

In the past, an emotional disturbance in the parent has been a necescessary and sufficient explanation for behavior deviations in the child. The data presented earlier would suggest that the child who is not responsive to social approval and overly responsive to disapproval is very likely to show maladjusted behaviors. It seems unlikely that variations in parental practices that relate to child responsiveness can be accounted for simply on the basis of emotional disturbance in the parent. Furthermore, it is equally unlikely that all parents who actually reinforce deviant behavior in their children are emotionally disturbed. If this is true, it seems possible that the clinician might actually have to leave his diagnostic tools in the office and observe child-behavior-parental-response contingencies in the home in order to plan his treatment program.

Most of our diagnostic techniques simply do not provide the detailed information necessary to plan the treatment programs being alluded to here. It is unlikely, for example, that the MMPI or the Rorschach is going to tell us that a mother is reinforcing dependency behavior in her child or that the overreaction of a sibling is reinforcing aggressive behavior. There is little doubt that as our clinical formulations change regarding the variables involved in behavior manipulation, a demand for rather different kinds of diagnostic procedures will result. Certainly, if these changes take place within the orientation of learning theory, it will require the development of techniques for observing and classifying interaction between the parent and the child.

# 8

## Studies of Interview Speech Behavior*

### JOSEPH D. MATARAZZO, ARTHUR N. WIENS,
### AND GEORGE SASLOW

The history of the interview, both as a therapeutic technique and as a research tool, is far too long to review here, and, further, there have been excellent reviews, particularly by Matarazzo (1962, 1965). Watson (1962) credits Rogers (1942) with launching "the research approach in behavior modification through psychotherapy." Rogers and his students (Rogers & Dymond, 1954) started the empirical investigation of the therapeutic process and have had a major influence on both research and therapy in American psychology. It is one of the major contributions of this chapter by Matarazzo et al. that it links this mainstream of clinical psychology to behavior therapy and in so doing enriches both. As will be seen in the present chapter, this is done by concentrating on the manipulation of selected formal characteristics of the interview situation. Matarazzo et al. measure the effects of these manipulations and relate them to diagnostic and therapeutic factors. It is this deliberate manipulation of variables rather than the investigation of an ongoing naturalistic process which places this research in a different category from that of Rogers. In fact, it is this procedure of programing the interviewer to maximize his effectiveness in altering behavior that puts Matarazzo in the field of behavior modification. This difference between Matarazzo et al. and traditional psychotherapists is illustrated by the contrast between their work and the Luborsky quotation with which they start their paper. Matarazzo et al. do not reify psychotherapy (Astin, 1961) but deal with it as an interpersonal transaction whose true purpose is the modification of behavior.

In the history of research on the interview (Matarazzo, 1962, 1965), many investigators, including Matarazzo (Matarazzo, Hess, & Saslow, 1962; Phillips, Matarazzo, Matarazzo, Saslow, & Kanfer, 1961; Matarazzo & Saslow, 1961; Matarazzo, Saslow, & Hare, 1958; Matarazzo, Saslow, & Matarazzo, 1956;

* The research described in this chapter was supported by research grants (M-735, M-1107, M-1938, and MH-01938) from the National Institute of Mental Health, of the National Institutes of Health, U. S. Public Health Service. The results of some of the studies presented here have been reported previously in different form, while some of the studies are being reported for the first time.

Matarazzo, Weitman, Saslow, & Wiens, 1963) have found formal noncontent variables to be remarkably reliable, valid, and consistent. This interest in reliability and validity, so characteristic of the research investigator, is markedly different from Freudian writings on the interview. American investigators, influenced by Freud, have stressed content, giving it various levels of interpretation, in contrast to other cultures, such as the Oriental, which have been more concerned with form and structure. Because formal, noncontent variables strongly affect interview behavior, it is imperative that the clinician become as interested in this aspect of his own behavior as he is in interpretations of content. Pauses, speed of response, interruptions, and length of speeches are important bits of behavior that the therapist can deliberately utilize once he realizes their importance. This information also has implications for training therapists. The view that therapists can learn to control their own behavior is in contrast to the view that therapists are weaned, toilet-trained, and analyzed into superperfect individuals (Krasner, 1963a). It is true that therapists have their blind spots, not only in terms of content areas (Bandura, Lipsher, & Miller, 1960), but also in terms of the formal qualities of their verbal behavior. Implicit here is the view that observation and feedback of the therapist's behavior is a more useful training device than a formal analysis.

Consistent with these comments on training has been the recent exciting experimental work on interviewer bias (Rosenthal, 1963). These studies have emphasized the role of noncontent variables in mediating bias. For example, Rosenthal, Fode, Vikan-Kline, and Persinger (1964) found that the bias of the experimenter was mediated by nonverbal cues, the exact nature of which were not completely understood by the investigators. The role of examiner bias is further elaborated by Sarason (Chapter 10).

The formal characteristics of speech are important determinants of how an individual carries out his social role (Sarbin, 1954). Such characteristics of speech as pitch, rate, density, length, pauses, and silences are aspects of social roles to which other individuals react. Changing these characteristics may systematically affect the reception an individual receives from the audience of his peers and significant others. It is often not what an individual says but the way he says it that influences how his peers react to him.

This chapter by Matarazzo et al. represents a link between the earlier chapters and the following chapters by Krasner, Kanfer, Sarason, and Hastorf, in which direct manipulation of speech through response contingent examiner behavior is discussed. In Hastorf's study (Chapter 12), leadership and other desirable roles are attributed to the individual who talks the most, irrespective of the content of the talk.

As others, such as Goldiamond (Chapter 6), have pointed out, the interview situation is not simply a matter of one-way influence, but it is a two-way association in which the subject's behavior alters the interviewer. Matarazzo et al. have devised and elaborated a method and a series of meaningful variables to evaluate the ways in which the subject may influence the examiner. Heller

(1963) and Goldstein (1962) review studies in which subject behavior was deliberately programed to affect interviewer behavior.

The Matarazzo *et al.* chapter calls attention to the potential matching of interviewer and interviewee in which the therapist can serve as a model of specific characteristics of verbal behavior for the patient. Thus, in addition to the training of therapists, we have the possibility of making deliberate use of natural characteristics of the therapist to maximize his effectiveness with certain patients. The concept of what is a good therapist may become specific to the needs of the patient. Many of the adjectives describing therapists, such as "warm" and "responsive," may, in the future, be analyzed into specific components that can be operationally defined and readily taught.

L.K.-L.P.U.

RESEARCH ON PSYCHOTHERAPY AND behavior modification from 1940 to 1955 appeared to focus on the global aspects of such phenomena as personality change and process in psychotherapy. Since 1955, more and more investigators appear to feel that these molar phenomena, important as they are, are not as amenable to immediate investigation as are smaller facets of the bigger problem. Thus, some research in the past decade has been focused on laboratory analogues of psychotherapy, while others have been directed to the study of *single* personality dimensions (rather than to such global phenomena as "personality" or "personality change"). The research to be described in the present paper is an example of the latter.

However, we are not unaware of the potential danger of investigative focus on seemingly sterile aspects of behavior and behavior change. Probably this concern has been voiced most candidly by Luborsky (1959, p. 337), who wrote:

> A number of rigidly quantitative studies which focus upon counting of words and silences or use an apparatus like the interaction chronoscope appear to be less fruitful than those which stick to more essential aspects of psychotherapy. These aspects of treatment seem to have been chosen primarily because they are more readily quantifiable. They are reminiscent of the now classic story of the logic employed by the drunkard looking for his lost housekey under a lamp post only because there was more light there.

Luborsky presents a superficially convincing argument. Yet, to press his classic story, one might ask: Given that a drunk (or sober individual) has lost his housekey and doesn't remember where and when he had it last, should he begin groping about at random in the dark, or might logic not suggest that he take advantage of the opportunity presented him by looking under the lighted lamp post *first?* If the key were truly lost, knowledge of probability theory suggests it has as much chance of being under the lighted lamp post as it does anywhere else he could search in the dark.

However, Luborsky's argument has been more convincingly met by Mowrer (1954a, p. 77) who, discussing a related problem, wrote:

> Those of us who are technically engaged in the study of learning have not, I think, devoted nearly as much time and thought as we should have to the problems and functioning of the "total personality," if I may use that hackneyed expression. I admit that there is a good deal more to human experience than our theories seem to imply, but I believe that we shall ultimately come to a real understanding of the quintessence of human personality only if we build slowly and securely upon basic principles which can be established by the tested methods of scientific inquiry. If we continue trying to understand man in a global molar manner, I can only foresee confusion being compounded with confusion.

Like Luborsky, the present writers are interested ultimately in erecting the psychodynamic penthouse of the skyscraper (personality). However, penthouses can be built first, without underpinning, no more easily in science than in architecture. We look upon the program of research next to be described as constituting a small part of the bricks and mortar of what hopefully someday will be the foundation, or first few floors, of the skyscraper called global personality, psychotherapeutic process, and the like. To date, along with a dearth of both basic facts and theories, a major obstacle to our better understanding of the admittedly richer, more global aspect of human personality functioning has been the *grossly* unreliable nature of the global opinions of individual psychotherapists, clinical psychodiagnosticians, and clinician-judges. The two studies by Raines and Rohrer (1955, 1960) are eloquent testimony to the fact that today we cannot trust the psychotherapist, or other clinician-judge-observer, to judge what is going on in psychotherapy and other clinical interactions. Much of this research recently has been reviewed by Matarazzo (1965). In the same year that Luborsky made his candid statement, Pasamanick, Dinitz, and Lefton (1959, p. 132), arguing for more, rather than fewer, objective psychodynamic measures wrote: ". . . more important [is] emphasis on the development of objective, measurable and verifiable criteria of classification based not on personal or parochial predilections but on behavioral and other objectively measurable manifestations."

The findings which we will report in this chapter derive from a program of research conducted by one research team over the past ten years. Until recently, and because of the "foundation-building-blocks" philosophy mentioned above, this research has concerned itself with the reliability and validity of single dimensions of the more formal, structural, or content-free aspects of the interview; namely, *frequency* and *duration* of single units of speech and silence. We also have looked at baseline, or natural history, aspects of the speech and silence dimensions; namely the anatomy of interview behavior.

## ANATOMY OF THE INTERVIEW

In order to acquaint ourselves and other interview and psychotherapy investigators with the normative characteristics of single units of interview action (speech) and silence behavior which occur in nondirective interviewing, we conducted and reported (Matarazzo, Hess, & Saslow, 1962) a study of 815 chronological speech units occurring in the 3 free periods of initial interviews of one interviewer with each of 20 interviewees. Similar data were reported for a second interviewer and 945 interviewee speech units. The interviews were typical, initial interviews in every way except that they were divided into 5 periods, during which the interviewer used either free interviewing (periods 1, 3, and 5) or introduced a stress tactic: silence (period 2) or interruption (period 4).

The results, although first presented by histogram (Matarazzo, Hess, & Saslow, 1962) and later in a frequency distribution curve (Matarazzo, 1965, Figure 3), revealed that single units of interviewee speech clearly formed a mirror-imaged J-shaped curve. The same was true for single durations of interviewee silence.

We recently studied 20 young normal male Ss, all applicants for the Civil Service positions of policeman and fireman. They constituted a *control group* for studies of interviewer influence on interviewee speech behavior which will be described below (and which are summarized in Figures 8-11 and 8-16). Although only for purposes of later analysis artificially divided into three 15-minute periods, these 20 control group interviews were *in reality* each a 45-minute, nondirective, clinical-employment interview. Thus they differed in form from the standardized 5-period interviews from which the earlier mentioned histograms and frequency distributions were constructed.

The 20 interviewee job applicants had a mean number of 81.4 single units of utterance per 45-minute interview, with a range of 43 utterances for one S and 119 for another. The number of single utterances for all 20 Ss came to a grand total of 1628. These 1628 single speech unit durations were tabulated into a frequency distribution curve in 1-second intervals from 1 second to 212 seconds. When grouped into larger intervals, the data from these 20 Ss, shown in Figure 8-1, also clearly reveal a mirror-imaged J shape. From Figure 8-1 it is clear that by far the largest number (522, or 32.1 percent) of interviewee utterances are 12 seconds or under in length; with 1215, or 74.6 percent of the 1628, being 36 seconds or less in duration.

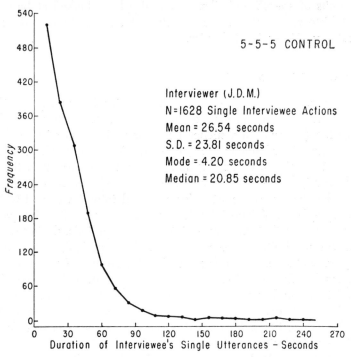

FREQUENCY DISTRIBUTION OF SINGLE UTTERANCES OF
20 DIFFERENT INTERVIEWEES WITH ONE INTERVIEWER

5-5-5 CONTROL

Interviewer (J.D.M.)
N=1628 Single Interviewee Actions
Mean = 26.54 seconds
S.D. = 23.81 seconds
Mode = 4.20 seconds
Median = 20.85 seconds

**Figure 8-1.** Frequency distribution of single utterances of 20 different interviewees with one interviewer.

We have analyzed a sufficient number of single units of interviewee utterances of both normal and patient groups to feel that the data in Figure 8-1 are highly representative, and that (a) most interviewees speak in utterances which *average* well under one minute,[1] and (b) these single interviewee utterances, when plotted, form a J shape.

The same is true of single units of interviewee silence, or latency. Figure 8-2 gives the distribution of latencies (or reaction times) during which the interviewee paused before answering (with the 1628 utterances of Figure 8-1) the interviewer's comment. From Figure 8-2 it is clear that the distribution for interviewee latency also is clearly J shaped. While different normal and different patient populations of Ss may give different means for latency (and utterance) behavior, our experience indicates that most Ss respond to an interviewer with an average latency per

---

[1] However, as will be seen later in this paper, duration of interviewee utterance is clearly a function of duration of interviewer utterance.

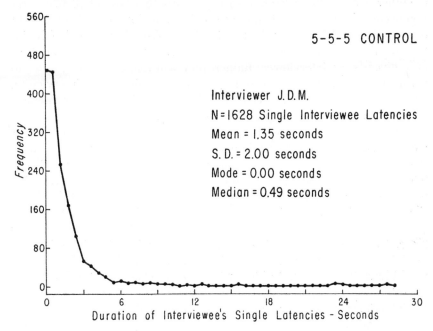

FREQUENCY DISTRIBUTION OF SINGLE LATENCIES OF
20 DIFFERENT INTERVIEWEES WITH ONE INTERVIEWER

5-5-5 CONTROL

Interviewer J.D.M.
N=1628 Single Interviewee Latencies
Mean = 1.35 seconds
S. D. = 2.00 seconds
Mode = 0.00 seconds
Median = 0.49 seconds

Duration of Interviewee's Single Latencies - Seconds

**Figure 8-2.** Frequency distribution of single latencies of 20 different interviewees with one interviewer.

interview of 1 to 2 seconds.[2] While some *individual* latencies in a 45-minute interview will reach an upper range of many seconds, the majority clearly are under 3 or 4 seconds. (Parenthetically, we have noticed this to be true also of most patient groups except those who are depressed.)

An interviewer's own habitual, idiosyncratic speech and silence behavior can have a profound effect on the absolute level of interviewee speech and silence means (see **Figure 8-11**). However, our study of this specific point reveals that the J shape of the distribution holds independent of the interviewer's own average speech and silence durations.

Another aspect of the silence dimension is important for understanding the anatomy of interview behavior. The latency variable plotted in Fig-

[2] In Figure 8-2, the *mode* for interviewee latency is shown as zero seconds. This value is probably an underestimate since the Interaction Chronograph is unable to record durations shorter than $\%_{10}$ of 1 second ($\%_{100}$ of a minute). Thus, many of the 448 zero latencies, out of the 1628 plotted in Figure 8-2, probably fell *between* zero and 0.6 seconds. To be more precise we probably should have plotted these 448 latencies not at zero but, rather, at their best estimate; namely, the *midpoint* between zero and 0.6 seconds. This would place them at 0.3, or one third of a second. Had we done this, the *mean* in Figure 8-2 would change from 1.35 seconds to 1.43 seconds.

ure 8-2 represents the passage of time (that is, reaction time) between the time that one participant (the interviewer) terminates his speech and the other person (the interviewee) begins. Another type of silence duration occurs in interviews when the second person (often the interviewer) does *not* respond following the termination of the other person's (the interviewee's) speech. Interviewers typically do *not* respond to each utterance given by an interviewee. Rather, they will remain silent in order to permit the interviewee to speak again even though he, the interviewee, has just contributed the last comment. While reaction time (or latency) would appear to be an appropriate term for the case where the interviewee responds to an utterance just contributed by the interviewer (or vice versa), the same term would not appear to be appropriate to describe the silence duration in those instances where the person, after a silence interval, *himself* contributes another utterance (without an intervening utterance from his partner). Chapple (1953, p. 24) has called this latter silence duration, before which an interviewee himself speaks again, *Quickness*. For our purposes, we prefer the operational term *Initiative Time*. Chapple, in developing the standardized 5-period interview we used in our earlier studies, maximized the chance that an interviewee would have to demonstrate his *Initiative Time* characteristics by having the interviewer (in period 2) 12 times remain silent, or fail to respond to the interviewee's last comment. In order to make allowance for an S who did not again take the initiative, in any single unit of exchange, Chapple set an upper limit of waiting by E of 15 seconds, after which E himself spoke. Thus having "restimulated" S, E again remained silent at the termination of that utterance by S.

The first type of silence behavior, that is, Latency or Reaction time, rarely exceeds 2 seconds for most interviewees. For the data with the 20 interviewees shown in Figure 8-2, the mean is 1.35 seconds.[3] In the previously published 5-period interview study (Matarazzo et al., 1962) the mean *Latency* (or *Reaction Time*) for the 20 interviewees with interviewer 1 of that study was a comparable 1.8 seconds, and with interviewer 2 it was 1.6 seconds. For these same 20 Ss, their *Initiative Time* was more than double these values (4.4 and 4.5 seconds, respectively). Analysis revealed that the 40 Ss in the two groups took the initiative in 64.6 per cent of the available opportunities when E purposely remained silent. In 36.4 percent of the 12 interviewer silence responses, S did *not* himself respond again, and E therefore spoke.

The two types of interviewee silence behavior, *Reaction Time* (1.8 and 1.6 seconds for the two interviewers) and *Initiative Time* (4.4 and 4.5 seconds), as well as this third type of interviewee silence, *Initiative Failure Time* (where S does not speak again for the full 15 seconds during which E waits for him to do so) are shown in Figure 8-3. It should be

[3] See footnote 2, *supra*.

# INTERVIEWEE SILENCES DURING INTERVIEWS

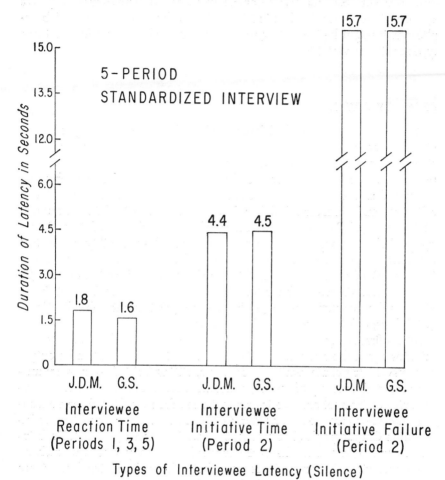

Figure 8-3.   Interviewee silences during interviews.

re-emphasized that *Interviewee Reaction Time* (or *Latency*) is measured in those instances (by far the majority in most interviews) when S responds to *E*'s comment; that is, *all* instances in which an S response follows a response by *E*. On the other hand, Interviewee Initiative Time and Interviewee Initiative Failure Time occur only in those instances where *E* does *not* respond to an S comment, or fails to speak before S himself speaks again. By setting an upper limit of 15 seconds of waiting for S to initiate (himself speak again) we were able to learn that our Ss did so in 64.6 percent of the available opportunities, and with an Interviewee Initiative Time of 4.4 (and 4.5) seconds. Only for 36.4 percent of the opportunities presented them did the interviewees not initiate again and, thus, these durations (of 15.7 and 15.7 seconds) were called Interviewee Initiative Failure Times. Since the data in Figure 8-3 are from young normal job applicants, it might be interesting to gather comparable values for the three types of silence variables from patient groups.

## RELIABILITY STUDIES

Before 1955 very little had been published on the reliability of interviewee speech behavior (that is, consistency of interviewee speech or silence characteristics from one interview to a second interview with the same S). Since then we have conducted and published five such reliability studies. Details of these five studies, as well as studies of interviewer reliability and observer reliability, have been summarized in Saslow and Matarazzo (1959). In these studies of the reliability of interviewee speech behavior, we concerned ourselves with the reliability across two *different* interviewers (or one interviewer doing both the test and retest interviews) of such speech variables as the average duration of each S's speech (and silence). The interval between the test and retest interviews in the five studies was: (1) 5 minutes; (2) 5 minutes (replication); (3) 7 days; (4) 5 weeks; and (5) 8 months.

In the first study, *two* interviewers each independently interviewed, 5 minutes apart, the same *new* patient (N of 20 interviewees) in an outpatient psychiatry clinic, while an observer, sitting behind a one-way mirror, recorded a variety of formal, noncontent measures of the interviewer–interviewee interaction. The instrument used for recording these noncontent interview (frequency and duration) dimensions was the Chapple Interaction Chronograph (Matarazzo, Saslow, & Matarazzo, 1956). Each interviewer talked about whatever content he typically would in such an initial interview. However, for reasons that will be clear later (see Figure 8-11), each interviewer was asked to limit all of his own interview comments to approximately 5 seconds.

The results with all 5 studies showed unusually high reliability for interviewee speech behavior from one interview to the next. The results (not previously published in this form) with one of these studies, the replication study of the test-retest interval of 5 minutes, are shown in Figure 8-4. This figure shows the *mean* duration of each *interviewee's* single units of speech during the total interview, graphed from the patient with the lowest mean (subject 1) to the one with the highest (subject 20) in order better to demonstrate the range of variability of such average patient speech durations. Patient 1's mean duration of single units of speech with Interviewer 1 was 7.2 seconds, and with Interviewer 2 it was 7.2 seconds; while the mean speech durations of Patient 19 with the two interviewers

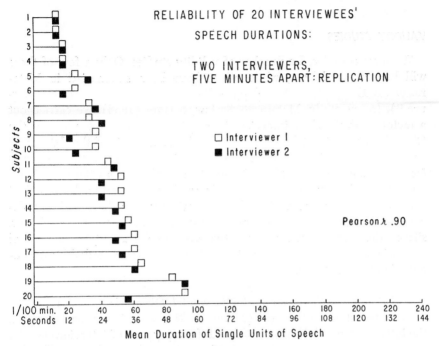

Figure 8.4. Reliability of 20 interviewees' speech durations: two interviewers, five minutes apart: replication.

was 52.2 and 55.8, and for Patient 20 the durations were 55.8 and 35.4 seconds, respectively.

Visual inspection of Figure 8-4, as well as the Pearson $r$ of .90 for the 20 patients across the two interviewers, provides clear and striking evidence that interviewee speech duration is a highly reliable variable. The reliabilities were similarly high in each of the four other studies (see Saslow & Matarazzo, 1959).

Although Guze and Mensh (1959) raised a methodological question about the *intra*interview reliability of interviewee speech behavior (the reliability of the *first* part of any interview with its *own* subsequent parts), a later study (Tuason, Guze, McClure, & Beguelin, 1961), utilizing a larger number of Ss in the replication study and a re-analysis of some of the data of the earlier Guze-Mensh study, clearly demonstrated a high reliability for both *inter*interview and *intra*interview speech behavior. In a more recent study, Dinoff, Morris, and Hannon (1963) repeated one of our 5 reliability studies almost in its entirety. Their results, obtained without communication with us, were a clear cross-validation of our results. (Their results were like those shown in Figure 8-4.) It would appear safe to conclude that interviewee speech and silence behavior are unusually reliable variables.

## VALIDITY STUDIES

We have completed a number of validity studies. Only a few of these will be presented here, while others have been summarizd in Matarazzo (1962, pp. 478-479 and pp. 479-490) and Matarazzo (1965, Figure 9). In one study, Matarazzo, Saslow, & Hare (1958), we carried out a factor analysis of 12 interview interaction measures recorded by the Chapple Interaction Chronograph. This factor analysis of the data of 60 Ss (and a replication study) revealed four independent factors; two major ones ("speech" and "silence") and two weaker ones ("initiative" and "adjustment"). As a result of this study, we have stopped analyzing all 12 Chapple variables, and their numerous derivative variables, and have focused our attention, instead, on the two strongest factors, speech and silence duration. Together, these two account for about 88 percent of the variance of the 12 interview interaction measures recorded by the Interaction Chronograph.

*Interviewee Behavior and Differential Diagnosis*

In one study in this area (Matarazzo & Saslow, 1961), we compared the interview speech behavior of five different groups of interviewees who were independently interviewed by four different interviewers. The five groups consisted of: (a) 19 state hospital back ward chronic psychotics (schizophrenics); (b) 40 neurotic and acutely psychotic patients from the inpatient and outpatient psychiatric service of a general hospital; (c) 60 outpatient clinic neurotics; (d) 40 normals (applicants for sales positions at a Boston department store); and (e) 17 normals (applicants for sales positions at a Chicago department store).

The results clearly revealed differences among these five groups in a variety of interviewee variables. The results with only one of these variables, average (median) interviewee speech durations, are shown in Figure 8-5. It is clear from Figure 8-5 that there were wide differences in the medians (means showed comparable differences) among the groups. Statistical analyses of these and the data from the other eleven Interaction Chronograph measures are given in Matarazzo and Saslow (1961). For the data presented in Figure 8-5, these analyses reveal that the two normal groups did *not* differ, one from the other, while each of them did differ statistically significantly from each of the three patient groups.

Figure 8-5 contains only the medians for each group. However, inspection of the mean interviewee speech duration for each of the Ss represented in the five groups revealed considerable *intragroup* individual differences. This is more clearly shown in Figure 8-6, where the mean interview speech duration for each interviewee is represented as a square. It is apparent from Figure 8-6 that, despite significant differences

## DURATION OF INTERVIEWEE SPEECH : DIFFERENT DIAGNOSTIC GROUPS

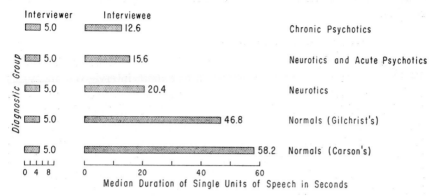

Figure 8-5.  Duration of interviewee speech: different diagnostic groups.

among *group* means, the wide individual differences in each group preclude the use of speech durations, alone, as adequate for differential diagnosis in the *individual case.* However, the results in Figures 8-5 and
8-6 would seem to lend credence to the prediction by Pasamanick *et al.*

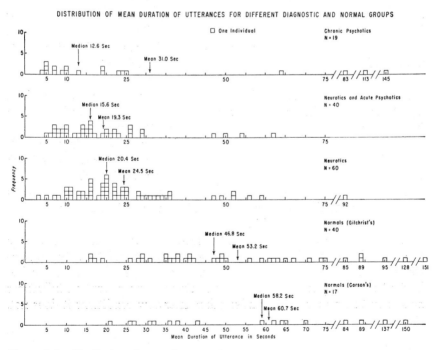

Figure 8-6.  Distribution of mean duration of utterances for different diagnostic and normal groups.

(1959, p. 132) that once objective indices of behavior are developed, differential diagnosis in clinical psychology or psychiatry will be more reliable.

### Studies of Interview Content

In one study (Phillips, Matarazzo, Matarazzo, Saslow, & Kanfer, 1961), we compared our structural, *noncontent* interviewee measures with the *content* of what the same interviewee was verbalizing in an initial clinical interview. The results revealed that *what* people say in the interview, that is, how they describe themselves as acting outside the interview situation (content, as analyzed from the transcribed tape recordings) correlated, albeit modestly, with the more formal characteristics of *how* (speech and silence noncontent variables) they talked during the interview itself, with the latter being recorded on the Interaction Chronograph.

In another content study (Matarazzo, Weitman, & Saslow, 1963) we experimentally controlled the content of the interview by having E purposely focus the talk during the whole of three 15-minute segments of a 45-minute employment interview on each (in counterbalanced order) of three content areas: family, education, and job history of each S. Whenever the interviewer talked during each 15-minute period, he did so in 5-second utterances, thereby standardizing how much he talked whenever he and S were discussing each of the three different content areas. The results (not reproduced here) revealed that the average duration of utterance of the 20 interviewees was the same for each of the three content areas (*p* not significant).

But in another content study (Kanfer, Phillips, Matarazzo, & Saslow, 1960), in which the interviewer was instructed beforehand to make *interpretations* (in period 2) about S's personality, motivations, etc., based on what the interviewee had revealed about himself (in period 1), it was found that this interviewer content-based tactic (interpretations) was associated with a *decrease* (*p* of .01) in the interviewee's average duration of speech. The results of these last two studies are presented in graphic form, similar to Figure 8-6, in Matarazzo, Weitman, and Saslow (1963), and are not repeated here.

It is clear from the three content studies we have carried out to date that the relationship between interviewee content and interviewee noncontent measures (frequency and duration of speech and silence behavior) is a complex one. Under some circumstances, content influences noncontent measures, while under other interview conditions it does not.

## INTERVIEWER INFLUENCE ON INTERVIEWEE
## SPEECH DURATION BEHAVIOR

Some of the studies presented above bear on this question. In addition we carried out a number of studies in which interviewer attempts to influence interviewee speech behavior (durations) were the direct focus of study. These will be described in this section.

### Control Group Study

This group of 20 Ss was designed to serve as a control group for the other studies that will be discussed below. The Ss were young normal male Civil Service applicants (7 policeman and 13 fireman). Mean age, education, and WAIS Full Scale IQ for these 20 Ss were: 24.6 years, 12.5 years, and 111.2, respectively. Similar values characterized each of the experimental groups to be described in this section. As indicated earlier (when discussing Figures 8-1 and 8-2 of the present chapter), each of these 20 control Ss was given a 45-minute, nondirective, clinical-employment interview. The interviewer artificially divided the 45-minute interview into three consecutive 15-minute segments, during each of which he devoted approximately 5 minutes to a discussion of each of three topics: family, education, and job history of each S.

Analysis of the unit by unit speech sequence of each interview permitted us to make up the frequency distributions described earlier (and presented in Figures 8-1 and 8-2), and also yielded us an average speech (as well as silence) duration for each S. Figure 8-7 presents the average interviewee speech duration for each S in each of the three 15-minute segments of the 45-minute interview. As can be seen, with the interviewer restricting himself to 5-second comments in each segement, the 20 interviewees spoke with a *grand* mean of 30.0, 30.5, and 28.1 seconds, respectively, in periods 1, 2, and 3 of the 45-minute interview.

Not surprisingly, statistical analysis of these three interviewee means revealed an *insignificant* p value. The three means for the interviewer (5.0, 5.2, and 5.2 seconds, respectively) likewise were not significantly different statistically.

It can be concluded from these control group results that if an interviewer confines himself to identical interviewing behavior (standardized duration and broad content areas) in each of three 15-minute segments of a 45-minute interview, interviewee speech durations (utterances) will remain unchanged from period to period. Likewise, the range of values of the means for individual Ss, from approximately 15 to 60 seconds for *average* single utterances, remains the same for all 3 periods with this control group.

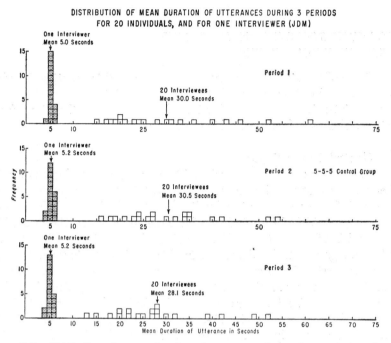

Figure 8-7.  Distribution of mean duration of utterances during 3 periods for 20 individuals, and for one interviewer (JDM).

## Influence of Increases in Interviewer Utterance Duration on Interviewee Duration

Three studies were done on this variable. The results of two of these (the 5-10-5- and 10-5-10-second studies) have been published previously (Matarazzo, Weitman, Saslow, & Wiens, 1963); while the results of the third (5-15-5-second study) have *not* previously been reported.

Each of the three studies utilized 20 Civil Service Ss and otherwise was similar in methodology (including the same interviewer) to the control group described above. In each of the three studies the method again involved a 45-minute clinical employment interview. The interview was divided into three 15-minute periods, during each of which the interviewer *controlled* only the duration of his own *speaking times* (with the content of what he said being restricted to family, education, and job).

In the first study, during the first and third 15 minutes (periods 1 and 3) the interviewer confined each of his comments to 5-second utterances, plus or minus slight error variance. However, during the experimental period (period 2) of this study, the interviewer increased the durations of *each* of his own utterances to 10 seconds.

The results are shown in Figure 8-8. With the interviewer aiming for 5-10-5-second single speech durations, and actually speaking in utterances

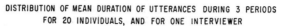

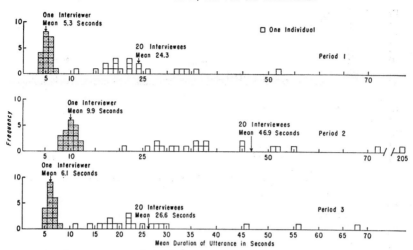

Figure 8-8. Distribution of mean duration of utterances during 3 periods for 20 individuals, and for one interviewer.

averaging (grand means) 5.3 seconds, 9.9 seconds, and 6.1 seconds, respectively, in periods 1, 2, and 3 ($p$ of .001), the average durations of single interviewee utterances were 24.3, 46.9, and 26.6 seconds respectively ($p$ of .01). Thus, as $E$ doubled his individual speech unit durations from period 1 to period 2, and halved them from period 2 to period 3, the effect on interviewee speech durations was marked and in the same direction. As $E$ doubled or halved his utterance lengths, so did $S$. In Figure 8-8, the range of means in periods 1 and 3, like that in the control group (Figure 8-7), was from approximately 11 to 68 seconds. With the introduction of an increase in $E$'s own speech durations in period 2, Figure 8-8 reveals that this period 2 range (21 to 205 seconds), like the mean, shifts toward the high end.

To control for a possible artifact in these results due merely to the *sequence* used by $E$ in periods 1, 2, and 3, a replication of this study was carried out, now utilizing a 10-5-10-second interviewer utterance sequence. The results of this study are shown in Figure 8-9. From Figure 8-9 it can be seen that average single interviewer utterances of 9.5, 4.9, and 9.5 seconds, respectively ($p$ of .001), produced average single interviewee utterances in the 20 Ss of this study of 41.1, 22.8, and 48.2 seconds, respectively ($p$ of .001). Again the range of interviewee means is comparable, and shifts in the direction of the change in $E$'s mean.

To test the limits of this interviewer influence one additional step, we designed a third study, one utilizing a 5-15-5-second interviewer sequence. For this third group of 20 Civil Service Ss, including 10 police-

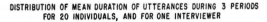

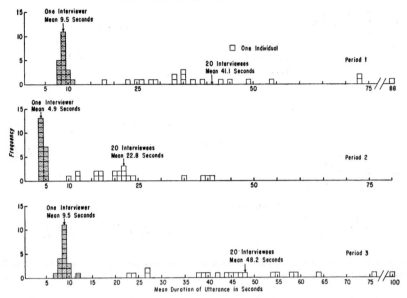

Figure 8-9. Distribution of mean duration of utterances during 3 periods for 20 individuals, and for one interviewer.

man and 10 fireman applicants, mean age (24.1 years), education (12.4 years), and WAIS Full Scale IQ (110.6) were similar to those obtained for the other groups (5-5-5; 5-10-5; and 10-5-10) constituting this series of studies.

The individual results of this study, not previously published, are given in Table 8-1.[4] For Subject 1 in this table, the interviewer aiming for single utterances of approximately 5-15-5 seconds across the 3 periods of the interview did, in fact, achieve mean durations of utterances of 4.8, 16.7, and 4.9 seconds per single unit of speech in the 3 periods. As is shown in the same row, the single units of speech of Subject 1 averaged 18.6, 30.1, and 16.8 seconds. The results of this one interviewer with each of the 19 other interviewees are also shown in Table 8-1. The grand means of these 20 individual means for both the interviewer and the 20 interviewees were 5.0, 15.2, and 5.5 ($F = 916.6$, $p$ of .001) for the interviewer, and 30.9, 64.5, and 31.9 ($F = 41.4$, $p$ of .001) for the 20 interviewees.

[4] Although not shown in Table 8-1, with the first interviewee, the interviewer spoke a total of 36, 18, and 37 times, respectively, in periods 1, 2, and 3 of the 45-minute interview. The corresponding numbers of utterances of Interviewee 1 in each of the same three periods were 36, 19, and 38 respectively. The range across all 20 Ss for the interviewer's number of units of speech in each of the three 15-minute interview periods was from 6 to 49 single utterances; while for interviewees the corresponding range was also from 6 to 49 single units of speech.

Inspection of the interviewee data in Table 8-1 indicates that 20 out of 20 Ss increased their *own* mean in period 2; with 15 out of 20 increasing the mean enough to reach statistical significance in the *individual case* (last column on the right in Table 8-1), in contrast to the group results shown at the bottom of Table 8-1.

*Table 8-1:* Concordance between Interviewer's and Interviewee's Mean Duration of Single Utterances across Three 15-Minute Periods of an Interview

| | Interviewer's Mean Duration of Each Utterance Periods | | | | Interviewee's Mean Duration of Each Utterance Periods | | | |
|---|---|---|---|---|---|---|---|---|
| Subject | 5 sec. | 15 sec. | 5 sec. | p | 5 sec. | 15 sec. | 5 sec. | p |
| 1 | 4.8 | 16.7 | 4.9 | .001 | 18.6 | 30.1 | 16.8 | .01 |
| 2 | 5.4 | 16.6 | 5.8 | .001 | 33.0 | 43.5 | 25.6 | |
| 3 | 5.0 | 17.6 | 5.6 | .001 | 20.4 | 46.0 | 18.9 | .001 |
| 4 | 5.0 | 15.7 | 5.6 | .001 | 15.3 | 36.9 | 13.1 | .001 |
| 5 | 5.5 | 15.9 | 4.9 | .001 | 22.1 | 34.2 | 19.4 | .01 |
| 6 | 5.3 | 16.9 | 6.2 | .001 | 75.2 | 139.1 | 134.0 | |
| 7 | 5.2 | 15.9 | 5.7 | .001 | 31.8 | 91.0 | 30.5 | .001 |
| 8 | 5.6 | 15.1 | 6.0 | .001 | 24.3 | 51.6 | 31.2 | .05 |
| 9 | 5.4 | 12.3 | 6.5 | .001 | 21.6 | 85.0 | 34.1 | .001 |
| 10 | 4.4 | 13.2 | 4.8 | .001 | 32.7 | 85.0 | 35.4 | .001 |
| 11 | 4.8 | 15.2 | 5.6 | .001 | 27.9 | 36.8 | 24.6 | |
| 12 | 4.8 | 14.1 | 5.6 | .001 | 36.9 | 93.9 | 27.2 | .001 |
| 13 | 4.5 | 14.1 | 5.3 | .001 | 34.8 | 101.0 | 33.7 | .001 |
| 14 | 3.9 | 15.4 | 5.4 | .001 | 40.7 | 86.1 | 25.9 | .001 |
| 15 | 5.3 | 13.6 | 5.8 | .001 | 15.4 | 33.6 | 15.8 | .001 |
| 16 | 4.7 | 14.2 | 6.1 | .001 | 38.4 | 51.9 | 32.4 | |
| 17 | 5.0 | 14.6 | 5.6 | .001 | 28.6 | 65.5 | 34.1 | |
| 18 | 4.7 | 16.3 | 5.1 | .001 | 15.3 | 31.9 | 11.0 | .001 |
| 19 | 5.0 | 14.7 | 5.0 | .001 | 45.1 | 61.2 | 32.5 | .05 |
| 20 | 4.7 | 15.3 | 4.8 | .001 | 40.3 | 86.3 | 41.6 | .05 |
| Mean of Means | 5.0 | 15.2 | 5.5 | .001 | 30.9 | 64.5 | 31.9 | .001 |

In order to facilitate comparison with the 5-10-5 and 10-5-10 studies of Figures 8-8 and 8-9, the data in Table 8-1 have been plotted in Figure 8-10. The marked influence of a threefold change in the interviewer's own average speech duration (from 5 to 15 seconds) is clearly shown in Figure 8-10. Except for Subject 6 (see Table 8-1), who earned period 1 and 3 means of 75 and 134 seconds, respectively, the range for the means of these 20 Ss is comparable to those in the other figures.

Detailed analysis of *E's content* in the 5-10-5 and 10-5-10 studies, and inspection of his content in the 5-15-5 study, *failed* to reveal that the influence shown in Figures 8-8, 8-9, and 8-10 was due to such potential arti-

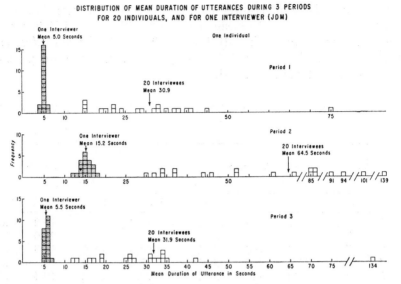

Figure 8-10. Distribution of mean duration of utterances during 3 periods for 20 individuals, and for one interviewer (JDM).

facts as: differential open-ended versus close-ended interviewing in the three periods; number of questions asked by $E$ per utterance; and possible interviewee "warming up" effect in period 1, or a fatigue effect in period 3 (Matarazzo, Weitman, Saslow, & Wiens, 1963).

These, and the additional data reported below, are of interest from another point of view. In our previous reports in the present series of studies on interviewer-interviewee behavior we have reported evidence for a verbal-interactional constant of roughly 5 to 1 or 6 to 1 between the average single speech durations of our nondirective interviewers and their groups of 20 interviewees. In Table 8-1, $E$'s period 1 *grand* mean of 5.0 seconds is associated with an $S$'s period, 1 *grand* mean of 30.9, yielding a ratio of 6.18 to 1. For periods 2 and 3 the comparable ratios are 4.24 to 1 and 5.80 to 1. These values are like those previously reported and recently summarized (Matarazzo, Wiens, Saslow, Allen, & Weitman, 1964); that is, the mean value of 27 such ratios reported earlier was 5.98 to 1. Thus, the data in Table 8-1, like our earlier data, represent continuing consistent evidence that, within the limits of duration set by our studies to date, and for the interviewers and the Ss and the conditions of this series of studies, the interviewer using nondirective interviewing elicits single durations of speech from his interviewees in a ratio of approximately 5 to 1 or 6 to 1.

The results of these three studies, plus the result of the control group, are shown graphically in Figure 8-11. The extent of the interviewer's influence from period 1 to period 2, in the four studies (reading down in

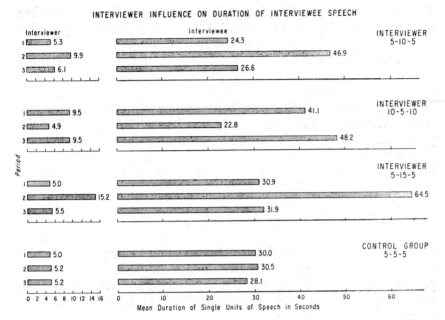

Figure 8-11. Interviewer influence on duration of interviewee speech.

Figure 8-11) was (a) an increase of 93 percent (5-10-5); (b) a decrease of 44 percent, or, better still, using the 5-second baseline of period 2, an increase of 80.2 percent (period 2 versus period 1), or an increase of 111.4 percent (period 2 versus period 3), in the 10-5-10 study; (c) an increase of 108.7 percent (5-15-5); and (d) no increase in the control group (5-5-5). Thus, it is clear that as the interviewer doubles, triples, or halves his own durations of utterances, the effect is an approximate 100 percent change in the duration of single units of interviewee speech duration, independent of the magnitude of change in E's own durations (that is, 2 to 1 or 3 to 1). It is difficult to predict whether or not we would continue to get only this 100 percent increase with still longer interviewer speech durations. That is, an increase in E's speech durations from 5 to 10 seconds, and from 5 to 15 seconds both increased S's average speech durations 100 percent, rather than 200 percent (that is, triple the base value) as in the case of the 5-15-5 study. Either the data in Figure 8-11 are (a) the result of an *asymptote* in E's influence (and no matter how much longer above 15 seconds we increase his speech durations we still will get only a 100 percent increase over S's baseline), or (b) a function of the values of the speech durations of E employed by us to date (ranging from 5 to 15 seconds), that is, possibly if we had used interviewer speech durations of 50-100-50 seconds, change from this larger, 50-second, baseline to 100 seconds might have produced *other* than a 100 percent increase; or (c) that 5 seconds, itself, is a "natural" or "critical" unit of interviewer speech duration, and *any* discriminable change from this 5-second natural baseline will produce a 100 percent increase in S's speech duration. Only further research can test these or other possible hypotheses.

That the influence shown in Figure 8-11 is not restricted to the single interviewer (JDM) who conducted all four studies in that figure, or to normal (job applicant) interviewees, has been reported in a study by Matarazzo (1962, Table 5, p. 489). In that study, four *different* interviewers interviewing the five diagnostic groups (shown in Figure 8-5 of the present chapter) were able to produce an increase or decrease in interviewee speech durations by modifications in the interviewer's own speech behavior. Interestingly, while two patient groups (the neurotic, and the neurotic and acute psychotic groups) were influenced in a manner identical to the two normal groups shown in the present Figure 8-5, the chronic psychotic (schizophrenic) group of the present Figure 8-5 did not increase or decrease its own speech durations in tandem with the interviewer. Although not as carefully controlled as the studies shown in Figure 8-11 of the present chapter, the results with these five diagnostic groups (Matarazzo, 1962, Table 5, p. 489) would suggest that the findings in Figure 8-11 probably can be generalized to other interviewers and other groups of interviewees.

The results in Figure 8-11 present some clear implications for behavior therapy: (a) it is conceivable, for example, that psychotherapist-interviewers might be able to induce depressed patients to talk in longer utterances by themselves speaking in longer utterances, or influence "manic" or loquacious patients (hysterics) to talk in briefer units by utilizing very brief speaking times with such patients; (b) without an *artificial* change in the habitual speech behavior of psychotherapists one could deliberately pair interviewers with known speech characteristics with patients whose own speech pattern can best utilize such a psychotherapist-patient combination.

*Interviewer Head-nodding and Interviewee Speech Durations*

To study the effect of the well-known interviewer tactic, head-nodding, on interviewee speech behavior, Matarazzo, Saslow, Wiens, Weitman, and Allen (1964) studied another group of 20 Civil Service Ss from the same population. Again the design utilized a 45-minute nondirective interview divided into three 15-minute periods. The interviewer confined himself to 5-second utterances in periods 1, 2, and 3. Only in period 2 did he introduce the experimental variable; that is, *each* time the interviewee began an utterance, E nodded his head *repeatedly throughout that whole utterance*. In the original study with 20 Ss, Interviewer 1 (JDM) nodded his head an average of 582 times while each S was talking in the 15-minute period 2; while, in the cross-validation study, Interviewer 2 (GS) nodded his head with his 20 Ss an average of 1241

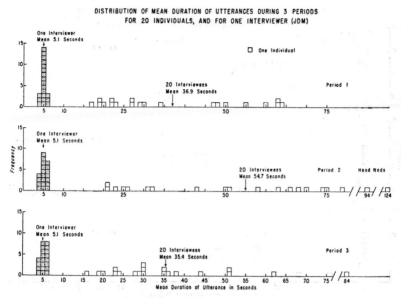

**Figure 8-12.** Distribution of mean duration of utterances during 3 periods for 20 individuals, and for one interviewer (JDM).

times (more than twice as often) with each S. These head nods were introduced at a rate of 44.0 per minute of interviewee speech by E-1 and at a rate of 97.5 per minute of interviewee speech by E-2. Throughout the whole 45-minute interview, each E took care not to introduce such additional social reinforcing stimuli as smiling, saying "mm-hmm," etc., and thereby contaminate the variable (head-nodding) under study.

The effect of Interviewer 1's head-nodding on average interviewee speech duration is shown in Figure 8-12; while that for Interviewer 2 is shown in Figure 8-13. With Interviewer 1 the interviewer and interviewee means were 5.1, 5.1, and 5.1 ($p$ not significant) and 36.9, 54.7, and 35.4 ($p$ of .001), respectively, a 48 percent increase from period 1 to period 2. Comparable values for Interviewer 2 were 5.1, 5.0, and 5.0 ($p$ not significant) and 25.2, 42.2, and 30.3 ($p$ of .001), a 67 percent increase.

*Interviewer "Mm-Hmm" and Interviewee Speech Durations*

We followed up the head-nod study with one identical in all respects except that only one interviewer (JDM) was used in both the original and cross-validation studies, and a second commonly employed interviewer tactic, saying "mm-hmm" (*throughout each of S's period 2 utterances*), was used as the verbal social reinforcing stimuli (Matarazzo, Wiens, Saslow, Allen, & Weitman, 1964). This experimental variable was introduced to each of the 20 interviewees an average of 160.6 times and

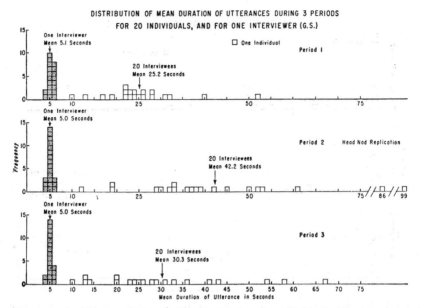

Figure 8-13. Distribution of mean duration of utterances during 3 periods for 20 individuals, and for one interviewer (GS).

191.0 times, respectively, in the 15 minutes of period 2 of the original and cross-validation studies, averaging a total of 12.4 times per minute of interviewee speech in the first study, and 14.8 times per minute of interviewee speech in the cross-validation study. The results are shown in Figures 8-14 and 8-15, and were, in the first study, 5.2, 5.3, and 5.3 ($p$ not significant) and 36.8, 48.3, and 39.1 ($p$ of .001), a 31 percent increase over period 1; and, in the second study 5.4, 5.6, and 5.4 ($p$ not significant) and 31.7, 58.3, and 28.6 ($p$ of .01), an increase of 84 percent from period 1 to period 2.

The results of the two head-nod and two "mm-hmm" studies, as well as those of the control group, are shown for purposes of comparison in Figure 8-16. The percentage increase from period 1 to period 2 in the 5 studies, reading down in Figure 8-16, was: (1) 48 percent; (2) 67 percent; (3) 31 percent; (4) 84 percent; and (5) none (control group). The values from these two interviewer tactics do *not* suggest a clear-cut value such as the 100 percent apparent asymptotic increase obtained by introducing changes in $E$'s own speech durations (Figure 8-11). Several possibilities suggest themselves: (a) head-nods and "mm-hmm," as presumed social reinforcers, do not belong in the same *identical* class of "social reinforcer" as do increases in an interviewer's own speech durations; (b) $E$'s use of head-nods and "mm-hmm" was not sufficiently skillful and that only in the study shown in Figure 8-15, where $E$ obtained an 84 percent increase, did

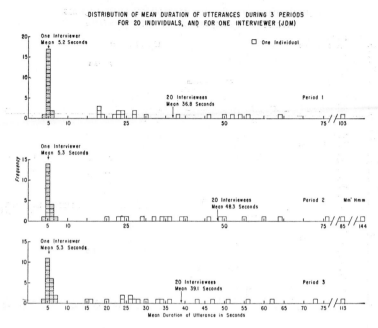

Figure 8-14. Distribution of mean duration of utterances during 3 periods for 20 indi-viduals, and for one interviewer (JDM).

he apply the reinforcement uniformly, or optimally; or (c) as rein-forcers, head-nods differ from "mm-hmm," and both of these differ from increases in E's durations. Again, only further research will answer these and related questions.

At this point one might ask, as we did, what is the *mechanism* whereby the interviewer is able to increase interviewee speaking duration by either himself speaking in longer duration (Figure 8-11) or by his use of such tactics as head-nodding and saying "mm-hmm" (Figure 8-16)? After discussing and discarding several potential artifacts in the increased duration study (Matarazzo, Weitman, Saslow, & Wiens, 1963) we specu-lated that the mechanism for E's influence on S's durations of utterance might be related to S's "greater satisfaction" when E, himself, talked longer or was more verbally active than when he talked in shorter utterances; a mechanism suggested by the findings of Lennard and Bern-stein (1960, pp. 182-184). The same "greater S satisfaction following E's more active participation" hypothesis can be tentatively specu-lated on as the mechanism for explaining S's longer individual speech durations while E is head-nodding or saying "mm-hmm." That is, it is possible again to speculate that, when E is head-nodding or saying "mm-hmm" while S is speaking, E is communicating more attention to, or showing more approval of S, than when he is not doing so, other con-

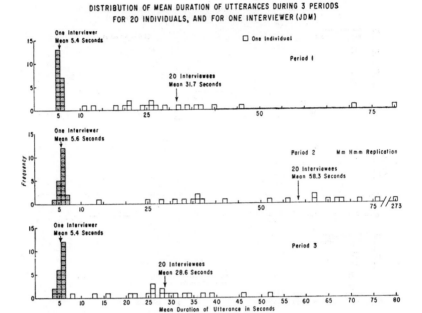

Figure 8-15.  Distribution of mean duration of utterances during 3 periods for 20 individuals, and for one interviewer (JDM).

ditions being equal. These various *E* behaviors are probably in a common *general* class of *nonverbal* generalized reinforcing stimuli, such that when they are emitted they produce profound changes in *S's* own nonverbal behavior (that is, increases in his speech durations). Whether the mechanism is brought into play because the interviewer is showing more approval of *S* by establishing a more permissive-accepting atmosphere, or by some other means must, at the present stage of our knowledge, remain speculative. Again, only further research will clarify this point.

To summarize the research presented in this chapter to this point, our studies have shown: (a) unusually high reliability for interviewee (and interviewer) speech and silence durations; (b) mirror-imaged J-shaped distributions for single units of interviewee speech and silence; (c) the ability of interviewee speech durations to differentiate broad diagnostic groups (but not all individuals within groups); (d) the complexity of the relationship between interview content and interviewee speech durations; and (e) the striking degree to which these highly reliable interviewee speech durations can be modified by such interviewer tactics as increasing or decreasing his own speech durations, head-nodding, and saying "mm-hmm." We also have studied the relationship between organismic and psychological test characteristics and interviewee speech behavior (Matarazzo, Matarazzo, Saslow, & Phillips, 1958) and between

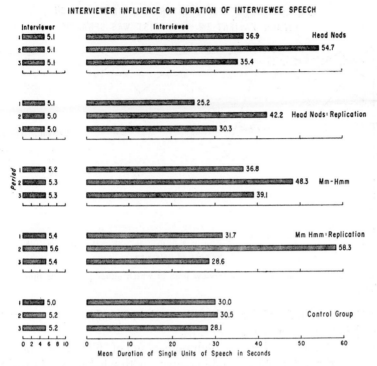

Figure 8-16.   Interviewer influence on duration of interviewee speech.

our noncontent interview measures and Bales content-derived interaction measures (Hare, Waxler, Saslow, & Matarazzo, 1960). The results of these two studies are too numerous to attempt to summarize here.

Taken together these various reliability and validity studies on *single,* initial interviews suggested we could proceed, with confidence in our measures and methods, to studies involving clinical psychotherapy series. This research has only now begun. Nevertheless, the results of several pilot studies are suggestive of the potential of our investigative approach. These pilot results will be presented next.

## STUDIES OF INTERVIEWEE SPEECH IN PSYCHOTHERAPY SERIES

The 3-period 45-minute clinical employment interviews utilized in the studies summarized in Figures 8-11 and 8-16 are characterized by the fact that (a) E was instructed always to respond to S in one second or less of silence, and (b) the average latency or silence to E's typical response shown by these Ss was approximately 1½ seconds. Since E's silences were under one second and S's silences averaged approximately 1½ seconds, this meant that almost 100 percent of the total 45-minute inter-

PERCENTAGE OF TOTAL INTERVIEW TIME IN WHICH
EITHER PATIENT OR THERAPIST WAS SPEAKING

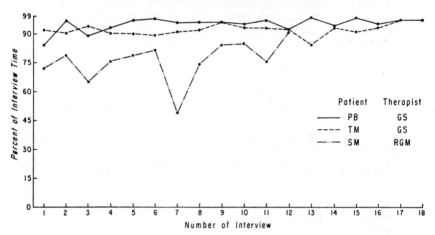

Figure 8-17.    Percentage of total interview time in which either patient or therapist was speaking.

view time was utilized by either *S* or *E* in *speaking* (in contrast to silence) in these interviews.

One might ask how this very high percentage of "filled time," or almost constant verbal interaction, would compare with what occurs in real psychotherapy interviews. Put another way, what is the "speech density" or "talk time" in clinical psychotherapy series? That is, for any given interview, what is the ratio of (a) total duration of time during which the therapist spoke *plus* total duration of time during which the patient spoke divided by (b) total duration of time consumed by the full interview? Thus, if in a 50-minute interview, *E* spoke a total of 15 minutes, *S* spoke a total of 25 minutes and they were *both* silent 10 minutes, the "filled time" or "speech density" of this interview is 80 percent (15 plus 25 is 40; 40 divided by 50 is 80 percent).

In our pilot studies to date we have examined three psychotherapy series: (a) a male psychotherapist (GS) with a neurotic ("schizoid") patient PB (a 33-year-old male engineer); (b) the same psychotherapist (GS) with a second patient (TM), a 59-year-old female patient with hysteria; and (c) a second (female) psychotherapist (RGM) with an 18-year-old suicidal female adolescent. These three psychotherapy series have lasted, to date, respectively, 18 sessions, 17 sessions, and 12 sessions.

Figure 8-17 presents the percentage of total interview time in which either patient or therapist was talking (that is, the "filled time" or "speech density" per psychotherapy session) in the three *series* of approximately 50-minute interviews. The two top curves show therapist GS with each of

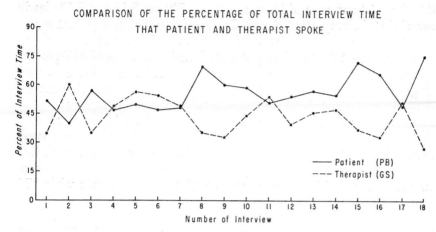

Figure 8-18. Comparison of the percentage of total interview time that patient and therapist spoke.

his two patients, and indicate that he in combination with each of his patients utilized, from session to session, approximately 93 percent of each 50-minute session in talking. There is very *little* deviation in this ratio from interview session to interview session with these two therapist-patient combinations.

The *separate* contributions of therapist and patient in talk time in each session for GS and each of these two patients are shown in Figures 8-18 and 8-19. Thus, while from Figure 8-17 the therapist-patient talk-time ratio (or speech density ratio) was the same (approximately 93 percent) with

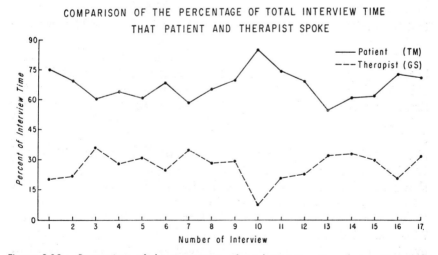

Figure 8-19. Comparison of the percentage of total interview time that patient and therapist spoke.

this therapist and *each* of his two patients, Figures 8-18 and 8-19 clearly reveal that the proportion of contribution of therapist and patient to this "constant" 93 percent ratio varied for the two patients. Figure 8-18 shows that with patient PB this therapist contributed an average of 43.7 percent of the talk time over each of the 18 sessions and PB contributed an average of 56.0 percent. The combined percentage (99.7 percent) is greater than the approximately 93 percent of total interview talk time because of simultaneous speech (approximately 6.7 percent of total interview time); that is, both therapist and patient interrupted each other and a small overlap in talk time resulted. On the other hand, Figure 8-19 reveals that with patient TM this same therapist contributed, from session to session, only an average of 26.7 percent of their 93 percent talk time while TM contributed an average of 67.1 percent.

The speculation (and *merely* that so early in this phase of our studies) from Figures 8-17, 8-18, and 8-19 that therapist GS "needs" 93 percent "filled time" per session and will adjust himself to the varying tempos of different patients is too striking to overlook even though it is based on one therapist and only two cases. We will, of course, follow up this possibility with additional research, while, at the same time, not overlooking the additional possibility that this finding may be due to a dynamic *inter-action* between him and his patients (rather than our seeking the explanation only in terms of a therapist variable, specifically).

Figure 8-17 reveals that the second therapist, RGM, and her patient, SM, earned a "speech density" ratio of 76 percent, with considerable *variation* from session to session (thereby differing from the marked stability in this ratio for GS and his two patients). The further breakdown, session by session, of the individual contributions of RGM and her patient to this 76 percent "filled time" is shown in Figure 8-20. There it is seen that the *variation* in the talk time ratio shown in Figure 8-17 is contributed *not* by therapist RGM, whose own percentage contribution across the 12 psychotherapy sessions remains a remarkably fixed 18.8 percent but, rather, by the oscillation in the talk time contribution of this 18-year-old suicidal girl. Two points are worth noting from Figure 8-20. First, the similarity between RGM's average 18.8 percent contribution with patient SM and GS's average 26.7 percent contribution with patient TM (Figure 8-19). Does this suggest that there are other similarities between patient SM and TM (for example, both are female), or between therapist GS and RGM as each interacts with a certain type of patient? Second, Figure 8-17 shows a marked dip in session 7 in the RGM-SM talk time ratio. Figure 8-20 reveals that this dip in session 7 was a function of a marked drop in the contribution of talk by patient SM. Interestingly, it was during session 7 that SM voiced suicidal threats and RGM decided to hospitalize her (for evenings and nights only) on an open ward in our general hospital. One might ask, were the suicidal verbalizations the cues which led RGM to

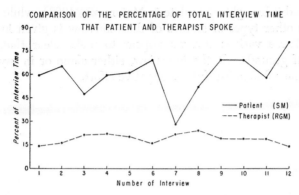

Figure 8-20. Comparison of the percentage of total interview time that patient and therapist spoke.

make the clinical decision to hospitalize; or was it the marked reduction in talk time; or a combination of these? It should be pointed out that the data in Figure 8-20 were computed only weeks *after* session 7 and, thus, therapist RGM had no quantitative knowledge of this dip in SM's talk time in session 7.

The pilot findings shown in Figures 8-17, 8-18, 8-19, and 8-20 are merely suggestive. That they point the way to "meaningful" clinical research in the sense that Luborsky was pleading for (as quoted in the introduction to this chapter) is, we hope, clear. This application to clinical psychotherapy of a series of precise, highly reliable speech measures has given us results (Figures 8-17, 8-18, 8-19, and 8-20) which are clearly similar to those of Lennard and Bernstein (1960, p. 109). These investigators independently have reported finding a *constant* speech time ratio for one therapist-patient combination (similar to our Figure 8-19), and an *oscillating* ratio for two patient-therapist pairs (similar to our Figure 8-20). They interpret these ratios in terms of an interesting theory of "equilibrium processes." Very recently, Jaffe (1962) has begun to study comparable psychotherapy session-to-session phenomena not unlike those of Lennard and Bernstein, and those in our Figures 8-17 to 8-20. The results of Lennard and Bernstein, Jaffe, and of our own group (Figures 8-17 to 8-20), when added to the striking reliability and validity findings presented earlier in this chapter, would appear to suggest that noncontent measures, either alone or, more likely, in combination with content-derived psychotherapy measures, appear to have a higher than average probability of furthering our understanding of "process" and related psychotherapy phenomena.

Review of the studies of other workers in this area was omitted in the present chapter. A full review of the noncontent studies of Chapple, Goldman-Eisler, and others is given in Matarazzo, Saslow, & Matarazzo

(1956), and is brought up to date in Matarazzo (1962); while a review of numerous other types of studies of the interview is given in Matarazzo (1965). These various reviews appear to make clear that, after two decades of groundwork, the interview, either alone or in psychotherapy series, is amenable to fruitful investigative effort.

# 9

## Verbal Conditioning and Psychotherapy*
### LEONARD KRASNER

K rasner's role identification has been as a clinical psychologist interested in treatment procedures (Krasner, 1963c). His research interests have
moved from using objective and projective techniques to investigate personality
variables (Krasner, 1953, Krasner & Kornreich, 1954) to assessing and modifying
behavior through operant conditioning techniques (Krasner, 1955, 1958a, 1958b,
1962a, 1962b, 1963a, 1963b, 1963c).

The studies described in this paper represent the collaboration of the editors
in a programmatic approach to investigating the variables involved in the
verbal conditioning situation. The clinical implications of verbal conditioning
studies are discussed both in this chapter and in the introductions to the chapters by Sarason and Kanfer.

Authors in previous chapters have called for new and different assessment
methods as well as treatment procedures. If we center on the maladaptive behavior itself, concepts such as "mental illness" and "schizophrenia" become
superfluous. There is genuine disagreement even among the experts who believe that there is a disease called schizophrenia and approach it from genetic,
biochemical, or Freudian viewpoints. Jackson (1960, p. 11), introducing a
volume entitled Etiology of Schizophrenia, wrote: "The term 'schizophrenic' in
medical circles carries almost as much of a ring of authenticity as 'diabetic' or
'tubercular.' Yet it is nearly as much a fiction as that lovely legal appelation
'reasonable man.' "

Significant results have been obtained via relatively short periods of reinforcement with central schizophrenic "symptoms" such as withdrawal (King,
Armitage, & Tilton, 1960; Ullmann, Krasner, & Collins, 1961); disorganized
thinking (Ullmann, Krasner, & Edinger, 1964), affect (Weiss, Krasner, & Ullmann,
1963; Salzinger & Pisoni, 1961), delusions (Ayllon & Michael, 1959; Ayllon &
Haughton, 1964; Rickard, Dignam, & Horner, 1960; Rickard & Dinoff, 1962)
and "neurotic defensiveness" (Ullmann, Weiss, & Krasner, 1963). If this can be

* Researches reported in this paper were supported in part by Research Grants
M-2485 and M-6191, from the National Institute of Mental Health, United States
Public Health Service, administered through Stanford University.

done, as it has been by different experimenters in different settings, there is prime evidence to support the point made by Ferster (Chapter 2) and reiterated throughout this book, that the medical model is inappropriate.

With this background, it seems reasonable and appropriate to treat maladaptive behavior directly. In his chapter, Krasner highlights both the similarities and differences between traditional psychotherapy and verbal operant conditioning, using the latter first as an analogue of psychotherapy and then as a form of treatment itself. He also presents material on the occurrence (often without the clinician's awareness) of verbal operant conditioning in situations in which influence is not apparent or is even denied.

L.K.-L.P.U.

FROM THEIR BEGINNING IN the early 1950's (Greenspoon, 1954), studies of verbal conditioning have been used as the basis of speculations and extrapolations to the process of psychotherapy. For example, Dollard and Miller (1950) cite Greenspoon's then unpublished doctoral dissertation as evidence that reinforcement in psychotherapy had effects that were "direct, automatic . . . unconscious." From that point on, most authors investigating verbal conditioning either derived their hypotheses from behavior observed in the psychotherapeutic situation or else discussed their results in terms of implications for psychotherapy. This chapter will present an overview of current research in verbal conditioning, describe some recent illustrative studies, and discuss the relevance of this research for psychotherapy.

Although Skinner's views of verbal behavior had been disseminated by his lectures and mimeographed material, the publication of his book (Skinner, 1957), which conceptualized human speech as "verbal behavior" subject to the same general laws as other behaviors, represented a major development. Skinner's work with verbal behavior goes back to 1936, to an ingenious technique, the Verbal Summator, which, ironically, first found its niche in psychology as a projective technique. The Verbal Summator is a phonograph recording of a vague pattern of speech sounds, played, at low intensity or against a noisy background, as often as necessary to evoke a response. Although it has not been widely used, it is a useful technique to elicit verbal behavior and offers many possibilities for research in the analysis of verbal behavior (Skinner, 1936).

## THE DEVELOPMENT OF VERBAL CONDITIONING

Historically, verbal conditioning is a research technique that grew out of an unlikely marriage between animal-based Skinnerian operant conditioning and clinical interest in verbal behavior, especially as it occurs in psychotherapy. Verbal conditioning is the systematic application of social reinforcements to influence the probability of another person emitting a specifiable verbal behavior. The examiner uses his own behavior systematically to cue the subject. These cues indicate that the examiner is listening, paying attention, perhaps even approving of what the subject is saying. For example, if the examiner desires the subject to verbalize material about his feelings, whenever the subject makes statements such as "I feel happy" the examiner may say "mm-hmm" or "good," or nod his head, or smile. The evidence is strong that, under certain combinations of circumstances, the subject will increase his verbalization of similar "I feel" statements. In this context, it becomes clear why some investigators, working with patients, noted similarities between this experimental technique and psychotherapy and labeled one procedure an analogue of the other (Krasner, 1955; Kanfer, Chapter 11).

Investigations of verbal conditioning started from two different but overlapping orientations. The first was an interest in general laws of verbal learning and was laboratory oriented. Experimental psychologists undertook studies, primarily with students, to investigate the variables that affect verbal performance, or to test learning concepts. The second, and larger, group of investigators approached verbal conditioning with an interest in the objective study of psychotherapy. Here at last seemed to be a situation which resembled the treatment process and in which one variable at a time could be manipulated and its effect explored.

Our own studies of verbal conditioning were initiated with this latter focus and were originally designed to test certain aspects of psychotherapy. Verbal conditioning is an excellent technique for learning how human verbal behavior is systematically influenced by situational events; what are the conditions for effectively modifying such behavior; what other behaviors are associated with changes in verbal behavior; and what is the effect on verbal behavior of the interaction of subject-examiner variables. Verbal conditioning and traditional psychotherapy are not the same process, nor is one an "analogue" of the other. Neither process is unique, and each is closely related to the other. Rather both belong to the broader category of behavior-influencing techniques that include attitude changes, placebos, role-taking and modeling, milieu control, and "brainwashing" (Krasner & Ullmann, in press). Our position is that verbal conditioning has progressed from a research technique to a type of treatment.

In an earlier paper (Krasner, 1958a), it was possible to cover the approximately 35 verbal conditioning studies then in the literature. The number of verbal conditioning studies have now increased to several hundred and have grown considerably more complex. For example, it is no longer possible to tabulate the percentage of studies which give positive results as against those which give negative results, and, further, such a comparison would be meaningless. A "negative" study, at this point, usually means that the investigator's hypotheses were not confirmed; conditioning may have been obtained, but the special relationships hypothesized were not.

A survey of the verbal conditioning studies would, at first, point to some conflicting results. However, as studies proceeded, it became obvious that the variables involved in verbal conditioning were very complex, and have not always been adequately controlled. The major uncontrolled variable in these studies, as Sarason points out (Chapter 10), has been the examiner—his expectancies, biases, and the interactions of his "characteristics" with other variables of the situation. Studies investigating several variables at the same time have demonstrated complex interactional effects (Sarason & Minard, 1963). The sensitivity of verbal conditioning to these many variables of human interaction underlies its usefulness as a research device.

## VERBAL CONDITIONING AND PSYCHOTHERAPY

Psychotherapy in this paper is used as a generic term for a behavior modification process between two people, one labeled by society as therapist, the other as patient. It covers many different techniques, ranging from nondirective therapy through more obviously directive approaches, and includes the various newer behavior therapies (Eysenck, 1960; Ullmann & Krasner, 1965). It has been argued that a comparison of verbal conditioning and psychotherapy is inappropriate because verbal conditioning is an "artificial laboratory" situation created for research purposes, whereas psychotherapy is a "natural" process. Butler et al. (1962), for example, compared the naturalistic investigation of psychotherapy to Darwin's observations of nature that resulted in the theory of evolution. Such a formulation may lead to false conclusions about the nature of the "reality" of the therapy situation. Psychotherapy involves the planned behavior of a professional person to assist a person seeking help and consequently is a highly unusual, artificial situation, of recent historical origin, rooted in a particular time, place, and culture.

In comparing verbal conditioning and psychotherapy, we should start with the metavariables that are appropriate to all influence situations. As a broad psychology of social influence emerges, we would first start with the social role definitions of the participants and the behaviors associated with these roles. Orne's term, "demand characteristics" (1962), is a way of conceptualizing the previously learned social role character- istics demanded of participants in a particular situation. We can first look at the influencer, realizing that "influencing" is not a one-way pro- cedure. Neither verbal conditioning nor psychotherapy are chance en- counters; in both, the influencer has performed certain behaviors that have set the occasion for this special meeting. By his initiation of these behaviors the influencer has gone a long way toward defining the na- ture of the roles in a specific societal setting. The experimenter has set up an experiment; he has labeled the situation "research." By this defini- tion, the "influencee" takes the role of "subject." Since the majority of subjects asked to perform verbal conditioning tasks are college students who are wise to the rules of the "research" game, they usually conform with what they think is expected of them unless there is strong reason not to. Orne (1962) illustrates the extent to which subjects will meet the demands of the experimenter. Similarly, the therapist has set up his own game and set of rules, which prescribe the behaviors of the patient (Krasner, 1959). For example, it is expected in psychoanalysis that the patient follow the "basic rule" of free association, and many patients feel they are not receiving full treatment if early childhood memories and sexual behavior are not fully probed.

Verbal conditioning takes place within both a research and "real" life framework. How these operants first came about, what gradual shaping, acquisition, one-trial learning, or no-trial learning were involved in their acquisition is, for purposes of modification, irrelevant. Irrespective of how the behavior developed, it was learned in a lawful way. The same can be said of the individual's behavior in psychotherapy. Patients have learned the "sick" role, which determines to a large extent their performance in psychotherapy. Sarbin discusses such role learning in his chapter on hypnosis. In this role, based on a medical model of pathology, the mal- adaptive behavior of an individual is viewed as symptomatic of an under- lying process in much the same way that a cough or high fever may be symptoms of underlying disease processes. The disease concept implies that there are psychodynamic forces within the individual that are re- sponsible for the observable behavior, the symptom. Yet studies such as those of Lennard and Bernstein (1960) and Murray (1956), among others, have demonstrated the lawfulness of verbal interactions even in traditional psychotherapy.

There are increasingly reported illustrations of verbal conditioning as psychotherapy. In one of the first of these studies Williams (1958) labeled his experimental interaction with students as "psychotherapy" and dem- onstrated significant changes in verbal behavior under such conditions. If changes in verbal behavior have consequences for changes in other kinds of behavior, then systematic modification of verbalization itself is treatment. Reece and Whitman (1962) reported verbal conditioning studies in which the therapist attributes of "warmth" and "coldness" were reproduced in a "free-association" situation and found that these attributes effected differential conditionability in college subjects. Dinoff, Horner, *et al.* (1960) used verbal conditioning to modify schizophrenic patients' verbalizations in a group therapy situation. Ayllon and Haughton (1964) used verbal conditioning to systematically modify schizophrenic verbalizations. One of our studies (Ullmann, Krasner, & Edinger, 1964) illustrates therapeutic modification of patient verbal behavior and will be described in detail below.

### TASKS IN VERBAL CONDITIONING

At this point, we will briefly discuss some of the technical problems involved in verbal conditioning research in order to understand its potentialities and limitations as a research and therapeutic procedure. We start with the task requirements of the verbal conditioning situation. Investigations have usually used one of two different task situations. There is, first, the task which offers the subject a limited choice of responses (Taffel, 1955). A card is presented with six pronouns, and the subject is asked to make up a sentence using one of these pronouns. Similar tasks involve making up sentences from a choice of verbs, or giving a "yes," "no," or "maybe" response to a paper-and-pencil personality inventory (Nuthmann, 1957). The Taffel-type task has become the most popular verbal conditioning technique, primarily because of its limited number of possible responses and consequent ease of scoring. However, for purposes of interpretation and extrapolation to more general behavior influence situations, this type of task involves a far too limited response repertoire. Further, this task has been criticized as not really representing a true operant conditioning situation, but rather a discrimination learning task.

What is involved in this kind of task from the subject's point of view? In most instances the context of the situation clearly labels it as a learning task, in which implicitly there is a right or wrong answer. In this instance "right" is the ability to discriminate the real "demands" of the examiner: "What does the experimenter want of me?" Further, the nature of the task is a fairly simple one, since most people can readily make up sentences. This allows for time and energy to speculate, to make hypotheses and to allow for "intentions"—"do I or don't I want to go along with what he wants me to do?" If your hypothesis about the real nature of the task is not confirmed by ensuing cues, then you can try again and evolve more hypotheses. "I thought that is what you wanted" is a frequent comment among students. All other things being equal, why not go along and give this fellow what he wants? This kind of simplification of reasoning may explain, in part, the relationship between performance and aware-ness found by some investigators (Dulany, 1962; Spielberger, 1962).

One may speculate as to why this type of task persists in verbal condi-tioning studies if it has such little generality. There are several reasons: it is relatively easy to incorporate into a design; it does not require training in identfication of a complex response class; it results in lawful interac-tions (under these limited circumstances); it allows for isolation of vari-ables and a careful control of interactions. Greenspoon (1962, p. 546), in a critique of this experimental paradigm, summarizes these critical points:

> It appears to the writer that some questions may be raised concerning the inclusion of research using the Taffel-type situation with the operant con-ditioning paradigm. This writer has serious doubts about its conclusions because an essential element of operant conditioning is missing. Skinner (1935) emphasized the importance of the generic nature of the concept of response in that a single response is unique and it is necessary to conceive of a class of responses, the members of which have certain common characteristics. The Taffel-type situation in which a specific personal pronoun is reinforced certainly does not provide for generalization within a class of responses. The modification of the Taffel-type situation in which hostile verbs, bodily active verbs, etc., are reinforced does provide op-portunity for generalization within the class of hostile or bodily active verbs. Some of the confusion in the results of research in verbal condition-ing may be a product of apparatuses, materials and procedures that do not fit within the operant conditioning paradigm.

The other type of verbal conditioning task takes the form of an inter-view or story-telling situation (Salzinger & Pisoni, 1958; Krasner, 1958a). The subject can respond to the task out of a broad behavior repertoire. Illustrations of this type of task include instructions such as "Say all the words you can think of" (Greenspoon, 1955); "Tell a story" (Krasner & Ullmann, 1958); "What do you see in these inkblots?" (Fahmy, 1953).

The free operant task is usually presented in somewhat disguised form. It should have a role or face-validity to it; it must make sense as an ex-perimental task as stated or the subject will attempt to hypothesize a real "meaning" to it. Thus, it sounds plausible to investigate "how people tell stories" or "use their imagination." Also, the task is usually one in which the subject can be fully preoccupied; for example, interview, conversa-tion, making up a story. There is little time or energy left over to make up hypotheses about the nature of the task, and if it is done, the specula-tions are usually in relation to the given task, for example, "you were saying 'mm-hmm' to hinder me, to interfere with my story telling."

The advantages to this type of task are that it more clearly approximates "real" life and other behavior influence situations such as traditional psy-chotherapy or brainwashing. The verbal units reinforced include emo-tional words (Krasner, Ullmann, Weiss, & Collins, 1961), affect statements (Salzinger & Pisoni, 1958, 1960), a particular content area (Quay, 1959), or self-reference statements (Adams & Hoffman, 1960; Rogers, 1960). Further, the relationships between variables are more complex, and thus there is less likelihood of the subject reporting awareness of the purpose of the study or the pattern of the examiner's reinforcing behavior. The clearer, less ambiguous a task, the more likely a well-motivated individual will perform it. Bandura (Chapter 15) has suggested that it is possible to obtain one-trial learning in verbal conditioning by simply telling the subject what is wanted of him. This certainly makes sense for the Taffel-type task in which one could inform the subject of the nature of the task, for example, "to make up sentences starting with I." He can then be given several illustrations, told that he will be well rewarded for proper task performance with approval and with class credit for his time. The examiner will thus have influenced the subject by his instructions, presented a model for him to follow, and will have rewarded his compliance. This is not as easy to do with a more ambiguous response class such as affect words. Here the response repertoire is under much less subject control. Even if his instructions were quite clear as to the task requirements he could not necessarily produce the desired operants. Further, measures of extinction strength may well differ between the one-trial model learning and reinforced learning with the latter procedure more resistant to extinction.

Insofar as task clarity is concerned, traditional psychotherapy itself has considerable ambiguity as to its requirements. Ambiguity is used as a technique to force from the patient material from "within" to fill the vacuum of the hour. If the patient is not completely clear as to what are the correct verbalizations, he will keep shifting his verbal repertoire until he hits the "correct" sequence, which will be rewarded by interest and attention. As we have emphasized, the behavior therapists have recently been rewarding their patients in a manner that brings the verbal conditioning task far closer to treatment than could have been surmised even a short time ago. To illustrate this point, we will describe a series of verbal conditioning investigations that demonstrate some of these procedures.

## INVESTIGATIVE PROCEDURE

The first task in our investigations was to isolate a verbal response class having certain characteristics: it had to be a demonstrably genuine response class; it had to have assumptive relevance for clinical material and for psychotherapy; it had to have a fairly high, but not too high, operant level, so that it would occur with enough frequency to elicit reinforcement, but not with so much frequency that it could not be improved upon; it had to be reinforceable and changeable; and, finally, it had to be presentable in the context of an acceptable task to the subject as part of a reasonable rationale for the existence of the study.

The first procedure we used to elicit verbal behavior was to ask the subject to tell a story, specifying the kinds of characters in the story, such as a mother, a father, a child, an animal (Krasner, 1958b). Then one of these verbal classes, such as *mother* (nouns and pronouns) was selected to be reinforced. Although this proved to be a useful technique, it was later modified into a procedure in which the subject was given a card with human figures on it, and asked to tell a story about the card. The response class was emotional words—those having special impact (Ullmann & McFarland, 1957). We selected this response class for several reasons: the importance attached to the use of emotional words in psychotherapy in various theoretical positions; the relationship between emotional words and other clinically meaningful material; the reliability of scoring this response class; the naturalness of the use of emotional words in a storytelling situation; and the relationship between emotional words and physiological changes. Our early expectations of the usefulness of this technique has been borne out in subsequent studies.

The next step was to determine an effective reinforcement. In the therapy situation, as in any behavior influence situation, there are many aspects of the influencer's own behavior that are utilized as reinforcing cues. These cues should be defineable and replicable behaviors. Most of the verbal conditioning studies have used minimal verbal cues of the examiner, such as "mm-hmm," on the basis that such cues indicate attention and interest, are quite natural and realistic, and are more effective than generally realized.

At first, it was thought by investigators that "mm-hmm" or "good" could be set up as objective types of responses, analogous perhaps to food pellets, which could be delivered in certain quantities with specifiable schedules. However, studies thus far have clearly indicated that the reinforcement could not be divorced from the "giver" of the reinforcement. Unlike animal studies, the magazine delivering the pellet is a crucial variable. Further, the "deliverer" can be either eliminated by "hardware" or can be incorporated into the design. For example, whereas in the early studies, care was taken to program the examiner so that the "mm-hmm" was clearly and carefully enunciated and controlled, and delivered only under certain specified conditions, in later studies (Krasner, Ullmann, & Fisher, 1964; Krasner, Knowles, & Ullmann, 1964), the examiner was programed differently. The nature of the verbal conditioning studies was explained to the examiner and included: the theory behind reinforcement procedure; the definition of reinforcement in terms of behavioral cues on the part of the examiner indicating interest and attention; examples of reinforcing cues such as "head-nodding," "smiling," "mm-hmm," and "good." The class of behavior to be reinforced was clearly defined for him, but the specific manner of reinforcement was left to himself to do what was most natural for him within these prescribed limits. Thus, the attempt was made to make use of a more natural unit of reinforcement, the examiner with his own natural human reinforcement qualities.

## INVESTIGATIONS

Using these response classes and reinforcers, we have investigated a number of the variables which influence verbal behavior. These have included the effects of examiner differences (Krasner, Ullmann, Weiss, & Collins, 1961); subject personality variables (Ullmann, Krasner, & Weiss, 1963); the relationship between awareness and performance (Krasner, Weiss, & Ullmann, 1961); the effects of instructional sets (Ekman, Krasner, & Ullmann, 1963); generalization effects (Ullmann, Krasner, & Collins, 1961); atmosphere effects (Weiss, Krasner, & Ullmann, 1960, 1963); the pleasantness of emotional words (Ullmann, Krasner, & Gelfand, 1963); physiological concomitants of changes in emissions of emotional words (Ullmann, Krasner, & Sherman, 1963b); changes in response class reinforced (Krasner & Ullmann, 1958); "placebo" effects (Gelfand, Ullmann, & Krasner, 1963); and relationship to other behavior influence situations such as hypnosis (Weiss, Ullmann, & Krasner, 1960; Bentler, O'Hara, & Krasner, 1963). We will describe in detail several recent studies that illustrate the general nature of the program.

Earlier studies reviewed by Krasner (1958a, 1962b) and Salzinger (1959) had offered strong evidence that the frequency of subjects' use of a specified class of verbal behavior can be influenced by minimal social reinforcement. In the course of our investigations of verbal conditioning effects, in five different studies (Ekman, Krasner, & Ullmann, 1963; Krasner, Ullmann, Weiss, & Collins, 1961; Weiss, Ekman, Ullmann, & Krasner, 1965; Weiss, Krasner, & Ullmann, 1960, 1963) we observed that in addition to changes in the frequency of emission, the emotional words used by the subjects became *pleasanter* (Ullmann, Krasner, & Gelfand, 1963). Further, the pleasantness of the emotional words used was significantly associated with psychological test measures of anxiety. There were three indications that this phenomenon was clinically as well as theoretically important. First, the definition of emotional words in these studies came directly from clinical material (Gurel & Ullmann, 1958; Ullmann, 1957, 1958; Ullmann & McFarland, 1957). Secondly, we had previously found that verbal conditioning of emotional words was significantly associated with clinically meaningful changes as measured by behavior in group therapy (Ullmann, Krasner, & Collins, 1961; Ullmann, Krasner, & Ekman, 1961) and recognition of threatening stimuli (Ullmann, Weiss, &

Krasner, 1963). Third, the "pleasantness" of emotional words was similar to the Dollard and Mowrer's (1947) Discomfort Relief Quotient (DRQ). There were two general purposes of the research to be described. At a first level, where previous work had dealt with the reinforcement of all emotional words, both pleasant and unpleasant, we now wished to determine whether we could be effective in differentially increasing or decreasing specific functional classes. That is, could pleasant emotional words be increased in frequency without a correlated increase in the emission of unpleasant emotional words. A second, and related purpose, was to test out the formulation of verbal conditioning as a direct form of therapy in itself. We wished to ascertain whether increasing a role behavior (saying things more pleasantly) which we assumed to be more acceptable and likely to elicit positive responses from other people (or had been associated more frequently in the subject's prior reinforcement history with favorable responses) would lead to reduction of "anxiety" as measured by generally used criteria.

In this study (Ullmann, Krasner, & Sherman, 1963b) we used 80 male psychiatric patients from an acute intensive treatment ward in a psychiatric hospital. Subjects in each of the four conditions to be described were balanced for diagnosis—two thirds psychotic, one third neurotic. The subjects first were connected to a Fels Dermohmeter. Then they were given a 24-item process-reactive scale (Ullmann & Giovannoni, 1964) followed by 35 MMPI items selected to predict emission of pleasant emotional words (Ullmann, Krasner, & Sherman, 1963a). The verbal conditioning procedures followed: subjects were given TAT-like instructions to make up stories to pictures. The stimuli cards were designed to depict "emotionally bland" situations. Five cards with 2-minute stories to each were used to obtain operant level. This was followed by another five-card trial (10 minutes). During this period the examiner's behavior differed for each of the four experimental conditions. In the first condition, the examiner continued to give no reinforcement. In the second, the examiner *reinforced all* emotional words by "mm-hmm." In the third, the examiner *reinforced pleasant emotional words only*, while in the fourth he *reinforced unpleasant emotional words only*. After completing the story-telling task, all subjects answered 34 additional MMPI items parallel to the initial 35 MMPI items.

In terms of differential control of types of emotional words emitted by the subjects, group I (no reinforcement) was used as the control group for the other three. As may be seen from Table 9-1, group I (which was essentially extinction) decreased in emission of (a) all emotional words, (b) pleasant emotional words, and (c) unpleasant emotional words, while group II, in which all emotional words were reinforced, increased in all three of these measures. For group III, in which only pleasant emotional words were reinforced, there was some increase in total number of emotional words, in pleasant emotional words, and a decrease in unpleasant emotional words. This indicated that within 10 minutes the examiner had obtained control over the reinforced response class. However, reinforcement of "unpleasant" emotional words did not lead to control of the selected response class. Similarly, in the Krasner, Knowles, and Ullmann (1964) study, we were unable to influence a "negative" attitude response class.

*Table 9-1:* Means and Standard Deviations for Change Scores in Four Groups of 20 Psychiatric Patients Each Receiving Different Reinforcement of Pleasant and Unpleasant Words

| | #EW [a] | | #P | | #U | | GSR [b] | | MMPI | |
|---|---|---|---|---|---|---|---|---|---|---|
| Group | M | S.D. | M | S.D. | M | S.D. | M | S.D. | M | S.D. |
| I | −2.80 | 9.35 | −1.25 | 6.00 | − .50 | 7.05 | +14.5 | 6.10 | +1.75 | 5.00 |
| II | +6.00 | 12.00 | +2.45 | 6.50 | +2.75 | 7.05 | +15.4 | 5.30 | +3.25 | 3.45 |
| III | +3.95 | 11.00 | +3.55 | 8.70 | − .90 | 6.45 | +16.2 | 4.70 | +2.90 | 4.25 |
| IV | +1.70 | 13.85 | +2.00 | 6.95 | −2.00 | 9.25 | +16.5 | 2.90 | +3.65 | 4.55 |

[a] #EW is greater than #P + #U because of words not relevant to the pleasantness–unpleasantness dimension and the presence of words scored at the mid-point of the pleasantness–unpleasantness scale.
[b] Scores are for changes in resistance, but the addition of a constant and rounding off to three significant figures means that averages do not refer to ohms.

Table 9-1 also presents change scores for pretest to posttest of GSR and MMPI measures. While further computation is necessary to eliminate regression effects and starting levels, it is interesting to note that if we take the actual behavior emitted by the subjects on both criteria, there is a similarity of progression. The control group decreased in anxiety as measured by skin resistance and MMPI items. However, the other three reinforced groups changed even more markedly in the same favorable direction on these two measures. Looking at the number of emotional words of the type to be reinforced, it seems that the progression is not associated with the number of positive reinforcements from the examiner, but rather the change in the patients' role.

Comparing groups I and II on change in use of *all emotional* words, the nonreinforced group (I) decreased in such usage whereas the reinforced group (II) increased ($t = 2.53$ in the predicted direction, significant at the .01 level with one-tail test). Comparing groups I and III on change in the use of *pleasant* emotional words, the nonreinforced group (I) decreased, the reinforced group (III) increased, ($t = 1.98$, in the predicted direction, significant at the .05 level with one-tail test). Comparing groups I and IV on changed use of *unpleasant* emotional words, both groups decreased, but the control group (I) decreased less than the experimental group (IV) ($t = 0.56$, statistically insignificant, and in the direction opposite to the one predicted).

Thus, we demonstrated the differential controllability of emotional words and the effects of changed verbal behavior on criterion measurements of "anxiety." The next study to be described (Ullmann, Krasner, & Edinger, 1964) is one of a continuing series dealing with social reinforcement of role behaviors of schizophrenics to alter their emission of disadvantageous responses. This experiment used men on one of the poorest prognosis wards in a psychiatric hospital (long-term, "chronic schizophrenics"). The design involved seeing the patient twice. In both times, the Sarbin-Hardyck Stick Figure Test (1955) was administered. This test had been previously demonstrated to have construct and criterion validity (Krasner, Ullmann, & Weiss, 1964). In the second session, the subject was given a word association test. After 20 operant words, half the subjects (experimental group) were reinforced for giving a common association, defined by those responses given by at least 100 cases (10 percent of normals) in Russell and Jenkins (1954). The other subjects, the control group, received no reinforcement. Analysis of covariance, correcting for starting level and regression effect was used. When the last 20 trials were compared with the first 20 trials, the experimental group increased while the control decreased significantly in the emission of common associations.

The results confirmed Sommer, Witney, and Osmond's (1962) finding that common associations by schizophrenics to word association stimuli may be brought under control by selective reinforcement. The use of different reinforcers, experimental design, examiners, and locales all added to the confidence which may be placed in this result. Whether disturbed association is a primary symptom from which secondary schizophrenic symptoms may be derived, or but one of many correlated symptoms, is not as important as the more general finding that such a symptom, even with a brief training period and long-term patients, can be influenced by social reinforcement. Of equal theoretical and practical interest is the decreased use of common associations by the control group. It seems reasonable that with schizophrenic patients social reinforcement is important in maintaining as well as changing common associations, and that in this respect the schizophrenics were the same as normals.

Both the present research and that by Sommer, Witney, and Osmond (1962) failed to obtain significant generalization of the training in common associations. It appears that the most useful line to follow in future research would be in specifically training patients to generalize from one training situation to another. It may be particularly necessary for the experimenter working with long-term patients to train the subject on every step of the task. Lines that might be followed include slowly decreasing the ratio of reinforcement, the use of different examiners, and a shifting from patients' responses to examiner introduced stimuli to interview type conversations and free associations.

From these two studies, we will move on to a description of two other studies investigating the relationship between change in the subject's attitudes toward the examiner and change in performance of an "important" required task. A major variable in behavior influence situations which affect the subject's performance is the subject's attitude toward the examiner or the patient's attitude toward his therapist. An important aspect of how well an individual plays the social role of the subject (Orne, 1962) or patient (Shapiro, 1960) is his understanding of the role and his desire to perform that role (Sarbin, Chapter 16). It is a reasonable assumption that, as in psychotherapy, the more favorable the subject's attitudes toward the examiner the more likely he is to be susceptible to influence.

In these studies the attitude toward the examiner was measured by a questionnaire designed to elicit opinions about the role of medical scientist in which the examiner was cast. In one study (Krasner, Ullmann, & Fisher, 1964), the first part of the investigation was concerned with the conditionability of the subject's attitudes by social reinforcement. The second part of this study dealt with the association between such attitude training and performance on a motor task of obvious importance to the examiner.

Previously, Ekman (1959), Hildum and Brown (1956), Nuthmann (1957), Staats, Staats, Heard, and Finley (1962), and Verplanck (1955) had illustrated that verbal conditioning can lead to significant changes in responses to opinion, attitude, and personality scales. The present study went one step further in investigating the association between such changes and consequent changes in an independent criterion situation.

The subjects selected were the mothers of children in a cooperative nursery school. This was a group of subjects with attitudes closer to the general population than the usual college sophomore and psychiatric patient samples. After preliminary oral arrangements with the school authorities, a letter was sent to the school asking for volunteers for an important research project to be run by a "physiological psychologist" within a medical research framework. The letter and the later instructions given by the examiner were designed to evoke a maximum of prestige, scientific aura, and face validity for participants. Subjects volunteered and were randomly assigned to the experimental and control groups. The examiner, in a business suit, introduced himself, as he had been described in the introductory letter, as a physiological psychologist, working for a U.S. Public Health Research project. A dynamometer was pointed out and the subject was told that it would be used to "measure psychomotor muscular coordination." Subjects were then asked to take the dynamometer in their preferred hand. A red light pressed by the examiner signaled them to start. At the onset of the light they were required to raise the dynamometer "exactly 4 inches above the table and to squeeze as hard as you can, and hold your squeeze at the maximum for as long as you can.

When you feel your grip weaken, place your hand back on the table. I'll give you a 10-second rest and signal you to begin again." Each subject was given six trials. The Medical Science Questionnaire, MSQ, was then read to the subjects. This questionnaire contains 54 items designed to measure attitudes toward the medical scientist-physician role. The rationale for the use of this questionnaire was that in a medical research experiment, the subject's response would be affected by his attitude toward two overlapping examiner roles, that of medical practitioner and that of medical scientist. All 54 items had been twice screened to insure internal consistency. The form used had a .91 corrected odd-even correlation for an N of 122 cases. The 24 (first) "operant" items and the 30 (succeeding) "reinforced" items were equated for percentage of subjects answering in a favorable direction, direction (agree or disagree) of a favorable response, and part-whole association. Example items were: "Doctors rarely make mistakes." "Scientists have too much power to control man." "The goals of science are the supreme goals of mankind." "Scientists sometimes mislead people in order to get monetary support."

In the experimental group, the first 24 items on the MSQ were given without any reactions on the part of the examiner. On the remaining 30 items the examiner reinforced favorable responses. The reinforcement consisted of a "mm-hmm," head-nod, smile, or any combination of these cues that the examiner felt would be most effective. The same procedure was followed with the control group except that reinforcement was not given. All 54 items were read without reinforcing reaction on the part of the examiner. After completion of the questionnaire, six additional trials on the dynamometer were given.

The experimental and control groups did not differ significantly ($t = 0.32$) on pretest dynamometer trials or on favorability toward medical science on the first 24 (operant) MSQ items ($t = 0.34$). Compared to the control group, the experimental group increased significantly both in its favorability of responses to medical science (at the .01 level, $t = 3, 15$) and in its dynamometer effort (at the .05 level, $t = 2.28$).

Thus the major findings confirmed the hypotheses. Favorableness of attitudes toward medical scientists can be influenced by social reinforcement. The finding that such attitudes can be conditioned in a task of this nature is consistent with previous studies. The results clearly indicate that the experimental manipulation, the social reinforcement of favorable attitudes, had a significant effect on the dynamometer performance. However, the results of this study were open to an alternative interpretation; namely, that the increased effort on the dynamometer was a response to social reinforcement, rather than a function of the specific change in attitude.

This alternative hypothesis was evaluated in the next study of this series (Krasner, Knowles, & Ullmann, 1964). The dynamometer performance of subjects treated like the reinforced subjects in the previous study was compared with that of subjects given equivalent degrees of reinforcement for responding to a questionnaire whose content was unrelated to the attitude under consideration. Thus, while one group of subjects received the MSQ and was reinforced for favorable responses, as in the earlier study, a second group of subjects was given a 30-item Medical Science Information Survey (MSIS) and reinforced, irrespective of the nature of the response, on a randomly selected 75 percent of the items. The statements comprising the MSIS were favorable or unfavorable comments upon the adequacy with which media such as TV, radio, and newspapers handled issues of psychological and physical health. This was considered an acceptable control procedure in that the MSIS had face-validity in the experimental situation, but did not reflect directly on the examiner's social role.

A third experimental condition was added in which MSQ responses unfavorable to the medical scientist role were reinforced. It was hypothesized that reinforcing such responses should result in decreased performance on the dynamometer task.

Finally, to control for the possibility of spontaneous changes in response from the first 24 to the remaining 30 items on the MSQ, a further control group was added. These subjects were given the MSQ and asked to complete the questionnaire privately.

The major results indicate that compared to the group that completed the MSQ in private, the group reinforced for favorable MSQ responses increased significantly in their favorability toward medical science. This result replicated the earlier study with a second examiner. For subjects reinforced for favorable MSQ attitudes, the degree of change in dynamometer performance was significantly associated with their change in attitude. The absence of a similar correlation in the nonreinforced control group confirmed the specificity of this association. The group receiving a fixed amount of reinforcement irrespective of response (MSIS) did not improve in dynamometer score, indicating that reinforcement, per se, did not affect performance. Contrary to prediction, but consistent with the findings of Ullmann, Krasner, and Sherman (1963b) described above, a significant change in the group reinforced for unfavorable attitudes was not obtained.

Thus, we feel that the results of these four studies can be used to emphasize the general themes we have been presenting in this chapter: verbal conditioning is a major aspect of traditional psychotherapy; verbal conditioning is prototypical of the social influence situation; verbal conditioning is a "treatment" procedure in its own right.[1]

---

[1] Further recent confirmation of these themes was obtained by Ullmann et al. (in press).

## SUMMARY DISCUSSION

As a focus for summarizing this general discussion of verbal conditioning and psychotherapy, we will comment briefly on comparisons made by Luborsky and Strupp (1962), which emphasize the differences between verbal conditioning and psychotherapy. Their seven arguments are as follows:

1. The role expectancies in operant conditioning and in psychotherapy are quite different. Patients in psychotherapy are ordinarily voluntary participants who want to change in certain areas. Subjects in an operant conditioning experiment do not experience themselves as being in a helping relationship; they participate for a variety of (often unrelated and unclarified) reasons. 2. The change that can be effected through operant conditioning may not be very deep, lasting or extensive. 3. The extent of the emotional involvement in operant conditioning experiments is considerably less than in psychotherapy. 4. Change in psychotherapy is mediated quite differently. 5. Individuals who do change via operant conditioning experiments are those who want to please. This is not necessarily true in psychotherapy. 6. The definition of reinforcement is too general in the operant conditioning experiments. It is unclear what is being reinforced. 7. The nature of that which is influenced in psychotherapy is much more complex than that which is influenced in operant conditioning; for example, in operant conditioning it is "plural nouns" or some such specific response. (Luborsky & Strupp, 1962, pp. 312-313)

Our discussion thus far has focused on the similarities between verbal conditioning and psychotherapy and emphasized that the assertion of these differences are not justified. The differences in role expectancy are of the same order as any differences in procedure between types of behavior influence. Further, these differences can themselves be altered by the manipulation of instructional sets (Ekman, Krasner, & Ullmann, 1963).

The extensiveness and length of the changes brought about by conditioning have been demonstrated repeatedly (Ullmann & Krasner, 1965). Throughout this volume, there are references to specific cases, which indicate that long-lasting effects may indeed be achieved through operant conditioning procedures. Further, we have presented evidence that changing verbal behavior has consequences for behaviors other than those directly changed (Krasner, Knowles, & Ullmann, 1964). It need not be emphasized, of course, that traditional psychotherapy itself has had considerable difficulty in demonstrating long-term effects (Eysenck, 1952, 1961).

The third point of Luborsky and Strupp, concerning lessened emotional involvement in verbal conditioning, is irrelevant. It brings into focus, as do the fourth and fifth points, the nature of change, and the variables involved. It is our contention that the variables effecting change in both instances are the same, and that they include expectancy of change and the interaction between examiner and subject variables. Thus, the subject's "desire to please" is a factor in both processes, as this attitude interacts with examiner or therapist characteristics, which facilitate or inhibit this "desire." Therapists believe that these interactions may be more complex in psychotherapy than in verbal conditioning. However, the interactions are equally lawful in both situations, and are clearer in the conditioning situation.

The sixth point, that the definition of reinforcement is too general in operant conditioning, is somewhat mystifying, since it is operationally clear as to what is being reinforced in verbal conditioning and how it is being reinforced. Finally, the psychotherapy situation has always been considered to be so complex that it defies adequate description. The operant conditioner would say that this is a criticism of psychotherapy itself, in that the procedures unnecessarily increase the complexity of issues. It is part of the task of the therapist to help simplify the patient's task, rather than extend its complexities.

As an over-all summary statement, we would emphasize the fact that the verbal conditioning studies have represented an important advance in investigating the process of changing deviant behavior. We have presented illustrations of this, and the next two chapters, by Sarason and Kanfer, further extend the points made in this chapter.

# 10

## The Human Reinforcer in Verbal
## Behavior Research*

### IRWIN G. SARASON

Sarason has produced a long and distinguished list of investigations of verbal behavior (Sarason, 1958a, 1958b, 1959, 1962; Sarason & Campbell, 1962; Sarason & Ganzer, 1962; Sarason & Minard, 1963). While the scope and complexity of these researches have steadily increased, Sarason has consistently related his work to psychotherapy. The title of one of Sarason's early papers (1958a) typifies the focus of his investigations: "Interrelationships among Individual Difference Variables, Behavior in Psychotherapy, and Verbal Conditioning." Sarason has used complex statistical designs to investigate relationships among subject, examiner, and situational variables through interaction terms. As he himself clearly points out, he has steadily introduced new variables in his investigations of verbal behavior.

In this chapter, which explicitly focuses on the role of the examiner-therapist-reinforcer, Sarason cogently brings together much of the material touched upon in previous chapters. Salzinger et al. and Patterson emphasized the importance of the human reinforcer and the changes brought about by his response contingent behavior. Chapters by Matarazzo et al. and by Krasner presented further details of the examiner's reinforcing behavior. In this chapter, Sarason presents evidence that if the reinforcer is defined as a contingent stimulus, the person dispensing the reinforcement is a significant aspect of that stimulus configuration. That is, the experimenter or therapist, when he uses his own behavior as the reinforcing stimulus, is an important and inseparable part of the reinforcement "machine" (Krasner, 1962b). Further, as pointed out by Orne (1962) and Rosenthal (1963), whom Sarason cites, there is a total social situation which includes the experimenter's attitudes and the very subtle cues which he emits. These cues, slight and subtle as they may be, are measurable and manipulable.

Sarason's research indicates how sensitive social influence situations are to the examiner's behavior. This evidence answers the often expressed criticism

* The preparation of this paper was facilitated by a research grant (M-3889) from the National Institute of Mental Health.

229

that the social reinforcement approach is too "mechanical" (Shoben, 1963; May, 1963). In fact, rather than being mechanical, the therapist is conceived of as an individual whose "stock in trade" is his behavior as a human being. In this framework, it is possible to translate into operational terms, as Sarason does, a concept such as transference, Like Matarazzo, Wiens, and Saslow (Chapter 8), Sarason implies that the therapist's knowledge of the effects of his own behavior is at least equal to if not better than a prolonged psychoanalysis. Sarason is somewhat critical of attempts to avoid problems of examiner influence by the introduction of "hardware." It is interesting to compare Freud and "hardware"-oriented behaviorists such as Lindsley (1956). Both think it desirable to eliminate examiner influence in the interpersonal situation. Freud attempted to do this by suggesting personal analysis to make the therapist aware of his own problems, by seating arrangements in which the therapist was unseen, and by a minimal amount of therapist verbalization. Lindsley (1962), on the other hand, uses "hardware" to the point where the therapist is in a room some distance away from the patient and can be seen and heard only on a television screen. However, the physical elimination of the examiner does not necessarily rule out examiner effects and remains one of the most important variables in the situation. Subjects and patients may still react to investigators or therapists, even when not physically present, because human beings emit all kinds of unpredictable ("imaginative") verbal stimuli in response to a situation in which another human being has placed them.

The major attribute of a science is the replicability of its experiments. Because of unmeasured examiner effects, Sarason questions (as do Orne and Rosenthal) the replicability of a large percentage of research with human subjects. Rosenthal and Fode (1963b) investigated the examiner variables in the area of animal learning and, even in this area of "pure" science, questioned the reproducibility of these studies.

If examiner differences are so important, they should be sampled and eventually controlled in the manner illustrated by Sarason. For clinical purposes, as Matarazzo, Wiens, and Saslow pointed out, therapist differences should be capitalized upon. An illustration of this view comes from placebo research (Krasner, Ullmann, & Fisher, 1964; Krasner, Knowles, & Ullmann, 1964). Whereas the problem had previously been conceptualized in terms of eliminating "placebo effects," it would seem reasonable to maximize placebo effects in the treatment situation to increase the likelihood of client change. The evidence is growing that "placebo effect" is a euphemism for examiner influence variables. Thus, while Sarason points out a source of behavior influence which must be measured and controlled in research, in treatment the therapist must be aware of these variables and use them. In addition to the overwhelming historical evidence of the effectiveness of the "powerful placebo" (Shapiro, 1960), studies using placebos to control for suggestion repeatedly indicate their potency in comparison with "real" medicine (Frank, 1961). Paul (1964) has offered convincing data to show that placebos, as a therapeutic device, were equal to the therapeutic manipulations of experienced psychologists using the therapeutic techniques of their choice. Goldstein (1962) offers many additional instances of the importance of both therapist and patient expectancies in the modification of behavior.

Studies of a more clinical nature also give strong support for the points made by Sarason. A good general review is presented by Masling (1960), who surveyed the examiner variable in diagnostic testing. The influence of the examiner was found to be so strong that the value of much of traditional diagnostic testing had to be questioned. Masling (1957) controlled interviewee behavior by using attractive female shills who were told to act in a "warm" or "cold" manner to male "examiners" giving them a personality test. The dependent variable was the interpretation given by these examiners (graduate students) to the "subject's" sentence-completion protocols. Masling found that the protocols of "warm" subjects elicited more favorable examiner interpretations than did the protocols of the "cold" subjects. Russell (1961) found that in an initial interview, "negative" clients generated more interview anxiety than did "positive" clients. Heller, Myers, and Kline (1963) using accomplices found that interviewers confronted with client friendliness responded with agreeable behavior. However, interviewers confronted with client hostility responded with subtle counterhostility. Further studies (Bandura, Lipsher, & Miller, 1960; Murray, 1956) show how the therapist or diagnostician influences and reacts to the content he obtains. In the same vein, Ullmann (1961) found highly significant differences among psychologists in designating patients as "testable" or "untestable." If such differences enter in the early stage of sample selection, then examiner differences will certainly influence the final results.

In short, Sarason supplements and extends the comments made by earlier contributors as to: the importance of the examiner in influence situations, the usefulness of the verbal conditioning paradigm for the investigation of social influence variables, and the direct applications of experimental results to the improvement of clinical effectiveness.

L.K.-L.P.U.

WHAT IS ATTEMPTED IN this chapter is to (a) show that characteristics of experimenters as possible sources of variability among subjects have been largely neglected in psychological research, and (b) suggest some of the ways in which these characteristics might be incorporated into the body of psychological knowledge. The procedure selected for making these two points is to start with a review of the general problem of the experimenter as an independent variable in psychological investigations and to cite examples of the problem's dimensions; and then, to attempt to narrow the focus to the area with which this series of papers is specifically concerned—changes in verbal behavior and verbal learning.

## REVIEW OF LITERATURE

A review of experimental literature in many fields of psychology reveals two incongruous conditions. The first is the strong motivation of psychologists to make the psychological experiment as powerful a tool as possible in their efforts to develop a science of psychology and to control and manipulate variables that might affect subjects' behavior. The second is that certain relevant, and possibly crucial, variables have to a large extent been neglected in psychological experiments—specifically, the need to assess the influences over subjects' behavior of (a) individual differences associated with experimenters, and (b) social contextual variables.

Brunswik (1956) and Hammond (1954), among others, have emphasized the importance of not only sampling subjects in experiments, but also experimenters and the situations and the contexts in which subjects and experimenters interact with each other. A recent paper by McGuigan (1963) has clearly demonstrated the relevance of the experimenter variable to problems of research design. Perhaps the areas in which the interpersonal or social aspects of experiments and situations have been most clearly recognized are those of (a) statistics and design of experiments, (b) clinical psychology and psychiatry, and (c) social psychology and personality.

Statisticians (for example, Edwards, 1960; Fisher, 1951; Lindquist, 1956) have been especially concerned with the generalizations which are drawn on the basis of statistically significant differences between groups. For example, in a study of learning in which one experimenter runs two groups of subjects using different methods with each, statistically significant differences between the groups may be difficult to interpret because of the confounding of the experimenter with the conditions of the experiment. Usually, investigators are interested in generalizing about obtained results. In this hypothetical experiment, however, there is no way of knowing whether another experimenter using the same methods could be expected to obtain results comparable to those obtained by the one used in the study.

In the fields of clinical psychology and psychiatry there has been a growing concern with the effects of patient-therapist, tester-testee, and subject-experimenter interaction on progress in therapy, diagnostic test findings, and results of clinical research. Numerous writers have called attention to the need for systematic study of the clinician and the context in which he functions as well as the need for studying the patient and his problem (Bandura, 1956; Bandura, Lipsher, & Miller, 1960; Frank, 1959, 1961; Goldman-Eisler, 1952; Hollingshead & Redlich 1958; Krasner, 1955, 1962b; Sarason, 1954; Strupp, 1962). It is interesting that Strupp (1962), in a review of the psychotherapy literature, expressed the view that the increasing concern with the variable of the therapist and his attributes is one of the most salutary recent developments in the clinical area.

## ROLE OF VARIABLES

There seems little question that "extraneous" variables such as the experimenter's characteristics and the context in which the experimenter and subject interact are receiving increasing attention and recognition from researchers. It would seem that what is currently needed is the step from simply recognizing the possible importance of these variables for psychological research to actual data-gathering in which the following sorts of factors are considered and manipulated and their effects assessed: (a) individual differences among subjects, for example, personality variables and sex; (b) individual differences among experimenters; (c) social, interpersonal, and situational variables, for example, the way in which the subject's task is structured to him, the instructional sets created, and the amount of verbal and social interaction between the subject and experimenter during the experiment.

There are many studies which relate to the first and third of these classes of variables. Researchers in many fields of psychology have found it worthwhile to incorporate the sex and personality characteristics of the subjects into research designs. For example, the experimental literature using anxiety scales may be viewed as one attempt to answer the question: what is the effect on the subject's performance of characteristics that he brings into the experimental situation? Thus, a number of investigators interested in learning have found it worthwhile to relate previously obtained subject's anxiety scores to the learning of different types of material (Axelrod, Cowen, & Heilizer, 1956; Krasner, 1958b; Matarazzo, Matarazzo, Saslow, & Phillips, 1958; Sarason, 1958b, 1959, 1960). Other illustrations of the increasing recognition and manipulation of questionnaire-inferred subject characteristics may be found in literature on need for achievement (Atkinson, 1958), introversion-extraversion (Eysenck, 1955, 1956), authoritarianism (Adorno, Frenkel-Brunswik, Levinson, & Sanford, 1950), and persuasibility and susceptibility to influence (Asch, 1956; Berg & Bass, 1961; Hovland, Janis, & Kelley, 1953; Janis, 1954). Recently, Carlson and Carlson (1960) have reviewed a sample of experiments in which sex of the subject was included as an independent variable. Their compilation showed that in 69 percent of the studies there were statistically significant differences due to this variable. In view of the heterogeneity of the problems studied in their sample, it would be difficult to think of many tasks or situations in which one could, a priori, rule out sex of the subject as a relevant variable.

The literature dealing with social, interpersonal, or situational variables is well exemplified by work that has been done on ego-involvement, instructional sets in relation to the subject's performance, and learning (Alper, 1946a, 1946b; Kanfer & Karas, 1959; Lazarus, Deese, & Osler, 1952; Sarason, 1960). Additional examples may be found in work on conformity and other areas of social psychology (Abelson, 1959; Asch, 1956; Back, 1951; Berg & Bass, 1961; Festinger, 1957; Kelman, 1956; McDavid, 1962; Schachter, 1959; Schutz, 1958). Interestingly, many investigators who have done work on instructional and situational variables have come to the conclusion that the value of manipulating aspects of the experimental situation is maximized when personality and other individual difference variables are also incorporated into the design of the experiments (Atkinson, 1958; Greenspoon, 1955, 1962; Lazarus, Deese, & Osler, 1952; Sarason, 1960; Tatz, 1956). In a general review paper dealing with effects of stress upon performance, Lazarus, Deese, and Osler (1952) have pointed out the marked lack of consistency in results of studies in this area. The authors point out that one factor contributing to the heterogeneity of findings is the unreplicability of experimental techniques employed in the various researches. Two of the points raised by the authors are: (a) the need to control and manipulate characteristics associated with the subjects, and (b) the need to control and manipulate characteristics of the experimenters, and of experimental stress situations. Although there has been some progress, since publication of this article in 1952, in the study of subject personality variables (for example, anxiety scales, introversion-extraversion indices, and MMPI measures), characteristics of the experimenters, who are presumed to create stress by means of verbal communications, are still largely unexplored and uncontrolled.

Despite the absence of systematic series of studies on experimenter variables and the social aspects of psychological experiments, there is a growing body of research that provides a basis for optimism that these variables are beginning to receive the attention they deserve as possible parameters in experiments. Riecken (1958, 1960) has called attention to the need for study of the impact of the many aspects of experimental situations on the subject. Orne (1962) has strikingly demonstrated the reasonableness of Riecken's concern. Orne found that highly intelligent subjects persisted for a long period of time in performing an apparently boring and repetitive task. Inquiry of the subjects after the experiment proper had ended indicated that the subjects' persistent behavior was a function of hypotheses which they had concerning the nature of the experiment and of the expectation of the experimenter. Riecken's and

Orne's papers make clear the need to recognize the subject as a nonpassive responder, and, furthermore, as a responder who may not respond only to stimuli formally presented to him by the experimenter, but, also, may respond to "extraneous" variables such as the experimenter's sex, personality, and manner. A conclusion to which both of these writers have come is that much more use must be made of postexperimental inquiry of the subjects in order to gain a better idea of their conception of the experimental situation. Additionally, this sort of postexperimental information could be very useful to researchers in directing their attention to variables hitherto ignored. Farber (1963) has reviewed some of the literature on verbal conditioning, particularly with regard to the question of the subject's awareness of the experimenter's reinforcements. His review led him to the conclusion that postexperimental inquiry should not be restricted simply to specific issues such as: was the subject aware of the experimenter's reinforcements? Rather, Farber recommends careful analysis of aspects of the subject's total response to the experimental situation:

> Subjects may not know exactly what is going on in an experiment or, for that matter, in a therapeutic session, but very few have no ideas at all. They may be mistaken, or they may be concerned with irrelevant matters, such as whether participation in the experiment is worth the time and trouble, or whether the counselor is as blase as he seems, or what's for lunch. The one thing psychologists can count on is that their subjects or clients will talk, if only to themselves. And, not infrequently, whether relevant or irrelevant, the things people say to themselves determine the rest of the things they do (Farber, 1963, p. 196).

## ROLE OF EXPERIMENTER

It has been suggested that the experimenter might be a significant aspect of any experiment whether the investigator recognizes it or not, and whether he wishes to be or not. What evidence is there that this suggestion has merit? Although the literature is scattered there have been several studies in which more than one experimenter was used and in which comparisons between experimenters were made (Binder, McConnell, & Sjoholm, 1957; Ferguson & Buss, 1960; Rosenthal, 1961, 1962; Rosenthal & Fode, 1963a; Rosenthal & Lawson, 1962; Salzinger & Pisoni, 1960; Verplanck, 1955). For example, Axelrod, Cowen, and Heilizer (1956) performed an experiment involving the stylus-maze learning of subjects differing in Taylor Manifest Anxiety Scale scores. The aim of the study was to evaluate certain hypotheses stemming from learning theory. Few of the results relating to the major concerns of the study reached statistical significance. However, significant results were obtained for the following interactions: Anxiety × Experiments, Anxiety × Sex of Subjects,

Experimenters × Subjects, and Anxiety × Experimenters × Sex of Subjects. Unfortunately, only three experimenters were employed in this experiment and there is no basis for inferring which experimenter characteristics led to the significant differences among them. The authors express concern over the absence of efforts in the anxiety and learning areas to explore systematically aspects of the experimenter variable.

An experiment by Binder, McConnell, and Sjoholm (1957) employed one male and one female experimenter in a verbal conditioning experiment using mildly hostile verbs as a response class with "Good" as the reinforcement. While reinforcement of the response class led to an increase in usage of the mildly hostile verbs, it was also found that the two experimenters differed significantly in the learning rates which they obtained from subjects. The authors concluded that ". . . future research could be profitably directed toward determining the specific personality and/or physical characteristics of experimenters which lead to differential learning effects, the types of learning situations in which such effects occur, and the constructs from learning and personality theory which account for the phenomena."

A recent study reported by Sapolsky (1960) supports the conclusions drawn by Binder, McConnell, and Sjoholm. Sapolsky investigated the effects of interpersonal factors in the experimental situation on verbal conditioning. Both subjects and experimenters were selected on the basis of Schutz's FIRO-B (1958). Sapolsky found that the effects of reinforcement on the subject's usage of the reinforced response class depended significantly on the compatibility or incompatibility of the subject and experimenter score patterns on this measure. The Sapolsky study is especially interesting because of its relationship to Schutz's interpersonal theory (Schutz, 1958) and because he not only included the experimenter as independent variable but, also, selected his experimenters on the basis of the same personality characteristic. Studies such as those of Axelrod, Cowen, and Heilizer (1956) and Binder, McConnell, and Sjoholm (1957) enable one to compare experimenters, but one does not know what there is about the different experimenters which might lead them to obtain different results.

A review of the experimenter variable would be incomplete without reference to the work of Rosenthal (Rosenthal, 1961, 1962; Rosenthal & Fode, 1963a; Rosenthal & Lawson, 1962), who has performed a series of experiments in which the set of the experimenter in running the subjects was experimentally manipulated. Rosenthal's findings provide evidence that the experimenter's attitudes toward his experiment and toward the subjects significantly influence the behavior of the subjects. Perhaps the most provocative aspect of Rosenthal's results was a study carried out with Lawson which indicated that the experimenter's set was as important in experiments using rats as subjects as in experiments with humans (Rosenthal & Lawson, 1962).

If this paper has been successful thus far, it is safe to assume that the importance of knowing as much as we can about the experimenters who conduct psychological research has been established. This means, of course, that the dangers of ignoring experimenter characteristics have been suggested effectively, also. If the assumption about the existence of the experimenter problem is correct, then, what do we do about it?

One solution, the one which has been predominant in psychology, is to ignore or perceptually defend against it. This solution is too close to the tendency of children and disturbed persons to deny the presence of anxiety-provoking stimuli to merit serious consideration. Another solution is to recognize that the experimenter may be confounded with manipulated experimental treatments and to eliminate this confounding by eliminating the experimenter. Many of the staunch proponents of brass-instrument psychology would appear to find this tactic an appealing one.

The solution of eliminating the experimenter, in addition to being a tempting one, is, also, a perfectly legitimate one. There is nothing wrong with using instrumentation in presenting problems to and communicating with subjects. The relevant point would seem to be that our subject matter should influence our instrumentation rather than the reverse being the case. There is no doubt that significant contributions can be made to the study of verbal behavior by use of many situations in which human intervention, in the person of the experimenter, is absent, and nonhuman signaling devices are used in his place. However, it should be noted that the use of a seemingly impersonal experimental set-up does not eliminate all social stimuli since subjects inevitably will have thoughts and hypotheses about the basis for and rationale of the experiment, and, implied in this interest, curiosity about the creator of the experiment, our old nemesis, the experimenter.

## PSYCHOANALYTIC APPROACH

Within the field of psychotherapy, another approach to the experimenter, or, in this case, the therapist, is to be found within the psychoanalytic framework. Obviously Freud was not interested in depersonalizing the therapy situation. But he was interested in gaining a measure of control and standardization over it. The concepts of transference and countertransference are certainly likely candidates for consideration as milestones in the study not only of unconscious processes, but, also, of social interaction. As we all know, the way in which Freud hoped that the psychotherapy situation could approach a degree of standardization was the therapist's awareness, through his personal psychoanalysis, of the implications of countertransference.

Important as Freud's contribution may be, the concept of countertransference does not appear to be the ultimate answer to the researcher's problems. To take what may be the weakest aspect of the application of the countertransference notion, the therapist's ability to cope with transference is dependent on the degree to which his personal psychoanalysis was a successful one. In the absence of highly reliable indices of the degree of this success, it would seem prudent for researchers to examine as many approaches as may suggest themselves to the study of the experimenter variable.

One starting point is to select a characteristic (or characteristics) in which we are interested and, then, to compare the behaviors of subjects as a function of experimenter difference on that characteristic. It seems likely that one of the reasons for the lacunae concerning the effects of the experimenter variable is the large number of organismic and personality differences on which experimenters differ. From which point along the shore of an unfamiliar body of water do we venture forth? Fortunately for the researcher, he can perform pilot work on the basis of which a decision can be made. It is probable that what will inevitably have to occur in the early stages of research on the experimenter variable is the performance of many experiments in which varieties of experimenters and other variables are manipulated. As was suggested earlier, three major classes of variables that merit simultaneous investigation are: (a) subject, (b) experimenter, and (c) situational, social, or contextual variables. Systematic study of these variables should prove of real value in developing theoretical frameworks within which the psychological experiment can be integrated.

It is hoped that the comments thus far have been more than a preamble to a consideration of aspects of the problem of reinforcement in effecting verbal behavior change. It is believed that the relevance of the experimenter variable to the social psychology of the experiment is even more dramatic in the case of general psychology than in the area defined by issues surrounding verbal conditioning research. But research on influencing changes in verbal behavior represents a powerful vehicle by means of which the impact of the human experimenter on the subject can be approached. There are two bases for urging the systematic use of more than one experimenter in studies of verbal behavior. On purely practical grounds it is important to know if two listeners or human reinforcers are, in some degree, comparable. When two different experimenters emit the "same" reinforcement, the effects on subjects may be quite different. These differences should be treated systematically and not haphazardly. On more theoretical grounds, knowing how different people affect others should contribute to our understanding of social behavior. In this sense, the verbal conditioning type of situation may be viewed as a prototype of one large class of social encounters, those in which reinforcements are employed, either consciously or unconsciously, to influence the behavior of someone else.

## STUDIES OF EXPERIMENTER ROLE

A good bit of the evidence that suggests the utility of studying the effects of reinforcement from the standpoint of personality and social psychology has already been mentioned. A few studies will now be discussed in somewhat more detail. These studies, because they did involve the simultaneous manipulation of subject, experimenter, and contextual variables seem especially germane to the strong emphasis that has been placed on the need for future research on these variables. The investigations to be discussed involve two classes of situations. One involves verbal conditioning and free verbalization paradigms. The other more closely resembles testing, learning, and achievement situations that have been of great interest to psychologists.

Several investigations which make a very strong case for the need to intensively study the variable of the experimenter will first be discussed. Winkel and Sarason (1964) performed a verbal learning experiment in which three organismic variables were examined. They were the test anxiety of subjects and experimenters and the subjects' sex. Test anxiety was inferred from the Test Anxiety Scale (Sarason, 1958a; Sarason & Ganzer, 1962). There were, also, two experimental variables: (a) preperformance differential motivating instructions, and (b) success-failure reports administered during learning.

The results demonstrated that the performance of the subjects was as much a function of the experimenter's level of test anxiety as of the subjects' own level. Furthermore, the effects of the experimental conditions on the subjects' performance were significantly influenced by the level of test anxiety of the experimenters. Winkel and Sarason (1964) interpreted these findings in this way:

> One cannot generalize from the present findings to the effects of the E variable for other kinds of tasks, settings, and research problems. However, on the basis of our results, it would appear that investigators studying diverse problems well may be flirting with danger if they ignore the potential "problems" posed by the E variable for other areas. For example, one wonders what effects E variables might have on S's behavior in a situation quite different from the one in which we have been interested, a simple psychophysical methods experiment. One would hope in such experiments to avoid E's influencing S's responses. However, unhappily, there might be unforeseen interactions of E variables with the very methods under study. It well may be that a major characteristic of E is his tendency, whether recognized or not, to serve as a discriminative, reinforcing cue for S. The point to be emphasized is that, at present, the dimensions of E-S variables are unknown. Our results provide encouragement to probe more deeply in these uncharted waters.

Another demonstration of the role of the experimenter may be found in a study carried out by Sarason and Harmatz (in press). These investigators were interested in the effects on verbal learning of positive and negative reinforcements administered by the experimenter. Some of their experimental groups were told in the course of learning that they were doing a fine job on the task on which they were working. Other subjects were told that they should work harder at improving their level of performance. The finding of the experiment of most relevance to the present discussion was that the effects of these experimentally manipulated comments interacted significantly with the characteristics of the experimenters who administered them. While, in general, favorable comments led to faster learning than did the unfavorable ones, it also was the case that the deliverer of the comments made a very real difference in influencing the performance of subjects.

Using as his experimental task a projective technique, Heath's Phrase Association Test, Barnard (1963) carried out a suggestive piece of research which bears directly on the question of the role of the experimenter or examiner in the testing situation. Barnard selected both subjects and experimenters on the basis of their scores on a hostility scale. This design, also, involved administration of the Phrase Association Test to both subjects and experimenters. Among the many significant results which Barnard obtained were the following:

1. Subjects tested by experimenters who themselves had shown a high degree of disturbance on the association task showed more association disturbance than subjects tested by experimenters who had shown little disturbance.

2. Subjects tested by low-hostile experimenters showed more association disturbance than did subjects tested by high-hostile experimenters.

3. Postexperimental questionnaires administered to the subjects (these questionnaires were not administered by the subject's experimenter) showed that experimenters who obtained high hostility scores were perceived by subjects as being more angry during the experiment than low-hostile experimenters.

4. For certain experimental subgroups, subjects' association disturbances appeared to be a function of the number of experimental sessions in which the experimenter had previously participated.

This last finding may provide us with a clue concerning a source of unreliability in many types of psychological research. The experimenters' behavior and attitudes may undergo significant change and adaptation as the number of *his* trials increases. In this connection, Barnard found that his experimenters did report a decided drop in their anxiety in the experimental situation as the number of sessions increased. Perhaps we should begin paying as much attention to distribution of practice among experimenters as among subjects.

Turning from performance and testing situations to those involving operant conditioning and free verbalization, there is evidence that the interaction of subject and experimenter characteristics can exert powerful influences over the degree to which the subject increases his usage of responses reinforced by the experimenter. Sarason (1962) and Sarason and Minard (1963) have found that the hostility of experimenters, as well as the hostility of subjects, influences verbal conditioning. Their results suggest that these influences occur whether the reinforced response class is hostile in connotation or seemingly neutral.

Symons (1964), in a recent experiment, obtained measures of nurturance and dominance on a sample of female experimenters. His subjects, who were also women, were categorized in terms of degree of anxiety. In his experiment, he had each experimenter interview a subject on three occasions spanning a three week period. The task for the subject on each occasion was to present a description of herself. Symons found that the personality characteristics of experimenters, as well as those of subjects, significantly influenced the ways in which the subjects talked about themselves. Campbell's findings (1960) concerning verbal conditioning tend to corroborate this finding.

Among the many specific relationships that turned up in Symons' research were these:

1. Subjects interviewed by high-dominant experimenters made more negative self-references than did subjects interviewed by low-dominant experimenters.

2. High-anxious subjects, regardless of the personality of the experimenter, generally made more negative self-references than did low-anxious subjects.

3. However, low-anxious subjects interviewed by high-dominant experimenters described themselves in more negative terms than did low-anxious subjects interviewed by low-dominant experimenters.

It is important in evaluating the influence of the experimenter or reinforcer to the experimental situation to be aware that this influence may be variable. This variability may, in part, be due to the type of experiment under consideration. Koenig (1962, 1963) and Winkel (1963) have found that subjects' postexperimental descriptions of themselves and their experimenters depended upon what went on during the experimental session. For example, Koenig found that subjects' reinforcement histories in a verbal behavior situation were related to their descriptions of the persons who had done the reinforcing, that is, the experimenters.

## SUMMARY

These verbal behavior experiments bear on the many studies that have shown that reinforcement exerts a powerful influence over individuals' utterances and their performance. They show that the agent (the experimenter), who performs the reinforcing operation, or who just listens, is of substantial importance. The more we know about him and the situation in which he operates, the closer will we come to converting the experimenter variable from an annoying, extraneous one to the theoretically interesting and meaningful one it should be.

In addition to the need for intensive study of subjects' and experimenters' personalities, together with their bodily and other individual difference characteristics, there are other variables (dependent and independent) and problems which eventually will have to be examined in the study of the psychological experiment. These include the following:

1. The degree of psychological sophistication of the experimenter and his level of training in research.

2. The degree to which the experimenter (as well as the subject) adapts to the situation in which he is functioning. Related to this point are considerations such as the number of subjects run by the experimenter over a given time period and the interval between experimental sessions. Most psychotherapists and physicians would probably agree that their behavior with patients at 4:00 o'clock in the afternoon is not the same as at 9:00 o'clock in the morning.

3. The effects of experimenter, subject, and contextual variables over time and over experimental experience. Do these effects change as a function of the number of subject-experimenter contacts?

4. The subjective and affective responses of subjects to experimenters, and the comparable responses of experimenters to subjects. Does the friendliness of the experimenter necessarily affect the subject's verbalizations or learning in the experimental situation?

5. To what extent do subject, experimenter, and situational variables have comparable effects over tasks? It seems possible that some experimenters might be better at eliciting certain response classes from certain types of subjects than from other subjects. Clinical evidence certainly suggests that psychotherapists vary in their handling of various types of patients.

In conclusion, a disclaimer is entered in order to avoid the appearance of arguing for the universal significance of the experimenter and related variables. The argument has not been that the personality, or sex, or socioeconomic status of the experimenter will always influence subject's verbalizations and performance. Rather it has been asserted that there is evidence that the experimenter is a relevant variable in certain types of situations involving social interaction between subjects and the experimenter. The conclusion is that it is high time to begin exploring the dimensions of these situations.

# 11

## Vicarious Human Reinforcements: A Glimpse into the Black Box*

### FREDERICK H. KANFER

Kanfer has published widely on the problems and variables of verbal conditioning (Kanfer, 1954, 1958; Kanfer & Karas, 1959; Kanfer & Marston, 1961, 1962a, 1962b, 1962c; Marston, Kanfer, & McBrearty, 1962), interview behavior (Kanfer, 1959, 1960b; Kanfer, Bass, & Guyett, 1963; Kanfer & McBrearty, 1962), reinforcement in learning (Kanfer & Matarazzo, 1959), relationships of psychotherapy to learning theory (Kanfer, 1960a, 1961, 1962), and problems such as awareness (Kanfer & McBrearty, 1961), self-reinforcement (Kanfer, Bradley, & Marston, 1962; Kanfer & Marston, 1963a, 1963c), and vicarious reinforcement (Kanfer & Marston, 1963b).

Self-reinforcement calls attention to the individual's own behavior as an important aspect of his environment. Vicarious reinforcement is important in the training of both therapist and patient. It is a common training procedure for a therapist to model his behavior upon that of his supervisor or other "expert." This is done through consultation, books, tape recordings, one-way screens, and clinical demonstrations. It is a frequent observation (Marmor, 1961) that the patient does in fact model his behavior after that of the therapist. The patient may use the therapist as a source of self-reinforcing stimuli, that is, "I asked myself what you would want me to do." Because the modeling is not used systematically by the therapist, the patient may become more similar to the therapist in ways that are irrelevant to the behavior that needs to be changed (Sheehan, 1951). Matarazzo et al. (Chapter 8) demonstrate how formal aspects of the therapist's speech can become patient models. There have been numerous clinical observations of patients displaying gestural and other motoric behaviors similar to their therapists. Here is a method of influencing behavior which therapists do not at present use systematically. However, it could be capitalized on by matching therapists with patients or by having the therapist alter his behavior in specified

* Studies reported in this paper were supported in part by research grants MH 06922-01 and -02 from the National Institute of Mental Health, United States Public Health Service.

244

ways to provide the model of most use for the patient. Both the Kanfer and Bandura research illustrate that vicarious reinforcement is also effective when peers are used as models. The therapist can utilize vicarious reinforcement principles in recordings or films in which model behavior can be explicitly demonstrated and reinforced (Schroeder, 1964). In this approach the repertoire of the therapist, the behaviors available to him, can be grealty extended. However, the use of such techniques imply that the therapist knows what behavior he wants to influence. This leads to the therapist explicitly taking responsibility for assessment of the situation, the goals to set, and the methods to achieve these goals. The therapist's assumption of responsibility for behavior modification may be contrasted with the traditional psychoanalytic conceptualization of the therapist as one who deals with patients' dynamic mechanisms as they slowly unfold. In such situations, failure to change the patient's behavior is attributable to unconscious conflicts over which neither the patient nor the therapist has control. This leads to a paradoxical situation in that the failure to help the patient is blamed upon the patient's internal dynamics, while the patient is absolved of blame because these dynamics are unconscious and, therefore, not under his control. Kanfer starts his chapter by emphasizing this new therapist role. Perhaps the strongest statement of these views was Goldiamond's (1963) comment that it is therapist incompetency rather than patient nonreadiness to receive help that underlies failure in psychotherapy.

In developing experimental analogues of clinical problems, Kanfer investigates the topic of awareness. His discussion is relevant to several controversies in experimental and clinical psychology. There is a long-standing controversy over the possibility of behavior change without awareness (Adams, 1957). The clinical analogue of this problem is whether patients' behavior can change without their having first achieved "insight." Kanfer's experimental results place him on the general side of authors such as Verplanck (1962), Krasner, Weiss, and Ullmann (1961), and Krasner and Ullmann (1963), all of whom question the central role of awareness and conclude that "report of awareness" is itself a verbal behavior subject to the same variables as verbal conditioning. Insofar as the clinical situation is concerned, Saslow (Chapter 13) discusses the relationship between insight and changed behavior. Is it necessary for a patient to verbalize insights in order for his behavior to change, or does changed behavior increase the likelihood of the patient's emitting the verbal behavior labeled by the therapist as "insight"? Changes in behavior by manipulation of environmental stimuli enable the patient to become aware of his own behavior because the contrast between new and old behavior gives him a basis for comparison.

Awareness seems a strange concept to be discussed by behavior-oriented investigators. The main consideration, however, is how the problem is approached. Investigating it as Kanfer does, with operational definitions and reproducible manipulations, makes the study of awareness a legitimate matter in a volume on behavior modification. Thus, Kanfer has taken awareness and self-reinforcement out of the "black box" and put them under the light of the laboratory. In so doing, he has extended social reinforcement to new areas and considerably widened the scope of behavior modification.

L.K.-L.P.U.

Today it is no longer necessary to present arguments for the utility of learning theory applications in clinical psychology. Even the most stubborn defenders of the right of the clinician to play by different rules of the game than his fellow psychologists in the laboratory will admit that much of human behavior with which the clinician deals is learned, and that personality, at least at some levels, can be conceptualized as a system of interrelated learned habits and behavior patterns. However, many clinicians stop at this point. The assumption that behavior is learned simply is used as a foundation upon which little is built except a new vocabulary. Therefore, we find many clinicians pursuing their traditional practices and perpetuating old myths but doing so in a new language, freely and carelessly using such terms as reinforcement, responses, extinction, generalization, instead of more traditional terms such as libidinal drive or transference. This is simply a substitution of terminology and does not seem to represent sufficient progress toward a "new" clinical psychology.

## CURRENT STATUS OF CLINICAL PSYCHOLOGY

Many authors of recent books in clinical psychology, while purporting to present a new approach, continue to use psychoanalytic and other traditional frameworks. They feel less inferiority vis-à-vis their experimental colleagues and have the firm conviction that they are in the mainstream of psychology because their approach is presented in learning terms. It is significant that the many attempts at translation of other theoretical schemas into learning terms did not lead to any major research developments which helped to put clinical psychology on a more objective basis. Part of the problem lies in the fact that what we need in clinical psychology is not a series of new justifications, but a totally new approach; an approach which fills in our gaps of knowledge by the same tedious step-by-step procedures used in all sciences until we have a coherent conceptual schema from which analysis and prediction of human behavior can be made despite all its complexity, and not just for the simplest form of maze learning or lever-pushing. Such a theoretical approach can benefit from its early theoretical ancestors *only* insofar as hundreds of years of observations have resulted in some shrewd guesses as to what might be the important independent variables in human behavior and how they might affect various facets of thinking, imagining, acting, or failing to act. However, an objective approach cannot benefit from the *conceptual* schemas of the past because we are obviously not satisfied with them as explanatory models of human processes. Our purpose then should be to gather research data so that eventually we can cover within one conceptual schema, somewhat independent from previous ones, all the complex human processes with which we deal as clinicians.

Clinical psychology is in a transition today because we have not yet been able to amass the amount of information which would allow a clinician, for example, to draw upon well-supported scientific principles in individual cases with any degree of specificity and predictability. Nor do we have enough information to go directly to the task of isolating antecedents of current conditions that resulted in the problematic behavior of a patient. In other words, we have a general viewpoint but not much more. We do not yet have the information, for example, to know what to look for when a patient with a particular problem comes in, to know what are the factors which are likely to produce one particular symptom rather than another, or to know how the patient would best respond to psychotherapy or other treatments. Consequently, the content of clinical psychology is still determined quite heavily by antiquated theories and traditional speculations about the nature of the human mind. In the last two decades our methods have improved to the point that we now have available a battery of diagnostic instruments that may be highly reliable and standardized. Yet, *what* these tests are essentially seeking to analyze is vague, and the test performances do not show a consistent relationship to everyday patterns of interpersonal relationships, or thoughts, or actions.

For example, there is a good deal of information about the TAT, and too many of us, looking at a Thematic Apperception protocol, will recognize "significant" material. To date we are not quite sure, however, *what* it signifies, and whether to expect a direct or inverse correlation between the themas and feeling expressed in TAT stories and the person's actual behavior, except perhaps in the area of aggression, where specific studies have investigated various determinants of aggressive content in TAT records.

A scientific approach to clinical psychology requires a science which has information about (a) the development of individual behavior, (b) the factors which maintain it, and (c) the conditions under which it can be changed. Until such time, much of our "clinicking" remains an art. Now the productions of an artist are certainly not to be ridiculed. They require sensitivity, great skill, and considerable effort and time. But an artistic production is a child of chance. It is difficult to foresee in advance how it will turn out, and usually it is not possible to set up conditions so that one guarantees positive effects. An artist creates a new and unique thing each time and so does a psychotherapist when he works with his patient. When we consider the obvious demand for mass-producing behavioral changes in this era of neuroses and anxieties, the clinical psychologist as an artist is simply as uneconomical, as inefficient, and as appropriate to the jet age as a horse and buggy.

The solution to the ills of clinical psychology also does not lie in a direct translation of results obtained from controlled research on the white rat, although this has been a popular pursuit by many people. In extrapolating from one species to another, many of us have cherished the fond hope that it will be necessary only to change a few parameters here and there, and that many clinical problems can be directly investigated and solved by studying the white rat, more cheaply and with much less personal involvement than required in human research. Unfortunately, this assumption is partially incorrect. The remainder of this chapter will attempt to illustrate some of the problems that make the psychology of Man somewhat different from rat psychology and therefore require separate experimentation rather than simple extrapolation. Several of the characteristics of the human preclude any utilization of such simple constructs as may satisfactorily explain the behavior of the rat; mind you, not of the rat in its natural environment in a wheat field or in the kitchen cupboard, but the rat who has been raised in the rather sanitary and sterile conditions of the laboratory, from litter to incinerator with beautiful control over his social relationships, his emotional experiences, his digestive processes, and his exposure to mazes or Skinner boxes. In fact, it is doubtful that much of our rat psychology is applicable even to the field mouse, much less to the adult human! In other words, many principles discovered in animal research have been extremely important and basic. They have allowed us to test methods and simple conceptual models. The detailed findings, however, simply do not fit the complexity of the uncontrolled everyday environment and the social environment for man or mouse or kangaroo. In part the reason for the difference between animal and human research in which we have become interested might be called the difference inside the little "black box." The black box, as usually used, is a very nice schema for avoiding responsibilities beyond certain areas. We say that we control the behavior which is fed into an organism, call this a stimulus; sometimes we do not even worry whether the recipient of the stimulus actually observes it. Then we record the output (behavior). If we can establish correlations between these two conditions, and we can vary these systematically, we have obtained some control in the modification of the behavior of the organism. It is quite obvious that the organism itself has certain characteristics which in turn modify what happens between these two observed events. We have been interested in a human being's response to certain environmental conditions, even when he is not forced immediately to make a response that is obvious to all of us.

In many interactions we do not specify at length the physical character-istics of the environment to which we respond. For example, only in small children is verbal behavior under close control of observed objects. As adults we take things for granted. We respond, thinking that the next fellow sees what we do. For example, I might say, "This is a beautiful curtain." I am looking at curtains and I could describe them in terms of their color, in terms of their size, and so on. Usually I don't do this. Some-where between my first sensory (discriminating) response to the visual stimulus and my verbal response other processes may intervene. Finally, of course, I make a statement that is a consequence of a chain of responses "inside the black box." I am not sure that our methods of looking inside the black box, or at cognitive processes, or, if one wishes, mental processes, need to be different from the methods we have used to study S-R relationships. In other words, it is feasible under experimental con-ditions to make a subject specify each step in the chain, to slow down this complicated process for analysis and then to modify independently his discrimination of what he is reacting to, his reaction to his own response, or any subsequent step in the sequence.

## CONTRIBUTIONS OF LEARNING THEORY

Learning theory can offer us some principles, a conceptual schema, and a methodology as a starting point. The empirical *content*, however, will have to come from research conducted directly on the phenomena which we wish to understand. Since any behavior modification, including psychotherapy, is essentially a learning problem, when we define learning as a change in behavior, it becomes easy to assume that the same con-ditions hold for psychotherapy, for example, as for the task of a human or a rat finding its way through a maze. Unfortunately, many blind alleys of learning theory, at least for human application, have been created by Purina Chow pellets and by electric grids. Neither of these superb meth-ods of controlling rat behavior have any resemblance to the complex motivations which, for example, determine the interaction of a six-year-old with his mother. In addition to increased complexity, we also find differences with regard to motivation as we try to translate from one species to another. Finally, we have differences as to what constitutes a reinforcement for a rat or a human.

We must look back upon our own early enthusiasm with some dis-appointment, and it must be admitted that attempts to treat humans as if they were simple, nonsocial, and nonverbal organisms do not always

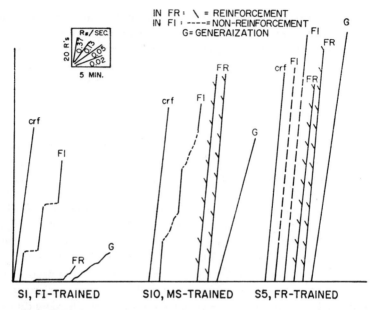

SI, FI-TRAINED          SIO, MS-TRAINED      S5, FR-TRAINED

Figure 11-1.    Individual cumulative records of college Ss working on Day 6 of a verbal conditioning study. (Kanfer, F. H., & Marston, A. R., "Control of verbal behavior by multiple schedules." Psychol. Rep., 1962, 10, 709.)

work. About 10 to 15 years ago researchers attempted for the first time to equate two kinds of procedures; bar-pressing by animals in the laboratory, yielding nice response curves, and human verbal behavior. These efforts gave rise to the area we know as verbal conditioning. Under some conditions humans do act very much like pigeons or rats.

Figure 11-1 gives the results of an experiment in which the subjects could be pigeon, rat, or human. The study was designed to investigate the effect of spacing reinforcements according to a certain time schedule. The study demonstrates that it is possible to get highly predictable curves with little variability and great precision. As a matter of fact, these curves are similar to Ferster and Skinner's (1957) curves that describe the response pattern in reaction to fixed-interval and fixed-ratio reinforcement.

Figure 11-1 presents the curves on fixed-ratio reinforcement of human subjects—college students in verbal conditioning—after these subjects had been trained for a period of several days. When one works with human beings long enough and consistently enough, much of the variability and many of the problems of self-instructions, complex self-correcting responses, or cognitive processes disappear. Even verbal behavior can become quite regular and predictable. These subjects were reinforced for talking in a situation similar to the analyst's free association. Every time they gave a word which was in the class of living animals they received a point, and when they had earned enough points they received money. Thus they sat and emitted words at a very high rate. The first day they didn't know what this was all about and their curves varied considerably. Gradually they quit thinking, guessing, testing hypotheses, or just playing games. Their behavior now came more fully under control of the experimental variables. The curves in Figure 11-1 were taken on the sixth day from different subjects who were trained in different ways. We actually wanted to see the differential effects of training on fixed-interval schedules, fixed-ratio schedules, and multiple schedules. The important point here is that under some conditions one can put a dependent variable under such tight control with human beings, even in verbal learning, which is probably the most complex activity that we can think of, so that the curves are quite regular, and we have results which would delight any scientist.

Direct application of these data is another story. Most of us are not in a situation in which we have people who are emitting verbal behavior for five or six consecutive days under relatively artificial conditions under consistent reinforcement for a limited class of responses. This kind of research is certainly feasible and necessary. In other situations, however, the human subject is trying to size up the experimenter; he wonders what this is all about, what the purpose of the experiment is, why he is here. Most often, unfortunately, we have used college sophomores who know very well they are here because they have to be. They may think about yesterday's date or tomorrow's date or many other things. In other words, in most human experimentation we have not been able to put the subject's behavior under total control.

What we finally see in this graph is a consequence of a combination of factors in addition to the ones we fed in. In other words, the experimenter feeds in one stimulus, the subject also provides some of his own. These are the situations that are the most challenging because they are the most revealing about the so-called natural behavior in humans. The problems in verbal conditioning have paved the way for two series of studies. Perhaps these experiments will shed some light on some of the processes inside the black box. The problems which we encountered are interesting because the original intent of researchers who first applied the verbal conditioning method to humans was to demonstrate the modifiability of verbal behavior with simple methods. It was hoped that there would be no need to concern ourselves with people's thinking or feeling about the experiment; we were going to concern ourselves only with the particular responses they make. As Figure 11-1 has shown, if we do this under certain specified conditions we can get people to act in a consistent fashion. However, partially because of the philosophical background of early behaviorism and its methodological emphasis we have often selected procedures yielding observable, instrumental, and nonverbal responses in artificially restricted laboratory situations. We have ignored much of our subject's concurrent activities, his response to the experimenter, the laboratory, the task requirements and so on. We have failed to ask our subjects what they are doing and to watch our subjects closely enough to see how they got to the answers which represented our dependent variable. There is no inherent merit in probing the private experiences and fantasies of our subjects. But it is possible to lose too much information by overzealous exclusion for the sake of methodological purity.

In situations in which human subjects attempt to test their notions about the purpose of an experiment, they are very much unlike any other experimental organisms. Humans may behave like rats or pigeons when the experimenter succeeds in putting a dependent variable under strict control of a single, powerful independent variable. More frequently, however, the human subject with his ability for a wide range of covert responses and a complex hierarchy of acquired reinforcements, responds not only to the experimentally controlled stimuli but also to his *own* varied reactions to them and to the total situation. The problems encountered in the study of verbal conditioning have pointed to what is a most important area of research for understanding human behavior, an area which had been naturally neglected on the basis of the general philosophy of early behaviorism as an "anti"-doctrine, and its attempts to deny the self-evaluating, self-motivating and self-instructing aspects of our human subjects. These psychological processes in humans are not necessarily sacred, mythical, or essentially different from other behaviors, but do require careful empirical study and consideration.

For a number of reasons described elsewhere (Kanfer, 1962), much of the difficulty in behavior modification on the human level lies in the fact that the human being is a self-correcting organism in whom much of the relevant behavior is verbal and sometimes nonvocal in nature. In other words, a person does lots of things at the same time, only some of which we observe. Many of the processes are difficult to observe, or even completely inaccessible under the *usual* experimental conditions. This does not mean, however, that we cannot eventually investigate and understand them if we arrange our conditions properly. It is interesting to note, by the way, that Skinner, who is notoriously known as a man who does not want to enter the black box, is the very same person who stands first among the few behaviorists who discusses the nature of private events. He even ventured to speculate about those behavioral processes that do go on in the black box (Skinner, 1953).

## INSIDE THE BLACK BOX

What is inside the black box first began to worry us in our early work on verbal conditioning. Although the task had been originally considered as the simplest type of operant conditioning, it became clear that the task in fact was, as Krasner pointed out in a previous chapter, a very complex one. After a series of studies we believed that to those subjects who weren't especially bored or preoccupied with other extraexperimental problems, the situation presented a challenge—to discover the purpose of the experiment and to understand "what was going on." A second and possibly *separate* event may be the gradual strengthening of the response class due to social reinforcement. Since solution of the former task, finding out what it is all about, may modify the latter, such findings as increased learning when subjects are "aware" or when instructions are less ambiguous would be expected. However, each process could be subject to modification by different variables and to different degrees. Thirdly, analysis of verbal conditioning data suggests that in many studies the training resulted not in operant conditioning or modification of a response class by reinforcement, but rather in discriminative learning. The subjects learned to attend to certain cues in the presented stimulus complex. Fourthly, the empirical data show a degree of variability which are considerably greater than in most laboratory learning studies. This finding further supports our speculation that personality (individual difference) variables, among others, affect this complex problem-solving behavior. In addition, in verbal conditioning studies extinction has usually not been obtained, nor has the gradual decrement in response strength that would reflect the modifiability of the newly acquired response been observed. Several investigators became interested in the problem of awareness, and they began to ask questions of the subject afterwards to find out what he remembers about the experiment, what he thought was going on, and so on. The failure to obtain extinction, the failure to obtain typical learning curves, the importance of subject's attitudes and guesses about the experiment, all substantiate our belief that the processes going on in verbal conditioning had been much oversimplified.

The nature of reinforcement in the verbal conditioning situation is rather vaguely defined. What is reinforcing to a human subject in a problem-solving situation, because of the built-in motivations found in most adults, may not be simply a verbal cue such as "mm-hmm" or "good," but also the attainment of information about the task. The reinforcing stimulus has informational and rewarding properties and both may function to strengthen a response tendency. When we first raised these questions about the nature of verbal conditioning (in 1959) we were not yet clear how to conceptualize the role of awareness. We asked whether awareness, in fact, occurred during the learning process, or whether the post-experimental questionnaire in itself represented a new problem-solving situation to the subject, to be solved by evaluating in retrospect the purpose of the study. Was it necessary for the subject to be aware of what the experimenter is trying to do to him, *prior* to learning, or could he learn *first* and *then* become aware?

The verbal conditioning procedure permits the full play of all of these factors because the subject is told very little about his job. In this sense this paradigm is very similar to psychotherapeutic endeavors. The patient very frequently also does not know what he is supposed to be doing in psychotherapy, and most therapists carefully guard this secret. This ambiguity may be an important parameter in human learning (Kanfer & Marston, 1961).

## EXPERIMENTAL PROCEDURE

In the experiment we cannot stop the subjects themselves while they are learning, to ask them whether they are aware or not. It occurred to us that we might get someone else to tell us. We decided to get some subjects to observe only and asked them to record their guesses about the experiment. We conducted the usual verbal conditioning experiment in front of a class with a stooge who, without the knowledge of the observing students, read previously determined responses from the stimulus cards presented to him.

The stooge and the experimenter conducted the experiment in the presence of a psychology class which was told that this was an examination (this always helps to increase motivation). The examination was intended to find out their ability to grasp the meaning of psychological research. Two such classes were run. The classes listened to 40 trials given to the stooge, who sat in front of the class with the experimenter. Six sentences were reinforced in the first block of 20 trials and 9 in the second block. We used the procedure first described by Taffel (1955), reinforcing *I* and *We* with the verbal response "mm-hmm." As the stooge went through each trial, the observing subjects were shown a slide projection of the appropriate stimulus card. They were asked to record their guesses about the purpose of the experiments on a sheet *during* the trials. After the acquisition procedure in front of the class, an extended questionnaire with 21 questions was also given to the class.

Originally we had intended to find out what happens to awareness during learning. Is it necessary for the person to be aware of what he is doing before he changes his behavior? We scored all the responses and found that the guess sheets provided more information than we expected. In these two groups, under the impression that the demonstration was a test of their ability to grasp the meaning of psychological research, 90 percent of all the observing subjects were fully aware of the response-reinforcement contingency. In other words, these two groups of students clearly picked up the notion that the subject had to pick a particular pronoun on a card, and when he did the experimenter said "mm-hmm." This didn't surprise us because we felt that instead of worrying about what to say next, these observers were in a better position to observe both the experimenter and the subject and to relate their behaviors.

We then ran two additional groups. In the next two classes we did not tell the students that this was a test. We just said this was a demonstration and asked them to watch and guess the purpose of the experiment. With these instructions only 35 percent of the subjects were aware of the response-reinforcement contingency. In other words, when they were not highly motivated, when there was no payoff, fewer students were able to report what the experiment was about. Taking the over-all sample, roughly 50 percent of the subjects were aware by the end of the questionnaire, even though they themselves never actually participated in the experiment. The results also showed that of all the subjects showing full awareness, 35 percent were aware on the guess sheet, that is, during the running of the experiment; another 26 percent showed awareness on the first post-experimental question, and 70 percent were aware by the time the second question was asked. All subjects who eventually indicated awareness did so by the end of question 6. In other words, if they were aware what was going on, they were aware quite early during the experiment itself or during the first few questions afterwards. These exploratory studies suggested that observation of the procedure rather than participation may be sufficient for verbalization of the response reinforcement contingency and that additional probing, by questionnaire items, may increase reported awareness.

Actually at this point our focus of interest changed. We had set out to inquire whether it is possible to modify behavior without awareness. The results suggested a much more fascinating question, namely, whether subjects who were observing the conditioning of someone else were also being conditioned.

In other words, it is one thing to ascertain that our observers knew what the demonstrators were doing. It is another to see whether these same observers would also do it if they were the subjects. Is it possible to change the behavior of another person not only by directly modifying his behavior by reinforcement but doing it vicariously, by having him listen to the reinforcement of another person? The second question was what goes on during the acquisition in the observer's covert behavior. What is he doing? What is he saying to himself? It occurred to us that part of the process might be represented by the observer rehearsing a response. It is as if one were watching a quiz program and gave the correct answer. When the quizmaster says "Why yes, you have won $10,000," one says to himself, "Gee, I was right. It's too bad I wasn't up there." In these vicarious situations we tend to say to ourselves, "that's fine" or "that's good" or "I was correct" when we observe reinforcement administered to another person, and when we participate, covertly or indirectly. The second notion led us to examine the concept of self-reinforcement. Is it possible for the human being, quite unlike animals, to withhold reinforcement until such time as the environment provides the information or cue that it is all right to reward yourself or reinforce your own behavior? (Kanfer & Marston, 1963a, 1963c; Marston & Kanfer, 1963b).

Two conclusions were suggested by these data. First, observation of another person's behavior and subsequent reinforcement coupled with the subject's covert rehearsal of the behavior may represent an important way in which human beings learn; secondly, it may be possible for the human to reinforce his own behavior in the absence of external feedback. The second conclusion will not be pursued in detail here, but the question is important to us because it implies that behavior also may be incorrectly self-reinforced. Especially when we deal with pathological or deviant behavior the person may say to himself, "I am correct," and strengthen the likelihood of the behavior recurring when it is, in fact, socially inappropriate. Since much behavior is not observed by others, no one else corrects the person and his response pattern may build up and increase in strength in the absence of "consensual" validation. Many of our ideas, attitudes, or conceptualizations about the world and about people are often made by ourselves. In social interactions we rarely get feedback from someone. For example, if we make a *faux pas* or behave improperly, nobody tells us about it. It is quite likely that self-reinforcement may be one mechanism by which we perpetuate socially undesirable or unacceptable behavior.

However, in this paper we will limit discussion to the effects of observing an experimenter administer reinforcement to another person and not to the subject.

Our next two studies in this series investigated verbal conditioning procedures in groups with the specific intent of comparing observation of the experiment with direct participation in the experiment. We reasoned that under appropriate motivational conditions the adminstration of reinforcement to a member of the group might be as effective in changing the behavior of an observing subject as direct reinforcement. In terms of applications, there are obviously potential mechanisms for what has often been called "identification" or the likelihood, for instance, that a child learns by seeing other people rewarded. These other people could be his siblings, or playmates, or parents, or other adults.

In the first study, undergraduate students reported to a classroom and were divided arbitrarily into a group of observers and participants. We seated the students on two sides of the room, with the middle of the room as a dividing line. Half of the group were observers; the other half were participants. The experimenter pointed to each person and said, "Give me a word, any word you can think of." When the word given consisted of a "human," for example, man, woman, child, teacher, or whatever, the experimenter said "good." Both groups received a preacquisition (operant) period during which no reinforcement was given. We called one complete sweep around the room a "round."

The sizes of the observation and participation groups were always equal but ranged from 5 to 13 in each replication. Each of two experimenters ran three groups. After 10 nonreinforced rounds for all subjects, the examiner continued with 30 reinforced rounds for the participation group only. Reinforcement consisted of the comment "good" whenever a word from the class "human" was used. Both groups were then given ten additional reinforced rounds and 20 extinction rounds. All subjects answered a post-experimental questionnaire to determine the degree of awareness of the response-reinforcement contingency.

A comparison of the groups on initial frequency of use of the critical response class yielded no significant differences. Degree of improvement from preacquisition to the last 10 reinforced rounds for both groups constituted the measure of learning. An analysis of variance of these data yielded no significant effect due to the observation versus participation variable. In other words, the change in the frequency with which human nouns were given was as great for those who just sat and listened as it was for those who were asked to give the word and to whom "good" was said. There was a significant difference, however, in the degree of rated awareness. Observers were higher than participants in their awareness of the response-reinforcement contingency. These findings are not inconsistent with the earlier results of considerable awareness when a class observed one subject. Both groups did yield a high percentage of subjects who could describe the response-reinforcement relationship.

We then wondered whether the effects of vicarious reinforcement required the physical presence of the observers and the feeling of group cohesion which may be obtained from treating the observers and participants as a unit. Therefore, a study was conducted in which we separated the two groups. We used adjacent classrooms separated by a one-way mirror. Auditory contact was provided by means of an intercom system. We modified our procedures slightly. The curtains allowing observation of the participation groups were opened only after both groups were given 10 preacquisition rounds. The observers watched 30 acquisition rounds in the participation group. Both groups then were given 30 extinction rounds separately.

In this study the observation and participation groups significantly differed in their improvement. The participation group did much better. However, the observation group also showed learning and $t$ tests of improvement scores, with a hypothesis of zero change, yielded $p$ values of less than .05. While the participation group learned somewhat better, both groups did learn, and observation alone resulted in a significant change in the probability of emission of the critical response class. Both groups extinguished, although the group which was not directly reinforced had not shown as much acquisition and their extinction curve was flatter.

One of the problems that arose was a question of mimicking or imitation. Was it possible that these people were simply giving the same words that they had heard others give? For this reason we decided to investigate systematically the effect of vicarious versus direct reinforcement.

It is very uneconomical to have 20 or 30 people sitting around a room for this research. Instead of having people sit around, we decided to tape-record the participation group. We taped a "fake" group conditioning procedure with nine graduate students who acted out the record of an actual "live" group session. The tapes were then available for use with individual subjects. The subjects sat in a room and they had a microphone in front of them. They wore earphones and each subject was encouraged to believe that he was one member of a group of people. We instructed subjects that their turn would come when a signal light blinked. Then they were to say a word. In effect, this procedure allowed us to use the tapes as the experimental variable. (See Kanfer & Marston, 1963b for details of this study.)

## REINFORCEMENT STUDIES

We used four experimental groups and four control groups. In the four experimental groups, in groups A and A', B and B', subjects heard a tape rigged in such a way that it seemed plausible that other people were doing the same thing next door. In these four groups we played a tape taken from the acquisition phase of an earlier group-conditioning session. Subjects were conditioned to increase the frequency of nouns of human content. The difference between the groups was as follows: in group A each time somebody on the tape gave the correct response, a human response, the reinforcement "good" was heard on the tape. When the subject gave a correct response he also was told "good." Group A' was given the same tape, but the subject was told nothing. In group B the same tape was used except no "good" was on the tape, but the subject was reinforced directly, if he gave a critical response. In B' neither the subject's response nor the tape was reinforced. The design is shown in Table 11-1.

In addition, groups C and C' represented controls for the tape content. The tape, after all, had a large number of human nouns because this increase reflected the effects of a learning procedure. In the C and C' tapes we used an operant session in which only 5 percent of the words on the tape were actually human nouns. In group C the subject was reinforced; in group C' he was not. Finally, in control groups D and D', no tape at all was played. In D the subject was reinforced; in D' he was not.

The questions posed were, "What is the relative effectiveness of direct and vicarious reinforcement? Is it sufficient to have vicarious reinforcement? Does direct reinforcement help further facilitate vicarious learning?" In other words, is it sufficient to see someone do things, or must we have the information that the person who is being observed is successful at it?

Table 11-1: Experimental Design of the Study Comparing Vicarious and Direct Reinforcement, Showing Tape Content and Direct Reinforcement Condition for S

|  | Condition | | |
|---|---|---|---|
| Group | Tape | RF to S | N |
| Experimental | | | |
| A | Acquisition, VR[a] | DR[b] | 9 |
| A′ | Acquisition, VR | — | 9 |
| B | Acquisition, No VR | DR | 9 |
| B′ | Acquisition, No VR | — | 9 |
| Control | | | |
| C | Operant, No VR | DR | 9 |
| C′ | Operant, No VR | — | 9 |
| D | No tape | DR | 9 |
| D′ | No tape | — | 9 |

[a] Vicarious reinforcement.
[b] Direct reinforcement.
From Kanfer and Marston, 1963b, page 293.

The frequency of correct responses was analyzed in blocks of trials. The addition of vicarious reinforcement on the tapes for groups A and A′ resulted in significantly more learning and significantly greater increments over blocks, demonstrating the facilitating effects of vicarious reinforcement. In this study, at least, it was necessary for some reinforcement to occur before people learned. It was not simply a matter of imitation. Group B′ was also exposed to an acquisition tape, containing 50 percent human nouns. Unlike the other experimental groups, group B′, in the absence of reinforcement, did not significantly increase in the critical class. The control groups, C, C′, D, and D′, did not change in mean frequency of critical responses. In extinction the groups aligned themselves much the same way as in acquisition. There was a large decrease when the experimenter stopped saying "good."

To establish the minimal conditions of reinforcement and tape content necessary for statistically significant evidence of learning in this task, Blocks × Ss analyses were run and significant values were obtained for groups A, A′, and B. The results indicate that only those groups that were exposed to acquisition tapes and received either direct or vicarious reinforcement showed learning.

Considering the failure of direct reinforcement to produce learning in groups exposed to tapes of operant sessions, that is, groups C and C′, it should be noted that in a usual verbal conditioning procedure subjects emit responses at the rate of approximately 20 words per minute. In the

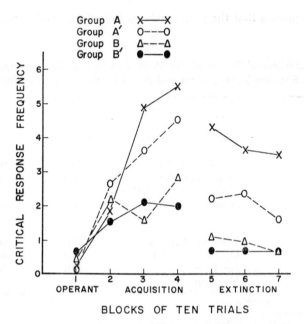

Figure 11-2. Acquisition and extinction curves for vicarious and direct reinforcement groups. Groups heard acquisition tapes under the following conditions: A: VR and DR; A': VR only; B: DR only; B' neither VR nor DR (Kanfer, F. H., & Marston, A. R., "Human reinforcement: vicarious and direct." *J. exp. Psychol.*, 1963, 65, 293.)

present study subjects had only 30 opportunities to make a response. Therefore a maximum of 30 reinforcements could be given. Neither group B' nor group C' showed large enough increases over blocks to yield evidence of learning. However, an *F* test between the groups indicated that exposure to a tape which contained 50 percent critical responses did result in significantly more critical responses than a tape in which critical responses were only 5 percent. In other words, when people listen to someone else giving a particular content they change somewhat, although not very much.

The results clearly indicate that exposure to contingencies between a critical response class and a social reinforcer in others can serve as an effective reinforcing stimulus for the observer. The conceptualization of vicarious reinforcement as a process, of course, is not quite as clear. Berger (1961) has called attention to the problem of separating vicarious reinforcement from direct reinforcement of the observer. Lewis and Duncan (1958) and others have suggested that reinforcement for the subject is mediated because there is arousal of an anticipatory goal response which is cued off by the model's behavior. If specific instructions are given to subjects, reinforcement for the subject may also be mediated because of the consequences that the subject anticipates for his own behavior after observing the model's reinforcement. Another approach might be to consider vicarious reinforcement as contributing to learning mainly because it provides information rather than because it provides reward. The variation between tapes in this study yields some evidence of the effect of making available to subjects a high or low degree of occurrence of critical responses as environmental cues. When neither vicarious nor direct reinforcement was given, it seemed that informational input alone did not increase the use of critical responses significantly. It is noteworthy that those subjects to whom vicarious and direct reinforcement were given pretty closely approximated the proportion of reinforcement that was given on the tape. In other words, these subjects matched pretty much the same rate of correct responses as given by the subjects whom they heard on the tapes.

In the absence of both vicarious and direct reinforcement, subjects failed to match the model in the prescribed manner suggested by Miller and Dollard (1941). On the other hand, groups A and A' approximated the mean frequency of critical responses during each block fairly well. It was noted that direct reinforcement did not result in learning when an operant tape was played. Thus the use of vicarious reinforcement in an acquisition tape considerably lowered the number of trials required for learning. We have already pointed out that there were only a few direct reinforcements because there were only 30 opportunities. In contrast to this, the subject heard 270 responses on tape.

This study suggested that people do not only mimic a model. When they hear someone else being successful, the probability of their imitating the observed behavior is greater. It also suggested that the process of vicarious reinforcement, that is, doing what we see others do successfully, is probably an important facet in human learning.

Our next study turned to the question of the contribution of the size of the group to which the subject listens. Is it important, for example, that there are many people who do the same thing or would the procedure be equally effective if the subject heard just one person do the same thing? In other words, in vicarious reinforcement the person may listen to either a large number of people or to a large number of incidents that are reinforced. Although he may have fewer opportunities for reinforcement, his behavior is modified nevertheless. The number of people and number of reinforcements to which he is exposed also have an effect. This study then addressed itself to the question of group size and number of vicarious reinforcements (Marston & Kanfer, 1963a).

Group size was varied in two ways because there are two ways in which we can change what the subject hears. First of all, we can increase the number of people on the tape. When we do this, the number of reinforced responses can either be held constant so that each person gets fewer when a new person is added, or we can keep the number of reinforcements constant by having each person give fewer correct critical responses on the tape. Our purpose was to investigate specifically the effect of varying group size by changing group size and keeping the number of reinforcements on the tape constant, and conversely by varying the number of reinforcements and keeping the group size constant. In the various groups the proportion of vicarious reinforcements of the tape was either constant or changing, and the group size was one, three, and five. Table 11-2 summarizes the design.

Table 11-2: Summary of the Experimental Design, Showing Proportion of Reinforced Responses on the Tape in Each of the 12 Groups

| VR Proportions | VR Group Size | | | VR + DR Group Size | | |
|---|---|---|---|---|---|---|
| | 1 | 3 | 5 | 1 | 3 | 5 |
| Constant | .30 | .30 | .30 | .30 | .30 | .30 |
| Changing | .60 | .20 | .12 | .60 | .20 | .12 |

From Marston and Kanfer, 1963a, page 595.

The procedure was similar to the previous one. The subject sat at a table in a darkened room. He looked at a board in front of him on which there was a signal light and a microphone. He wore a set of earphones and was told to respond whenever the light went on. The simulated groups were tape-recorded by male graduate students who read prepared lists of words taken from earlier protocols. Six tapes were recorded, varying the number of voices on the tapes and the number of reinforced correct responses on the tape. Following each correct response on the tape, the word "good" was spoken by an experimenter. On all tapes, 50 rounds of responses were recorded and each round consisted of a series of responses in which each voice had a turn. Regardless of the total number of correct responses on a tape, their absolute number per block of 10 rounds increased over 5 blocks. In other words, we simulated a learning curve so the number of critical responses showed an increase over blocks approximating a 45° angle.

This design was replicated in one case with only vicarious reinforcement (VR), in the other case with vicarious (VR) and direct reinforcement (DR). In addition to listening to the tapes, subjects in the VR + DR groups also were told "good" for every correct response. This represents a 3 × 2 × 2 × 6 factorial design, with six blocks of trials as the repeated measure. The first factor, group size, had three levels, one, three, or five voices. The second factor concerned the relationship of the number of reinforced responses on the tape to the group size. At one level, as group size increased the proportion of reinforced responses remains constant,

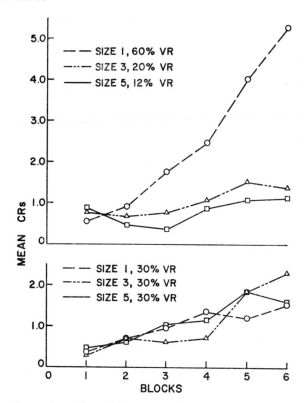

Figure 11-3. Comparison of acquisition curves in groups varying in size, shown separately for constant and changing proportions of VR on the tapes (Marston, A. R., & Kanfer, F. H., "Group size and number of vicarious reinforcements in verbal Learning." *J. exp. Psychol.*, 1963, 65, 595.)

increasing the number of reinforced responses. In these groups, each voice added to the tape contributed another unit of 15 reinforced responses. At the second level, the number of reinforced responses remained constant, but the proportion changed. The third factor is represented by vicarious reinforcement alone, and vicarious plus direct reinforcement together.

Figure 11-3 indicates that the most important factor was the proportion of reinforcements heard by the subjects. In other words, the most effective conditioning was obtained when 60 percent of the responses were reinforced for only one other person. This finding indicates, of course, that within the limits of our experimental design, the more effective and economic procedure is to have a subject listen to one other person who is reinforced frequently, rather than to a large group reinforced less frequently.

The results indicate that the effects of vicarious reinforcement follow the same principles as those of direct reinforcement. Grant, Hake, and

Hornseth (1951) and others have shown that the strength of a response is directly related to the *percentage* of reinforcement rather than to the fixed number of reinforcements. The social factor, that is, the effectiveness of having a subject listen to many people do the same thing, is not as important as having consistency or saturation with regard to one person doing it quite frequently. The addition of DR in the replication did not enhance learning. To summarize, using simulated groups to provide vicarious reinforcement, the relationship of vicarious reinforcement to group size was investigated. Size was varied by controlling the number of reinforced responses observed and controlling the percentage of reinforced responses. The effect of adding direct reinforcement to the observing subject was nonsignificant. Whether the subject himself was told "good," or whether he simply listened to others being told "good" did not make a difference. It was found that decreasing the proportion of reinforced vicarious responses by increasing group size resulted in significantly lower learning.

Our interest turned next to an examination of the effects of information inherent in the vicarious reinforcing stimulus. In the preceding studies "good" was used as a reinforcer. This social reinforcer may have several different properties in vicarious learning. First, its administration implies approval and achievement. This effect may be even stronger when given by the exprimenter in a situation in which the subject has little knowledge of the "rules of the game" (Kanfer & Marston, 1961). Secondly, when "good" is said after selected response it also conveys to the subject information that may serve him as a guide for future responses. Would the subject benefit from observing a model receiving reinforcement even if no useful information is conveyed? If the subject benefits in the absence of information, then the VR effect may be mainly motivational rather than informational.

In the following study we attempted to separate these two effects by varying the degree of relevance (information) of the observed performance by the model. We further varied the subject's motivation for attending to the model's performance by using cooperation and competition instructions.

We used 80 female college students as subjects. They were split into two groups. One group was given cooperative instructions and the other worked with competitive instructions. A stooge, who was actually an experimenter, worked in a booth adjacent to the subject. It seemed to the subject that two people were working as a team. The subject in the cooperative group was told that "you are going to see cards exposed one at a time; your task is simply to select one word on the card and say it out loud. When you select the correct one I'll flash a light. Each time the light flashes it means you have scored a point. Try to get as many points as you can.

"You have a partner in the other cubicle who will be performing a similar task. Pay attention to her response. You two will act as a team. Whenever she gets a point a red light will flash, and this will count as a point for you also. Thus you can earn points in two ways—first when you are correct, secondly, when your partner is correct."

The competitive instructions were similar except that "when your partner gets a correct response, that you ought to try to do better than she, and you will be competing with her to see which one of you can score more points."

We had four groups that varied with regard to the vicarious experience. On each trial a card was presented with four words printed on it. Each of these words came from four content classes. One was an animal word, one a shape word, one a human word, and one a plant word. In the vicarious experience zero group (zero VR) the subject was told that she wouldn't be able to hear her partner at all. All she would see were the points gained by her teammate. Would the knowledge that someone else was working with or against the subject modify the subject's responses? In the second group, the irrelevant reinforcement group, the subject was reinforced whenever she gave an animal word which was correct for her. But the partner was reinforced when she gave a word which was not even on the card. Her critical class comprised words in the area of cosmetics. Whenever she said "lipstick," "powder," and so on the stooge was reinforced, whereas the subject was reinforced only for animal words. The purpose of this group was to have someone else reinforced for something completely different, so that the subject received no information but points were still accumulated. In the partial vicarious reinforcement group the stooge was reinforced for one of the words on the card but not in the same class as the subject's critical class, that is, animals. Finally, in the full vicarious reinforcement group both subject and stooge were reinforced for the same class.

All stooges read their responses from prepared lists. They gave and were reinforced for four critical responses in each block of 10 trials. In the groups in which the partner was not reinforced for animals, the partner never used a response that the subject made. At the end of one operant block 10 reinforcement blocks were given. The subject was reinforced on a 50 percent schedule. The design consisted of eight groups. The two independent variables were two levels of motivating instructions—cooperation versus competition—and four levels of vicarious experience—zero, reinforcement with irrelevant information, reinforcement with partially relevant information, and reinforcement with completely relevant information.

The results indicated that there were no differences between the cooperative versus competitive conditions. The groups were therefore pooled in subsequent analyses. Figure 11-4 shows the learning curves for

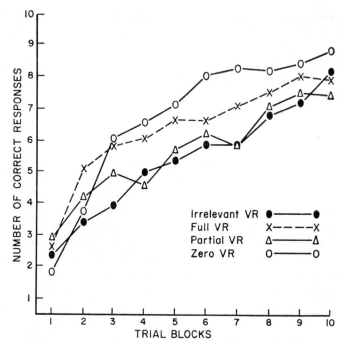

Figure 11-4. Acquisition curves for groups with varying relevance (information) of VR to S's experimental task.

the four VR conditioning groups. All the girls learned extremely well. In fact, the ease with which the task was learned suggests that the task may have been too simple to allow observation of the effects of the independent variables. As the graph in Figure 11-4 shows, the VR groups did not differ from each other in rate of learning.

We compared the effects of the two sets of instructions on incidental learning on the frequency of the number of responses used by the stooge which the subject remembered. Here some differential effects of instructions were noted on vicarious learning. Subjects receiving cooperative instructions tended to use and remember significantly more of their partner's responses than those with competitive instructions. In other words, under cooperative instructions the subject recalled better what the partner said; under competitive instructions she may have paid less attention to her partner.

The fact that the group which received no vicarious reinforcement (zero VR) performed equally well is difficult to interpret in light of our earlier results. Again the ease of the task may have precluded the effects of additional cues from VR. Also, in this situation the subject worked by herself. In this situation, perhaps the response of the partner, if anything, provided distraction or noise rather than information for the subject. In the earlier studies subjects actually listened to larger groups and their own task was not as clearly defined, nor were point rewards used. All of these factors may account for the different results. In any case, this study failed to show the effects of increasing information in VR. Since the task turned out to be too easy we will need to repeat this study with a different task before answering the question.

## SUMMARY

To summarize, one of the new areas of research that has emerged from earlier attempts to apply learning theory directly to human behavior has been discussed. It is clear that the efforts using models derived from animal studies can open new directions for research on human behavior. Hopefully this approach will eventually contribute substantive knowledge about human behavior, and provide a broad experimental basis for a behavior theory which can encompass human social behavior in all its complexity. One day it may even heal the painful dissonance created by the use of behavioral language and method in the animal laboratory and the reliance on crude common sense, dualism, intuition, and personal experience when we deal with individuals in the clinic, or people in their natural complex habitat.

The studies reported here have investigated the parameters of vicarious learning. It is probable that in everyday life much learning in childhood and in social situations occurs most effectively by the observation of others. There are some obvious ways in which our results may be applied. There is great efficiency and economy in the use of learning and reinforcement techniques in which the individual can be taught by observing others. Instead of conducting individual retraining in psychotherapy it may be possible to train a group of patients with some common behavioral problem by systematic observation of successful execution of some behavioral pattern in others. If our results from the laboratory can be generalized at all, they suggest that much learning can take place equally effectively in situations other than individual therapy, in which a person is isolated and works on his own behavior. These studies also suggest that the teaching machines may not be the final answer to our problems in education. In a classroom in which students observe the behavior and reinforcement of others such vicarious reinforcement may provide considerable learning experience. The area of vicarious learning therefore appears to be an exciting area for further study.

# 12

## The "Reinforcement" of Individual Actions in a Group Situation[*]

### ALBERT H. HASTORF

Hastorf has published in the fields of personality, cognitive, and social psychology (Hastorf, 1950; Hastorf & Bender, 1952; Hastorf, Bender, & Weintraub, 1955; Hastorf & Cantril, 1949, 1954; Hastorf & Kennedy, 1957; Hastorf & Knutson, 1949; Hastorf & Myro, 1959; Hastorf & Piper, 1951; Hastorf & Way, 1952; Hastorf, Richardson, & Dornbusch, 1958). He has the distinction of being the only author in this volume who does not see himself as directly involved in the modification of behavior in a clinical setting. Yet, as Hastorf himself points out, his research has major implications for clinical psychology. For example, the research he presents in this chapter is relevant to Saslow's ward research because of its implications for group therapy and ward decision-making.

Hastorf not only presents points of linkage between clinical and social psychology, but brings into focus what is implied by many of the other authors in this volume, namely, that much of clinical psychology is, in essence, applied social psychology. This point has been made by authors such as Luchins (1959) and is implicit in the behavioral engineering of Ayllon and Michael (1959). If one wants to manipulate the environment, there are probably few stronger secondary reinforcers than other people. Instead of using only the experimenter, Hastorf indicates how other people, for example, fellow students or patients, might be used systematically.

One approach to Hastorf's group work would put it in the context of leadership and group research. Petrullo's (1962) work on small group research and Bass's (1960) work on leadership, psychology, and organizational behavior provide excellent and comprehensive summaries. One of the first studies to apply reinforcement in a group situation was by Bachrach, Candland, and Gibson (1961). They point out that the same variables which apply to the individual situation also apply to the group, namely, prior history of reinforcement, the

[*] This research was supported by the National Science Foundation, Grant No. G 24137. I should like to express my thanks both to Alex Bavelas, my collaborator in this research, and to Alan Gross and Richard Kite, graduate students in the Department of Psychology at Stanford.

268

reinforcing stimulus, the schedule and amount of reinforcement, the behavior upon which reinforcement is contingent, and the change in rate of response.

McNair (1957) studied the effect of a bell-tone, defined by instructions as signifying approval, on rate of verbalization in an 18-person discussion-type group. In that study, subjects were shown pictures depicting interpersonal situations and were instructed to talk about them. Results indicated that rate of verbalization was influenced by reinforcer and varied as a function of the schedule of reinforcement.

Cieutat (1959) reported the effects of nonverbal gestural cues on rate of verbalization in a seminar-type situation. Positive reinforcement consisted of attention directed toward the subject, that is, he was looked at and given occasional nods. Negative reinforcement consisted of inattention, that is, the subject was ignored. Cieutat found that the amount of time during which a subject spoke was positively associated with attention and negatively associated with inattention.

Oakes, Droge, and August (1960) developed an important procedure for investigating the effects of positive and negative reinforcement on rate of speech in a free operant situation. Oakes et al. investigated the effect on rate of verbalization in a discussion-like situation of (a) the presentation of nonverbal reinforcers (positive and negative) and (b) the withholding of such reinforcers after they had been established. The reinforcing stimulus was a light that was defined for half the subjects as indicative of their having made an insightful statement. For the other half of the subjects the light indicated that they had made a statement lacking "psychological insight." The topic under discussion in the four-person groups was a clinical "case history." The authors concluded that the light signifying "insight" or "lack of insight" was a very powerful reinforcer. Some subjects receiving positive reinforcement got to the point where they seemed to be saying anything that came to mind just to keep talking, while subjects receiving negative reinforcement exhibited a great deal of hesitancy in their speech. In one case a negatively reinforced subject, upon receiving a light flash, stopped in the middle of a sentence and remained silent, obviously frustrated, for the next 20 minutes. Furthermore, positively reinforced subjects frequently made comments at the end of the session indicating that it had been very interesting and enjoyable for them. Negatively reinforced subjects, on the other hand, usually left the session quietly, looking either dejected or relieved.

Oakes, Droge, and August (1961) obtained similar results when reinforcing a more restricted response (choice from among three alternatives) in a group discussion. A work by Oakes (1962a) illustrated the importance of prestige, in that the most effective reinforcer in the group discussion was a light signifying that the subjects' statements indicated insight or lack thereof as judged by statements made by the professional team that originally worked with the patients, while the least effective reinforcer was a light signifying that the subjects' statements agreed or disagreed with statements made by a group of laymen during a previous discussion of the case. In a further study, Oakes (1962b) found that the verbal response class "giving opinions" could be significantly reinforced in a group situation.

A series of studies by Shapiro and Morningstar (1963), Shapiro (1963), Levin and Shapiro (1962), and Leiderman and Shapiro (1963) investigated the effect of reinforcement in a group situation in terms of social responses such as the order of speakers in conversation, the number of initiations individuals made to one another, and decision-making activity. These papers illustrate that such behaviors can be manipulated under different reward conditions. Walker and Heyns (1962, p. 75) found that ". . . groups can be made to appear as 'individualists' or 'conformists' almost at will through subtle but nevertheless effective differential reward for the two forms of behavior." Aiken (1963) reports a study which replicates the findings presented by Hastorf in this chapter. Dinoff, Horner, et al. (1960) and Salzberg (1961) indicate that the control of verbal behavior in group situations extends to "therapy" groups including schizophrenics.

In these studies, feedback to the subjects that they were "right," "showed insight," and so on acted as reinforcers and increased specific verbal outputs. The manipulation of a preselected verbal behavior as a treatment procedure is suggested in Krasner's chapter and illustrated clinically in Saslow's chapter. In the context of Hastorf's research, however, talking, per se, is part of a "leadership" role, recognized as such in the culture from which the subjects came. Increasing one aspect of a social role led to improvement in how the subject rated himself and in how others rated his behavior. This finding has implications for the therapy of "self-esteem" (Saslow, Chapter 13), role theory (Sarbin, Chapter 16), assertion training (Wolpe, 1958; Stevenson & Wolpe, 1960), role-taking as a therapeutic technique (Kelly, 1955), and "behavior rehearsal" (Lazarus, 1963).

Leadership, like creativity and intelligent behavior, has been frequently treated as a trait. In the present work, in a remarkably brief period of time, leadership, as observed by others, was enhanced by manipulation of the environment. Knowing the antecedents of the behavior can lead people to question whether the behavior is "real" and whether the person has truly changed. It seems that if an observer does not know the antecedents, the behavior is attributed to the person, while if he has knowledge or control, he is inclined to consider the behavior to be superficial. We are so ingrained with the concept that people should be responsible for the production of their own behavior that when the effect of changing environmental conditions is demonstrated, there is a tendency, even by those who instigated the conditions, to denigrate the influencees by calling them "suggestible" or "conforming." However, the observed behavior is real and the people who are influenced are responding to alterations in their environment. Once behavior has been changed, the new behavior elicits further changes in the environment. Hastorf provides a dramatic illustration of how audience reaction shapes behavior in a group situation and, thereby, supplies a technique that could be readily adopted for systematic use in clinical situations.

L.K.-L.P.U.

The experiments described in this report are characterized by two major conditions: a group of four men discuss, in one sitting, three problem cases; and during the discussion of the second case, each group member receives, privately, evaluations of his behavior from "experts" who are watching and listening in an adjoining observation room.

The four men sit around a table which is unobstructed except for a microphone and four small boxes all grouped at the center of the table. The boxes are radially oriented, each one pointing at one of the participants. Each box houses two small lights, which are the means by which the experts' evaluations are made know. The boxes are so built that only the person at whom they point can see the lights, and they are visible to him without peering into the box.

The central question in each of the experiments is whether the evaluations received during the discussion of the second case will affect the behavior and the perceptions of the participants. Will they talk more or less? Will their views of their own and the others' behavior change? Will their estimates of their own and the others' effectiveness of participation change? And if changes occur during the discussion of the second case, will they persist into the discussion of the third case?

The primary data, therefore, are measures of verbal activity, rankings of effectiveness of participation which each group member makes of himself and of the others, and the answers to a number of questionnaire items concerning the over-all process.

Before going into greater detail as to the experimental procedure, it would seem worthwhile to summarize what it is hoped to accomplish in this chapter. First, to report some of the background of this research, primarily as to how we got started and what problems concerned us; second, to describe some of the questions that we asked following our first exploratory investigations; third, to describe our procedure in some detail, and the data that were obtained; finally, to speculate a little, both as to some of the implications of this research and as to some of the questions that might be explored further.

## BACKGROUND OF STUDIES

Essentially these studies are concerned with the attempt to experimentally modify the structure of the group by differentially reinforcing the behavior of individuals while they are participating in group problem solving. There is a rather interesting paradox as to the setting of this research. Contemporary social psychologists have been rather ardent proponents of the experimental method for the study of social interaction. Interestingly enough, they have not made much use of the various techniques for the experimental modification of behavior. If one takes a look at the history of social psychological studies of group behavior, one finds the retrospective studies as exemplified by the work of Bales (1950). In these studies, group discussions are set up and the experimenter attempts to trace what happens by recording what goes on and by asking the participants to report their perceptions at the end of the session. On the other hand, one finds the more experimentally orientated attempts to manipulate either the behavior or the perception of the subject through the use of instructions or through the use of confederates.

One of the issues that we will be concerned with is exploring the perceptions of group members when the behavior of one individual in the group changes rather markedly. If you have hired people to act as confederates and to nod and smile when another person talks, you may get marked behavior change; but the perceptions of the group members (confederates) are not going to be especially interesting. They are mainly going to report that they were being paid a dollar or so an hour. Interestingly enough, clinical psychologists who have historically not been so experimentally orientated have been much more concerned with the experimental modification of behavior.

The notion of experimentally modifying behavior in a group situation grew out of some discussions between Alex Bavelas and the writer. Over the past three or four years, he had been exploring some of the psychological consequences of the use of noncontingent reinforcement. What do people do when one gives them an apparently reasonable task, such as guessing when the correct pattern of lights is on. The subject perceives this as a concept-formation task. Actually, the feedback as to his performance is noncontingent. Specifically, the experimenter has preset both the pattern and the ratio of right and wrong responses. In general, subjects, being both reasonable and trusting people, perceive this as a truly contingent situation and they search for the "rule." If the subject is made right a good deal of the time, he usually evolves a rather simply stated rule. If the number of times that he is told that he is correct is markedly reduced, the subject reports at the end of the session that he has not discovered the rule, but he has not given up. He acts a little like a methodologist, saying something like: "I don't know the rule, but I think I know how to find it out." This type of research is one part of the history of this project (Wright, 1960).

The other part of the background of this research was some exploratory work by the writer. We became interested in the conditions under which a group decides to engage in a revolution and overthrow its leader. We set this up as a noncontingent situation in which we had three group members who were to solve a task in which, prior to the feedback, every member of the group gave his individual guess as to whether a pattern was "right" or not. What we arbitrarily did was to pick out a member of the group and said to ourselves, not to them, "We're going to make this fellow right 90 percent of the time. Won't he emerge as the leader in the group?" The subjects were going to discover that this individual's guess was usually correct and would infer that he understood the job and knew the rule. The question we were asking was what would happen when we created a leader, where we had made a person right 90 percent of the time, as compared to what would happen when we made a leader by making him right only 60 percent of the time. Our hunch was that if we put the created leader on an extinction schedule where he was right only a chance number of times or even below chance, the group would stick with the 60 percent fellow for a long time. They would say, "Well, he's having a bad run but he really understands it" whereas they'd get rid of the 90 percent fellow in a great hurry.

We had some troubles with this. Interestingly enough, in the group situation we obtained a much greater incidence of subjects perceiving the noncontingency. The individual who was right 90 percent of the time did not behave exactly as Bavelas' subjects had. When he was asked "Why do you think you were right?" he said, "I don't know. It's kind of funny. Sometimes I didn't even think I'd be right when I guessed and I turned out to be right." Although I feel that this procedure should be explored further, it serves as the other part of the history of this project.

The question arose as to whether we might combine the two techniques to see if it would be possible to change the behavior of an individual in a free-floating group discussion. Our first attempt entailed the use of two subjects. They were provided with a simple task and instructed that we would sound a buzzer whenever they had said something on the right track. We did not define what we meant by "the right track" and we set up a predetermined schedule of buzzes, such that one person was to receive three times as many buzzes as the other. It turned out to be a very dull and halting two-person discussion. One of the reasons that it was halting is that subjects immediately responded to this as if it were a game, somewhat like "Twenty Questions." When one subject received a buzz, he quite naturally decided that he was on the right track and he pushed that point of view. Given our predetermined reinforcement rules, we wouldn't necessarily buzz him again when he kept on with the same approach. The situation rather soon became chaotic and messy, including considerable irritation on the part of the subjects. We then decided to alter our procedure so that there would be more subjects, the reinforcements would be private, and the apparent contingencies for reinforcement quite vague.

## EXPERIMENTAL PROCEDURE

The typical experimental procedure went as follows. Four subjects arrived to participate in a study of group problem solving. The subjects were seated around a circular table and were instructed that they would work as a group on the solution of some human relations problems. They were allowed 10 minutes for the discussion and solution of the first case. No intrusions were made during their discussion, but they were observed from behind one-way mirrors and records were kept of the total number of times each individual talked and the total length of time that he talked. This provided us with a measure of the number of outputs per subject, and the total amount of time consumed by each subject. At the end of this discussion a brief sociometry questionnaire was distributed and each subject was asked to rank-order the group, including himself, on four questions: (a) Who would you say talked the most? (b) Who would you say had the best ideas? (c) Who would you say did the most to guide the discussion? (d) Who would you say was the group's leader? It was not especially surprising to us that these four sociometric questions were highly correlated; after all, it had only been a 10-minute discussion. We therefore combined them into a general measure of the perceived status hierarchy in the group. We also had available to us the previously mentioned measures of behavioral output. In general the behavioral output data correlated quite highly with the sociometric data. This enabled us to obtain a general status ranking in the group.

While this ranking was going on, group members were reading the next case. Our procedure was to select the individual who ranked third in the hierarchy, that is, next to the bottom. He was selected as the *target person*. His selection was quite naturally not announced to the group. The group members were then instructed as follows: "You've now discussed one case. This research is concerned with the influence of feedback on group discussion." There then followed a statement concerning the fact that in many group discussions the chairman does not really give the members any feedback on how they are doing; all he does is direct the discussion, call on people, and maintain proper order. They were told that they were to be a feedback group and that they were going to be given evidence as to how they were doing. Each subject, as they sat in a circle, had a little box in front of him with a green light and a red light. The subjects were told that they were going to be given feedback concerning their performance in the group and that there were "human relations experts" in another room, who were very skilled in the general phenomena of group discussion. The experts were going to give the subject feedback of the following sort. "Whenever you make a contribution to the discussion which is helpful or functional in facilitating the group process your green light will go on. Whenever you behave in a way which will eventually hamper or hinder the group process your red light will go on." The contingency was vague since it was clearly possible that one could say something that would receive either a red or a green light, but that might be because the expert deemed that it would help or hinder later activity. But the subject's directions clearly implied some contingency between what they did in the group and the presence of either red or green lights. There seemed to be no doubt that the subjects believed the instructions.

Subjects were further instructed that they should not mention the fact that they had received either a red or green light. It should be kept in mind that they were unable to see the other people's lights, because the lights were placed in boxes which shielded any one subject's lights from the view of the other participants. We therefore have a situation where the subjects are prepared to engage in a 20-minute case discussion, where they expect to receive reasonable and frequent feedback on their participation.

What is special about the whole situation is that the experts back of the one-way mirrors are actually the experimenters, and they were going to follow somewhat different rules than the subjects had been told. An experimenter controlled the distribution of red and green lights given to the subject who ranked three in the status hierarchy (the target subject). The experimenters also tried to influence the behavior of the other participants. The experimenter who was going to try to control the behavior of the target person had the task of trying to make him the leader of the group. The experimenters also had the task of trying to make the other three subjects followers. Only the most informal rules were agreed to by the experimenters. We did not attempt to formally define leadership. We did not attempt to prescribe just what behaviors should be reinforced or punished on the part of the target person or on the part of the followers.

During the first trials of this procedure the experimenter who was hooked up with the target person usually said things like, "My fellow was awfully quiet during the first discussion; I've clearly got to get him talking." By the same token, the experimenter who was hooked up to the number 1 man in the status hierarchy usually said something like, "I'm going to have to try and shut this fellow up." During the first trial there was a general feeling on the part of the experimenters that the natural tendency on the part of some people to talk and engage in leadership acts, and on the part of others to be quiet and submissive, was very great. In fact, they were very doubtful that they could alter behavior in a mere 20-minute acquisition period. We shall soon see that they were surprisingly successful.

There was one bit of informal evidence that it might be possible to bring about change of this kind. Researchers had explored the technique of inviting one member of a group to "try and act important" in a group discussion. The evidence was that although subjects were very hesitant about trying this, sociometric evidence indicated considerable success.[1] Beyond this, there is an investigation by Oakes, Droge, and August (1960)

[1] Richard E. Farson, a personal communication, 1963.

that reports changes in the verbal output in four-person groups as a function of two subjects receiving positive reinforcement and two subjects receiving punishment. In that situation, however, the subjects were unable to see each other and their concern was primarily with change in verbal output.

Our acquisition session lasted for 20 minutes. We again made records of total number of outputs and talking time consumed by each subject; and at the conclusion of this session, the same sociometry questionnaire was distributed. Subjects were asked to rank the group on the same four questions. We were interested in not only the question as to whether we could change behavior, but also the question as to whether this behavior change was reflected in the perceptions of group members.

Reference to Table 12-1 under Condition B, which is the condition we have been describing, indicates the rather dramatic change in both the number of outputs and the amount of time consumed on the part of the target person or "leader." We will return to this table in more detail later, but the rather dramatic improvement that occurred in the sociometric status of the target person should be noted. In fact, a colleague, upon learning of our first results, described our procedure as "the mouse that roared."

There then followed a third session that lasted for ten minutes. At the start of the session the subjects were told that there would be no feedback lights. We again took measures of actual performance and obtained sociometric rankings. Following this, the subjects were given a brief questionnaire regarding their total experience, and the entire procedure was explained to them.

Before going to some general questions that might be asked, it might be helpful to make a few informal observations. First of all, the experimenter hooked up with the target person found that he had to use red lights early in the acquisition session; in essence, he had to punish silence on the part of the target person. He found a rather quick response to this. The target person said something which he immediately reinforced with a green light. As time went along the target person increased output and this output could be maintained with an occasional green light. Experimenters attempting to control the behavior of the first and second persons in the status hierarchy found that they had to punish talking early in the acquisition session, but that in time they could give some green lights to reinforce agreement with the target person. We even noticed postural changes on the part of our subject. The target person appeared to be slouched down in his chair at the beginning of the acquisition session; halfway through the session he was actually quite upright and looking rather attentive and eager.

## OBJECTIVES OF STUDIES

Let us now turn to some general questions that might be asked, the answers to some of which have already been implied. One might first question whether the lights really would make a difference, and could we really change the verbal output of our subjects? Secondly, one might ask just what the import is of the rather vague instructions given to the experimenters. The experimenters were all social psychologists, and we might assume that they could apply their sophistication concerning group behavior and be especially adept at selecting out the behavior that is to be reinforced or punished. In other words, is it really important that qualified experimenters select the behavior that is reinforced? Perhaps a machine that gives reinforcements where the only contingency was on verbal output would do just as well. One can push this a little further and raise the question as to whether the reinforcements need be contingent on verbal output. Perhaps one can preset a certain number of reinforcements and punishments for each subject and have them contingent on nothing but time.

Note that we have been operating on all four members of the group. Perhaps one can get the same effect by only reinforcing and punishing the target person and doing nothing to the other three members; or we may be able to raise the status of the target person by doing nothing to him but encouraging the other three members to be followers, so that the target person is almost forced to act like a leader because everyone else is acting like a follower. These are questions that we shall return to shortly with some data that bear on their answer.

Another question that we might ask relates to the perseverance and generalization of this effect. If we do get some behavior change, does it carry over to the nonfeedback session? Reference to Table 12-1 indicates that there is some carry-over in the third session. Beyond this, one might ask if it would carry over to another group? Can we employ this therapeutic technique on a quiet person and have it carry over to other social situations? This and the above questions all relate to the technology of behavior change.

Another set of questions are concerned with the ways people perceive this behavior change. What is the target person's perception of the situation? Does he notice a change in his own behavior? Does this change go above or below his own adaptation level? Does he say, "I talked more"? Does he like talking more? There are psychologists who believe that people have their own adaptation level toward participation in group discussion and if forced above or below their adaptation level they become unhappy. In general, the evidence is that target persons whose behavioral output was stepped up seemed to be pretty pleased with talking more. A second and possibly more interesting question concerns the reaction of the other subjects to the target person. If behavior change occurs, do the others notice it? If they do notice it, what do they make of it?

Behavior change would appear to be a rather significant stimulus for our perception and evaluation of others. Heider (1958) has stressed the fact that in order to make an evaluation of another person's behavior we must make certain inferences as to the causality of the behavior. His primary distinction has been between internal and external causality. For example, if one perceives another's behavior as having been internally caused and it happens to have been "good" behavior, we will evaluate that individual as being a "good" person; whereas, if we perceive another person as behaving in the way he did for external reasons, that is, because some external force made him behave that way, then we are not in a position to necessarily infer that he is a "good" person; we cannot be sure.

It would appear that this issue applies rather directly to inferring the quality of "leadership." More specifically, if our group members notice an increase in the verbal output of the target person and also raise that person's status on such dimensions as best ideas and leadership, one would have to guess that they experience him as talking more because he wanted to. Compare this with the perception that another person is talking more only because some external force is making him do it. It should be noted at this point that the group members under condition B raised the status of the target person on all the sociometric dimensions. They appear to be willing to make certain attributions concerning his behavior change. We shall return to this issue after a discussion of the experimental conditions that have been run and the data that have been obtained.

### RESULTS

Table 12-1 presents our results. Note that six conditions have been run, and that for each condition data are presented for both sociometric rankings and for length and frequency of talking. All values refer to the behavior of the target person and to the sociometric rankings given him by the other three group members. The target person's own sociometric ratings are excluded. The three case discussions are referred to as: operant 1 (10 minutes), acquisition (20 minutes), and operant 2 (10 minutes).

Condition C refers to the control condition in which four subjects discussed cases 1, 2, and 3 under instructions that they were a nonfeedback group. In other words, the lights were not operated at all. There were no significant changes in either output or sociometric status in this situation. It should be noted that there is a small increase in the target persons output and sociometric status at the end of the acquisition period. These changes do not approach statistical significance. This may well be some

|  | SOCIOMETRIC RANKINGS Average rankings received by TP from other group members (1 to 4) | | | LENGTH OF TALKING Total time talked by TP expressed as percentage of length of session | | | FREQUENCY OF TALKING Total utterances by TP expressed as percentage of total group utterances | | |
|---|---|---|---|---|---|---|---|---|---|
| Condition | OPER 1 | ACQ | OPER 2 | OPER 1 | ACQ | OPER 2 | OPER 1 | ACQ | OPER 2 |
| C | 3.05 | 2.81 | 2.80 | 15.3 | 18.2 | 18.1 | 19.5 | 22.5 | 22.9 |
| (N = 9 groups) | | | | | | | | | |
|  | *p*.01 | *p*.06 | | *p*.01 | *p*.01 | | *p*.02 | *p*.01 | |
| B | 3.23 | 1.70 | 2.30 | 13.4 | 35.5 | 24.6 | 17.2 | 31.2 | 25.4 |
|  | | *p*.01 | | | *p*.01 | | | *p*.01 | |
| (N = 9 groups) | | | | | | | | | |
|  | *p*.02 | | | *p*.10 | | | | | |
| D | 3.18 | 2.13 | 2.36 | 15.4 | 26.9 | 28.6 | 22.6 | 30.9 | 29.4 |
|  | | *p*.02 | | | *p*.02 | | | | |
| (N = 7 groups) | | | | | | | | | |
| E | 3.12 | 2.80 | 2.75 | 17.5 | 18.7 | 18.8 | 22.0 | 21.6 | 20.5 |
| (N = 7 groups) | | | | | | | | | |
| V | 3.08 | 2.66 | 2.82 | 16.4 | 21.4 | 20.6 | 20.4 | 26.0 | 27.2 |
| (N = 7 groups) | | | | | | | | | |
| W | 3.24 | 2.95 | 3.11 | 18.6 | 20.5 | 17.0 | 20.7 | 22.6 | 24.3 |
| (N = 7 groups) | | | | | | | | | |

Only *p* values of .10 or less are indicated. All tests are two-tailed.

OPER 1–ACQ differences for all experimental conditions are compared with OPER 1–ACQ differences for control (C) groups by the Mann-Whitney test.

Significance levels for ACQ–OPER 2 and OPER 1–OPER 2 differences were computed by the Wilcoxon matched-pairs, signed-ranks test.

sort of a regression effect. The changes in all other conditions were compared with the control condition.

*Condition B* is the experimental condition that was described earlier in the report. Group members participated in a 10-minute case discussion followed by a 20-minute acquisition period in which they were given red and green lights. The meaning of these lights, from the standpoint of the participants, was that they were evaluative of their contributions to the group; however, the experimenters operating the lights were attempting to raise the level of participation of the target person and to lower the level of participation and encourage follower-type behavior on the part of the other three group members.

The operant 2 session immediately followed in which no lights were given and no lights were expected. Reference to Table 12-1 indicates that the acquisition period led to a significant increase in both the output and the sociometric status of the target person. In the operant 2 session, there was a significant drop in both the output and the sociometric status of the target person. However, it should be noted that the target person's output and status do not fall to their original position, but remain significantly above the original position.

The effects of the acquisition experience appear to carry over to an immediately following discussion.

Two things should be stressed in regard to this finding. First of all, we have not only succeeded in bringing about behavioral change, but we have found that group members are aware of the change. Secondly, an experimentally increased incidence of talking is correlated with an increase in sociometric status on the leadership dimension. Previous research has usually demonstrated a high correlation between talking and leadership, but one could never be quite sure how this came to be. Was it that people who were perceived as having "leadership qualities" were encouraged or permitted to talk a lot, or did the sheer amount of talking create an impression of leadership? These findings appear to indicate that if one can increase the incidence of any person's talking, it will increase the likelihood that that person will be seen as a leader.

One comment should be noted in regard to these data. It is conceivable that the increase in the target person's status could be the result of the other three group members reducing their self-ranking because they had received red lights. However, if we eliminate their self-ranking they still increase the status of the target person.

*Condition D* was run in order to explore the importance of selecting specific behaviors to be reinforced or punished. The directions to the subjects were exactly the same as under condition B; however, a preprogramed machine was responsible for giving red and green lights to the participants. The experimenters' job was to let the machine know that a participant had talked. The machine was programed so that the target person would get quite a few green lights and very few red lights; the other three participants would get a greater incidence of red lights for talking and a small number of green lights. The program was set so that if all subjects talked about the same amount as they had under condition B, each of the participants would get about the same number of lights as he had under condition B.

The program was set so that the target person received three green lights for each five outputs and a red light at the end of a 45-second period of continuous silence. The other participants received seven red lights and two green lights for each 25 outputs. Note that under this condition the experimenter was allowed to make no selection of the verbal behavior that would be rewarded or punished. Surprisingly enough, the results of condition D are remarkably similar to those of condition B. This is especially remarkable in that the increase of talking on the part of the target person was not quite as great as it was in condition B. This of course reduced his chances of getting green lights and, as it turned out, more green lights were given to the target person under condition B. Even with this reduction in the incidence of controlling stimuli, sociometric status follows the same general pattern as in condition B. Interestingly enough, in condition D the target person appears to maintain his gains of the acquisition period during the operant 2 session.

It appears that the primary difference between the two conditions was in the first 2 minutes. It is at this time that the experimenters under condition B worked most heavily on the target person in order to "get him started." With a preprogramed machine, this was not possible under condition D.

*Condition E* was run in order to determine whether the effect could be obtained when the lights were not contingent on verbal output. Again, the subjects were instructed in the same manner as before; however, this time in the acquisition period the lights were preprogramed on the basis of time. In other words, the target person was going to receive about the same number of green lights that he had received under condition B, but they were to be given at certain times and contingent on nothing but time.

Reference to Table 12-1 indicates that there were no significant changes in either the output or the sociometric status of the target person. Quite obviously the phenomenon of increase in output and increase in status is not a function of merely the number of reinforcements given. Quite clearly there must be some contingency between the lights and talking in order to get the effect.

*Conditions V and W* are similar enough so that they will be discussed at the same time. They represent our preliminary explorations into reinforcing only certain members of the group. Condition V entailed an exploration of the effect on the target person of the attempt to create a leadership vacuum in the group. The target person was instructed by private written directions that he was in a nonfeedback group and that there would be no lights during the acquisition period. The other three group members were instructed by private written directions that they would receive lights. The experimenters attempted to suppress the verbal output of the other three group members to see if the target person would increase his behavior in order to fill the vacuum we had created. Reference to Table 12-1 indicates that this was not successful. There was a slight tendency for the target person to talk somewhat more, and there was a slight increase in his sociometric status; these changes did not approach significance.

Interestingly enough, there was a slight increase in the amount of "dead air" during the acquisition period. By this we mean there was an increase in the amount of time when no one in the group was talking. This seems to imply that we had made the other group members somewhat more hesitant about talking, but apparently the target person did not leap in to fill the gap.

Condition W is essentially the mirror image of condition V. One might describe it as a wedge. In this condition the target person received written instructions indicating that he would receive lights during the acquisition period and he was given a regular "leadership" schedule of lights, just as in the B condition, whereas the other group members were given private instructions that they would not receive lights. We were curious to see if we could create the effect by merely operating on the target person. Reference to Table 12-1 indicates that we were not successful. It is worth noting that if you conceive of adding together condition V and W, you get condition B. However, if you add together the behavioral effects of conditions V and W you do not approach the size of effect that you get in condition B. It would appear that one must have the operations combined at the same time.

## SUMMARY

Let us summarize what we now know. The procedure that has been described permits us to bring about rather dramatic behavior changes when we use lights as both rewards and punishments. We also know that these lights must in some way be contingent on talking, although it does not seem to be necessary for the experimenters to make decisions as to what classes of talking should be reinforced. We also know that it appears to be necessary to influence all group members to get the effect. Beyond this, it is apparent that the group members notice the behavior change on the part of the target person, and that they appear to be willing to alter their perception of his status. It is also clear that if the lights are removed, the output and the sociometric status of the target person tends to fall, but they do not fall to their original position. The target person maintains some of his gain.

This all seems to imply that in a very short period of time we can take a person of fairly low status and make him a leader, at least in the eyes of the members of his group.

Let us briefly survey some of the questions that might be raised for further exploration. The first set of questions are related to the general question of behavior change itself. What is the effect of all this on the target person? The target person reports, following the entire procedure, that he enjoyed most the discussion that we have called the acquisition period. Furthermore, he reports that the lights "helped him." Is it possible to change a person's adaptation level for participation in group activities by this means? Is it possible to demonstrate that he will generalize this to other group situations?

Another class of questions under the heading of behavior change might be called experimental studies of group structure. Can this technique be used for the experimental study of clique formation? Can we create a status fight (conceive of putting both rank 1 and rank 2 on leadership schedules)? It would appear that this technique would make possible the experimental manipulation of various types of group phenomena.

A third set of questions relates to the use of behavior change as a stimulus for social perception. Earlier in the chapter, we referred to the necessity for making inferences about the causality of behavior change in order to make certain evaluations of the behavior itself. Interestingly enough, the experimenters were somewhat surprised when they saw the rather dramatic change in the sociometric status of the target person under condition B. Clearly they were aware of the change in the behavior of the target person; why were they surprised? We must keep in mind an important difference in the perceptual situation of the group members as compared with the experimenters. The group members could not see the lights that were being given to other people and might infer that a person who was talking a lot was getting green lights from "experts" for "good behavior." The experimenters had an extremely different perception of the causality of the behavior change. In Heider's (1958) terminology, the experimenters were in an almost ideal situation to perceive the behavior change on the part of the target person as having stemmed from external causes. The experimenters were operating the lights and may have been making causal attributions different from those of the participating group members. It may be difficult to positively evaluate an individual's ideas when you perceive this output of ideas as occurring only because the lights are making him talk. This may be a question of very great importance, both to social psychologists and to clinical psychologists. Certainly one of the activities of the clinical psychologist is the intentional bringing about of behavior change.

It would seem important to explore the evaluations people make of behavior change in a situation such as this when they are in the role of observers, having been told just what the participants have been told, and not being aware of the experimenters' rules. They ought to perceive the situation essentially as the participants themselves do. What if observers are informed about the experimenters' rules? Would they have a tendency to perceive the behavior change as externally caused (the lights made him talk), and thus not positively evaluate his ideas? What if the observers actually operate the lights? An important facet of this situation may be the active conscious attempt to influence another person's verbal output. It is possible that this situation could lead to an even less positive evaluation of an individual's ideas and leadership activity. Exploration of these situations are of considerable theoretical importance to social psychology. They also strike us as being of overwhelming concern to the clinical psychologist. The clinical psychologist is in the business of behavior change and it would seem crucial to understand how he perceives and evaluates the changes that he brings about.

# 13

## A Case History of Attempted Behavior
## Manipulation in a Psychiatric Ward *

### GEORGE SASLOW

Saslow's background includes a doctoral degree in physiology as well as in medicine. As a physician and psychiatrist he starts his presentation with analogies to cardiac disease and makes acute observations on psychoanalysis. His multidiscipline experience includes contributions to psychological research on interviewing and treatment (Saslow, 1952; Saslow & Chapple, 1945; Saslow & Matarazzo, 1959, 1962; Saslow, Matarazzo, & Guze, 1955; Matarazzo & Saslow, 1956, 1961), and on verbal conditioning (Matarazzo, Saslow, & Pareis, 1960).

The setting in which he works enables Saslow to put into practice several of the concepts and ideas expressed in previous chapters by Kanfer and Hastorf. His experimental procedures of focusing on the single case link him with the earlier chapters as well. He shows the actual operation of behavior modification in a hospital setting.

Saslow demonstrates that the aim of assessment is not categorization, but treatment. It is the treatment program that determines the kind of assessment questions that are asked. Saslow's approach is to treat disadvantageous behavior directly with techniques based on learning principles. Viewing behaviors as disadvantageous rather than symptomatic or sick leads to new diagnostic questions which may be formulated as follows: (a) What are the disadvantageous behaviors that interfere with more socially desirable behavior? (b) What situations (stimuli) elicit these behaviors? (c) What new, socially acceptable responses can be associated with these stimuli? (d) What effective environmental reinforcers are available and can be manipulated?

The focus of the assessment procedures is on the individual's behavior with other people. Psychological tests are more useful as standardized situations in which to observe the subject's behavior than as measures of internal dynamics, ego-strength, or patterns of pathology. The assessment procedures which stem from Saslow's approach involve the total social environment, including the pa-

* The experimental observations described were planned and carried out in collaboration with Professor F. H. Kanfer.

tient's home and the locale in which treatment takes place. Saslow's experimental in-treatment program parallels the nursery school program described by Bijou in the fourth chapter. Bijou's collaborators have provided instances in which disadvantageous behavior was ignored and more appropriate behavior reinforced (Wolf, Risley, & Mees, 1964). In these studies, the reinforcing contingencies were reversed to indicate clearly the necessary role of the therapeutic program in modifying behavior.

Saslow's discussion of the doubtful attitudes of many of the staff people, such as nurses, points to an important problem. It takes a certain "toughness" to carry through such a program (Ayllon & Sommer, 1960). Many workers in the mental health field have been trained to respond favorably to the help-eliciting cues of the patient. More often than not such staff reinforcement of "sick role" behavior occurs for lack of systematic training in more effective responses. The behavior modification approach aims for two types of long-term "kindness." The first is helping the patient increase advantageous behavior. The second is testing the efficacy of the program to measure the individual's progress. If such progress is not forthcoming the program can be changed. Each program that is found effective increases the clinician's repertoire for dealing with similar patients in the future.

If one conceives of a treatment program in an institutional setting as designed to elicit and maintain new and more desirable behaviors, then such a program should involve everybody with whom the patient has contact. Saslow discusses a problem to which others (Allyon & Michael, 1959) have alluded—that of programing the staff as well as the patients. The institution provides a situation in which the therapist has far more control than in an outpatient setting. In the institutional setting the therapist should make use of this control to manipulate the environment so that there may be effective generalization, shaping, chaining, role retraining, and role maintenance.

L.K.-L.P.U.

DESPITE A NUMBER OF innovations in psychotherapeutic procedures in the last decade or two, the most frequent approach to psychotherapy is still that dominated by Freud's contributions. In this approach one attempts to uncover and resolve the various intrapersonal or intrapsychic conflicts of the patient by helping him achieve insight into the origin and significance of these conflicts. It is then hoped that this insight will lead to improved verbal and nonverbal behavior in the patient's talks with his therapist and that there will follow similar improved behavior with other people. There are at least three underlying assumptions. First, insight into one's difficulties is considered to be essential before any change occurs. Secondly, there is the assumption that if one's thoughts or feelings about one's problems and oneself change, there will be new actions. Third, it would follow from the first two assumptions that simply changing any present symptom, even though it may be particularly disadvantageous behavior, without achieving insight, will lead only to other symptoms appearing as a consequence of the lack of insight into the supposed underlying conflict.

For some period of time there have been observations available from a variety of sources which suggest that these are not the only assumptions that one might make about attempting to influence another person's behavior by psychotherapeutic means. There are observations suggesting that we should be considering assumptions alternative to these, and if we do consider such alternative assumptions, we probably will think of alternative procedures to the Freudian one. For instance, in 1946, Alexander and French published the first observation in the psychoanalytic tradition that indicated that changed behavior on the part of the patients they were working with led to less frequent repression of early events in the person's life. Significant traumatic memories were recovered better, and various kinds of dream material of significance to the early history were communicated for the first time, only after new and improved behavior had already occurred. Thus Alexander and French began to observe something that suggests assumptions rather different from those in which they themselves had been trained.

Another related significant observation comes from a field that is perhaps somewhat simpler than psychotherapy, the field of the diagnosis and treatment of cardiac disease. The American Heart Association has for some time been aware that even a considerable amount of knowledge about the etiology of a particular cardiac difficulty is not enough to predict the degree of present incapacity. That is, the etiologic agent could be known, the nature of the anatomic damage to the various structures of the heart could be identified by careful clinical observation and improved laboratory methods, and the physiological incapacity of the heart and circulatory system could be defined. After these three dimensions of cardiac difficulty had been determined, it was discovered over and over again by cardiologists that one person with pathology as defined above would be bed-ridden, unable to work, unable to carry on any ordinary life, while another person with apparently the same pathology might be active occupationally and socially as if he had zero cardiac difficulty. In other words, when it came to determining the functional capacity of the person as a whole, as a behaving organism, it turned out that fairly precise etiologic, anatomic, and physiological data were often not at all predictive of the total functional capacity. Thus, the complete cardiac diagnosis as recommended by the American Heart Association for the past 15 years requires that there be an independent determination of the person's present functional capacity quite apart from the other three (etiological, structural, physiological) determinations.

It has been felt for a long time, and the available psychiatric experience supports the view, that in the field of human behavior the relationships between early causative events, no matter what insight we have about them, and the present behavioral capability were often just as oblique and unpredictable as in the field of cardiac diagnosis. The relationships are probably just as tenuous. In the last few years observations that supply the evidence for such a view have been made in various places.

## BACKGROUND STUDIES

There have been a number of studies carried out with chronic schizophrenic persons who are given the chance to learn new occupational skills (Poindexter, 1962; Blachly, Stephenson, & Levy, 1963). The results were that the ability of severely handicapped schizophrenics to learn and to sustain occupational skills had no relationship whatever to the severity of their psychiatric disability as conventionally and clinically defined, to the psychiatric diagnostic label, or to their current degree of disorganization. Thus present behavioral capability has to be conceived of as frequently, if not generally, independent of much past historical information and present personality diagnostic formulation.

There have been a number of observations indicating that the behavior of numerous people suffering from severe disability can be modified without their attaining insight into what they are doing and without any extensive personal examination of the origin of these difficulties. For example, Ayllon and Haughton (1962) have reported the improvement of severely disadvantageous eating behavior in a whole ward of chronic schizophrenic patients by the use of carefully planned reinforcement procedures in relation to the desired kind of eating behavior. They provide evidence that the behavior of human beings in a group of considerable size may be independent of clinical disorganization, and that the behavior of all the group members can be markedly influenced for the better without following the usual pathways and assumptions that the dominant psychoanalytic approach requires.

An additional observation suggesting the wisdom of alternative assumptions is that one notices fairly often that the particular behavior a patient shows may be so disadvantageous to him that it creates many additional difficulties. An example is working with a person (such as one to be described) who talks only about his symptoms at interminable length and alienates everyone. If one could reduce this symptom talk noticeably the patient could shift to some other way of relating himself to other people. By achieving this one change in his behavior the patient would be permitted many otherwise unavailable interpersonal opportunities for which he may possess an effective social repertoire. It is important to consider whether this would not be a desirable approach to certain problems.

A final observation relates to the difference between verbalization of one's difficulties and how one actually behaves. In the days when frontal lobotomy was much more popular than it is now, it was not uncommon, after frontal lobotomy had been done for the intractable pain of cancer involving the structures of the face and head, that one could meet such a person postoperatively and notice certain changes in his behavior. By comparison with his behavior before the operation, he did not wince when the physician approached him, nor did he grimace or turn his head when the physician approximated his hand to the patient's face. He did not have the look he had had before the operation, a look easily interpreted by all observers as that of a person in considerable apprehension, pain, and discomfort. He seemed, in fact, to be quite comfortable. But if the physician stopped by his bedside and asked the patient how he was feeling or what his pain was like, the physician would hear a faithful repetition of exactly the same statements about the patient's suffering, pain, and complaints that he had heard before the operation. It was a somewhat pallid emotional statement by comparison perhaps, but it was strikingly reminiscent of what one had heard before the operation and was unrelated to the patient's apparently much more comfortable behavior.

Putting together observations such as those mentioned above, we may conclude that there is no reason to think that the sequence of insight (into early problems and early difficulties) and behavior alteration must always go in one direction. It is accepted in fields outside psychiatry, apparently much more easily than within it, that, although feelings, ideas, and sentiments can lead to new action, actions can lead to new feelings, ideas, and sentiments just as well. There is no compelling evidence that the sequence works only in one direction. It probably works in both, and we should be free to decide which way we want to push the sequence or to push it first one way and then the other.

## DIRECT MANIPULATION OF BEHAVIOR

There are various ways of dealing directly with the undesired behavior itself if we decide to concentrate on this way of pushing the sequence, and this is what this book is about. One way of dealing directly with the undesired behavior itself, which I shall not cover here, has to do with manipulating the entire physical and social environment—the milieu—of the person. This is discussed in its numerous variants in a recent book by Cumming and Cumming (1962).

Another way of dealing directly with behavior disadvantageous to the patient will now be discussed. This method attempts to apply the principles of reinforcement to specific types of response classes of undesired behavior. This assumes that most human behavior is amenable to change by such means. It assumes also that the therapeutic effort has two components, either of which one can work with directly. One component is a change in the perceptual discriminations of the patient in his approach to perceiving, classifying, and organizing the stimuli to which he attends. One can directly provide a subject with finer, more precise, or different discriminations of input stimuli. The second component in dealing directly with behaviors that are undesirable has to do with producing a change in the person's long-established patterns of response to himself and to others. (Kanfer, 1961).

### Analysis of Behavior

The first step in dealing with behavior directly is to analyze the patient's behavior in a search for those classes of response, those aspects of his behavior, that it is desirable to modify. After finding such response classes, the second step is to devise procedures for modifying them. There is a variety of situations we can use to help determine the kinds of responses with which we should deal directly. We need information of several kinds in order to carry out the necessary analysis of the ways in which the patient's behavior is ineffective or to suggest ways of modifying it. We can obtain this information in special situations, and a number of these will be listed. We tend to use all of them routinely on our small open psychiatric ward in a general hospital.

The conventional behavior of verbal self-report such as one finds in patient-therapist encounters is a good beginning. We do not pay much attention (when we are interested in modifying behavior directly) to the verbal reports as equivalents of actual events, but we look upon them as telling us about the patient's manner of speaking and acting. Does he speak and act in such a way, no matter what the verbal content, as to alienate people? We also listen to his verbal self-reports in order to make some guesses about his attitudes toward himself and others, about the way he deals with his past experience, or how he uses fantasy. A second situation which is a source for the material we need for analysis of the patient's behavior is direct observation of a therapist-patient encounter or a patient-patient encounter. The behavior of a patient with a particular therapist of whom we know something or with a particular patient who is known to us may give us information useful for behavior analysis. For example, one may make the simple observation that a given patient talks only to the men on a ward or that he never talks to the men.

Another kind of situation which is useful for the types of clues we are searching for has to do with what can be observed in a psychological test setting. Here we are not paying attention to the usual psychological test performance and report. We are looking for the way the patient reacts to a partly ambiguous situation in which he has to be task-oriented and intermittently frustrated. We may find that he gives up very easily but that the psychologist can help him sustain his effort by coaxing. We can observe in the standardized psychological test situation that certain behaviors of the psychologist produce describable and predictable responses on the part of the patient. We can ask ourselves whether this kind of observation has anything to do with the patient's difficulties outside this particular miniature interpersonal situation. The psychologist can provide useful observations, too, if he notices that by giving the patient smaller gradations in a required task, the patient performs at a higher level, or that if he allows the patient more time on a speed-pressure test the patient turns in a superior performance. These observations may be useful to us in the context of treatment.

Next, we use reports from other informants, people who know the patient, such as family members and friends. Here we can compare the way that the patient perceives events with the way that significant other people in his life perceive the same events. We can make observations of the patient on the psychiatric ward by means of other patients who observe him, as well as by means of the staff. The staff, particularly nurses, are in frequent contact with the patient and can furnish us with observations of his behavior toward himself and others in a variety of settings such as industrial, recreational, or occupational therapy, small group therapy, ward meetings, and informal social activities and games. All these observations will be useful in our behavior analysis. One can also use records of the patient's activities and obtain tape recordings of his performance in interpersonal encounters such as individual or group therapy. A closed circuit TV monitoring system might be used for this purpose. Another useful source of observations might be the patient's way of dealing with his own family. These observations can be made by inviting the family to the ward to participate in small group or ward meetings, or to meet specific nurses or therapists. The patient in interaction with his entire family can be observed from behind a one-way window. We can get a picture of the way the patient deals with the people closest to him. Finally, in this series of settings that provide useful information for behavior analysis, one could make use of the techniques of assigning planned roles to specific staff such as nurses. These assignments could be brief standardized roles with regard to a given patient. For example, during a given shift on duty, a nurse could be assigned the role of initiating general social conversation in a certain way, briefly, or at length, a certain number of times per shift, or for some particular duration of time. Or the brief standardized role might be to initiate pair or group activity of a social, instructional, recreational, or athletic kind. The patient's responses could then be observed for indications of what behavior is available in his current repertoire in the presence of known stimuli.

Observations in these various settings can be made as soon as the patient enters a ward for study. Decisions then can be made about the response classes that one will try to change. In general these response classes will be of two main categories: self-defeating social behaviors of major magnitude or subjective complaints of major incapacitating effect. Some people will need both changed. We try to discover from the behavioral analysis, in any and all of the settings described, eliciting conditions and reinforcing stimuli that might be especially approprate to the particular individual and that could be used to bring about and to sustain the desired changes in behavior.

### Motivational Devices

There are a number of motivational devices or reinforcing stimuli that are useful in attempting to modify patients' behavior. One can use external rewards such as special arrangements about food or special food, ward privileges, staff attention, special behavior of a therapist, or special conditions that bring about tension discharge or discharge of hostility in a patient. Such rewards can be deliberately and repetitively planned and can be made contingent upon certain desired behavior. One can try internal rewards such as self-reinforcement, self-esteem, self-knowledge, the understanding of others, and changes in self-concept. The more a patient can use such internal reinforcing conditions, the better he will be able to manage his own affairs in his community. We are particularly interested in seeing how skillful we can become in using self-esteem as an internal reward because studies clearly show that many of the difficulties patients have are highly correlated with low self-esteem (Rosenberg, 1962). To summarize these studies: The person with low self-esteem is a person who tends to feel alienated from others, tends to report himself as experiencing many psychosomatic symptoms, tends to deal with himself in terms of a compensatory striving for perfection, has a very low tolerance for frustration and for criticism, and has a very high anxiety level. There would be many obvious benefits if we were able to devise effective techniques for raising one's level of self-esteem.

Among the motivational devices may be the incorporation by the patient of procedures that are in some way imitative of the therapist. We hear these reported by patients from time to time. For example, when a patient says to a therapist, "Now at that time I remembered what you had said about a similar problem that I had," the patient is telling himself something that is imitative of the therapist's way of solving a problem. Sometimes a patient will cut out a photograph of his therapist that has appeared in the paper and say, "I looked at your photo that I carried around, and it gave me the courage to go ahead and do this or that." It is possible to devise procedures that will enhance the likelihood of imitating the therapist.

Another motivational device that is useful is one that brings about a reorganization of the previous hierarchy of needs or motives in the patient. Imagine, for example, that a person has a recurrent conflict between his need for social recognition, that is, keeping up with the Joneses, and his need for economy, not drawing checks in excess of his bank balance. Such a conflict can be resolved by the patient's learning to give more appropriate priorities to each of these needs through repetitive practice.

An important motivational device that is constantly being used by significant others in the patient's life is the threat of cessation of meaningful reinforcements. The implied threat, "I won't have anything to do with you," is very influential in inducing various kinds of behavior. It is possible to think of using these to induce behavioral change, for instance, by systematically building up a high frequency and intensity of an interpersonal relationship with a staff member or therapist, and then unexpectedly reducing the frequency of these encounters or the intensity of the relationship contingent on some undesired behavior. The original nature of the relationship can be restored contingent upon the development of more acceptable behavior.

## EXPERIMENTAL CASE STUDIES

Given this approach, which is based upon assumptions different from those of traditional psychotherapy, the treatment of three patients on our small open psychiatric unit will be described. No patients can be legally committed to this ward, and we accept patients of all ages, both sexes, and any kind of problem that can be dealt with without the patient's running away or deceiving us so thoroughly and successfully (as in drug addiction) that therapy on an open ward is useless.

### Case I

The first case deals with a young woman whom we shall call Lucy. She was a 20-year-old, bright college student who was admitted with a diagnosis of acute schizophrenic reaction. In her recent past she had made a considerable number of nearly successful suicide attempts by a variety of the most frequently used methods. She had a long history going back to age eight or nine of emotional and behavioral instability. On this particular admission, drug treatment for the acute episode had been tried and was not effective. We observed her for a number of weeks in the various settings such as those mentioned above and, putting together the information that we obtained, decided to focus upon certain classes of response in her behavior repertoire. She repeatedly talked about being useless to anyone and of feeling dead. Appropriate to such talk was a very narrow range of affective verbal responses. Despite the great variety of human beings available, we also noticed in a variety of situations conspicuous failure to initiate conversation with anyone and an almost total failure to ask anyone for anything even when this would have been socially expected. We often noticed an acceptance of something that was needed but was not asked for. We tried, without success, various procedures to alter these behaviors.

We evolved the following procedure: In a session with an experimenter present, Lucy was given a tape recorder to manage herself. She was to start and stop the tape recorder herself. She could obtain any help she wanted from the experimenter but only when she asked for it. When she asked for aid, because something wasn't working right on the recorder, she would always be rewarded for doing so with "that's good, that's fine," and she would always be helped. She recorded her own readings from selected plays. We had told her that such tape recordings could be useful to blind patients in the hospital and to patients temporarily blinded after eye operations. Thus she would be doing something useful for others. As soon as we hit upon this idea and gave her plays to read so that she could make these recordings under her own control, we were surprised by the immediate exhibition of an extraordinary range of inflections of an emotional kind and of well-modulated verbal expressions. Up to this time nobody on our ward had observed such verbalizations, and her mother told us she had not heard these expressions for years before Lucy's present episode of illness. In addition to our apparently having hit upon a way of evoking a much wider range of affective response than she had seemed to possess, Lucy was rewarded (as she listened to the recordings) for any comment that she made about her own performance. She was praised whenever she showed awareness of her own performance as a reader.

In group therapy sessions (where previously she had participated not at all), she was advised to participate by giving information to the other members through making a minimum number of comments per session. Later Lucy made tape recordings of stories that were to be played to bedridden children on the pediatrics ward. While making these, she was rewarded immediately, emphatically and invariably for erasing poor tape, because she was now discriminating poor from better reading. She was rewarded similarly for asking questions and for being spontaneous. As she moved ahead in her responsiveness, she was assigned to the pediatrics ward to help feed the children and to read stories to certain bed-ridden children. During the period of these procedures, we made observations about her in a number of the other settings in which she lived. For example, the nurses (who had been given minimal information about our experimental procedures) reported in their notes that there was a noticeable improvement in the way she talked about herself. Her self-esteem was evidently higher. She was more spontaneous on the ward in interactions with both patients and staff, and on one occasion she danced very happily, something that had not been seen before. She became more active in contributing to group therapy sessions, and she changed her attitude toward her therapist. Her attitude had been one of "no one can help me; I am dead; I am of no use," and so on, but she now began to show interest in the possibility of some kind of meaningful life after leaving the ward.

As it happened, after a few days on the pediatrics ward, an interesting event occurred. There was an emergency requiring the immediate attention of the nurses on duty. The nursing supervisor, who knew Lucy well and with whom her activities had been carefully discussed, was absent. In the helter-skelter of activities that were going on Lucy was not told what to do. At that time, she was reading to the children, as she had been doing regularly, but was told by the other nurses, who were worried about other matters, that she was in the way while she was reading to the children. She never returned to her assignment—an interesting example of how fragile such persons may be.

Sometime shortly after this, for a variety of reasons, the specific procedures were discontinued. Lucy very promptly relapsed to her original behavior. In another week or two she was discharged home and two months later was recommended for legal commitment. There seemed to have been no subsequent recovery of what she had gained during the time that the specific behavior-influencing procedures were being carried on. A striking feature of our experience with a person as disadvantaged as she, was the patient, even tedious, search which we had to conduct for appropriate reinforcing circumstances. For years, positive self-attitudes or behaviors had not been in evidence to anyone including members of her own family.

### Case II

The second patient with whom we used these procedures was a 55-year-old man named Frank. He had been a steady worker in a skilled trade until he was about 40 years of age, at which time he had a minor accident and fractured a bone in one foot. He never worked again, and we saw him in the hospital 15 years later. He is one of those persons who have been described by Dr. Herbert Modlin of the Menninger Clinic, who suffer an apparently minor injury with profound persistent consequences for personality functioning. He complained of great difficulty with his foot and back, had a number of operations, mainly on the foot, and had been in several psychiatric hospitals because of symptoms of depression. In his most recent admission to a psychiatric hospital, a half year before we knew him, he had had electroconvulsive therapy without benefit. When he was admitted he talked only about his foot and back and his inability to work, and complained, "I can't form a mental image of anything." He would add to this, "I can't think," or "I can't remember." He could spend an hour talking on minor variants of these three themes.

We observed the assigned therapist through a one-way window when he interviewed Frank on several occasions. He was nondirective in the interviews with Frank, vigorously nodding his head often, as the patient described his symptoms. We have made observations on head-nodding in studies on interview behavior; Dr. Matarazzo summarized this work in a previous chapter of this book. We found that one can increase by 50 percent how long a person talks about whatever he's talking about if one nods his head intermittently. Our therapist was very vigorously reinforcing by head-nodding the kind of talk which he himself was complaining about in supervisory sessions. The patient persisted in this kind of symptom talk in session after session with the therapist. From the other kinds of observations we made, we learned that Frank rarely left his room and remained aloof from all other patients and ward activities. When one took the initiative and engaged him in conversation, Frank always gave the same stereotyped reasons for his nonparticipation: "I can't think, I can't remember, I just can't form a mental image of things."

After collecting a number of these observations we decided upon the following specific procedures: Symptom talk would not be rewarded; it would be ignored and, in fact, interrupted. Reward would be given for any talk about things he had done or could do and anything he was currently doing. We would reinforce doing or talking of doing but not symptom talk. If Frank paused while talking about symptoms in order to ruminate about more symptoms, which is what we had observed him doing with the assigned therapist, this would be discouraged by the experimenter's prompt intervention. The experimenter, in his interventions, would try to get Frank to talk about what he could do, or, if necessary, what he had done when he was well and a steady worker

Table 13-1: Frank: Interview Analysis with Assigned (A) and Experimental (B) Therapists

| | | Patient Utterances (means) | | | Therapist Utt. |
|---|---|---|---|---|---|
| Therap. | Utt./min. | Duration (seconds) | Latency (seconds) | % Talk of total | Duration (seconds) |
| A | 1.6 | 25.5 | 1.3 | 84.5 | 5.9 |
| B | 3.7 | 3.9 | 0.7 | 65.2 | 5.5 |
| Ten days later | | | | | |
| A | 0.9 | 23.9 | 0.3 | 91.6 | 6.3 |
| B | 4.2 | 4.6 | 3.3 | 66.7 | 4.8 |

Table 13-1 demonstrates the differences in Frank's emitted behavior with the experimental therapist and with the assigned therapist. The first column gives measurements based on two pairs of interviews. Although we gave no instruction about this, both the assigned therapist and the experimental therapist, as a matter of chance, happened to talk about 5 or 6 seconds each time they talked. As Matarazzo reports previously in this book, when one talks 5 seconds in a nondirective way in an interview, the patient tends to talk about 25-30 seconds. As indicated in Table 13-1, Frank averaged 26 seconds. These data are consistent with Matarazzo's report of carefully controlled interview data. The duration of time that the therapist talks is a highly influential factor in the amount of time the patient talks. In this case, however, this was not the significant variable. There was considerable difference between the two therapists in their behavior with the patient in two sessions that were roughly 10 days apart.

With the assigned therapist, who was behaving in his nondirective supportive way, Frank talked about 1.6 times per minute; he talked 25½ seconds at a time. Frank talked 85 percent of the total talk in the interview. The experimental therapist talked more often and elicited more talk per minute from the patient. However, the patient was talking for a considerably briefer period (about 4 seconds) and, of the total talk during the interview, Frank talked only about two thirds of the time. Ten days later we repeated these observations; many interesting things had happened in the interval. The assigned therapist had become very curious about certain changes in the patient's behavior with him. (He had been asked not to observe or inquire about the experimental therapist's specific procedures.) Nevertheless, he was interviewing the patient in precisely the same way as previously. Frank was talking about once a minute for about 25 seconds, and accounting for 90 percent of the total talk in the interview. The experimental therapist was still hewing to the previously prescribed line.

After the first interview with the experimental therapist, there were some remarkable changes in Frank's behavior. These were noticed by the assigned therapist and soon began to be noticed by personnel on the ward. After one of these experimental interviews, the patient was reported to have been more spontaneous with the assigned therapist, to have talked less about his symptoms, and to have stayed longer on other topics. Further, there occurred a phenomenon which is always surprising even though it has happened frequently in the past under similar circumstances. In the next interview, the patient introduced totally new content which he had never told anybody else and which the therapist had not realized existed. This was a history of overt homosexuality and bestiality going back 40 years. He told the therapist that he had not talked about these matters to anyone else previously. He had not thought about them for many years. Thus "new" kinds of memories, as Alexander and French (1946) have pointed out, can be released as behavioral changes are induced by the planned action of an experimental therapist. There were seven experimental sessions spread over about a month. During this period Frank showed a number of changes in some of the other settings available to us for observation. For instance, he made an increasing number of contributions in group therapy sessions, which he began to attend regularly. He showed increased participation in ward activity including social activities; he was even observed to play basketball. He had previously complained of such pain in his foot and back that he could not walk, or stand up long enough at one time to hold a job; he was now playing basketball without any comment. He did not talk in his usual complaining way. He also completed a toy house as a Christmas gift for one of his grandchildren. He began working in occupational therapy and in industrial therapy; at first he worked a few hours a week, but by the end of the month he was working 30 hours a week. In addition, following a suggestion of the occupational therapist, he was teaching other people on the ward certain carpentry skills that had been in his repertoire for many years.

We became aware at this point that his family was behaving with him precisely as if they had been traditional interns in our program, trained to do nondirective supportive therapy. His family was reinforcing his symptom talk. We observed that they were always very sympathetic when Frank talked about his symptoms. In our discussions with the family we pointed out the consequences of their behavior in rewarding symptom talk, and indicated ways of extinguishing such behavior by nonreward. After several such family interviews, Frank was discharged. In some ways he was like the frontal lobotomy patients previously described in that, if we gave him the slightest encouragement, the old patterns of verbalization recurred: "I can't think, I can't remember, I can't form a mental image of things, I can't do anything." Thus, while he was actually working regularly 30 hours a week, if asked whether he could work, he would reply that he was unable to work.

### Case III

A third patient, Bill, was a 53-year-old, twice-married professional man. He had been an alcoholic, an overt homosexual, and had had a number of episodes of depression, with several serious suicide attempts. Nevertheless, Bill had been very successful professionally, socially, and politically and had been a well-known figure in his state. He was observed in a variety of settings. It was noticed that he was very facile in language, very perceptive about the difficulties of the other patients, and was always discussing the other patients and their difficulties, criticizing them, admonishing them, and acting like an assistant therapist. After a while many patients began to tell Bill that they did not like this behavior and that as far as they could see it was his way of evading facing his own

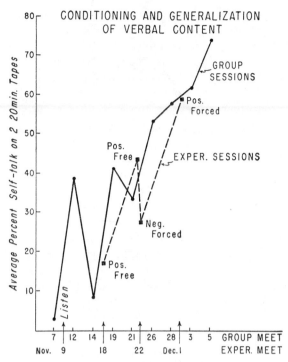

Figure 13-1. Bill—self-reference in experimental and test sessions.

problems. Consequently Bill was being subjected to rather powerful negative group attitudes. However, his behavior of not talking about himself continued. In this instance, group sanctions alone were not adequate to change behavior.

To help Bill rectify the balance between exploration of his own difficulties and directing attention to others' difficulties, we then decided to concentrate on the response class "talking about oneself." Figure 13-1 contains the observations which we made with Bill.

The experimental sessions are shown on the dotted line, and the full line shows the ongoing ward group therapy sessions which met several times a week. We obtained permission from the group to have tape recordings made which we could then work on with Bill in the experimental sessions. On the left, at the point marked "listen, November 9th," he was given two 20-minute samples of the tape recording of the preceding group therapy session. He was, of course, not the only one who had spoken. Bill was asked only to listen to these two 20-minute selections of tape. In the next group therapy session (full line, November 12), when he was talking, the percentage of time (on two 20-minute tapes) that he talked about himself went up from below 10 to nearly 40. In the following group therapy session, this increase in talk about himself was not sustained; he was nearly back to the pre-experiment level. What we next tried is described on the dotted line under the label of "positive free reinforcement." During a 20-minute group therapy tape recording, Bill was asked to listen and to stop the tape and comment on it any time he wished. He was strongly reinforced and could go on if he made a comment which included a reference to himself. After that kind of session, in the next group therapy session, the average percentage of talk about himself in relation to his total talk increased to about 40. Another such experimental session was held some days later and is labeled "positive free reinforcement." In the following group therapy session, Bill nearly maintained the increase in percentage of time that he talked about himself. The procedure in the next experimental session (labeled "negative forced reinforcement") was different. The tape was managed by the experimental therapist in this way: every two minutes (in a sample of Bill's talk) the tape was stopped. Although not specifically told to do so, Bill was invited to make a comment on what he had said in such a way as to include some reference to himself. If he did so, the tape was played forward for another two-minute sample. But if Bill did not refer to himself, the same two-minute talk sample was played again (as a mildly aversive stimulus). We set ourselves the punishment limit of playing one sample no more than five times. We never had to play the same sample more than three times. As is evident in the two following group therapy sessions, the percentage of time that Bill talked about himself reached new high levels.

In the last experimental session, labeled "positive forced reinforcement," the tape was played for a two-minute sample that included a remark by Bill. He was given a chance to comment, and if he said something which included a remark about himself, he was rewarded by the playing of another two-minute segment. During this period, Bill was never punished by repetition of a sample. In the ten-group therapy sessions that followed, the percentage of the time that he talked about himself in relation to his total talk became still higher and remained high.

Figure 13-2 presents a different point in which we became interested. We compared three different ways in which we used the tape, by computing the average time in seconds that Bill talked about himself during each specific procedure, in relation to the first third of the tape, the middle third of the tape, and the last third of the tape. In the last third of the "negative forced reinforcement" sample, dated November 22, Bill showed a great increase in the number of seconds he talked about himself as he was subjected to this mildly punishing situation. In the "positive forced reinforcement" session, he remained at a fairly high level. With the "positive free reinforcement" technique he started low, and the amount of talk about himself in a number of seconds increased. In the negative forced session, he was definitely uncomfortable as we would play the tape over and over; his lips were dry, he would repeatedly moisten them, he

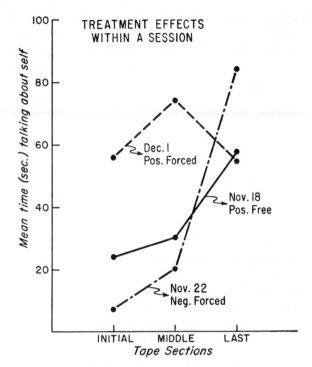

Figure 13-2.  Bill—differential effects of different reinforcement procedures.

seemed to squirm around a good deal, there were long pauses—quite unusual for him—between one kind of statement and another, and he
seemed very anxious during the entire session.

His behavior of including himself in his conversations with other people
was sustained for several months after the experimental sessions were
discontinued. He showed, in general, a much greater acceptance of the
other people on the ward. He had the very difficult and realistic problem
of finding a new kind of work that was acceptable to him in terms of his
previous status, professional training, financial need, and age. He went
through a number of employment disappointments which he handled
far better than he had previously, without relapsing more than once or
twice into the old episodes of alcoholism, homosexuality, suicide attempts,
and so on.

We interpreted the events that helped him to get through these crises
as follows: His most successful periods during his adult life had been in
close and meaningful relationships with a strong woman; his wife in two
instances and a woman superior in a third. But these people were through
with him for good. When the people on the ward began to accept him because he seemed more like one of them instead of a fake therapist or staff
member, their acceptance of him helped him to deal with rebuffs when

he no longer had a significant woman figure in the picture. If this were the case, it would be an example of a situation in which a particular behavior, apparently not overly significant by itself, can paralyze nearly all other opportunities for growth and gratification in the patient's life. Thus if some positive improvement in this behavior can be effected, new opportunities and new sources of strength are made available to the person as he works on other problems.

## DISCUSSION

Some general observations arise from the study of these three patients. In any given social situation, as on our ward, an individual has multiple interpersonal relations. How can a research design take into account the effects on the patient of our specific procedures when so many other important influences are active in the same period? Can it always be done as neatly as by observing the temporal sequence of events, as when the dramatic change in Frank, after one experimental interview, simply overwhelmed the assigned therapist the next time he saw him? We will not always have things that dramatic, but observation in terms of temporal sequence can be helpful in dealing with a problem as complicated as Frank's. Another way of dealing with these multiple relationships would be the repeated introduction and abandonment of the specific procedures we use. This means that our whole staff has to be willing to watch a patient improve and then watch the patient relapse. This is what happened in the case of the first patient. Will we be able to do this deliberately? This is an important point involving the morale of a whole staff.

As we carried out our observations, we found that the attitudes of both our medical and our nursing staff were extremely important. For example, we didn't want to contaminate our experiments by letting people know, when we first started, what we were doing in the experimental sessions. It was very obvious after Frank's first session that he was behaving differently on the ward. Everybody knew that something about him had changed. They tried to find out what was going on, but the experimenters desired to keep their procedures uncontaminated. They were denying everyone else on the ward staff information, while apparently doing wonderful things. Ideally, we would like to try out such procedures in ways similar to those used to test out a drug, with a placebo for contrast in the double-blind experiment. We would like the other members of the staff not to know what we were doing, so they would make, without prejudice, the kinds of observations that they ordinarily would. But if we are at all successful in changing behavior, the staff's curiosity is aroused. Therefore, we have to find some way of having the staff act as we need them to, and yet wait until the experiments are over to find out about the specific procedures used. We did not solve this problem. We realized that we had taken for granted certain things about members of our staff that we should not have taken for granted. It was particularly the nursing staff, because of their tradition of emphasizing patient care, who had problems in accepting the research attitude of the experimenters. Nurses are trained to give care and to help. However, it is clear that, in some of the things we need to evaluate, the most important thing the nurses can do is to stop being so helpful. We would like them not to intervene, yet to remain interested in what is happening, and to make careful observations. We have taken for granted that it is feasible for a staff to collaborate in this way. However, we actually were putting the nurses into serious internal conflict about this, because it is by no means an easy kind of behavior to practice. Many psychotherapists have the greatest difficulty in doing research about psychotherapy because of this kind of emotional involvement. Thus, this is not a problem limited to nurses. We have thought of such things as trying to create a different climate for everybody on the staff. Our initial mistake was to limit this climate to the research workers. Perhaps we should have involved the nurses in a more effective and comfortable way by making it clear that we were doing experimental work with a certain patient and that we would describe the program at a staff meeting as soon as we were ready. Perhaps a better technique is to find a way of involving a member of the nursing staff and of every other professional group on a ward as participants in the research effort itself. Thus everybody would know that he would have a chance to contribute to the research activity on the ward. All staff members could then be aware of the difficulties of research investigators, especially in terms of the problems involved when staff knowledge of the nature of the experiment would itself change the very nature and results of that experiment. As experimenters, we must be able to keep certain information to ourselves for a time without feeling that we are dishonest with our colleagues.

It is clear that if these procedures are worth pursuing, then we are dependent upon a careful prior analysis of the patient's behavior as manifested in a number of different settings. These include behavior with a therapist, behavior with one or more members of his family, behavior in the industrial therapy situation where he works for his employer, and behavior with other patients. In all these observations the question arises whether we are interfering with his privacy. We do not always think about this because we take the view that we are inquiring about his behavior for his own ultimate good. Patients will, in fact, sometimes raise questions such as, "Will everything I say to a nurse go into the nurse's notes and get back to you?" Patients will often also say, "I want to thank you for having behaved in such and such a way, for example, shared information about me or induced me to try this or that. I wouldn't have done it by myself, but I can see that I am now managing things better. I want to thank you for making me do it this way." A patient can be coerced in his own interests. He can thank the staff for this coercion because he now feels as if he is a real member of his society, whatever that society may be. Dr. Kanfer and I, as well as others, think that there are important ethical problems about privacy which we are not quite sure how to resolve. We feel that there are such problems because the kind of language just quoted from our patients in the United States in 1964 is no different from the kind of language which one will read in Lifton's book (1961) describing Chinese totalism. Lifton describes the talk of university students who had been "brainwashed" and the talk of people who had been sent to concentration camps. They were coerced against their will and they came out very different beings. They belonged to a people and a society to which they had not belonged previously, and they were very grateful that now they belonged to somebody since it had been miserable to be alienated. The similarities of attitude of those whose behavior has been altered, in societies that seem so different, raise interesting and important questions that people in our society who use controlling and privacy-invading procedures such as we have been describing must face.

Finally, the persistence and generalization of the behavior alterations brought about by the type of procedure described are unknown. The kinds of stimulus situations that will have to be built into the subsequent living arrangements of such patients to maintain the behavior altered by therapy are also unknown. However, while there is a great deal of empirical work which can and must be done, the application of the new assumptions we discussed seems exciting and very promising.

# 14

## Things to Come: Designing Neurotic Computers
### KENNETH MARK COLBY

olby is a trained psychoanalyst who has done empirical research and is now extending his investigations to the field of computer simulation. The very titles of Colby's books indicate this unique combination of interests: *A Primer for Psychotherapists* (1951); *Energy and Structure in Psychoanalysis* (1955); *A Skeptical Psychoanalyst* (1958); and *An Introduction to Psychoanalytic Research* (1960a). Colby's researches have also included studies of the effects of the therapist's presence or absence on the production and content of free associations (Colby, 1960b) and of the relationship between therapist "input" and patient free association (Colby, 1961a).

In this chapter, which draws on the growing field of computer simulation (Borko, 1962; Colby, 1964; Colby & Gilbert, 1964; Tomkins & Messick, 1963), Colby outlines his search for methods to increase his ability or "leverage" to influence his patients. His goal is to find the therapist's responses that will most effectively alter the patient's behavior. The verbal response labeled "interpretation" is the analyst's major vehicle for bringing about a change in the patient. Numerous authors have attempted to identify various types of interpretation and their differential effects (Bordin, 1955; Dittmann, 1952; Raush *et al.*, 1956). Within the operant conditioning model there have been a series of investigations which have compared the effects of interpretations with the effects of other social reinforcers (Adams, Butler, & Noblin, 1962; Adams, Noblin, Butler, & Timmons, 1962; Noblin, Timmons, & Reynard, 1963).

In this chapter Colby defines the patient as an information processing system (Colby, 1961b) and the analyst's task as the input of the information most likely to change the system. A computer may help scan the bits of information available and aid in the selection of the most effective alternatives. The therapist, then, is seen as being that part of the machine system that delivers the information selected by the computer. In short, the psychoanalyst is the automatic pellet dispenser of a Skinner box.

Colby's research, if successful, will tend to decrease considerably the time involved in training a psychoanalyst. It takes the ordinary analyst many years of contact with patients and other analysts to learn the correct verbal responses to emit in the patient's presence. Colby is enlisting the aid of modern computer science to eliminate this trial-and-error process to make therapy more effective.

The implication of Colby's paper, in terms of the use of computers, the search for techniques of leverage, and the new views of therapist and patient roles, is fascinating and provocative. Whether he agrees or disagrees with Colby's approach, in coming to grips with Colby's concepts the reader will test and clarify his own formulations.

L.K.-L.P.U.

RATHER THAN ENTER INTO a discussion of the technical details of computer programing, I shall try to say what we hope to accomplish with this method.

A psychotherapist is faced with the problem of trying to modify neurotic processes in persons who come to him. With clinical experience he begins to realize not only his own limitations but the limitations of techniques currently available. He gets good results in some cases but not in others. He wants to do better, to have more powerful techniques, than he has at present. He looks to research to discover something useful.

In psychotherapy research the approaches to problems are roughly categorized as naturalistic and experimental. In a naturalistic approach we study the events of ongoing therapy and try to find out what is happening in this two-person situation. The measurement operations are usually limited to counting, and the investigator comes up with statistical answers in the form of percentages. In experimental approaches, instead of trying to cover the whole process of therapy, one isolates a particular event or group of events and reproduces it experimentally. One hopes thereby to gain control over elusive variables.

Both of these approaches are purely empirical. They search for observable regularities. They try to find dependable generalizations and construct laws that will apply to a general population. But the question is: Does this give us what we want? Certainly we have gained some information in this way. Yet all of the psychotherapy research for the past 15 or 20 years has had no effect on the actual practice of psychotherapy because a statistical answer does not help the individual therapist in making proper decisions with an individual patient. It does not give a therapist what he wants, namely, increased influence or leverage with a particular person. The failure of conventional research approaches to this problem forces us to consider alternatives, to seek novelty, to try anything that looks promising.

## COMPUTER SIMULATION

One such novelty is the area of computer simulation. There are many areas of inquiry in which computers are now being used in an attempt to understand complex situations. The strategy of this approach differs somewhat from the strategy of conventional science. It involves model-building as a type of theory construction rather than a search for laws. In most model-building we start off with something we call a real system which is observable in the world, for example, there are planets and there are persons. We observe this real system and note some kind of behavior, output, or activity—not necessarily a regularity. For instance, what we observe about persons in a psychotherapeutic situation is their utterances. From this behavior we postulate a purely hypothetical system and assume that this system is generating the observed behavior. The hypothetical system is not intended to account for all of the behavior of the real system but only for some of its cardinal aspects.

The "accounting for" represents a group of explanations by theory rather than an explanation by summary. If we heat a piece of metal and it expands, one might ask "Why does it expand?" An explanation by summary would state "All metals expand when heated." An explanation by theory would postulate a model, stating "Metal is composed of tiny particles moving in space; as they become heated they move faster and away from one another and thus the metal expands."

Let us view a person as a large, complex system with many idiosyncratic elements. It is a dynamic system that changes in time and is never in exactly the same state twice. It is an information-processing, symbolizing system that bestows meanings on symbols and comprehends those meanings. It is an evolutionary system that can directly generate new combinations and by selective mechanisms sort out from the many combinations which are good and which are bad, thus improving in time. Finally it is a decision-making system that can choose one course of action when faced with alternatives. If we view a real system, a person, as having these properties, why not use another real system that also has these properties to simulate it? A computer can be programed to exhibit these properties, which we feel to be characteristic of persons. Until the computer came along we could not handle multivariate systems of this great order of symbolic complexity.

Among the many objections that can be voiced against this approach of computer simulation, two are outstanding. First, the theories of the model are not known to be true and in fact may be known to be false. This could be fatal for a scientific theory that purports to be true. But a computer program does not attempt to yield only true conclusions. Only some of its outcomes are expected to have confirmable contact points with reality. Second, in an attempt to simplify, the boundary conditions may be too narrow. Again this is not bothersome at the moment. The only way one can judge what are the appropriate boundary conditions is to try out alternatives until one is satisfied. Assumptions regarding boundary conditions must be first actualized and run in a program. Decisions regarding them cannot be made entirely from the armchair.

The data for simulation programs comes from observing real persons. If one wished to simulate a cognitive process such as chess-playing, the way to go about it is to observe a person playing chess. Ask him to think out loud and record on a tape recorder the descriptions of self-observation reported by the player. This description will contain not only thoughts about decisions to be made but thoughts about thoughts and perhaps this sort of meta-thinking down to three or four levels. Then one writes a program that will play chess, using heuristics similar to those used by the person. A person may or may not be aware of the heuristics he is using. When he is not, they are supplied to the program by the programer. Thus a program contains not only copies of observations regarding the real world but also the programer's notions and inferences regarding the real world.

In the case of the psychotherapeutic situation, we first try to write a program that simulates the behavior output of a particular patient. Then we attempt to modify its behavior by making inputs into the system much as a therapist does. A computer provides an ideal experimental situation in a true laboratory. It is ideal because it represents the extreme of an artificial simplified system that can be deliberately interfered with, using independent variables entirely under our control. In experiments with real persons the deceptions, duping, and game-playing involved make it difficult to evaluate what the independent variables actually are. Also, even with experimental subjects we cannot do or say anything we want to them. Words are powerful explosives and can do persons harm. But with computer programs the ethics of nonhurting do not apply. An interesting paradox will arise when, as computers become more and more like persons, the question will come up "Is it ethical to hurt them?" If a program can pass all the tests we subject a person to in order to tell if he is a person, then we may have to consider it as deserving of the ethics we apply to persons. Do these machines feel? I don't know. Do they think? No, they just think they think.

## UNANSWERED QUESTIONS

How will we know when these programs correctly represent a neurotic process in a person? There are no decision criteria available for establishing the approximate truth of such models. One might consider a form of Turing's test. Turing (1950) proposed that if a machine could answer every question a person could answer, if their outputs were indistinguishable, then the machine was an adequate representation of a person. In the case of a neurotic program, we might show to clinicians 10 examples of a series of sentences from the machine and 10 from the patient. If a clinician could not distinguish them at better than chance probability we could begin to think we have a good approximation. But we need better tests and measures than clinicians' judgments.

One could also take the position that truth is created and not found. Is space really three-dimensional and Euclidean or is it curved and Riemanian? It depends on how human observers decide to view reality for coping with their particular problems. If neurotic processes are viewed as programs, does that get us anywhere with the problem of understanding and influencing neuroses in a psychotherapeutic situation? The answer to this question remains to be seen.

# 15

## Behavioral Modifications through Modeling Procedures*

### ALBERT BANDURA

$B$andura has made contributions to work on child development (Bandura, 1963a), aggression (Bandura, Ross, & Ross, 1961, 1963a; Bandura & Walters, 1958, 1959), modeling (Bandura, 1963b; Bandura & Huston, 1961; Bandura & Kupers, 1964; Bandura & McDonald, 1963), and social learning (Bandura, 1962b; Bandura, Ross, & Ross, 1963b, 1963c; Bandura & Walters, 1963). His research on psychotherapy has ranged from investigations of the relationship between psychotherapists' characteristics and patient behavior (Bandura, 1956; Bandura, Lipsher, & Miller, 1960) to important reviews of behavior therapy (Bandura, 1961, 1962a). In the present chapter, Bandura reviews his systematic program of research on a particularly effective behavior modification technique. He tests the conditions under which modeling procedures facilitate the emission of particular behaviors. In these situations, reinforcement plays a major role just as it played a vital part in learning to model per se. Once learning to model is in the individual's repertoire, the focus of research becomes twofold: under what conditions will modeling behavior occur, and under what conditions will performances be more quickly learned by modeling than by procedures such as chaining and shaping?

Bandura's distinction between performance and learning is of major importance. For example, it can be linked to Sarbin's view of hypnosis as a role-playing situation. The concepts of performance and self-reinforcement are importance ingredients in a subject's evaluation of the effects of playing certain roles. In this instance, self-reinforcement may also be related to the subject's estimate of his own ability to elicit rewards (level of aspiration) by the manner in which he performs his role. Sarbin is also interested in the way in which an individual adopts model behavior when he learns to act like a hypnotized subject.

Bandura raises theoretical questions which lead to a broadening of the scope of social reinforcement theories to include concepts such as plans (Miller, Ga-

* The experiments reported in this paper were supported in part by Research Grant M-5162 from the National Institutes of Health, United States Public Health Service.

lanter, & Pribram, 1960), modeling, and vicarious reinforcement, as discriminative stimuli (Skinner, 1963). Further, Bandura discusses some of the classic topics of personality and psychotherapy, such as delay of gratification, and brings them within the scope of social reinforcement. Bandura's argument is not with operant conditioning procedures per se, but rather against the restriction of explanatory concepts to exact analogues of the rodent in the Skinner box. That is, all applications of reinforcement principles that are effective with infrahuman animals will be effective with humans but not all applications of reinforcement principles that are effective with humans will be effective with infrahumans.

Once an individual is under the control of the discriminative stimuli of other people's behavior, these stimuli may be used to alter his future behavior. That is, there will be "no-trial learning" when the person has learned to attend to other people as sources of information. Once this has been achieved there can be a determination of the conditions under which modeling is the behavior modification technique of choice. For example, Jones (1924) reports an instance in which one child was used to demonstrate a lack of a fear of a small animal to another child. Unexpectedly, the model acquired the other child's fear instead of vice versa. This is an instance in which modeling effectively changed behavior but in a direction opposite to the one desired. We may compare the Isaacs, Thomas, and Goldiamond (1960) shaping of a mute patient's speech with an approach using modeling (Staples, Wilson, & Walters, 1963). In this latter study, the investigators selected patients whose verbal behavior was minimal. Two series of slides were presented to the patients with the instructions to talk about what they saw. Some of the patients were exposed to a talkative model who freely described and commented on the slides between the exposures of the first and second series. The other half of the patients listened to music between the two slide presentations. Compared to the patients exposed to the music, patients exposed to the talkative model showed a marked increase in verbal behavior. Additional examples of modeling in a therapeutic context are given by Chittenden (1942), Jack (1934), and Page (1936).

Bandura suggests the use of modeling in a hierarchic progression. Such a procedure is similar to Wolpe's use of behavioral hierarchies in his technique of systematic desensitization (1954, 1958). Both methods involve taking an individual through a series of progressively more difficult behaviors. In modeling, a person views an adequate handling of these situations, while in desensitization he associates a more adjustive response to the stimulus situations.

Similar to behavior modification techniques which have been in the literature for many years (Burnham, 1924; Hollingworth, 1930; Jersild & Holmes, 1935; Guthrie, 1938), modeling is a technique that is once again being studied because of research such as that by Bandura and the other authors in this book.

L.K.-L.P.U

MOST THEORIES OF BEHAVIOR assume that, in order for learning to occur, the subject must perform a response and experience prompt response-contingent reinforcing consequences. This conceptualization of the learning process presents two important theoretical problems.

First, it requires the subject to perform some approximation of the response before he can learn it. In cases in which a behavioral pattern contains a highly unique combination of elements selected from an almost infinite number of alternatives, the probability of occurrence of the desired response, or even one that has some remote resemblence to it, will be zero. Nor is the successive-approximations shaping procedure likely to be of much aid in altering this probability value. It is highly doubtful, for example, that an experimenter could get a mynah bird to sing a chorus of "Sweet Adeline" during his lifetime by differential reinforcement of the birds squeaks and squawks. Nevertheless, a recent appearance of a gifted mynah bird on television demonstrated how a young housewife who had employed modeling procedures succeeded, not only in training her feathered friend to sing this sentimental ballad with considerable fidelity, but also developed in the bird an extensive verbal repertoire.

Second, traditional behavior theories assume that the subject somehow suspends learning until the occurrence of reinforcing consequences following the termination of the response. Thus, if an experimenter were to inform a child that Columbus discovered America in 1492, the acquisition of this knowledge is presumably delayed and made contingent on the occurrence of a rewarding payoff. While consequent reinforcing events can alter significantly the future probability of occurrence of preceding responses, these events can hardly serve as a necessary precondition for their acquisition.

In this chapter I shall present some research supporting a theory of *no-trial learning*, a process of response acquisition that is highly prevalent among Homo sapiens, exceedingly efficient and, in cases where errors are dangerous or costly, becomes an indispensable means of transmitting and modifying behavioral repertoires. For example, one does not employ trial-and-error or operant conditioning methods in training children to swim, adolescents to drive an automobile, or in getting adults to acquire vocational skills. Indeed, if training proceeded in this manner, very few persons would ever survive the process of socialization. It is evident from informal observation that the behavior of models is utilized extensively to accelerate the acquisition process, and to prevent one-trial extinction of the organism in situations where an error may produce fatal consequences.

In assessing the relative efficacy of modeling and operant conditioning procedures in promoting behavioral change, it is important to distinguish learning from performance. Operant conditioning is an exceed-

ingly reliable and efficient method for strengthening and maintaining responses that already exist in the behavioral repertoire of an organism.
Through careful management of incentives, the frequency, amplitude,
latency, and the discriminative patterning of responses can be readily
modified. Most of the psychotherapeutic applications of this principle
have, in fact, been concerned with problems of performance rather than
of learning. By selecting an adequate reinforcer and arranging the appropriate response-reinforcement contingencies, a therapist can induce a
mute catatonic, who possesses a language repertoire, to emit linguistic responses; schizophrenics who have previously acquired adequate eating
repertoires can be impelled to feed themselves within specified time
schedules, and college students who command an abundant supply of
personal pronouns can be subtly prompted to emit these verbal responses
at a relatively high rate.

While operant conditioning methods are well suited for controlling existing responses, they are often exceedingly laborious and inefficient for
developing new behavioral repertoires. The fact that a patient and persistent experimenter may eventually develop a novel response in an organism through the method of successive approximations, *provided he
carefully arranges a benign environment in which errors will not produce
fatal consequences,* is no proof that this is the manner in which social responses are typically acquired in everyday life. Let me illustrate this
point by referring to Bachrach's (1963) case of Rodent E. Lee, a southern
cousin of Barnabus, the Barnard rat (Pierrol & Sherman, 1958, reported in
Lundin, 1961, pp. 178-184). Through a long series of training sessions,
based on differential reinforcement, the rat ultimately learned a relatively
complicated chain of responses in which he climbed a circular stairway to
a second landing, lowered a draw bridge to cross the miniature room, rode
a cable car down an inclined plane, climbed a second set of stairs to a
third story, struck two piano keys on a miniature Steinway, crawled
through a wire tunnel, and after entering an elevator, the winded rodent
pulled a chain that lowered the elevator to the ground floor where he received a well-earned delectable pellet, immediately after striking a bar.

Let us expand this rodent colonial mansion to human proportions, enlist
a resurrected Rodent E. Lee as the performing subject, and substitute a
bottle of bonded bourbon for the pellets. In getting him to master this sequential task, would one embark on a similar training program requiring
Rodent E. Lee to engage in a lengthy series of random trial-and-error
behavior, in which correct responses are reinforced positively, while inappropriate or incorrectly sequenced responses are left unrewarded? I
seriously doubt that anyone would so choose to accomplish the training
objective. Obviously, the simplest and most commonly employed procedure would be to provide the General with either a skilled model who
demonstrated the correct responses in their appropriate sequence, or a

symbolic model presented pictorially or through verbal descriptions. It is a safe prediction that the General would exhibit the entire novel repertoire on the first trial without having had to engage in tedious and haphazard trial-and-error experimentation.

Much social learning is fostered by exposure to real-life models who perform, intentionally or unwittingly, patterns of behavior that may be imitated by others. Once a learner has developed an adequate verbal repertoire, however, increasing reliance is placed on the use of verbally or pictorially present symbolic models. A psychological trainee, for example, can learn the complex repertoire necessary for administering an intelligence test simply by matching the responses described in the instructional manual. Since, however, an actual performance is apt to provide substantially more relevant cues with greater clarity than can be conveyed by a verbal description, a combination of verbal and demonstrational procedures is usually most effective in transmitting new patterns of behavior.

## RELATIVE EFFICACY OF OPERANT CONDITIONING AND MODELING PROCEDURES

The relative superiority of modeling procedures over operant conditioning techniques in promoting behavioral change is most apparent in learning situations in which there is no reliable eliciting stimulus for the desired responses apart from the discriminative cues provided by social models as they exhibit the behavior. If a child had no occasion to hear the word "successive approximations," for example, it is doubtful whether this verbal response could ever be shaped by differential reinforcement of the child's random vocalizations. Even in cases where some stimulus is known to be capable of eliciting an approximation to the desired behavior, the process of learning can be considerably shortened and accelerated by the provision of models. This is particularly true when the presence of strong dominant repertoires limit the opportunity for reinforcing the desired subordinate responses because of their infrequent occurrence. An experiment designed to test the validity of Piaget's stage theory of moral development provides a laboratory illustration of the latter point (Bandura & McDonald, 1963).

According to Piaget (1948), one can distinguish two clear-cut stages of moral orientations demarcated from each other at approximately seven years of age. In the first stage, defined as objective morality, children judge the gravity of a deviant act in terms of the amount of material damages, and disregard the intentionality of the action. By contrast, during the second or subjective morality stage, children judge conduct in terms of its intent rather than its material consequences. The sequence and timing of these stages are considered by Piaget to be predetermined and invariant.

Children who exhibited predominantly objective or subjective moral

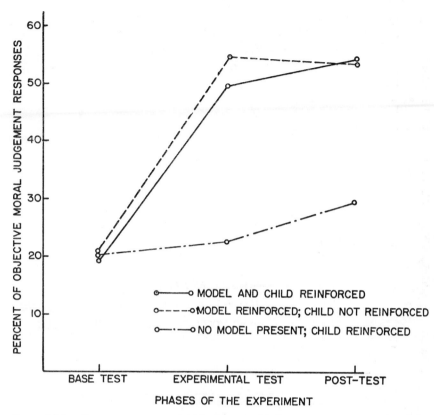

Figure 15-1. Mean percentage of objective moral-judgment responses produced by subjective children on each of three test periods for each of three experimental conditions. [M. R. Jones (Ed.), *Nebraska Symposium on Motivation*. Lincoln, Neb.: University of Nebraska Press, 1962.]

orientations were assigned to one of three experimental conditions. One group of children observed adult models who expressed moral judgments counter to the group's orientation and the children were reinforced with approval for adopting the models' evaluative responses. A second group observed the models, but the children received no reinforcement for matching the models' behavior. In both of the modeling treatment conditions, the model and the child were administered alternately different sets of stimulus items, with the model receiving the first item, the child the second one, and so on. The third group had no exposure to the models, but each subject was reinforced whenever he expressed moral judgments that ran counter to his dominant evaluative tendencies. Thus the experimental design permitted a test of the relative influence of direct social reinforcement and of the behavior of models, and these two factors combined in shaping children's moral judgments.

The provision of models was found to be highly effective in altering the

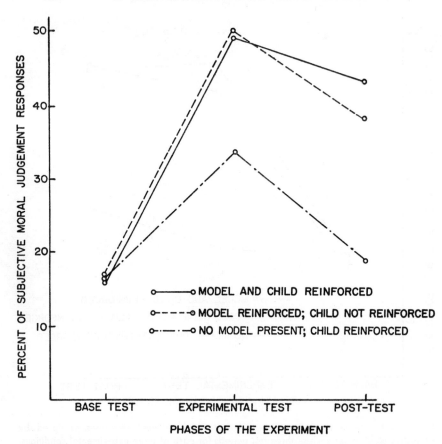

Figure 15-2. Mean percentage of subjective moral-judgment responses produced by objective children on each of three test periods for each of three experimental conditions. [M. R. Jones (Ed.), *Nebraska Symposium on Motivation*. Lincoln, Neb.: University of Nebraska Press, 1962.]

children's judgmental responses. Objective children modified their moral orientations toward subjectivity; similarly, subjective children became considerably more objective in their judgmental behavior (Figures 15-1 and 15-2). Moreover, the children maintained their altered orientations in a new test situation when models and social reinforcement were absent. Operant conditioning alone produced slight response increases in the direction of the social influence but not of statistically significant magnitude.

Inspection of the test protocols from the acquisition phase revealed that in the operant conditioning groups, the subordinate responses were either totally absent or occurred so infrequently that there was little opportunity to influence them through reinforcement. For example, only 9 percent of the children who were exposed to the objective models failed to produce a single objective judgmental response, whereas 38 percent of the chil-

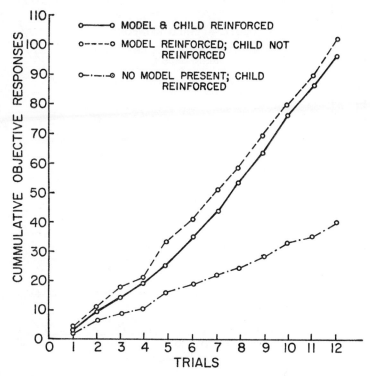

Figure 15-3. Cumulative frequency curves of the acquisition of objective responses from subjective children in each of three experimental conditions.

dren in the operant conditioning groups did not emit a single objective response. As shown in the cumulative frequency curves (Figures 15-3 and 15-4), modeling procedures produced the appropriate matching responses early in the learning sequence and maintained them at a relatively high level.

It is interesting to note that in both replications of the experiment, children who were nonrewarded for emitting matching responses that produced positive social reinforcements for their respective models displayed a similar rate of matching behavior as subjects whose imitation was continuously reinforced. These experimental findings are somewhat analagous to evidence from informal observation that children often persist in their efforts to reproduce through imitation child-prohibited adult-role activities that are observed to be highly rewarding to parental models.

Some additional evidence for the relative efficacy of modeling techniques in promoting learning, even in the case of subhuman species, is provided in studies reported by Warden and his associates (Warden, Fjeld, & Koch, 1940; Warden & Jackson, 1935). The investigators spent a considerable amount of time in training rhesus monkeys, by the trial-

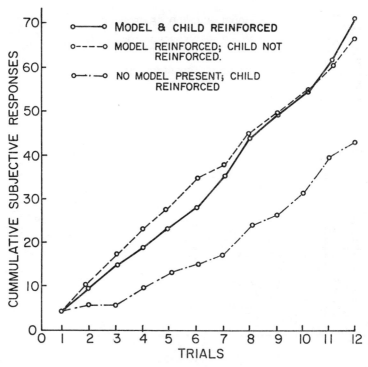

Figure 15-4. Cumulative frequency curves of the acquisition of subjective responses from objective children in each of three experimental conditions.

and-error method, to master four problem-solving tasks in which the animals opened doors to obtain raisins by pulling chains, turning knobs, or manipulating latches. Following training, the primate models manipulated the puzzle devices while naïve monkeys, presented with a duplicate set of problems, observed the skilled performers. It was found that naïve observers displayed instantaneous imitative solutions in 76 percent of the test trials!

If the proverbial Martian were to review earth-man's psychological literature he would undoubtedly be quite puzzled by the fact that researchers interested in the learning process have focused their attention almost exclusively on the slower and more laborious trial-and-error procedures, to the relative neglect of more prevalent and economical processes and methods.

Skinner has, of course, recognized the utility of "echoic" procedures for "short-circuiting of the process of progressive approximation" in the development of verbal operants (Skinner, 1957). This is not surprising, since operant conditioning procedures alone would be totally ineffective in shaping linguistic responses. As illustrated in the introductory section of this chapter, verbalizing models are not only helpful, but actually indispensable in promoting language learning. Had Skinner extended the application of modeling procedures to other classes of responses, the amount of attention devoted by current researchers to experimental analyses of imitative or observational learning would probably be more commensurate with the obviously important contribution of modeling variables to social learning in everyday life.

In a recent article, Skinner (1963) expressed some reservations about the use of modeling procedures in learning experiments because they circumvent the operant analysis of behavior. It is true that modeling techniques typically produce rapid acquisition of patterned responses and, therefore, throw relatively little light on the behavioral processes that characterize the slower operant conditioning procedure. This outcome, however, can hardly be considered a regrettable state of affairs. Indeed, the fact that organisms can readily acquire through observation complex operants without undergoing hazardous consequences and needless experimentation has contributed more to man's longevity than all the remarkable advances in medical science.

Skinner's arguments against the utilization of models in social learning are somewhat puzzling. It is highly debatable, for example, that modeling procedures that teach a person how to operate a machine are not concerned with problems of response acquisition:

> Verbal instruction may be defended when the resulting behavior is not the primary object of interest; for example, the experimenter may show a subject how to operate a piece of equipment rather than shape his behavior through reinforcement so long as he is not concerned with the acquisition of the response but with what happens to it later. Verbal communication is not, however, a substitute for the arrangement and manipulation of variables. (Skinner, 1963, p. 510)

On the contrary, modeling procedures are most efficacious in transmitting new response patterns, whereas operant conditioning methods as applied to human behavior are typically concerned with the management and control of previously learned responses.

The argument that verbally presented models may have limited applicability because they are ineffective with nonverbal organisms ("The scope of the verbal substitute can be estimated by considering how a nonverbal organism, human or otherwise, could be similarly 'instructed'" [Skinner, 1963]), simply highlights the inadvisability of relying too heavily on infrahuman organisms for establishing principles of human behavior. The social training of children at a preverbal developmental level is partly achieved through the use of nonverbal demonstrations of the desired responses. It would be interesting, for example, to record the total time required to train a young child to tie his shoelaces by means of operant conditioning without the aid of response-guidance modeling procedures.

As verbal repertoires are gradually extended through social imitation, behavioral demonstrations are frequently replaced by their verbal equivalents. It is often implicitly assumed, for reasons that are not entirely clear, that human behavioral processes do not constitute genuine or important phenomena unless they have been reproduced in animals. This reasoning would lead one to conclude that verbal communication in humans is of limited significance because no experimenter has ever succeeded in teaching a pigeon or a rodent to articulate in any known human language system.

The preceding discussion has emphasized the indispensibility of models, particularly in situations fraught with potentially perilous consequences, and in developing highly novel responses as illustrated by language learning. It might be argued that in the latter case a successive regression of learners would eventuate in a single individual with no model for imitation and, consequently, our lonesome survivor could never develop linguistic responses. The initial occurrence of a given verbal operant, however, poses no problems for language learning since any vocal response can be selected arbitrarily to symbolize a particular object or event. A person who studies human behavior, for example, could be labeled arbitrarily a "zoogrozyconologist." The language learning problem arises, however, when a cultural agent is assigned the delightful task of teaching a second person the word "zoogrozyconologist" without the aid of a verbalizing model.

Most behavioral innovations are struck upon by individuals more or less without design, and the patterns that generate rewarding consequences are rapidly adopted by other group members and transmitted to succeeding generations. Similarly, individuals who have attempted provisionally, or performed unwittingly, responses that generate aversive consequences, by their examples progressively limit the range of trial-and-error behavior exhibited by contemporary and future generations. Once certain behavioral repertoires have thus become an enduring part of a culture, its members are spared the travail of trial-and-error discovery. It would be difficult to imagine a culture in which its language, mores, vocational and avocational patterns, familial customs, and its educational, social, and political practices were shaped in each new member through a process of operant conditioning, without the response guidance of models who exhibit the accumulated cultural repertoires in their own behavior.

## THREE EFFECTS OF MODELING INFLUENCES

Exposure to the behavior of models may have three rather different effects that may be reflected in the topography, frequency, or magnitude of the observers' subsequent behavior (Bandura, 1962b, 1963a; Bandura & Walters, 1963). In the first place, the observer may acquire new responses that did not exist in his behavioral repertoire. In demonstrating this *modeling effect* experimentally, the model exhibits responses that the observer has not yet learned to make, and he must reproduce them in substantially identical form (Bandura, Ross, & Ross, 1961, 1963a). The component responses that enter into the development of more complex novel patterns are usually present in the observers' behavioral repertoires as products either of maturation or of prior social learning. Consequently, learning is most frequently reflected in the unique combination of response components, or the evocation of previously learned responses by new stimuli.

Exposure to models may also strengthen or weaken inhibitory responses in the observer. These *inhibitory* and *disinhibitory effects* are evident when the frequency of imitative and nonmatching responses increases or decreases, often as a function of rewarding or punishing response consequences to the model (Bandura, 1963b; Bandura, Ross, & Ross, 1963c; Walters, Leat, & Mezei, 1963). The observable changes produced by vicarious reinforcing events may reflect several different processes. Reinforcers administered to a model undoubtedly serve a discriminative function, signifying the probable reinforcement contingencies associated with the modeled classes of responses. In addition, rewarding consequences may result in vicarious extinction of inhibitory responses. Conversely, observed aversive outcomes tend to establish conditioned emotional responses (Bandura & Rosenthal, 1964; Berger, 1962) that help to support avoidant and inhibitory repertoires.

Finally, the behavior of models may elicit previously learned responses that match precisely or bear some resemblance to those exhibited by the model. This *response facilitation effect* can be distinguished from disinhibition when the behavior in question is not likely to have incurred punishment and, therefore, any increase in responsivity is not attributable to the reduction of inhibitory responses.

These three effects of the observation of models are clearly illustrated in a study that was designed to investigate the social transmission of novel aggressive responses (Bandura, Ross, & Ross, 1961). Nursery school children were assigned to one of four treatment conditions, or to a control group. One group of children observed an aggressive model who exhibited relatively unique forms of physical and verbal aggression toward a large inflated plastic doll; a second group viewed the same model behave in a very subdued and inhibited manner, while children in the control group had no exposure to the models.

It might be expected, on the basis of saliency and similarity of cues, that the more remote the model is from reality the weaker his modeling influence. This investigation was therefore later extended (Bandura, Ross, & Ross, 1963a) in order to compare the relative efficacy of real life, and pictorially presented symbolic models who differed on the reality-

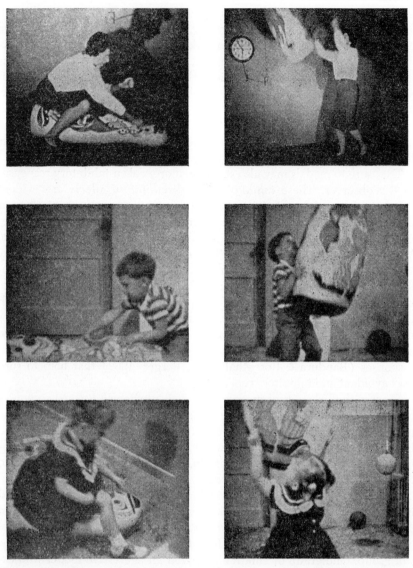

Figure 15-5. Photographs of children reproducing the behavior exhibited by an aggressive model. [M. R. Jones (Ed.), *Nebraska Symposium on Motivation*. Lincoln, Neb.: University of Nebraska Press, 1962.]

fictional stimulus dimension. Children in the human film-aggression group viewed a movie showing the adults who had served as models in the earlier experiment performing the same novel aggressive acts; children in the cartoon-aggressive group were presented a movie in which the model costumed as a cartoon cat exhibited the aggressive behavior toward the plastic doll.

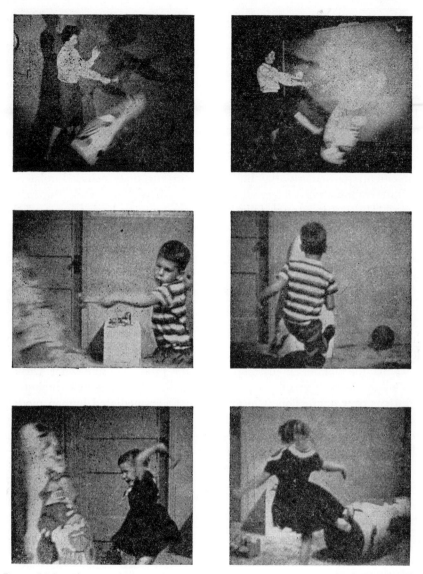

Figure 15-5. Photographs of children reproducing the behavior exhibited by an aggressive model. [M. R. Jones (Ed.), *Nebraska Symposium on Motivation*. Lincoln, Neb.: University of Nebraska Press, 1962.]

During the acquisition period, the children simply watched the model's behavior but could not perform the responses he exhibited; consequently, any learning that occurred was purely on an observational or covert basis. This same no-trial learning procedure was employed in all of the experiments in the program of research discussed in this chapter.

After exposure to their respective models, all children, including those in the control group, were mildly frustrated and then tested for the amount of imitative and nonmatching aggressive behavior.

Children who observed the aggressive models displayed a great number of precisely imitative physical and verbal responses, whereas such behavior rarely occurred in either the nonaggressive-model group or the control group. Illustrations of this modeling effect are provided in Figure 15-5, which depicts a boy and a girl reproducing the behavior of the female model whom they had observed in the film condition. These new repertoires were developed through a 10-minute exposure. Had the investigator attempted to shape these responses gradually by differential reinforcement, particularly the linguistic patterns that included relatively unique combinations of verbal elements such as "Pow, sock him in the nose," "He sure is a tough fella," "He keeps coming back for more," the research assistants would undoubtedly still be toiling in the laboratory.

The behavior of the models not only effectively shaped the form of the children's aggressive responses, but it also produced substantial disinhibitory effects. Children who had observed the aggressive models exhibited approximately twice as much aggression as did subjects in either the nonaggressive-model group or the control group. By contrast, children who witnessed the subdued nonaggressive models displayed the inhibited behavior characteristic of their model and expressed significantly less aggression than the control children (Figure 15-6).

While the nonhuman cartoon character produced somewhat weaker modeling effects, nevertheless it was equally influential in reducing inhibitions over aggression. The finding that film-mediated human models can be as effective as real-life models in transmitting and disinhibiting responses suggests that televised models may play an important role in shaping and modifying social response patterns.

The results of these experiments also provide some evidence for facilitation effects. In one of the four physically imitative acts, for example, the model pummelled the doll with a mallet. Relative to children in the nonaggressive-model and control groups, subjects who had observed the aggressive models displayed significantly more behavior in which they pounded a peg board with the mallet (Bandura, 1962b). Since this type of play activity is socially sanctioned, the heightened responsivity reflects primarily the operation of a facilitative or enhancement effect, rather than a disinhibitory process.

## CATHARSIS AND BEHAVIORAL CHANGE

It has been widely assumed on the basis of psychoanalytic theory and other hydraulic energy models of personality that either vicarious participation in or the direct expression of aggressive behavior serves to discharge "pent-up energies and affects" and thereby to reduce, at least tem-

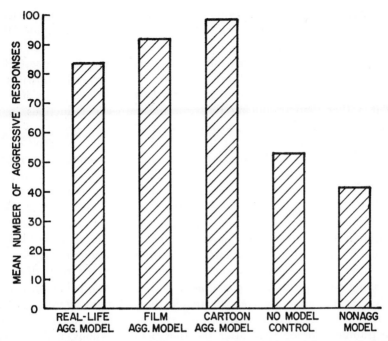

Figure 15-6. Mean frequency of aggressive responses performed by control children and by those who had been exposed to aggressive and inhibited models. (Reprinted from *The Journal of Nursery Education*, April 1963, *18*, permission of the National Association for the Education of Young Children.)

porarily, the incidence of aggressive behavior. Guided by this catharsis theory, many parents, educators, rehabilitation workers and psychotherapists subtly or openly encourage hyperaggression children to participate in aggressive recreational activities, to view highly aggressive televised programs, and to aggress in psychotherapeutic playrooms and permissive interview settings.

In contrast to this "drainage" view, social-learning theory would predict that the provision of aggressive models, and the inadvertent positive reinforcement of aggression, which inevitably accompanies the encouragement of cathartic expressions, are exceedingly effective procedures for enhancing aggressive response predispositions. The research findings cited above, and evidence from other modeling studies employing behavioral dependent measures (Bandura, Ross, & Ross, 1963c; Lovaas, 1961; Larder, 1962; Siegel, 1956; Walters & Thomas, 1963), provide unequivocal support for the social-learning theory. An experimental situation simulating psychotherapeutic interviews in which angered students directly expressed their hostility to a permissive, accepting, and sympathetic "physician" similarly resulted in postexperimental increases rather than decreases in aggression (Kahn, 1960). It should be noted in passing that advocates of the catharsis hypothesis rarely recommend vicarious participation in sexual activities as a means of reducing sexual behavior (Bandura & Walters, 1963).

The over-all evidence from laboratory studies strongly suggests that psychotherapies employing "abreaction" procedures may be unwittingly maintaining deviant behavior at its original strength or actually increasing it, rather than producing the expected cathartic reductions in response strength. By contrast, therapy based on social-learning principles would concentrate on shaping the desired alternative patterns of behavior. Proceeding on this basis, Chittenden (1942) employed symbolic modeling procedures in modifying children's aggressive reactions to frustration. Children who were excessively domineering and hyperaggressive in their social interactions observed a series of plays in each of which dolls exhibited alternatively an aggressive and a prosocial cooperative frustration reaction under circumstances that the children were likely to encounter in everyday situations. In addition to modeling these two competing response patterns, the experimenter depicted rewarding and punishing consequences for cooperative and aggressive behavior, respectively. The therapy effectively decreased the children's aggressive domineering responses, assessed from nursery school observations made before training, immediately after the therapeutic sessions, and a month later.

In preceding sections operant conditioning and modeling procedures were compared and contrasted. They should be regarded, however, as complimentary methods for shaping, maintaining, or disinhibiting social response patterns. Jack (1934) and Page (1936) provide illustrations of the combined use of modeling and social-reinforcement procedures to increase the assertiveness of relatively inhibited children.

The psychotherapeutic application of modeling procedures is not confined to young children. Kelly's (1955) role-prescription methods and Lazarus' (1963) behavior-rehearsal techniques, for example, essentially represent approaches in which adult clients are provided a real-life or a symbolic model of the desired behavior, and conditions are arranged so that the appropriate matching responses are promptly reinforced. Although the possibilities of modeling procedures have yet to be fully explored, they seem to hold considerable promise.

It is evident that people do not reproduce the responses of every model whom they may happen to observe, nor do they imitate each element of behavior exhibited even by models whom they have selected as their primary sources of social behavior. The set of experiments to be discussed next was designed primarily to isolate some of the variables that determine the selection of models, and the degree to which their behavior will be imitated.

## INFLUENCE OF THE MODEL'S REINFORCEMENT CONTINGENCIES

The occurrence of imitative behavior is partly a function of the reinforcing consequences experienced by the model. These consequences may either follow immediately the models' responses, or be inferred from certain discriminative symbols, attributes, and skills possessed by the model that tend to be regularly correlated with differential reinforcements.

The manner in which immediate response consequences to the model enhance or inhibit imitation is demonstrated in an experiment (Bandura, Ross, & Ross, 1963c) in which children observed either an aggressive model rewarded, an aggressive model punished, or highly expressive prosocial models. A control group of children had no exposure to the models. The models were two adult males presented to the children on film. In the aggression-rewarded condition the model appropriated the prize possessions of the other adult through physically aggressive behavior. The film shown to the children in the aggression-punished condition was identical to that shown to the aggression-rewarded group, except the aggression displayed by the model resulted in his being severely punished. After observing the models, the children were tested in a different experimental situation designed to assess the incidence of postexposure aggressive responses.

Children who observed the aggressive model rewarded displayed more imitative physical and verbal aggression than children who witnessed the model punished. An analysis of aggressive responses that were not precisely imitative revealed that boys and girls were differentially influenced by the behavior of the models and its response consequences. Boys were inclined to inhibit aggression when they either observed an aggressive model punished or had no exposure to displays of aggression, whereas observation of rewarded models produced substantial disinhibitory effects. By contrast, exposure to prosocial models had its greatest inhibitory effect on the girls' expression of aggression. These findings demonstrate how behavioral control can be transmitted vicariously either by the administration of punishment to the model, or by the presentation of incompatible prosocial examples of behavior.

## RESPONSE CONSEQUENCES TO THE MODEL AND THE ACQUISITION OF MATCHING RESPONSES

In evaluating the role of reinforcement in modeling processes it is important to distinguish learning from performance. The experiment discussed above demonstrated the facilitating and inhibiting effects of rewards and punishments administered to the model on the *performance* of imitatively learned responses. It is widely assumed that the occurrence of imitative or observational *learning* is also contingent on the administration of reinforcing stimuli either to the model or to the observer.

According to the theory propounded by Miller and Dollard (1941), for example, the necessary conditions for learning through imitation include a motivated subject who is positively reinforced for matching the rewarded behavior of a model during a series of trial-and-error responses. Since this conceptualization of observational learning requires the subject to perform the imitative response before he can learn it, this theory evidently accounts more adequately for the emission of previously learned matching responses, than for their acquisition.

Mowrer's proprioceptive feedback theory (1960) similarly highlights the role of reinforcement but, unlike Miller and Dollard, who reduce imitation to a special case of instrumental learning, Mowrer focuses on the classical conditioning of positive and negative emotions to matching response-correlated stimuli. Imitative learning can occur, according to Mowrer, either through direct pairing of the model's response with reinforcers dispensed to the observer, or by means of vicarious conditioning.

There is some recent evidence that imitative behavior can be enhanced by noncontingent social reinforcement from a model (Bandura & Huston, 1961), by response-contingent reinforcers administered to the model (Bandura, Ross, & Ross, 1963b; Walters, Leat, & Mezei, 1963), and by increasing the reinforcing value of matching responses through direct reinforcement of the participant observer (Baer & Sherman, 1964). Nevertheless, these reinforcement theories of imitation fail to explain the learning of matching responses when the observer does not perform the model's responses during the process of acquisition and for which reinforcers are not delivered either to the model or to the observers (Bandura, Ross, & Ross, 1961; 1963a).

The acquisition of imitative responses under the latter conditions appears to be accounted for more adequately by contiguity theory of observational learning (Bandura, 1965; Sheffield, 1961). According to this theory, when an observer witnesses a model exhibit a sequence of responses the observer acquires, through contiguous association of sensory events, symbolic or representational responses possessing cue properties that are capable of eliciting, at some time after a demonstration, overt responses corresponding to those that had been modeled.

Some suggestive evidence that the *acquisition* of matching responses takes place through contiguity, whereas reinforcements administered to a model exert their major influence on the *performance* of imitatively learned responses, is provided in the foregoing experiment (Bandura, in press). Although children who had observed aggressive responses rewarded subsequently reproduced the model's behavior while children in the model-punished condition failed to do so, a number of subjects in the latter group described in postexperimental interviews the model's re-

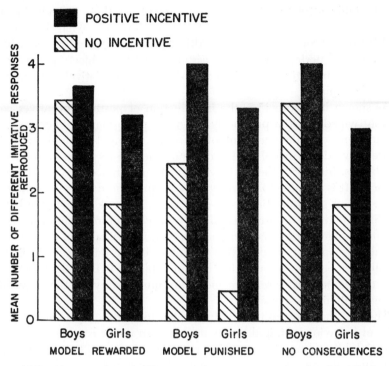

Figure 15-7. Mean number of different matching responses reproduced by children as a function of response consequences to the model and positive incentives.

sponses with considerable accuracy. Evidentally, they had learned the cognitive equivalents of the model's responses but they were not translated into their motoric form.

In order to investigate more systematically whether reinforcement functions primarily as a performance or a learning-related variable, a second experiment was conducted in which children observed a film-mediated model who exhibited novel physical and verbal aggressive responses. In one treatment condition the model was severely punished, in a second, the model was generously rewarded; while the third condition presented no response consequences to the model. Consistent with the findings from the earlier experiment (Bandura, Ross, & Ross, 1963c), a postexposure performance test of imitation revealed that differential reinforcement had produced differential amounts of imitative behavior. Relative to subjects in the model-punished condition, children in the model-rewarded and the no-consequences groups spontaneously performed a significantly larger number of imitative responses (Figure 15-7). Moreover, boys reproduced substantially more imitative responses than girls, the differences being particularly marked in the model-punished condition.

Following the performance test, children in all three groups were offered highly attractive incentives contingent on their reproducing the model's responses in order to activate into performance what the children had learned through observation. Although learning must necessarily be inferred from performance, it was assumed that the subjects' behavior under positive incentive conditions would provide a relatively accurate index of learning.

As shown in Figure 15-7, the introduction of positive incentives completely wiped out the previously observed performance differences, revealing an equivalent amount of learning among the children in the model-rewarded, model-punished, and the no-response-consequences conditions. Similarly, the initially large sex difference was substantially reduced. It is possible to interpret these acquisition data as reflecting the operation of generalization from prior reinforcement of imitative behavior. Since both the occurrence and the positive reinforcement of matching responses, whether by accident or by intent, is inevitable in the course of social development, no definitive resolution of the reinforcement issue is possible in experiments utilizing human subjects. It is evident, however, that contemporaneous reinforcements are unnecessary for the acquisition of new matching responses.

The fact that most of the children failed to reproduce the entire repertoire of behavior exhibited by the model, even under conditions designed to disinhibit and to elicit matching responses, indicates that factors other than mere contiguity of sensory stimulation undoubtedly influence imitative response acquisition.

Exposure of a person to a complex sequence of stimulation is no guarantee that he will attend to the whole range of cues, that he will necessarily select from a total stimulus complex only the most relevant stimuli, or that he will even perceive accurately the cues to which his attention is directed. Motivational variables, prior training in discriminative observation, and the anticipation of positive or negative reinforcement contingent on the emission of matching responses may be highly influential in channeling, augmenting, or reducing observing responses, which is a necessary precondition for imitative learning (Bandura, 1962b). Procedures that increase the distinctiveness of the relevant modeling stimuli also greatly facilitate observational learning (Sheffield & Maccoby, 1961).

In addition to attention-directing variables, the rate, amount, and complexity of stimuli presented to the observer will partly determine the degree of imitative learning. The acquisition of matching responses through observation of a lengthy uninterrupted sequence of behavior is also likely to be governed by principles of associative learning such as frequency and recency, serial order effects, and other multiple sources of interference.

Social responses are generally composed of a large number of different behavioral units combined in a particular manner. Responses of higher-order complexity are produced by combinations of previously learned components that may, in themselves, represent relatively complicated behavioral patterns. Consequently, the rate of acquisition of intricate matching responses through observation will be largely determined by the extent to which the necessary components are contained in the observer's repertoire. A client who possesses a very narrow repertoire of behavior, for example, will, in all probability, display only fragmentary imitation of a competent model; on the other hand, a person who has acquired most of the relevant elementary skills is likely to perform precisely matching responses following several demonstrations. In the former case, the desired complex pattern would have to be reduced to smaller subunits of behavior, each of which could be developed through modeling and operant conditioning procedures.

In the acquisition of psychomotor skills, which are governed largely by proprioceptive stimuli that are neither observable nor easily described verbally, exposure to modeling behavior is insufficient for learning; consequently, varying amounts of overt practice are generally necessary.

It is evident from the above discussion that imitation is not a passive observational matter, but an active process in which modeling stimuli combine with other variables in shaping response patterns.

## VICARIOUS ACQUISITION OF SELF-CONTROLLING RESPONSES

Theory and research relating to the process of internalization and self-control have typically focused on resistance to deviation and the occurrence of self-punitive responses following transgression. Perhaps even more prevalent and important behavioral manifestations of self-control are the manner in which a person regulates the self-administration of highly rewarding resources over which he has control, and his willingness to defer immediate rewards in favor of delayed, larger reinforcers.

It is generally assumed that most self-controlling responses are originally developed through direct aversive conditioning. However, the studies described earlier demonstrate that children can acquire inhibitions over aggression by observing models undergoing aggression-contingent negative reinforcement. The vicarious acquisition of other behavioral manifestations of self-control is also revealed in laboratory investigations of self-rewarding responses and delay-of-gratification patterns.

## TRANSMISSION OF SELF-REINFORCEMENT PATTERNS THROUGH MODELING

Although the controlling power of external reinforcing stimuli cannot be minimized, self-administered primary and conditioned rewards may frequently outweigh the influence of external stimuli in governing social behavior. The latter phenomenon, however, has been virtually ignored both in psychological theorizing and experimentation, even though it is apparent from informal observation that most human behavioral repertoires are maintained to a large extent by self-administered positive and negative reinforcers. The experimental preoccupation with learning processes established in work with infrahuman organisms may partly account for the neglect of self-reinforcing behavior. Unlike human subjects, rats or chimpanzees are disinclined to pat themselves on the back for commendable performances, or to berate themselves for getting lost in cul-de-sacs.

In order to determine whether self-reinforcing responses may be products of imitative learning, the following experiment was conducted (Bandura & Kupers, 1964):

Children participated in a bowling game with an adult or a peer model, the scores, which could range from 5 to 30 points, being controlled by the experimenter. At the outset of the game, the children and their models were given access to a plentiful supply of candy, from which they could help themselves as they wished. In one condition of the experiment, the model adopted a *high criterion for self-reinforcement;* on trials in which the model obtained or exceeded a score of 20, he rewarded himself with candy and made self-approving statements, while on trials in which he failed to meet the adopted standard he refrained from taking any candy and berated himself. In a second condition the model displayed a similar pattern of self-reward and self-disapproval, but adopted the relatively *low self-reinforcement criterion* of ten points. There was also some minor variation in the magnitude of self-reinforcement; the models helped themselves to one piece of candy when they scored at, or slightly above, criterion, and two pieces when they performed well above their adopted minimum level. A control group of children had no exposure to the models.

After completing his trials the model departed, the experimentor generously refurnished the candy supply, and the child played 15 games in which he received scores ranging from 5 to 30 points according to a pre-arranged program. The performances for which the child rewarded himself with candy and imitative positive or negative self-evaluative verbal responses constituted the dependent measure.

Whereas children in the control group administered rewards to themselves more or less independently of performance level, subjects in the experimental conditions made self-reinforcement contingent upon achievements that matched the self-reward criteria of their respective models. Thus, children who had been presented with low-criterion models were highly self-indulgent and self-approving for comparatively low achievements; by contrast, children in the high-criterion condition dis-

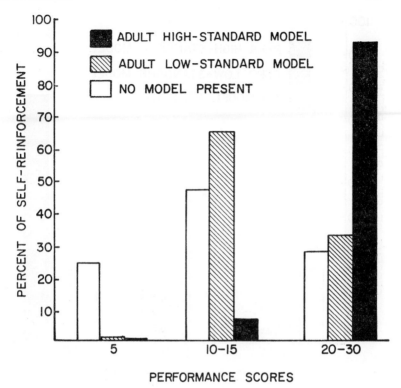

100 ┬
 90 ┤        ■ ADULT HIGH-STANDARD MODEL
 80 ┤        ▨ ADULT LOW-STANDARD MODEL
 70 ┤        □ NO MODEL PRESENT

PERCENT OF SELF-REINFORCEMENT

        5              10-15            20-30

PERFORMANCE SCORES

Figure 15-8. Regulation of self-reinforcement as a function of level of performance by children in the control group and by those exposed to adult models adopting high and low criteria for self-reinforcement. (*J. abnorm. soc. Psychol.*, 1964, 69, 5.)

played considerable self-denial and self-derogation following identical accomplishments. The children not only adopted their models' self-rewarding patterns of behavior, but they even matched the minor variations in magnitude of self-reinforcement exhibited by the models.

A comparison of the results obtained with adult and peer models revealed that children were less influenced by the standard-setting behavior and self-reinforcing responses exhibited by peers. The matching behavior of children in the peer-model condition was somewhat less precise, and a higher percentage rewarded themselves in excess of their model's maximum amount than did children who had observed adult models. Figures 15-8 and 15-9 present graphically the distribution of self-reinforcements as a function of level of performance for each of the three groups of children.

Although the subjects acquired positive and negative self-reinforcing responses without the mediation of direct external reinforcement, it is probable that the evaluative properties of performances which fall short of, match, or exceed a given reference norm are the resultant of past dis-

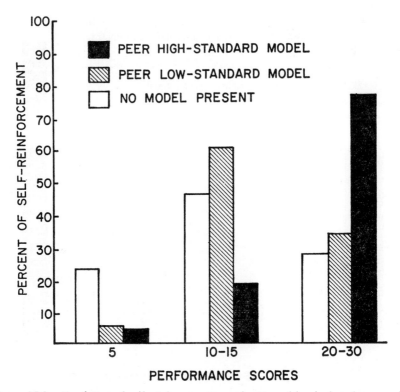

Figure 15-9. Regulation of self-reinforcement as a function of level of performance by children in the control group and by those exposed to peer models adopting high and low criteria for self-reinforcement. (*J. abnorm. soc. Psychol.*, 1964, *69*, 5.)

criminative reinforcements. Through the repeated pairing of performance deficits with aversive consequences and successfully matched behavior with rewards, differential achievement levels per se eventually acquire positive and negative valence. It should be noted, however, that performance-produced cues have relatively little evaluative significance independent of the accomplishments of models whom the subject has chosen for comparison.

Once the evaluative properties of differential accomplishments are well established, adequate or inadequate matches are likely to elicit similar self-evaluative responses, irrespective of the class of behavior being compared. Thus, a person who has received repeated negative reinforcements in a variety of different situations for accomplishments that fall at the mean of his reference groups is likely to evaluate subsequent average performances as inadequate, regardless of the content of the particular activity. At this stage the whole process becomes relatively independent of external reinforcement and the specific contingencies of the original training situations. As demonstrated in the experiment discussed above, subjects will adopt the particular criteria for reinforcement exhibited by a reference model, evaluate their own performance relative to that standard, and then serve as their own reinforcing agents.

In discussions of psychopathology and psychotherapy, attention is frequently directed to the presence of behavioral deficits, or to anxiety-mediated inhibitory and avoidance response patterns. A large proportion of the clients who seek psychotherapy, however, present relatively competent repertoires and are not excessively inhibited in their social behavior. These are clients who experience a great deal of self-generated aversive stimulation and self-imposed denial of positive reinforcers stemming from their excessively high standards for self-reinforcement, often supported by comparisons with historical or contemporary models noted for their extraordinary achievements. This process frequently gives rise to depressive reactions, a lessened disposition to perform because of the unfavorable work to self-reinforcement ratio, and efforts to escape the self-generated aversive stimulation through alcoholism, grandiose ideation, and other modes of avoidant behavior. In these cases, the modification of standards for self-reinforcement would clearly constitute a principal psychotherapeutic objective ( Bandura, in preparation ).

## INFLUENCE OF MODELS IN MODIFYING DELAY-OF-GRATIFICATION BEHAVIOR

According to the psychoanalytic theory of delay behavior ( Singer, 1955; Freud, 1946), aroused impulses press for immediate discharge of tension through overt motoric activity. As a result of repeated association of tension reduction with goal objects, and development of greater ego organization, absence or imposed delay of satisfying objects results in the substitution of hallucinatory satisfactions, and other thought processes that convert free cathexes into "bound" cathexes. The capacity to delay or inhibit motor discharge by substituting cathected ideational representations presumably reflects the gradual shift from primary-process activity to reality-oriented secondary-process thinking.

Dr. Mischel and the writer recently conducted an experiment to test a more parsimonious theory of delay of gratification, according to which preferences for immediate or delayed reinforcers are partly determined by the delay patterns displayed by social models ( Bandura & Mischel, in press).

Children who showed decided preferences for immediate or delayed reinforcers were exposed to adult models who exhibited a consistent delay pattern that was counter to the children's dominant orientations. The models were presented pairs of objects including edibles, money, and recreational items, in each of which the model made a choice between a small reward that could be obtained immediately, or a more valued item contingent on his willingness to wait for a period of 2 to 3 weeks. With children who characterically preferred reinforcers that were immediately available, the model selected the more valued, delayed rewards, and commented periodically on his postponement-of-gratification philosophy of life. Similarly, with children who preferred delayed rewards, the model selected the less valuable items that could be obtained immediately, and expounded his immediate-gratification pattern of life.

Half of the children in each of the experimental groups participated with real-life models, and half were shown the objects between which the model had supposedly made choices earlier that day, and the children simply read his choices and the accompanying philosophy-of-life commentary. The mode of model presentation was varied in order to compare the relative efficacy of real-life and verbally presented symbolic models.

Immediately following the models' performances the children made choices between a different set of paired items, and their preference for either immediate or delayed rewards was recorded. In order to assess the generality and stability of changes in delay patterns produced by the modeling procedures, the children were readministered the original set of selection items in an entirely different setting approximately three weeks following the experimental session. A control group of children made choices between the same sets of items except they had no intervening exposure to models.

The modeling procedures proved to be quite successful in modifying the children's delay-of-reward patterns. Children who had shown a delayed-gratification pattern exhibited an increased preference for the immediate, smaller rewards (Figure 15-10).

It is of particular interest to note that, while the real-life and verbally presented models were equally effective within the immediate social-influence setting, the changes produced by the symbolic model were significantly less stable over time.

Immediate-gratification children exposed to the delay models similarly increased their willingness to wait for larger, delayed rewards. The final analyses of this set of data, however, have not yet been completed.

### REWARDING POWER AND IMITATION

In the studies to which reference has been made, subjects were exposed to only a single model. In everyday life, however, individuals have extensive contact with multiple models who may differ widely in their behavior and in their relative influence. Therefore, a further study, designed to test several different theories of identificatory learning, utilized three-person groups representing prototypes of the nuclear family (Bandura, Ross, & Ross, 1963b).

In one condition of the experiment an adult assumed the role of con-

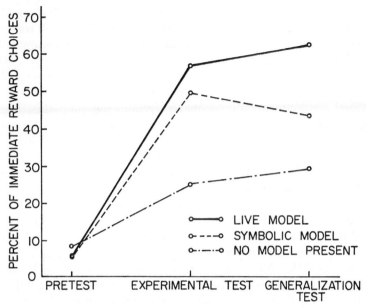

Figure 15-10. Mean percentage of immediate reward choices by children who exhibited delayed-gratification patterns.

troller of highly rewarding resources that included attractive play material, appetizing foods, and high-status objects. Another adult was the recipient of these resources, while the child, a participant observer in the triad, was essentially ignored. In a second condition, one adult controlled the resources; the child, however, was the recipient of the positive resources, while the other adult was assigned a subordinate and powerless role.

An adult male and female served as models in each of the triads. For half the boys and girls in each condition the male model controlled and dispensed the rewarding resources, simulating the husband-dominant home; for the remaining children, the female model mediated the positive resources as in the wife-dominant home. Following the experimental social interactions the adult models exhibited divergent patterns of behavior in the presence of the child, and measures were obtained of the degree to which the child patterned his behavior after that of the models.

According to the status-envy theory of identification proposed by Whiting (1959, 1960), where a child competes unsuccessfully with an adult for affection, attention, food and care, the child will envy the consumer adult and consequently identify with him. This theory represents an extension of the psychoanalytic defensive identification hypothesis that identification is the outcome of rivalrous interaction between the child and the parent who occupies an envied consumer status. In contrast to the status-envy hypothesis, the social power theory of identification (Maccoby, 1959; Mussen & Distler, 1959), predicts that children will reproduce more of the behavior of the adult who controls positive resources than that of the powerless adult model.

The secondary reinforcement theory of identification (Mowrer, 1950, 1960) assumes that as a model mediates rewards for a child, the model's behavioral attributes acquire secondary reinforcing properties through the process of classical conditioning. On the basis of stimulus generalization, matching responses attain rewarding value for the child in proportion to their similarity to those exhibited by the model. Consequently, the child can administer conditioned reinforcers to himself simply by reproducing as closely as possible the model's positively valenced behavior. This theory would predict, therefore, that the condition in which children received direct positive reinforcement would produce the greatest amount of imitation, with the model who dispensed the rewards serving as the main source of behavior.

The manipulation of rewarding power produced differential imitation of the behavior exhibited by the two models. In both experimental triads, regardless of whether the rival adult or the children themselves were the recipients of the rewarding resources, the model who possessed rewarding power was imitated to a considerably greater extent than was the competitor or the ignored model (Table 15-1). Moreover, power inversions on the part of the male and female models produced cross-sex imitation, particularly in girls.

Children who were directly rewarded by the controller exhibited significantly more total matching responses than the subjects who were ignored. However, the effect of combining direct reinforcement of the child with resource ownership was primarily to increase imitation of the ignored competitor, rather than to enhance imitation of the model who dispensed the positive rewards. In fact, boys who were the recipients of rewarding resources mediated by the female model tended to favor the ignored male as their object of imitation (Table 15-1). This finding is particularly surprising since an earlier experiment based on two-person groups (Bandura & Huston, 1961), demonstrated that the association of a model with noncontingent positive reinforcement augmented the occurrence of matching behavior. Postexperimental interview data revealed that the discrepant results arose from the fact that the rewarded boys felt sympathetic toward the ignored male and were mildly critical of the controller for not being more charitable with her bountiful resources. These two sets of data show how learning principles based on a two-person model may be subject to strict limitations, since the introduction of additional social variables can produce significant changes in the functional relationships between relevant variables.

Although the subjects adopted many characteristics of the model who

*Table 15-1:* Mean Number of Imitative Responses Performed by Subgroups of Children in the Two Experimental Triads

| | Objects of imitation | | | |
|---|---|---|---|---|
| Subjects | Male controller | Female consumer | Female controller | Male consumer |
| Girls | 29.00 | 9.67 | 26.00 | 10.00 |
| Boys | 30.17 | 18.67 | 22.33 | 16.17 |
| Total | 29.59 | 14.17 | 24.17 | 13.09 |
| | Male controller | Female ignored | Female controller | Male ignored |
| Girls | 22.00 | 16.17 | 31.84 | 22.17 |
| Boys | 29.17 | 16.67 | 26.83 | 34.50 |
| Total | 25.59 | 16.42 | 29.34 | 28.34 |

possessed rewarding power, they also reproduced some of the elements of behavior exhibited by the model who occupied a subordinate role. Consequently, the children were not simply junior-size replicas of one or the other model; rather, they exhibited a relatively novel pattern of behavior representing an amalgam of elements from both models. Moreover, the specific admixture of behavioral elements varied from child to child. These findings provide considerable evidence for the seemingly paradoxical conclusion that imitation can in fact result in considerable response innovation.

## CONCLUDING REMARKS

Most conceptualizations of psychotherapy as a learning process depict the therapist as a *source of reinforcements* that can be manipulated in a contingent manner so as to develop and to maintain the clients' behavioral repertoires. However, relatively little attention has been paid to the importance of therapeutic agents as a *source of behavioral repertoires.* The laboratory studies reviewed briefly in the present chapter demonstrate clearly that the provision of models can be an exceedingly effective method for transmitting entire behavioral repertoires, for disinhibiting or inhibiting existing response patterns, or for serving as discriminative or response facilitative stimuli.

The establishment of complex social repertoires and the modification of persistent anxiety-mediated behavior is generally achieved through a gradual process in which the client must pass through an orderly learning sequence that guides him in progressive steps toward the final form of the desired behavior. Consequently, the efficacy of psychotherapeutic modeling procedures will depend to a large extent on the care with which the modeled performances are programed. In the modification of anxiety-avoidant responses, for example, the client might observe initially a model responding positively toward relatively weak anxiety-provoking cues. Once these stimuli have lost their aversive properties for the observer, gradually increasing anxiety-arousing stimuli can be presented until the most potent cues have been successfully neutralized. When the anxiety responses are elicited primarily by independent environmental stimuli, the treatment can be graded by varying the number of aversive elements in the total stimulus complex to which both the client and the model are exposed; in cases where the anxiety arousal is primarily generated by response-correlated stimuli, the client might observe the model exhibiting gradually increasing intensities of the negatively valenced social responses, preferably with positive response consequences.

The systematic use of modeling techniques, whether singly or in conjunction with other treatment methods, is likely to accelerate substantially the successful achievement of therapeutic outcomes. It is interesting to note that modeling procedures are utilized extensively in shaping the behavioral repertoires of psychotherapists, but seldom employed in modifying the behavior of clients.

# 16

## Hypnosis as a Behavior Modification Technique

### THEODORE R. SARBIN

$S$arbin has made many contributions to the field of personality, social psychology, and clinical psychology (Sarbin, 1943, 1952, 1954, 1956, 1960, 1961, 1963, 1964; Sarbin & Andersen, 1963; Sarbin & Hardyck, 1955; Sarbin & Jones, 1955; Sarbin & Lim, 1963; Sarbin, Taft, & Bailey, 1960). These contributions have two basic consistencies, a rigorous adherence to scientific method, and a role theory formulation. A role formulation permits the investigator to work with diadic, culturally oriented, socially meaningful, and readily identifiable units of behavior. Within this framework, larger and more complex social patterns of behavior (roles) can be used as dependent variables within a social reinforcement approach. The research presented in Sarbin's chapter illustrates this point. He takes a highly complex area which has involved considerable mysticism, controversy, and presumed discontinuity with "normal behavior." By a careful use of base rates and control groups, Sarbin identifies hypnotic phenomena as normal behavior under particular social-influence conditions. That is, the manipulation of the environment which is called "hypnosis" and the subject behavior called "being under hypnotic control" are reduced to special instances of social influence in which the important variables are the same as those in psychotherapy, verbal conditioning, placebo, modeling, brainwashing, and, to some extent, sensory deprivation (Orne & Scheibe, 1964).

Sarbin is one of the investigators of hypnosis whose approach is "skeptical" rather than "credulous" (Sutcliffe, 1960, 1961). This is an important distinction because the skeptical—credulous dichotomy is also applicable to other social influence situations. There are some investigators of social influence situations as, for example, psychotherapists, who believe that they are dealing with a unique phenomenon which is an "entity" in its own right. In contrast are those investigators who believe they are dealing with phenomena that are all special instances of a more general process. Sutcliffe makes this distinction for hypnosis as follows:

> A traditional opposition runs through the many viewpoints about the nature of hypnosis. . . . What might be called the "credulous" view takes the hypnotic subject's testimony on faith. For example, it is suggested to a subject in trance that

a blank card is a photograph of a person's face; if the subject says that he can see the face and goes on to describe its detail, the "credulous" view is that in some sense the subject does "see." The perceptual process is assumed to be akin to that which is produced by an actual set of stimulus conditions. Erickson (1937) is quite explicit in his view that hypnotically produced "unconsciousness," "deafness" (1938a, 1944), "colour blindness," and "after-images" (1938b) are like the naturally occurring organic conditions. In opposition there are those who doubt the subject's testimony and contend that he actually perceives the situation as it is while acting as if it were as suggested by the hypnotist. This might be called the "sceptical" point of view; and White's (1941) position is of this sort. The "credulous" and "sceptical" viewpoints diverge on certain questions of fact, particularly on that of the subject's perceptions, and it is of interest to take stock of the large body of pertinent evidence which has been accruing (Sutcliffe, 1960, p. 73).

More often than not studies which are held to provide evidence for the "credulous" point of view prove to be inconclusive. The occasional well designed study tends to refute the "credulous" view; and so all told the evidence can be said to directly support or be consistent with the "sceptical" point of view (Sutcliffe, 1960, p. 97).

Further evidence for the "sceptical view" of Sutcliffe and Sarbin has come from Orne, whose work is discussed by Sarbin, and from Barber in a series of studies (Barber, 1962, 1964; Barber & Glass, 1962). Barber summarizes his research with the following suggestions as to the pertinent variables in hypnosis:

In conclusion, research concerned with delineating the factors involved in hypnotizability and suggestibility should place greater emphasis than heretofore on attitudinal and motivational variables. To formulate comprehensive theories in this area, however, we require precise data not only with respect to the direct effects of attitudinal-motivational factors but also with respect to the confluence of personality factors, attitudinal and motivational factors, and situational factors. We should therefore proceed to study both the direct effects and the interactive effects on hypnotizability and suggestibility of such variables as: S's attitudes toward and relationship with the investigator; S's goals and motives with respect to the assigned tasks; S's enduring personality characteristics; investigator's attitudes and characteristics; and a host of situational variables such as the specific instructions and experimental procedures employed (Barber, 1964, p. 316).

The variables suggested above by Barber, and discussed in detail by Sarbin in this chapter, are variables that are modifiable and common to all social influence situations. Viewing hypnosis as a special instance of social influence, approachable within a role and social reinforcement framework, leads to the assertion that there is a definite social role in our culture called "being hypnotized." Sarbin points out how this role has changed historically, and his description of Orne's (1962) experiment shows how this role is continually redefined by modeling procedures. Similarly, both the "sick" role and the "patient-in-psychotherapy" role have changed considerably within recent times. Szasz (1961b) presents a well-documented historical perspective on the "patient" or "sick" role.

Szasz (1961b) and Bockoven (1963) help us see how the patient role is a function of time, place, and society. Goldstein (1962) brings together the research on patient and therapist expectancies and indicates how the individual learns the kinds of behaviors expected of him in the psychotherapy situation. This role-learning influences the outcome of psychotherapy.

Another situation in which the variables discussed by Sarbin are relevant is the one usually labeled "placebo." It is increasingly acknowledged that the active ingredient in the placebo situation is not the inert or nonspecific substance in the capsule, but is the social influence process. Every aspect of Sarbin's discussion of hypnosis is directly relevant to the placebo situation (Frank, 1961).

Given the proper environmental conditions, human beings have the ability to make an enormous number of different role enactments. There is increasing evidence that enacting a role can also lead to measurable physiological changes (Platonov, 1959; Sarbin, 1956; Shapiro, 1960). If it is true that emitting the behavior required for a specific social role enactment can influence bodily functions, then it is likely that there are many conditions that have been called "psychosomatic" that can be ameliorated by behavior modification techniques.

We may parallel Sarbin's analysis of hypnosis as metaphor by noting that the concept of metaphor is equally applicable to psychotherapy. Frank (1961) has noted that psychotherapy creates its own demand and Astin (1961) has discussed the "functional autonomy" of psychotherapy. Much of the research on the "naturalistic" psychotherapy process is similar to investigations of the "special phenomenon" of hypnosis by "credulous" investigators who are unable to specify just what hypnosis *is*. Formulation of psychotherapy from a social reinforcement viewpoint facilitates investigation of the process and eliminates much that is irrelevant. A clinician can systematically apply the variables discussed by Sarbin to increase the likelihood of obtaining changed patient behavior. The view that a trained individual can change the behavior of another through the judicious manipulation of environmental stimuli is the major focus of Sarbin's chapter just as it has been in all the chapters in this volume.

L.K.-L.P.U.

THIS PRESENTATION IS AN attempt to describe a particular conception of hypnosis and how the conception fits into the general problem of behavior modification. It is not the intention to discuss the techniques of hynosis that might be used in studies of behavior change.

The traditional conception of hypnotism is that of a two-person interaction in which one person, the hypnotist, engages in verbal behavior, and the second person, the patient or subject, engages in both verbal and motoric behavior. The result of this interaction in the traditional conception demands a different kind of explanation than if the interaction had occurred in a nonhypnotic setting. It is here proposed to show that the concepts that have been demonstrated to be useful in accounting for interaction between people in other social psychological settings are equally applicable to the hypnotic setting.

## ROLE OF METAPHORS

As an introduction to this point of view, the role of metaphors in science will be briefly discussed. A metaphor is a term that has denotative "concrete" meaning in one idiom and is applied to a phenomenon from another idiom. For example, metallurgists talk about "metal fatigue," borrowing the term "fatigue" from muscle physiology. All that is intended in the borrowing is that certain effects can be colorfully described by likening them to effects with which we are familiar. The use of the metaphor does not carry with it the meaning that metals and muscles are alike. It is frequently the case, however, that the original literal meaning somehow drops out and we tend to focus on the metaphor as if it had denotative meaning. In the history of hypnosis, as in the history of any other field, various metaphors have been introduced that carry different implications for research, for therapy, and for explanatory efforts, usually in medical or psychological domains. The metaphor that Mesmer used 200 years ago to account for the observed "crisis" behaviors was "magnetism." He referred to the process that produced remarkable, dramatic changes in his patients as a form of animal magnetism. Until that time no concept of animal magnetism had been systematically used, although the concept of mineral magnetism was well known. By borrowing the term *magnetism* Mesmer also borrowed the set of concepts associated with it, including induction (the transference of magnetism) which was utilized in his invention, the *baquet*. Through this device, a large number of people could be treated simultaneously by grasping iron rods which had been placed in a large oval shaped vessel and which presumably contained animal magnetism induced by Mesmer.

Another metaphor was used a few decades later by Braid, who coined the term "hypnosis" to account for certain observations, some of which had been made by Mesmer. Braid used the term *hypnosis*, which is Greek for *sleep*, and various combinations of the root, *hypno*, with other forms such as hypnology, the study of a special kind of sleep. Viewing the phenomenon as sleeplike had certain implications for scientific theorizing and for treatment. The theorizing originally led to studies of hypnosis based on the physiology of sleep. Braid first worked out a theory that related the phenomenon to fatigue of the muscles controlling the eyelids and had a rather extensive formulation that was congruent with the neurology of the time. Later he had to discount the theory because hypnotic performances occurred in the absence of ocular fixation.

Another metaphor was used by Charcot in the 1880's. He saw hypnosis as a variant of hysteria. At that time, hysteria was seen as a form of neuropathology. Thus, if hypnosis was artificial hysteria, then scientists could study hypnosis with the aid of the reflex hammer and with a checklist of reflexes, signs, and symptoms such as were employed at that time by trained neurologists.

Each of these metaphors, and others as well, has had a life and has declined and died because they were replaced by metaphors more in keeping with concurrent scientific vocabularies. Also, as we know from the history of science, inventions and discoveries in other areas provided a cognitive framework for establishing a new metaphor.

The present century witnessed the development of the discipline of social psychology. This discipline has coined new terms, borrowed concepts from other disciplines, and—most significant—developed research methods. One could have predicted from the controversy of a hundred years ago that when a social psychological vocabulary was constructed, the description of hypnosis would be based on social psychological concepts. The particular social psychological concept that has been widely used in connection with hypnosis has been that of role. Drawn from the theater and from everyday life, this formulation regards the actions of the hypnotist and of the subject as determined in large part by the situation in which both participants are trying to play or act reciprocal roles. When one looks at hypnosis in this way, of course, the implications are quite different from that which follows when one looks at hypnosis as a physiological event or as an event mediated by animal magnetism. The implications for theory and practice are drawn from the study of persons working in the theater, and emphasize among other things interaction, acting skill, and the function of the audience, particularly the latter, both in providing cues to maintain the proper role and in providing reinforcements for specific enactments.

The theme in this introduction is that when we try to account for any behavior, particularly complex behavior, we are forced to use metaphors, and the metaphors that we choose direct our search for facts and our practical applications of these facts. Some will criticize the use of the role metaphor because they regard acting as being at the level of sham behavior. While it is true that professional acting sometimes does carry such a meaning, acting in the general sense does not require this qualification. At the present moment we are all acting. I am acting in the role of writer and you are acting in the role of audience and each of us has expectations for the other no different in principle from any other interaction. This view will be developed further below.

## HISTORICAL ROLE OF HYPNOSIS

If one were to review the literature of hypnosis, some of it going back two hundred years, he would be impressed with the fact that behavior of almost any kind is modified through the intervention of hypnosis. One can point to such events as modifications in psychosomatic conditions, the removal of phobias and fears, the changing of habitual responses, and many others. These behavior modifications are reported as consequent to the patient engaging in the role of hypnotic subject. These reports contain an implicit premise that the hypnotic induction produced mental or other internal changes within the person which, in turn, were responsible for changes in overt behavior. But the precise nature of these internal changes has never been spelled out. Some authors have tried to write a neurophysiological view of how the message gets into the auditory channels, then spins around in the brain, and comes out in behavior, but these speculations are not much different from Mesmer's theories in their connections with reality. The belief is widely held that the mediating event between the utterances that the hypnotist makes to the patient and the patient's overt behavior is the "trance," that is, it is the "trance" that somehow intervenes between the stimulus and the response.

The word *trance* as used in the literature on hypnosis is not usually defined. Most often, it is treated as a primitive word that presumably everyone understands with the same denotation. If necessary, a person will demonstrate what is meant by *trance* by walking around with hands outstretched as a sleepwalker is supposed to do. When the theorist who employs the trance metaphor is pushed into defining *trance* in objective terms, he asserts that it is a change in mental state. In an effort to find some kind of empirical test for the mental state notion, the person who believes in the existence of a trance may refer to a change in attention, that attention is shifted from one hypothesized *internal mental object* to another. Proponents of trance theories will argue from reports of some subjects in hypnosis experiments who will say, "Well, of course I was in a trance because I don't remember what happened between 12:10 and 12:20." However, the subject can readily be made to remember what happened during the interval by the hypnotist reciting a ritual statement such as, "Now you're hypnotized again and now you remember all." When the person does report the events that presumably had been lost to recall, what is the status of the trance concept? I propose that we can better describe hypnotic conduct by eliminating the word from our vocabulary.

Another point to be made before describing how hypnosis functions in behavior change is related to the problem of individual differences. The earlier hypnotists were not concerned with the fact that while some people responded to the hypnotic induction and performed the acts expected of them, others did not. In Mesmer's time, individual differences were attributed to inauspicious astrological conditions or to failures in technique. Later nonperformances were regarded almost entirely as failures in technique. Such nonperformances were regarded as lacking in importance for mention in a scientific report. Thus the early reports all contain accounts of persons who were successfully hypnotized, and hardly any of those who did not perform according to expectations. In contemporary psychology the notion of individual differences is a profound one and inescapable. Any attempt to explain hypnotic behavior must take into account the fact that not all persons respond in the same way to standard induction procedures. One must raise the question: what are the conditions under which persons respond according to expectations when assigned the hypnotic role?

## HYPNOTIC ROLE ENACTMENT

The content of large numbers of clinical reports that indicate behavior change following hypnotic induction leads us to the conclusion that *enacting the hypnotic role* is a necessary antecedent to the behavior changes monitored (Sarbin, 1964). Since individual differences are demonstrable, we are obliged to raise the further question: what accounts for observed differences in hypnotic role enactment?

A word is in order about the referent for the expression *hypnotic role enactment*. Today we employ a standard set of signs that we regard as characteristic of the hypnotic role. This standard set of signs has been codified in various kinds of scales. Friedlander and Sarbin (1938) prepared such a scale 25 years ago. More recently Hilgard and his associates at Stanford (Weitzenhoffer & Hilgard, 1959) prepared a similar scale which contains the behaviors presumably descriptive of or associated with the phenomenon of hypnosis. These signs, as it turns out, are quite arbitrary and are modified from time to time. For example, in Mesmer's time the "crisis," something similar to an hysteroepileptic convulsion, was regarded as one of the signs of a trance. If he had had the background, wisdom, and skill to construct a scale such as the Stanford Scale, he would have included the crisis as one of several items. When Braid began to work with influence phenomena some 50 or 60 years later, none of the subjects exhibited the crisis, so this sign was not incorporated in his descriptions of hypnosis. In the standard set of signs that currently are grouped together in hypnotic scales are (a) catalepsy and other motoric behaviors; (b) posthypnotic behavior, that is, the subject receives an instruction during the treatment period which is carried out at some later time; (c) amnesias, that is, the person "forgets" certain events that occurred during the hypnotic performance; and (d) the modification of perceptual behavior, for example, forming hallucinations.

It can be demonstrated that most people who have been exposed to the mass media of communication, such as radio, television, newspapers, books, comic magazines, and so on, are familiar with a standard set of beliefs about hypnosis. From time to time in our classes at the university we have distributed questionnaires to undergraduates and asked them to indicate the kinds of behavior that are characteristic of hypnosis. We find a surprising consensus among our subjects, many of whom have never witnessed a hypnotic performance but know about it only vicariously through the mass media. Thus, if a person who has been exposed to the mass media volunteers for an experiment in hypnosis, he is not naïve and uninformed. He comes to the experiment with a set of expectations in regard to his own conduct and that of the hypnotist. Similarly, the hypnotist has a list of expectations of how the subject is supposed to perform. In the case of the Stanford Scale, these expectations are incorporated in the list of signs and are tested in a predetermined order. If one performs according to this scale, then he is considered a good hypnotic subject, he is enacting the role according to the experimenter's expectations. If the subject responds only to half the items in the scale, then he is called moderately hypnotizable. If he responds to none, then he is considered to be unhypnotizable. If he is hypnotizable by this standard, and some change in behavior occurs after the induction of hypnosis, it is assumed that the hypnotic induction, or the effects of the induction, mediated the behavior change. We must address ourselves to the question: What are the characteristics of the person or of the interaction that account for differences in hypnotic performance, that account for the fact that some people and not others enact this special role?

## SUBJECT VARIABLES

When we observe two people interacting in a hypnosis setting, we can describe their conduct from our present knowledge in terms of a set of social psychological variables, each of which has a contribution to make to the total performance. These will be discussed *seriatim*.

### Role Expectations

First, there is the validity of the subject's role expectations. It has already been pointed out that we acquire these role expectations from the mass media and, it should be added, from communications in face-to-face settings. The hypnotist will generally not depend entirely on the fact that the subject has been exposed to mass media but will also include in the beginning of his induction a statement subtly outlining his expectations. He expects the subject to cooperate, to listen carefully to everything he has to say, and so on. A personalized set of expectations are built upon those brought to the laboratory by the subject. If the subject is resistant to the expectancy statements made by the hypnotist, such as might occur when the subject is a member of a religious group that has a negative evaluation of hypnosis, then he probably would not perform according to the hypnotist's expectations. However, the subject might have these expectations for the behavior of another person who was asked to play this role. An experiment of Orne's (1959) illustrates the way expectations function. He used two classes of undergraduates for his experiment. In one class he demonstrated hypnotic phenomena in which he used a subject who had previously been hypnotized and had been given the instruction that when he accepted the hypnotic role there would be a catalepsy of the dominant hand. For the second class of undergraduates, he did not give this instruction to the subject. To recapitulate, there were two undergraduate classes, one witnessing a standard hypnotic demonstration and one a standard demonstration *plus* spontaneous pathology of the dominant hand of the subject. In the course of the demonstration, Orne casually remarked that in hypnosis there is usually a spontaneous catalepsy of the dominant hand. Then he went on to other facts. Subsequently he called for volunteers from both classes. These volunteers came one at a time to the laboratory and were tested by one of Orne's associates, who was uninformed in regard to the antecedent conditions. As expected, those students who had witnessed the demonstration during which the catalepsy-of-the-dominant-hand expectation had been built in showed this behavior when they accepted the hypnotic role. In the second sample, where this expectation had not been built into the demonstration, the phenomenon was absent. A number of other experiments have been reported that show unmistakably that the expectations one brings to a situation function in the outcome. This of course applies to any social psychological situation, not only to the hypnotic one.

### Role Perception

A second variable, accuracy of role perception, is one that is related but less important in our experimental work because of the fact that we usually employ as subjects college students who have more or less uniform beliefs. In a standard psychological experiment the subject is told, or knows because he has volunteered, that he is to play the role of the hypnotic subject when he perceives himself in a situation with a hypnotist. This perception follows from his recognition of the cues that he is supposed to initiate in the enactment of the role. His knowledge is such that when he comes into the waiting room and sees a secretary, he perceives her as the secretary and not as the experimenter. Consequently, he does not enact the hypnotic role or "go into trance" but waits until the man in the white coat escorts him into the laboratory or consultation room. Then the subject has the opportunity to perform according to his beliefs and expectations. Role perception turns out *not* to be a variable of importance in our experimental work with college students but *is* a variable of importance in clinical work. The role of patient is not the same as the role of subject. The patient voluntarily asks to be treated according to hypnotic methods or is referred by his physician or psychiatrist. Under these conditions, he sometimes must be taught what cues are supposed to trigger off the enactment of the role.

### Specific Skills

A third variable has to do with the specific skill that a person brings to the hypnotic situation. When we look at hypnosis from the point of view of the dramatic role metaphor, we think of actors and directors, and of individual differences in skill in histrionics, in dramatic performing. Anyone with the briefest experience in amateur dramatics recognizes the fact that there are some who respond readily to a role assignment and others who are awkward and unconvincing. When we examine the items that comprise the usual scale of hypnotizability we find that many of these items have to do with motoric and gestural behavior. Sarbin and Lim (1963) performed an experiment in order to test whether, in fact, it was true that persons who responded well to the hypnotic induction were particularly skillful in role enactment in a nonhypnotic setting. A number of volunteers were hypnotized one at a time according to a standard method (Friedlander & Sarbin, 1938). They were tested on a scale not too dissimilar from that developed by Hilgard and his associates. From 1 to 2 weeks later each of these students appeared at the Department of Dramatic Arts, where they individually engaged in pantomime improvisations. Members of the staff of Dramatic Arts rated the subjects on acting ability, not knowing what the subjects' scores were on the hypnotic scale. In general, those subjects who were particularly adept at taking the hypnotic role, which demanded certain kinds of gestural and other motoric behavior, were also rated high on the convincingness of their pantomime improvisations.

In this connection, we have recently completed a study to determine the base rates for motoric acts often used as "signs" in hypnotic scales. Eight tasks from the Stanford Hypnotic Susceptibility Scales (Form A) were presented to a sample of 120 nonvolunteers as "imagination tasks." No hypnotic induction was employed. The performances of this sample were comparable to the performances of 124 hypnotized subjects, the original Stanford standardization sample (Anderson & Sarbin, 1964).

By establishing base rates for skills in nonhypnotic settings, we have a standard from which to assess the effects, if any, of the hypnotic induction.

In addition to the motoric skills, the hypnotic performance may call for perceptual skills, such as in the production of hallucinations. An experiment was designed to illustrate a widespread misunderstanding in hypnosis and to meet a methodological problem. The experiment that served

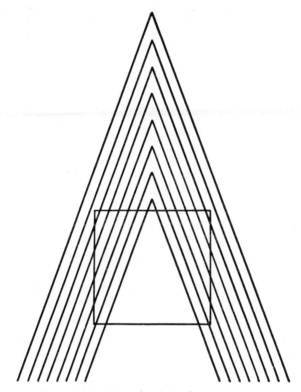

Figure 16-1.   Example of stimulus presentation.

as the stimulus for the present one was reported by Underwood (1960), in which he presumably demonstrated that induction of hypnosis was antecedent to producing perceptual changes tested by a little-known illusion. Underwood started with a pool of about 200 volunteer student subjects, and hypnotized each of them individually. He identified six subjects who met all his criteria for being "deeply hypnotized." Included in his criteria were not only the usual items drawn from a standard scale but also the ability to visualize vividly. In fact, he mentions that these subjects were selected mainly because they were able to produce hallucinations. Then he proceeded to test the hypothesis that hypnotic induction produces changes in perceptual processes by comparing these six subjects with the rest on a perceptual illusion test.

In the standard illusion, the presence of a set of inverted Vs distorts a superimposed quadrangle (see Figure 16-1). When a perfect square is superimposed, the top of the square appears narrower than the bottom. By superimposing, one at a time, a number of quadrangles that vary in their degree of "squareness," the experimenter can determine the amount of distortion produced by the set of inverted Vs. In this experiment, the quadrangles were first presented in the absence of the field or ground, the inverted Vs. Underwood instructed his six subjects to hallucinate the field. If they could hallucinate the field, then their perception of the quadrangle would be distorted in the same way as when, in a later session, the actual inverted Vs were presented. Underwood reported that the hypnotic hallucination of a nonpresent field produced the degree of distortion in the perception of the quadrangles similar to that produced by the actual presence of the inverted Vs. Thus the conclusion was drawn, although cautiously, that being hypnotized changed the perceptual apparatus in such a way that the visual functions were modified.

We repeated this experiment without hypnotizing anyone. We used 120 subjects in three classes in undergraduate psychology. We presented the same material except that we instructed the subjects to imagine vividly the presence of the inverted Vs, and to throw themselves into the task, and to use their imagination. There was no mention of hypnosis, no hypnotic induction, only instructions to use their "powers of imagination." Of these 120 subjects, 11 (9 percent) were able to report the distortion of the squares in the absence of the background. In Underwood's experiment, six hypnotic subjects were able to report the distortion out of a total of almost 200, that is, 3 percent. The conclusion to be drawn from this study, and other studies not reported here (Barber, 1961) is that the hypnotic induction is unnecessary in order to obtain changes in behavior either of a motoric kind or of a perceptual kind. Rather, behavioral changes may follow from unwitting preselection of subjects on the variables under study (Sarbin & Andersen, 1963).

This returns us to the problem of base rates. Many of the dramatic phenomena associated with hypnosis are mainly events that occur with extremely low frequency in the general population, such as a pathological Babinski. It has been assumed by workers in this field that a pathological sign has *zero* frequency in the general population. On this assumption, the presence of, say, a positive Babinski in a hypnotized subject would be attributed to the effects of the hypnotic induction or "trance." Once the experimenter or clinician recognizes that the zero frequency assumption is untenable, he will be less likely to assume a causal connection between infrequently appearing behavior and hypnosis (Barber, 1962).

### Congruence of Role Requirements with Characteristics of the Self

Another variable that is readily applicable to everyday behavior as well as to hypnotic behavior is the congruence of the role requirements with characteristics of the self. Andersen has recently completed a study (1963) in which he called this variable "role comfort" in connection with the acceptance of a role which is dissimilar to one's usual roles, which calls for a high degree of commitment, and which is potentially embarrassing.

All of us feel more comfortable in some roles than in others. Presumably we can do a more convincing job of enacting a role if we are comfortable in it. How do we test whether a person is comfortable in the role that he is asked to perform? A number of studies done in this country and elsewhere are leading us to an understanding of this variable. Aas (1962), Shor, Orne, and O'Connell (1962), and Andersen and Sarbin (1963) have approached this problem by creating specially designed questionnaires to tap self-characteristics that presumably make the hypnotic role a comfortable one. One of these, for example, is *absorption in the role.* Most of the roles in which we engage in everyday life require only a minimum of concentration or absorption. A person engaged in his daily occupations may be called upon to become deeply absorbed in some aspect of his work, and as a result pays no attention to incidental stimuli.

Analysis of the questionnaires used by Andersen and Sarbin revealed three classes of item responses which correlated with assessed hypnotic performance. The first class of items refer directly to the hypnotic role, for example, "There are things that would worry me about being hypnotized" (answered *no* by "good" subjects). The second class of items refer to the ability to become deeply absorbed in a role, for example, "I sometimes find that when I'm studying hard I don't notice the passage of time" (answered *yes* by the "good" subjects). The third class of items refer to the ability to resist distraction, for example, "I find it difficult to read or study in a noisy or busy place" (answered *no* by "good" subjects). When hypnotic performance and performance on hypnoticlike (imagination) tasks were used as criterion measures, and scores on the three classes of questionnaire items as independent variables, we obtained some interesting correlations. With hypnotic performance as the criterion measure, role absorption items tend to produce higher correlations than ability to resist distraction items. Aas (1962) reported similar findings. The class of items that referred directly to the role of hypnosis subject, however, tend to yield the highest correlations with criterion performance.

### Sensitivity to Role Demands

Sensitivity to role demands is another in this set of variables that presumably account for individual differences in role enactment. When a therapist and patient or an experimenter and subject interact there must be considered not only the expectations that each brings to the situation, not only the perceptions of each other, not only the skills that each possesses, but also the demands of the situation. The demands of the situation are overriding and have been described in other contexts as the sensitivity to subtle mores. Experiments from another domain may be used as illustrative. A decade ago a number of experiments were reported which appeared to show the operation of a process called perceptual defense. To caricature briefly these experiments, subjects were shown a list of words flashed on a screen, some "taboo," others, neutral. In general, subjects seemed to have difficulty in correctly recognizing taboo words. The premature inference that was drawn at that time was that the inability to recognize the taboo words was due to the operation of "perceptual defense." Later experiments showed that subjects, when they are proper ladies and gentlemen, are not likely, in the presence of an experimenter, to vocalize such taboo words, even though the instructions to report are clear. They not only were enacting the role of experimental subjects, but they were also enacting their *proper* social roles, taking into account the mores or role demands. These studies are somewhat caricatured in order to simplify them, but the description is close to the facts. The subtle role demands were not taken into account (Sarbin & Chun, 1964).

Orne (1959) also performed an experiment that showed unmistakably the operation of role demands. He designed an experiment in which a sample of subjects had been hypnotized, that is, they had been tested on their ability to perform the hypnotic role. A second set of subjects had been motivated to *simulate* the hypnotic role. Orne and other experienced hypnotists were unable to distinguish whether a subject was hypnotized or simulating. Earlier experiments, such as Hull's (1933), had demonstrated only that waking behavior was somehow a little different from hypnotic behavior. These differences were not seen as attributable to differential role demands, however. In Orne's study the situation was so constructed that the simulating subjects were strongly motivated to perform and to convince the experimenter that they were genuinely enacting the hypnotic role.

In the entertainment situation in which a multiple audience is present, there is an implied contract between the experimenter and the subject, indicating "if you do something for me, I will do something for you in return," a form of the standard contract in any social interaction. In a public setting, the possibility exists that the experimenter may be embarrassed if the subject does not perform according to expectations. To prevent embarrassment is a potent role demand in our polite society. A few years ago a TV hypnotist received a lot of advance publicity for his act. A volunteer co-ed had been previously hypnotized. One hundred thousand dollars in paper currency was placed on the table. The hypnotized subject sat three feet away from the money and was told by the hypnotist that if she reached over and took the money she could have it all. But earlier, before he had given this challenge, he had used an instruction of this nature: "You cannot get out of this chair. No matter what you do, you can't get out of this chair." In order to reach the money she would have to remove herself from the chair. The subject, of course, did not budge. A person versed in role theory would not have been surprised by this at all: first, a relationship had been built up between these two interactants on the basis of prior sessions, and second, there may have been 40,000,000 people in the audience and taking the money would have been a great embarrassment to the hypnotist. Anyone reconstructing his own social experiences will recall the lengths to which he will go to prevent himself or others from meeting an embarrassing situation.

Thus far, we have discussed five conceptions that individually or in combination account for individual differences in responsiveness to the hypnotic induction. If hypnosis is a prerequisite to some instances of behavior change, then the study of these variables are prerequisite to an understanding of behavior change.

### Social Reinforcement

The sixth variable contains the notion of social reinforcement. In keeping with the role metaphor, we employ the figure, *reinforcement provided by the audience.* The audience in most hypnotic experiments is singular, the therapist or experimenter, but audiences may be multiple, such as when hypnosis is used in an entertainment or clinical setting.

An important difference must be taken into account. In considering size of audience, it has frequently been noted by experienced hypnotists that for a larger audience, the number of volunteers who can perform hypnotic behaviors is greater than for a small audience. This suggests that the size and the nature of the audience is a potent factor in determining performance.

Experiments have been reported in the literature that indicate clearly that the depth of hypnotic response is greater when the hypnotist (a one-person audience) is a prestigious person, such as a professor, a doctor, or a therapist, than when the hypnotist is a student (Das, 1960). This occurs even when the same person is enacting the role of hypnotizer, at one time introducing himself as "Doctor so-and-so" and at another time as "Mr. so-and-so." Thus the role of the potentially reinforcing person (the audience) has something to do with the outcome, as we know from other contexts, as well as the number of persons who make up the audience. At the present time, we are in the midst of testing this experimentally in our laboratory by having audiences of various sizes available to observe a person as he performs the hypnotic role. Results thus far seem to fit the theory that with a large audience, subjects will respond differently than with a one-person audience. The reinforcing properties of audiences are documented in other papers in this book and need not be further detailed here. Suffice it to say that the acts emitted by the subject in the hypnotic situation may be reinforced or not by the one- or many-person audience, and that the reinforcing act may be exceedingly subtle.

## SUMMARY

The burden of this paper is that hypnosis is not an occult entity. Hypnosis is a word that is left over from an earlier metaphor, the metaphor of sleep, to describe a set of social conditions, usually between two interactants, although more may be involved. If we never had had a term such as hypnosis and the derivative concept of the trance, the question occurs: would we have hypnotic phenomena? It can be demonstrated that persons who are knowledgeable and experienced, such as Orne and the writer, can be easily deceived by persons pretending to be hypnotized. Does this mean that for 200 or more years patients and experimental subjects have been deceiving us? In part, it does mean this, if we avoid casting the word *deceive* in a pejorative mold. As we know from observing ourselves and others, we are all in a position to deceive others in order to promote group or individual goals. Every society provides institutionalized ways of employing such deceptions.

A critic will offer as contradictory evidence the fact that subjects who have been hypnotized may frequently report unusual kinds of experiences or bizarre thoughts, sometimes will break into tears and cry, sometimes will spontaneously report an hallucination—behaviors not called for in the standard hypnotic role, nor asked for by the experimenter. How then to account for this? At first glance this appears not to fit into the role model. Again, we have to look at these phenomena in the same way we look at any others. We stand back and ask the question: do these same kinds of events occur occasionally without the intervention of a hypnotist? We have to answer in the affirmative. For example, some persons will report occasionally breaking into tears. When we analyze this carefully we find that they have recalled something to memory that was sad or associated with grief. Most persons can report bizarre kinds of implicit phenomena occurring just before awakening or even while asleep. It is true that many subjects take the sleep instructions literally when they are told to go to sleep by the hypnotist and thus engage in psychological behavior that is indistinguishable from dreaming. Under these conditions they may exhibit brief depressive or elated episodes. Again we have to apply the notion of base rates to these unusual experiences, which are sometimes taken as the critical differences between role enactment, using the acting model, and "genuinely experiencing" so-called trance phenomena.

Finally, should we follow the apparent implications of this paper and do away with hypnosis if it is no more than role enactment? The implication does not follow any more than saying we should do away with psychotherapy because we can account for what occurs by means of variables that are drawn from stimulus-response theories or from social psychological theories. We must take into account the fact that many disordered or unhappy persons will approach therapists with the expectation that the therapist will use a hypnotic induction. The therapist may participate in the beliefs of the patient and employ the hypnotic induction as a part of the ritual associated with the therapeutic enterprise. The fact is inescapable that whatever kind of behavior change methods we use, there are entrance and exit ceremonies. These may be highly ritualized, as in psychoanalysis, or may be more casual, as in childrens' play therapy. It is a decision for the therapist whether to expand the entrance ceremony to include the ritual of the hypnotic induction because this meets the role expectations of his client.

To summarize, the outcomes of the behavior modification enterprise called hypnosis are related to individual differences in a special kind of role enactment. These individual differences in the convincingness with which one performs the hypnotic role are related to at least six variables, which are applicable to all social psychological events. We have identified these six variables as (a) validity of role expectations, (b) accuracy of role perception, (c) general and specific skills, (d) congruence of self and role, (e) sensitivity to role demands, and (f) the nature of the reinforcing audience.

# 17

## SUMMARY AND IMPLICATIONS

THE material presented in this volume has the effect of blurring a number of traditional distinctions. The foremost of these is the distinction between clinical and experimental psychology. While for purposes of exposition we will refer first to the influence of the clinical setting on the laboratory and then to the influence of the laboratory on the clinic, the major point is that the clinic and the laboratory no longer are separate. In the present volume this is made manifest by the backgrounds of the authors themselves and the reciprocal clinical and experimental implications of their work. In the future this trend is likely to be accelerated by an increase in the number of investigators in this area coupled with more psychologists actively interested in applying the results of these experimental investigations.

### EFFECTS OF CLINIC ON LABORATORY

Because of this growing interest, it is likely that clinical concerns will have an increasing effect on the selection of problems for experimental investigation. Another effect of the clinical interest in experimental results may well be an increase in work such as that of Goldiamond, Salzinger, Staats, and Bijou in which the subject is observed repeatedly over long periods of time rather than during a single experimental session.

Another future effect on the laboratory will be a blurring of the distinction between experimenter and subject. As indicated in the chapters by Sarason and Matarazzo, the experimenter will, and perhaps must, become the object of research, that is, the subject. Two areas for future research are the influences on the influencer (examiner-experimenter-therapist) and the communication of examiner bias to the influencee.

Another likely impact of the clinical orientation on the laboratory may well be manifested in the selection of the populations and settings for research. The majority of important human interactions are not single meetings with strangers. Patterson has illustrated the possibility of having socially meaningful "experimenters" (parents) act as the agents of influence. Bijou has discussed the mobile research laboratory, and throughout the book there are references to research with subjects such as retardates and handicapped children who differ markedly from college sophomores. Logical extensions of the interest in behavior influence, studies of the influencer, and the desire to work with socially important criteria, are studies set in the field (classroom and ward) and the use of socially meaningful criteria such as reading and leadership. It would be interesting and important to extend such work to include the study of nurses, teachers, politicians, managers, and deans, that is, the people who in everyday life are influencers by virtue of their societal roles.

Just as there has been a blurring of the clinical-experimental distinction, so have traditional subject areas merged. For example, the supposed topic areas of set, demand characteristics, placebo, and examiner bias are hard to separate from each other because all may be viewed as instances of the same phenomenon. Another reason why topic areas are increasingly less well defined is that a social influence procedure may be either an independent or dependent variable. For example, verbal conditioning, as discussed in Krasner's chapter, may be an independent variable evaluated in terms of differences between groups in emission of a particular response, or it may be a dependent variable used to measure response to certain social conditions, atmospheres, or reinforcers. Subareas of behavior influence also move together because response to one social influence situation may be used both to predict and to facilitate response to another social influence technique. For example, we have identified the role played by a number of social influence procedures such as verbal conditioning in psychotherapy. The combination of social influence techniques within a single procedure raises the interesting question of how general is susceptibility to social influence, and the even more interesting question of what are the discriminative stimuli, the conditions under which the same person will be susceptible or resistive to social influence.

Still another likely effect of the clinic on the laboratory is an emphasis on increasingly large, complex, and socially important units of behavior. Social role enactments are likely to become the units for measurement of response to and emission of culturally meaningful behavior. In the same manner, the environmental setting should be the subject of increasingly extensive and rigorous study. Social institutions and bureaucratic organizations may limit the individual's range of socially acceptable behavior. Behaviors that are adjustive in prisoner-of-war camps, jails, corporations, and psychiatric hospitals may be disadvantageous in other social situations. An analysis of what behaviors are selected for reinforcement in specific situations will provide a method for developing a psychology of social influence.

The environment, including reinforcing stimuli, may be viewed as a flow of information. Many of the traditional problems of psychology may be approached within a social reinforcement framework with fresh insights, methodologies, and hope for useful results. Kanfer's approach to the "black box," Bandura's researches on the ramifications of modeling, Bijou's work on concept formation, Hastorf's work on leadership, and Sarbin's work on hypnosis are examples of this possibility. It seems reasonable to expect that research involving manipulation of the environment will make use of decision theory and probability learning formulations. Topics such as intelligence, creativity, arousal, and novelty may be approached either as sources of reinforcing stimuli or as problems that may be elucidated by recourse to social reinforcement concepts.

In the foregoing material we have tried to sketch the manner in which clinical interest in experimental results may influence future laboratory investigations. It is important to realize that just as experimental work has had a major impact on clinical psychology, so we may expect a reciprocal process in which clinical interests, needs, and research opportunities will have an effect on experimental psychology.

### EFFECTS OF LABORATORY ON CLINIC

Turning to the effects of laboratory work on clinical practice, we may note that the starting point of clinical work is a desire to change people in a preselected, socially desirable manner. The concepts of preselection and social desirability have two implications: the first is a change toward greater therapist responsibility and the second is the more general social problem of values. The goal of wanting to change people leads to selection of techniques to accomplish the stated purpose. Experimental data provide the best basis for choosing appropriate clinical procedures. When laboratory work has been the basis of clinical practice, the results have been very promising in terms of speed, number of successes, and types of subjects. However, selecting the most appropriate techniques leads to far-reaching implications for the clinical setting. We will discuss these implications in terms of therapist, assessment, treatment, and training.

A major implication of the use of experimental work is a change in the identification and role behavior of the psychologist engaged in treatment. The psychologist engaged in behavior modification sees himself as a stimulus that he can manipulate appropriately, meaningfully, even ingeniously, but never mechanically. The psychologist responds to subjects' behavior in terms of a preselected program. For example, if the psychologist decides that his goal is to reduce delusional speech, he will respond with attention and pleasure to rational, nondelusional verbal behavior and ignore or respond coldly to bizarre verbalizations. There are many issues touched on by this example. The psychologist, after assessment, formulates a program of treatment and assumes the responsibility of selecting behaviors whose emission by the patient are to be increased or decreased. The psychologist is also active in eliciting, reinforcing, shaping, providing models, changing characteristics of his speech or nonverbal behavior, making suggestions, increasing his own leverage (even to the point of depriving the patient of cigarettes, candy, or some pleasurable stimulation, if this is needed to develop an effective reinforcing stimulus), assigning tasks, recording changes in response frequency, latency, and amplitude, and, finally, evaluating the results of his program. The person engaged in behavior modification may be said to be tough rather than tender-minded, sceptical rather than credulous, and behaviorally rather then medically oriented. The modifier of behavior is a person whose primary goal is to be effective in assisting the patient rather than being loved. This involves discipline, delay of gratification, and resistance to short-term temptations on the part of the therapist.

The focus of the psychologist engaged in behavior modification is reliably observed behavior and not internal dynamics. This is consistent with a behavioral model and is different from work within a medical model, which posits that overt behaviors (symptoms) are a function of an underlying cause and must be treated indirectly and in terms of that cause. This focus on behavior has the effect of providing the psychologist with constant feedback about the effectiveness of his efforts. If progress is not made, the recordings of the target behavior will make this evident, and the psychologist will alter his technique.

The focus on behavior and movement away from a medical model alter the therapist's relationship with his patient in the direction of making the treatment endeavor far more a partnership of interdependent equals. Behavior modification procedures can usually be explained directly to the patient. The concept that lack of progress is due to difficulties in application of reinforcement principles changes the evaluation of the patient's behavior; for example, criticism of the therapist is no longer explained away as the result of overdetermined transference characteristics. Rather than nonevaluative acceptance of everything the patient does, the nub of treatment is that behavior has immediate and meaningful consequences in that situation just as it does in the community. The relationship between a psychologist practicing behavior modification and his client is far more that of teacher and student than doctor and patient.

## ASSESSMENT AND TREATMENT

Assessment and treatment are inseparable. Assessment starts with questions of what behaviors are disadvantageous, what reinforcers maintain current behavior, what new behaviors could replace the disadvantageous behavior, and what reinforcers can be manipulated in order to increase or maintain socially appropriate behavior. Assessment based on current behavior rather than internal dynamics is of the total social situation and centers on the development of new behaviors rather than the sorting of deficient or bizarre behaviors into categories which have little impact on therapeutic strategy. Assessment provides the information on which the therapeutic program is devised and continues into therapy as the measurement of progress and evaluation of success.

Treatment may involve many different techniques or specific applications of social reinforcement principles, but in all cases the goal is the development of new and more advantageous responses to the stimuli that previously elicited maladaptive behavior. The method is direct, ahistorical, and utilizes any and all appropriate social influence techniques. An important difference from psychotherapy within a medical model is a point made most explicitly by Saslow: the prime goal of treatment is changed behavior with significant others rather than insight. There is evidence that changed behavior may precede insight, and possibly produce it.

Because there is a unity of principles for changing behavior, therapists may be trained in the same manner as children or patients. The techniques used for teaching include modeling and selective reinforcement. Of great importance for purposes of communication is that the material to be taught is operationally defined. This level of communication has been achieved with intelligence tests and there is no reason why psychotherapists should be naturally endowed with highly valued but randomly defined traits such as warmth and intuition. Rather, if such traits can be identified in the form of overt behaviors, they can be taught. Once there is an overt behavior that the teacher has identified as germane, training becomes a matter of technique.

Given an appropriate background, the person engaged in behavior modification has a clear framework within which he can evaluate his own behavior. This leads him to formulate how his behavior is contingent on the patient's behavior through asking himself questions such as, "What am I reinforcing?" and "What am I teaching?" While these comments have dealt with the training of therapists, it should be noted that behavior *influencees* may be taught to become behavior *influencers*. This is explicit in the teaching of *self*-control and in the encouragement of behaviors which will increase reinforcing responses from significant others.

## SOCIAL VALUES INVOLVED IN BEHAVIOR MODIFICATION

The very effectiveness of behavior modification, the use of terms such as *manipulation, influence,* and *control of the environment,* and the concept that the therapist has the responsibility to determine the treatment program, all lead to concern with social values. Behavior modification, as an area of social influence, shares this problem with advertising, public relations, and education. These areas have in common individuals who have the interest and the ability to alter the behavior of other people, that is, one person determining what is desirable behavior for another. There are circumstances in which this is beneficial for the individual and society and circumstances in which this is not the case. The ethical problem is not whether behavior influence is proper or improper, but a specification of the circumstances under which behavior influence is appropriate. This view reduces the problem from a general one to a more specific operational one. While a crucial variable is the behavior to be modified, other circumstances that must be taken into account are the methods of influence used and the impact on society of the individual's changed behavior. If a person is being supported by society (as in a psychiatric hospital), then it is appropriate for an authorized agent of society to alter his behavior. On the other hand, behavior modification is inappropriate if the person is a self-supporting, contributing member of society. The ultimate source of values is neither the patient's nor the therapist's wishes, but the requirements of the society in which both live. This broadens the framework in which behavior is evaluated by stressing the relativity involved in time, place, and person.

## LONG-RANGE GOALS

We would suggest as positive, long-range goals the increase of the person's frequency and range of socially appropriate behaviors. The goal is to permit the individual to have as wide a choice of appropriate responses as possible. There are basic requirements for life within a society, and they cannot be avoided. Once these basic demands have been met, the individual should be given both the skills and the freedom to realize his full potentialities. An individual does not have the right to perform maladaptive behavior that will be harmful either to himself or to other members of society. Further, we do not think that the emission of harmful behaviors indicates that the individual has freedom. Just as ignorance of antecedents does not define freedom, so knowledge of antecedents of behavior does not reduce freedom.

Values, in terms of appropriate ends and the means to them, are social behaviors and cannot be conceived as the result of anything other than human behaviors. Values should be the focus of research in the same manner that other behaviors such as creativity, intelligence, or socially valuable flexibility and nonconformity are the subjects of research.

An integral part of training therapists is the recognition of the socially appropriate application of behavior modification techniques. Given increasingly effective behavior modification techniques, the area of values must not be overlooked or allowed to go untouched. The point we wish to make is that the material in this volume implies the need for research on social values, and that the results of such research should be central in the training of therapists.

This volume started with a concept of behavior modification as the application of experimental findings to the alteration of behavior in the clinical setting, and has presented relevant research and implications stemming from this orientation. In so doing there have been clear indications of new clinical techniques, new research opportunities, and new social obligations.

# References

Aas, A. A note on distractibility and hypnosis. *Amer. J. clin. Hypn.*, 1962, 5, 135-137.

Aas, A. Hypnotizability as a function of nonhypnotic experience. *J. abnorm. soc. Psychol.*, 1963, 66, 142-150.

Abelson, H. I. *Persuasion.* New York: Springer, 1959.

Adams, H. E., Butler, J. R., & Noblin, C. D. Effects of psychoanalytically-derived interpretations: a verbal conditioning paradigm? *Psychol. Rep.*, 1962, 10, 691-694.

Adams, H. E., Noblin, C. D., Butler, J. R., & Timmons, E. O. Differential effect of psychoanalytically-derived interpretations and verbal conditioning in schizophrenics. *Psychol. Rep.*, 1962, 11, 195-198.

Adams, J. K. Laboratory studies of behavior without awareness. *Psychol. Bull.*, 1957, 54, 383-405.

Adams, J. S., & Hoffman, B. The frequency of self-reference statements as a function of generalized reinforcement. *J. abnorm. soc. Psychol.*, 1960, 60, 384-389.

Adamson, R. Inhibitory set in problem solving as related to reinforcement learning. *J. exp. Psychol.*, 1959, 58, 280-282.

Adorno, T. W., Frenkel-Brunswik, Else, Levinson, D., & Sanford, R. N. *The authoritarian personality.* New York: Harper & Row, 1950.

Aiken, E. G. Interpersonal behavior changes perceived as accompanying the operant conditioning of verbal output in small groups. *Tech. Rep. 11, Western Behav. Sci.*, Oct. 1963.

Alexander, F., & French, T. M. *Psychoanalytic therapy; principles and application.* New York: Ronald, 1946.

Allen, K. Eileen, Hart, Betty M., Buell, Joan S., Harris, Florence R., & Wolf, M. M. Effects of social reinforcement on isolate behavior of a nursery school child. *Child Developm.*, 1964, 35, 511-518.

Alper, Thelma G. Memory for completed and incompleted tasks as a function of personality. *J. abnorm. soc. Psychol.*, 1946, 41, 403-420. (a)

Alper, Thelma G. Task-orientation vs. ego-orientation in learning and retention. *Amer. J. Psychol.*, 1946, 59, 236-248. (b)

Andersen, M. L. Correlates of hypnotic performance: an historical and role-theoretical analysis. Unpublished doctoral dissertation, Univer. Calif., Berkeley, 1963.

Andersen, M. L., & Sarbin, T. R. Correlates of responsiveness on hypnotic-like tasks. Unpublished manuscript, Univer. Calif., Berkeley 1963.

Andersen, M. L., & Sarbin, T. R. Base-rate expectancies and motoric alterations in hypnosis. *Int. J. exp. clin. Hypn.*, 1964, 12, 147-158.

Asch, S. E. The doctrine of suggestion, prestige, and imitation in social psychology. *Psychol. Rev.*, 1948, *55*, 250-276.

Asch, S. E. Studies of independence and conformity. I. A minority of one against a unanimous majority. *Psychol. Monogr.*, 1956, *70*, No. 9 (Whole No. 416).

Astin, A. W. The functional autonomy of psychotherapy. *Amer. Psychologist*, 1961, *16*, 75-78.

Atkinson, J. W. (Ed.) *Motives in fantasy, action, and society*. Princeton: Van Nostrand, 1958.

Axelrod, H. S., Cowen, E. L., & Heilizer, F. The correlates of manifest anxiety in stylus maze learning. *J. exp. Psychol.*, 1956, *51*, 131-138.

Ayllon, T. Intensive treatment of psychotic behaviour by stimulus satiation and food reinforcement. *Behav. Res. Ther.*, 1963, *1*, 53-62.

Ayllon, T., Conditioning procedures in the rehabilitation of psychotic patients. Paper presented to 1st Int. Cong. Soc. Psychiat., London, Aug. 1964.

Ayllon, T., & Haughton, E. Control of the behavior of schizophrenic patients by food. *J. exp. Anal. Behav.*, 1962, *5*, 343-352.

Ayllon, T., & Haughton, E. Modification of symptomatic verbal behavior of mental patients. *Behav. Res. Ther.*, 1964, *2*, 87-97.

Ayllon, T., & Michael, J. The psychiatric nurse as a behavioral engineer. *J. exp. Anal. Behav.*, 1959, *2*, 323-334.

Ayllon, T., & Sommer, R. A directive or a permissive approach. *Ment. Hosp.*, 1960, *11*, No. 9, 45-48.

Azrin, N. H., Holz, W. C., & Hake, D. F. Fixed-ratio punishment. *J. exp. Anal. Behav.*, 1963, *6*, 141-148.

Azrin, N. H., & Lindsley, O. R. The reinforcement of cooperation between children. *J. abnorm. soc. Psychol.*, 1956, *52*, 100-102.

Bachrach, A. J. (Ed.), *Experimental foundations of clinical psychology*. New York: Basic Books, 1962.

Bachrach, A. J. Psychotherapy as a response chain. Paper presented at V. A. Hospital, Palo Alto, March 1963.

Bachrach, A. J., Candland, D. K., & Gibson, J. T. Group reinforcement of individual response experiments in verbal behavior. In I. A. Berg and B. M. Bass (Eds.), *Conformity and deviation*. New York: Harper & Row, 1961, 258-285.

Bachrach, A. J., Erwin, W. J., & Mohr, J. P. The control of eating behavior in an anorexic by operant conditioning techniques. In L. P. Ullmann and L. Krasner (Eds.), *Case studies in behavior modification*. New York: Holt, Rinehart and Winston, 1965.

Back, K. W. Influence through social communication. *J. abnorm. soc. Psychol.*, 1951, *46*, 9-23.

Back, K. W., Hood, T. C., & Brehm, M. L. The subject role in small group experiments. Paper presented to Southern Sociol. Soc., 1963.

Baer, D. M. A technique of social reinforcement for the study of child behavior: behavior avoiding reinforcement withdrawal. *Child Develpm.*, 1962, *33*, 847-858. (a)

Baer, D. M. Laboratory control of thumbsucking by withdrawal and re-presentation of reinforcement. *J. exp. Anal. Behav.*, 1962, *5*, 525-528. (b)

Baer, D. M., & Sherman, J. A. Reinforcement control of generalized imitation in young children. *J. exp. child Psychol.*, 1964, *1*, 37-49.

Bales, R. F. *Interaction process analysis; a method for the study of small groups*. Cambridge, Mass.: Addison-Wesley, 1950.

Bandura, A. Psychotherapist's anxiety level, self-insight, and psychotherapeutic competence. *J. abnorm. soc. Psychol.*, 1956, *52*, 333-337.

Bandura, A. Psychotherapy as a learning process. *Psychol. Bull.*, 1961, *58*, 143-159.

Bandura, A. Punishment revisited. *J. consult. Psychol.*, 1962, *26*, 298-301. (a)

Bandura, A. Social learning through imitation. In M. R. Jones (Ed.), *Nebraska symposium on motivation: 1962*. Lincoln: Univer. Nebr. Press, 1962, 211-215. (b)

Bandura, A. The role of imitation in personality development. *J. nursery Educ.*, 1963, *18*, 207-215. (a)

Bandura, A. Behavior theory and identificatory learning. *Amer. J. orthopsychiat.*, 1963, *33*, 591-601. (b)

Bandura, A. Influence of model's reinforcement contingencies on the acquisition of imitative responses. *J. pers. soc. Psychol.*, in press.

Bandura, A. Vicarious processes: a case of no-trial learning. In L. Berkowitz (Ed.), *Advances in experimental social psychology*, Vol. II. New York: Academic Press, 1965.

Bandura, A. *Principles of behavioral modification*. New York: Holt, Rinehart and Winston, in preparation.

Bandura, A., & Huston, Aletha C. Identification as a process of incidental learning. *J. abnorm. soc. Psychol.*, 1961, *63*, 311-318.

Bandura, A., & Kupers, Carol J. Transmission of patterns of self-reinforcement through modeling. *J. abnorm. soc. Psychol.*, 1964, *69*, 1-9.

Bandura, A., Lipsher, D. H., & Miller, Paula E. Psychotherapists' approach—avoidance reactions to patients' expressions of hostility. *J. consult. Psychol.*, 1960, *24*, 1-8.

Bandura, A., & McDonald, F. J. Influence of social reinforcement and the behavior of models in shaping children's moral judgments. *J. abnorm. soc. Psychol.*, 1963, *67*, 274-281.

Bandura, A., & Mischel, W. Modification of self-imposed delay of reward through exposure to live and symbolic models. *J. pers. soc. Psychol.*, in press.

Bandura, A., & Rosenthal, T. L. Vicarious classical conditioning as a function of arousal level. Unpublished manuscript, Stanford University, 1964.

Bandura, A., Ross, Dorothea, & Ross, Sheila A. Transmission of aggression through imitation of aggressive models. *J. abnorm. soc. Psychol.*, 1961, *63*, 575-582.

Bandura, A., Ross, Dorothea, & Ross, Sheila A. Imitation of film-mediated aggressive models. *J. abnorm. soc. Psychol.*, 1963, *66*, 3-11. (a)

Bandura, A., Ross, Dorothea, & Ross, Sheila A. A comparative test of the status envy, social power, and secondary reinforcement theories of identificatory learning. *J. abnorm. soc. Psychol.*, 1963, *67*, 527-534. (b)

Bandura, A., Ross, Dorothea, & Ross, Sheila A. Vicarious reinforcement and imitative learning. *J. abnorm. soc. Psychol.*, 1963, *67*, 601-607. (c)

Bandura, A., & Walters, R. H. Dependency conflicts in aggressive delinquents. *J. soc. Issues*, 1958, *14*, 52-65.

Bandura, A., & Walters, R. H. *Adolescent aggression*. New York: Ronald, 1959.

Bandura, A., & Walters, R. H. *Social learning and personality development*. New York: Holt, Rinehart and Winston, 1963.

Barber, T. X. Antisocial and criminal acts induced by "hypnosis." *Arch. gen. Psychiat.*, 1961, *5*, 301-312.

Barber, T. X. Experimental controls and the phenomena of "hypnosis": a critique of hypnotic research methodology. *J. nerv. ment. Dis.*, 1962, *134*, 493-505.

Barber, T. X. Hypnotizability, suggestibility, and personality: V. A critical review of research findings. *Psychol. Rep.*, 1964, *14*, 299-320.

Barber, T. X., & Glass, L. B. Significant factors in hypnotic behavior. *J. abnorm. soc. Psychol.*, 1962, *64*, 222-228.

Barnard, P. G. Interaction effects among certain experimenter and subject characteristics on a projective test. Unpublished doctoral dissertation, Univer. Wash., 1963.

Barrett, Beatrice H. Reduction in rate of multiple tics by free operant conditioning methods. *J. nerv. ment. Dis.*, 1962, *135*, 187-195.

Barrett, Beatrice H., & Lindsley, O. R. Deficits in acquisition of operant discrimination and differentiation shown by institutionalized retarded children. *Amer. J. ment. Defic.*, 1962, *67*, 424-436.

Bass, B. *Leadership, psychology and organizational behavior.* New York: Harper & Row, 1960.

Becker, W. C. The relationship of factors in parental ratings of self and each other to the behavior of kindergarten children as rated by mothers, fathers, and teachers. *J. consult. Psychol.*, 1960, *24*, 507-527.

Bender, Lauretta. *A visual motor Gestalt test and its clinical use.* New York: Amer. Orthopsychiat. Assoc., 1938.

Bentler, P. M. An infant's phobia treated with reciprocal inhibition therapy. *J. child Psychol. Psychiat.*, 1962, *3*, 185-189.

Bentler, P. M., O'Hara, J. W., & Krasner, L. Hypnosis and placebo. *Psychol. Rep.*, 1963, *12*, 153-154.

Berg, I. A., & Bass, B. M. (Eds.) *Conformity and deviation.* New York: Harper & Row, 1961.

Berger, S. M. Incidental learning through vicarious reinforcement. *Psychol. Rep.*, 1961, *9*, 477-491.

Berger, S. M. Conditioning through vicarious instigation, *Psychol. Rev.*, 1962, *69*, 450-466.

Berlin, J. I., & Wyckoff, B. The teaching of improved interpersonal relations through programmed instruction for two people working together. Paper presented to annual meeting, Amer. Psychol. Assoc., Phila., Aug. 1963.

Biderman, A. A., & Zimmer, H. (Eds.) *The manipulation of human behavior.* New York: Wiley, 1961.

Bijou, S. W. Therapeutic techniques with children. In L. A. Pennington and I. A. Berg (Eds.), *An introduction to clinical psychology.* (2nd ed.) New York: Ronald, 1954.

Bijou, S. W. Patterns of reinforcement and resistance to extinction in young children. *Child Develpm.*, 1957, *28*, 47-54.

Bijou, S. W. A child study laboratory on wheels. *Child Develpm.*, 1958, *29*, 425-427. (a)

Bijou, S. W. Operant extinction after fixed-interval schedules with young children. *J. exp. Anal. Behav.*, 1958, *1*, 25-29. (b)

Bijou, S. W. Discrimination performance as a baseline for individual analysis of young children. *Child Develpm.*, 1961, *32*, 163-170.

Bijou, S. W. Theory and research in mental (developmental) retardation. *Psychol. Rec.*, 1963, *13*, 95-110.

Bijou, S. W., & Baer, D. M. *Child development: a systematic and empirical theory.* New York: Appleton, 1961.

Bijou, S. W., & Oblinger, Barbara. Responses of normal and retarded children as a function of the experimental situation. *Psychol. Rep.*, 1960, *6*, 447-454.

Bijou, S. W., & Orlando, R. Rapid development of multiple-schedule performances with retarded children. *J. exp. Anal. Behav.*, 1961, *4*, 7-16.

Bijou, S. W., & Sturges, Persis T. Positive reinforcers for experimental studies with children—consumables and manipulatables. *Child Develpm.*, 1959, *30*, 151-170.

Bilger, R. C., & Speaks, C. E. Operant control of non-fluent speech in normal talkers. *Asha*, 1959, *1*, 97. (Abstract)

Binder, A., McConnell, D., & Sjoholm, Nancy A. Verbal conditioning as a function of experimenter characteristics. *J. abnorm. soc. Psychol.*, 1957, *55*, 309-314.

Bindra, D. *Motivation: a systematic reinterpretation.* New York: Ronald, 1959.

Birnbrauer, J. S. Applications of reinforcement theory to clinical problems. Paper presented to Amer. Assoc. Ment. Def., Portland, Oreg., 1963.

Birnbrauer, J. S., Bijou, S. W., Wolf, M. M., & Kidder, J. D. Programed instruction in the classroom. In L. P. Ullmann and L. Krasner (Eds.), *Case studies in behavior modification.* New York: Holt, Rinehart and Winston, 1965.

Birnbrauer, J. S., Bijou, S. W., Wolf, M. M., Kidder, J. D., & Tague, Cecilia. A programmed instruction classroom for educable retardates. Unpublished manuscript, Univer. Wash., 1964.

Blachly, R., Stephenson, W. F., & Levy, L. A demonstration of work as therapy, *Summaries of Scientific Papers*, Paper No. 191, Amer. Psychiat. Assoc. annual meeting, St. Louis, 1963.

Black, J. W. The persistence of the effects of delayed side-tone. *J. speech hear. Disord.*, 1955, *20*, 65-68.

Bloodstein, O. Hypothetical conditions under which stuttering is reduced or absent. *J. speech hear. Disord.*, 1950, *15*, 142-153.

Bockoven, J. S. *Moral treatment in American psychiatry.* New York: Springer, 1963.

Bond, I. K., & Hutchison, H. C. Application of reciprocal inhibition therapy to exhibitionism. *Canad. med. Assoc. J.*, 1960, *83*, 23-25.

Bonney, M. E. Relationships between social success, family size, socio-economic home background, and intelligence among school children in grades III to V. *Sociometry*, 1944, *7*, 26-29.

Bordin, E. S. Ambiguity as a therapeutic variable. *J. consult. Psychol.*, 1955, *19*, 9-15.

Borko, H. (Ed.), *Computer applications in the behavioral sciences.* Englewood Cliffs, N. J.: Prentice-Hall, 1962.

Bradley, C. *Schizophrenia in childhood.* New York: Macmillan, 1941.

Brady, J. P., & Lind, D. L. Experimental analysis of hysterical blindness. *AMA Arch. gen. Psychiat.*, 1961, *4*, 331-339.

Braine, M.D.S. On learning the grammatical order of words. *Psychol. Rev.*, 1963, *70*, 323-348. (a)

Braine, M.D.S. The ontogeny of English phrase structure: the first phase. *Language*, 1963, *6*, 1-13. (b)

Bronfenbrener, U. Soviet methods of character education: some implications for research. *Amer. Psychologist*, 1962, *17*, 550-564.

Brunswik, E. *Perception and the representative design of psychological experiments.* Berkeley: Univer. Calif. Press, 1956.

Burnham, W. H. *The normal mind.* New York: Appleton, 1924.

Butler, J. M., Rice, Laura, N., & Wagstaff, Alice K. On the naturalistic definition of variables: an analogue of clinical analysis. In H. H. Strupp and L. Luborsky (Eds.), *Research in psychotherapy*, Vol. II, Washington, D. C.: Amer. Psychol. Assoc., 1962.

Cairns, R. B. The influence of dependency inhibition on the effectiveness of social reinforcement. *J. Pers.*, 1961, *29*, 466-488.

Cairns, R. B. Antecedents of social reinforcer effectiveness. Unpublished manuscript, Indiana Univer., 1962.

Cairns, R. B., & Lewis, M. Dependency and the reinforcement value of a verbal stimulus. *J. consult. Psychol.*, 1962, *26*, 1-8.

Cameron, N. A. *Personality development and psychopathology*. Boston: Houghton Mifflin, 1963.

Campbell, J. M. Verbal conditioning as a function of the personality characteristics of experimenters and subjects. Unpublished doctoral dissertation, Univer. Wash., 1960.

Carlson, E. R., & Carlson, Rae. Male and female subjects in personality research. *J. abnorm. soc. Psychol.*, 1960, *61*, 482-483.

Case, H. W. Therapeutic methods in stuttering and speech blocking. In H. J. Eysenck (Ed.), *Behaviour therapy and the neuroses*. New York: Pergamon, 1960.

Cattell, R. B. *Personality and motivation: structure and measurement*. New York: Harcourt, 1957.

Chapple, E. D. The standard experimental (stress) interview as used in Interaction Chronograph investigations. *Hum. Organization*, 1953, *12*, No. 2, 23-32.

Cherry, C., & Sayers, B. McA. Experiments upon the total inhibition of stammering by external control, and some clinical results. *J. psychosom. Res.*, 1956, *1*, 233-246.

Chittenden, Gertrude E. An experimental study in measuring and modifying assertive behavior in young children. *Monogr. soc. Res. child Develpm.*, 1942, *7*, No. 1 (Serial No. 31).

Chomsky, N. *Syntactical structures*. Gravenhage: Mouton, 1957.

Cieutat, V. J. Surreptitious modification of verbal behavior during class discussion. *Psychol. Rep.*, 1959, *5*, 648.

Cofer, C. N., & Foley, J. P. Mediated generalization and the interpretation of verbal behavior: I. Prologemena. *Psychol. Rev.*, 1942, *49*, 513-540.

Cohen, D. J., & Lindsley, O. R. Catalysis of controlled leadership in cooperation by human stimulation. Unpublished manuscript, 1963.

Colby, K. M. *A primer for psychotherapists*. New York: Ronald, 1951.

Colby, K. M. *Energy and structure in psychoanalysis*. New York: Ronald, 1955.

Colby, K. M. *A skeptical psychoanalyst*. New York: Ronald, 1958.

Colby, K. M. *An introduction to psychoanalytic research*. New York: Basic Books, 1960. (a)

Colby, K. M. Experiment on the effects of an observer's presence on the imago system during psychoanalytic free-association. *Behav. Sci.*, 1960, *5*, 216-232. (b)

Colby, K. M. On the greater amplifying power of causal-correlative over interrogative inputs on free association in an experimental psychoanalytic situation. *J. nerv. ment. Dis.*, 1961, *133*, 233-239. (a)

Colby, K. M. Research in psychoanalytic information theory. *Amer. Sci.*, 1961, *49*, 358-369. (b)

Colby, K. M. Experimental treatment of neurotic computer programs. *Arch. gen. psychiat.* 1964, *10*, 220-227.

Colby, K. M. & Gilbert, J. P. Programming a computer model of neurosis. *J. math. Psychol.*, 1964, *1*, 405-417.

Coleman, J. C. *Abnormal psychology and modern life*. (3rd ed.) Chicago: Scott, Foresman, 1964.

Cowden, R. C., & Ford, L. I. Systematic desensitization with phobic schizophrenics. *Amer. J. Psychiat.*, 1962, *119*, 241-245.

Crowne, D. P., & Marlow, D. A new scale of social desirability independent of psychopathology. *J. consult. Psychol.*, 1960, *24*, 349-354.

Cumming, J., & Cumming, Elaine. *Ego and milieu*. New York: Atherton, 1962.

Dailey, C. A. An experimental method for improving interpersonal understanding. *Psychol. Rep.*, 1963, *13*, 240.

Das, J. P. Prestige effects in body-sway suggestibility. *J. abnorm. soc. Psychol.*, 1960, *61*, 487-488.

Davison, G. The training of undergraduates as social reinforcers for autistic children. In L. P. Ullmann and L. Krasner (Eds.), *Case studies in behavior modification*. New York: Holt, Rinehart and Winston, 1965.

DeMyer, Marian K., & Ferster, C. B. Teaching new social behavior to schizophrenic children. Unpublished manuscript, 1964.

Dinoff, M., Horner, R. F., Kurpiewski, B. S., Rickard, H. C., & Timmons, E. O. Conditioning verbal behavior of a psychiatric population in a group therapy-like situation. *J. clin. Psychol.*, 1960, *16*, 371-372.

Dinoff, M., Morris, J. R., & Hannon, J. E. The stability of schizophrenic speech in a standardized interview. *J. clin. Psychol.*, 1963, *19*, 279-282.

Dinoff, M., Rickard, H. C., Salzberg, H., & Sipprelle, C. N. An experimental analogue of three psychotherapeutic approaches. *J. clin. Psychol.*, 1960, *16*, 70-73.

Dittmann, A. T. The interpersonal process in psychotherapy: development of a research method. *J. abnorm. soc. Psychol.*, 1952, *17*, 236-244.

Dollard, J., & Miller, N. E. *Personality and psychotherapy*. New York: McGraw-Hill, 1950.

Dollard, J., & Mowrer, O. H. A method of measuring tension in written documents. *J. abnorm. soc. Psychol.*, 1947, *42*, 3-32.

Dulany, D. E., Jr. The place of hypotheses and intentions: an analysis of verbal control in verbal conditioning. In C. W. Eriksen, (Ed.), *Behavior and awareness*. Durham, N. C.: Duke Univer. Press, 1962.

Dunlap, K. *Habits their making and unmaking*. New York: Liveright, 1932.

Easterbrook, J. A. The effect of emotion on cue utilization and the organization of behavior. *Psychol. Rev.*, 1959, *66*, 183-201.

Edwards, A. L. *Experimental design in psychological research*. New York: Holt, Rinehart and Winston, 1960.

Ekman, P. Conditioning of opinions about capital punishment as a function of verbal and nonverbal reinforcement. *Amer. Psychologist*, 1959, *14*, 347. (Abstract)

Ekman, P., Krasner, L., & Ullmann, L. P. Interaction of set and awareness as determinants of response to verbal conditioning. *J. abnorm. soc. Psychol.*, 1963, *66*, 387-389.

Emmerich, W. Family role concepts of children ages 6-10 years. *Child Develpm.*, 1961, *32*, 609-624.

Epstein, R., & Liverant, S. Verbal conditioning and sex-role identification in children. *Child Develpm.*, 1963, *34*, 99-106.

Erickson, M. H. Development of apparent unconsciousness during hypnotic reliving of a traumatic experience. *Arch. Neurol. Psychiat.*, 1937, *38*, 1282-1288.

Erickson, M. H. A study of clinical and experimental findings on hypnotic deafness: I. Clinical experimentation and findings. *J. gen. Psychol.*, 1938, *19*, 127-150. (a)

Erickson, M. H. A study of clinical and experimental findings on hypnotic deafness: II Experimental findings with a conditioned response technique. *J. gen. Psychol.*, 1938, *19*, 151-167. (b)

Erickson, M. H. An experimental investigation of the hypnotic subject's apparent ability to become unaware of stimuli. *J. gen. Psychol.*, 1944, *31*, 191-212.

Eysenck, H. J. The effects of psychotherapy: an evaluation. *J. consult. Psychol.*, 1952, *16*, 319-324.

Eysenck, H. J. A dynamic theory of anxiety and hysteria. *J. ment. Sci.*, 1955, *101*, 28-51.

Eysenck, H. J. Reminiscence, drive, and personality theory. *J. abnorm. soc. Psychol.*, 1956, *53*, 328-333.

Eysenck, H. J. Learning theory and behaviour therapy. *J. ment. Sci.*, 1959, *105*, 61-75.

Eysenck, H. J. (Ed.), *Behaviour therapy and the neuroses.* New York: Pergamon, 1960.

Eysenck, H. J. The effects of psychotherapy. In Eysenck, H. J. (Ed.), *Handbook of abnormal psychology: an experimental approach.* New York: Basic Books, 1961.

Eysenck, H. J. Behaviour therapy, spontaneous remission and transference in neurotics. *Amer. J. Psychiat.*, 1963, *119*, 867-871.

Fahmy, Sumaya A. Conditioning and extinction of a referential verbal response class in a situation resembling a clinical diagnostic interview. *Dissertation Abstr.*, 1953, *13*, 873-874.

Fairbanks, G. Selective vocal effects of delayed auditory feedback. *J. speech hear. Dis.*, 1955, *20*, 333-346.

Farber, I. E. The things people say to themselves. *Amer. Psychologist*, 1963, *18*, 185-197.

Ferguson, D. C., & Buss, A. H. Operant conditioning of hostile verbs in relation to experimenter and subject characteristics. *J. consult. Psychol.*, 1960, *24*, 324-327.

Ferster, C. B. Reinforcement and punishment in the control of human behavior by social agencies. *Psychiat. Res. Rep.*, 1958, *10*, 101-118.

Ferster, C. B. Positive reinforcement and behavior deficits of autistic children. *Child Develpm.*, 1961, *32*, 437-456.

Ferster, C. B. The repertoire of the autistic child in relation to principles of reinforcement. In L. Gottschalk (Ed.), *Methods of research in psychotherapy.* New York: Harper & Row, 1965.

Ferster, C. B., & DeMyer, Marian K. The development of performances in autistic children in an automatically controlled environment. *J. chron. Dis.*, 1961, *13*, 312-345.

Ferster, C. B., & DeMyer, Marian K. A method for the experimental analysis of the behavior of autistic children. *Amer. J. Orthopsychiat.*, 1962, *32*, 89-98.

Ferster, C. B., Nurnberger, J. I., & Levitt, E. B. The control of eating. *J. Mathetics*, 1962, *1*, 87-109.

Ferster, C. B., & Skinner, B. F. *Schedules of reinforcement.* New York: Appleton, 1957.

Festinger, L. *A theory of cognitive dissonance.* New York: Harper & Row, 1957.

Fisher, R. A. *The design of experiments.* (6th ed.) New York: Hafner, 1951.

Flanagan, B., Goldiamond, I., & Azrin, N. H. Operant stuttering: the control of stuttering behavior through response-contingent consequences. *J. exp. Anal. Behav.*, 1958, *1*, 173-178.

Flanagan, B., Goldiamond, I., & Azrin, N. H. Instatement of stuttering in normally fluent individuals through operant procedures. *Science,* 1959, *130*, 979-981.

Frank, J. D. The dynamics of the psychotherapeutic relationship: determinants and effects of the therapist's influence. *Psychiatry,* 1959, *22*, 17-39.

Frank, J. D. *Persuasion and healing.* Baltimore: Johns Hopkins Press, 1961.

Franks, C. M. (Ed.), *Conditioning techniques in clinical practice and research.* New York: Springer, 1964.

Freud, S. Formulations regarding the two principles in mental functioning. In *Collected Papers.* Vol. IV. London: Hogarth Press, 1946, pp. 13-21.

Friedlander, J. W., & Sarbin, T. R. The depth of hypnosis. *J. abnorm. soc. Psychol.,* 1938, *33*, 453-475.

Fuller, P. R. Operant conditioning of a vegetative human organism. *Amer. J. Psychol.,* 1949, *62*, 587-590.

Ganzer, V. J., & Sarason, I. G. Interrelationships among hostility, experimental conditions, and verbal behavior. *J. abnorm. soc. Psychol.,* 1964, *68*, 79-84.

Gelfand, Donna M. The influence of self-esteem on rate of verbal conditioning and social matching behavior. *J. abnorm. soc. Psychol.,* 1962, *65*, 259-265.

Gelfand, S., Ullmann, L. P., & Krasner, L. The placebo response: an experimental approach. *J. nerv. ment. Dis.,* 1963, *136*, 379-387.

Gerard, H. B., & Rabbie, J. M. Fear and social comparison. *J. abnorm. soc. Psychol.,* 1961, *62*, 586-592.

Gewirtz, J. L. Three determinants of attention-seeking in young children. *Monogr. Soc. Res. Child Develpm.,* 1954, *19*, No. 2 (Serial No. 59).

Gewirtz, J. L., & Baer, D. M. The effect of brief social deprivation on behaviors for a social reinforcer. *J. abnorm. soc. Psychol.,* 1958, *56*, 49-56. (a)

Gewirtz, J. L., & Baer, D. M. Deprivation and satiation of social reinforcers as drive conditions. *J. abnorm. soc. Psychol.,* 1958, *57*, 165-172. (b)

Goffman, E. *Asylums.* New York: Doubleday, 1961.

Goffman, E. Mental symptoms and public order. In *Disorders of communication* vol. xlii. Res. Publ., Assoc. Res. Nerv. Ment. Dis., 1964.

Goldiamond, I. The temporal development of fluent and blocked speech communication. Air Force Com. Cont. Develpm. Div., T.R. 60-38, 1960.

Goldiamond, I. The maintenance of ongoing fluent verbal behavior and stuttering. *J. Mathetics,* 1962, *1*, 57-95. (a)

Goldiamond, I. Perception. In A. J. Bachrach (Ed.), *The experimental foundations of clinical psychology.* New York: Basic Books, 1962. (b)

Goldiamond, I. Machine definition of ongoing silent and oral reading rate. *J. exp. Anal. Behavior,* 1962, *5*, 363-367. (c)

Goldiamond, I. Justified and unjustified alarm over behavioral control. Paper presented to Annual Conv., Amer. Psychol. Assoc., Phila., Sept. 1963.

Goldiamond, I., Atkinson, C. J., & Bilger, R. C. Stabilization of behavior and prolonged exposure to delayed auditory feedback. *Science,* 1962, *135*, 437-438.

Goldman-Eisler, Frieda. Individual differences between interviewers and their effect on interviewees' conversational behaviour. *J. ment. Sci.,* 1952, *98*, 660-671.

Goldstein, A. P. *Therapist-patient expectancies in psychotherapy.* New York: Pergamon, 1962.

Goldstein, K., & Scheerer, M. Tests of abstract and concrete behavior. In A. Weider (Ed.), *Contribution toward medical psychology,* vol. II. New York: Ronald, 1953.

Graham, C. H. Color theory. In S. Koch (Ed.), *Psychology: a study of a science.* Vol. I. New York: McGraw-Hill, 1959.

Grant, D. A., Hake, H. W., & Hornseth, J. P. Acquisition and extinction of a verbal conditioned response with differing percentages of reinforcement. *J. exp. Psychol.,* 1951, *42,* 1-5.

Green, E. J. *The learning process and programmed instruction.* New York: Holt, Rinehart and Winston, 1962.

Greenspoon, J. The effect of two nonverbal stimuli on the frequency of members of two verbal response classes. *Amer. Psychologist,* 1954, *9,* 384. (Abstract)

Greenspoon, J. The reinforcing effect of two spoken sounds on the frequency of two responses. *Amer. J. Psychol.,* 1955, *68,* 409-416.

Greenspoon, J. Verbal conditioning and clinical psychology. In A. J. Bachrach (Ed.), *Experimental foundations of clinical psychology.* New York: Basic Books, 1962.

Gurel, L. & Ullmann, L. P. Quantitative differences in response to TAT cards: the relationship between transcendence score and number of emotional words. *J. proj. Tech.,* 1958, *22,* 399-401.

Guthrie, E. R. *The psychology of human conflict.* New York: Harper & Row, 1938.

Guthrie, E. R. *The psychology of learning.* (2nd ed.) New York: Harper & Row, 1952.

Guze, S. B., & Mensh, I. N. An analysis of some features of the interview with the Interaction Chronograph. *J. abnorm. soc. Psychol.,* 1959, *58,* 269-271.

Hammond, K. R. Representative vs. systematic design in clinical psychology. *Psychol. Bull.,* 1954, *51,* 150-159.

Hare, A. P., Waxler, Nancy, Saslow, G., & Matarazzo, J. D. Simultaneous recordings of Bales and Chapple interaction measures during initial psychiatric interviews. *J. consult. Psychol.,* 1960, *24,* 193.

Harris, Florence R., Johnston, Margaret K., Kelley, C. Susan, & Wolf, M. M. Effects of positive social reinforcement on regressed crawling of a nursery school child. *J. ed. Psychol.,* 1964, *55,* 35-41.

Hart, Betty M., Allen, K. Eileen, Buell, Joan S., Harris, Florence R., Wolf, M. M. Effects of social reinforcement on operant crying. *J. exp. child Psychol.,* 1964, *1,* 145-153.

Hartup, W. W. Sex and social reinforcement effects with children. Paper presented to the annual meeting of the Amer. Psychol. Assoc., New York, 1961.

Hastorf, A. H. The influence of suggestion on the relationship between stimulus size and perceived distance. *J. Psychol.,* 1950, *29,* 195-217.

Hastorf, A. H., & Bender, I. E. A caution respecting the measurement of empathic ability. *J. abnorm. soc. Psychol.,* 1952, *47,* 574-576.

Hastorf, A. H., Bender, I. E., & Weintraub, D. J. The influence of response patterns on the "refined empathy score." *J. abnorm. soc. Psychol.,* 1955, *51,* 341-343.

Hastorf, A. H., & Cantril, H. Some psychological errors in polling—a few guides for opinion interpretation. *J. educat. Psychol.,* 1949, *40,* 57-60.

Hastorf, A. H., & Cantril, H. They saw a game: a case study. *J. abnorm. soc. Psychol.,* 1954, *49,* 129-134.

Hastorf, A. H., & Kennedy, J. L. Emmert's law and size-constancy. *Amer. J. Psychol.,* 1957, *70,* 114-116.

Hastorf, A. H., & Knutson, A. L. Motivation, perception and attitude change. *Psychol. Rev.*, 1949, *56*, 88-94.

Hastorf, A. H., & Myro, G. The effect of meaning on binocular rivalry. *Amer. J. Psychol.*, 1959, *72*, 393-400.

Hastorf, A. H., & Piper, G. W. A note on the effect of explicit instructions on prestige suggestion. *J. Soc. Psychol.*, 1951, *33*, 289-293.

Hastorf, A. H., Richardson, S. A., & Dornbusch, S. N. The problem of relevance in the study of person perception. In R. Tagiuri and L. Petrullo (Eds.), *Person perception and interpersonal behavior*. Stanford, Calif.: Stanford University Press, 1958, 54-62.

Hastorf, A. H., & Way, K. S. Apparent size with and without distance cues. *J. gen. Psychol.*, 1952, *47*, 181-188.

Hanfmann, Eugenia. Concept formation test. In A. Weider (Ed.), *Contributions toward medical psychology*. Vol. II. New York: Ronald, 1953.

Haughton, E., & Ayllon, T. Production and elimination of symptomatic behavior. In L. P. Ullmann and L. Krasner (Eds.), *Case studies in behavior modification*. New York: Holt, Rinehart and Winston, 1965.

Heider, F. *The psychology of interpersonal relations*. New York: Wiley, 1958.

Heller, K. Experimental analogues of psychotherapy: the clinical relevance of laboratory findings of social influence. *J. nerv. ment. Dis.*, 1963, *137*, 420-426.

Heller, K., Myers, R. A., & Kline, Linda V. Interviewer behavior as a function of standardized client roles. *J. consult. Psychol.*, 1963, *27*, 117-122.

Hess, R. D., & Torney, Judith V. Religion, age, and sex in children's perceptions of family authority. *Child Develpm.*, 1962, *33*, 781-789.

Hildum, D. C., & Brown, R. W. Verbal reinforcement and interviewer bias. *J. abnorm. soc. Psychol.*, 1956, *53*, 108-111.

Hingtgen, J. N., Sanders, Beverly J., & DeMyer, Marian K. Shaping cooperative responses in early childhood schizophrenics. *Amer. Psychologist*, 1963 (Abstract). In L. P. Ullmann and L. Krasner (Eds.), *Case studies in behavior modification*. New York: Holt, Rinehart and Winston, 1965.

Holland, J. G. Teaching machines: an application of principles from the laboratory. *J. exp. Anal. Behav.*, 1960, *3*, 275-287.

Holland, J. G. New directions in teaching-machine research. In J. Coulson (Ed.), *Proceedings of the conference on applications of digital computers to automated instruction*. New York: Wiley, 1963.

Holland, J. G., & Skinner, B. F. *The analysis of behavior*. New York: McGraw-Hill, 1961.

Hollingshead, A. R., & Redlich, F. C. *Social class and mental illness: a community study*. New York: Wiley, 1958.

Hollingworth, H. L. *Abnormal psychology*. New York: Ronald, 1930.

Holz, W. C., & Azrin, N. H. Discriminative properties of punishment. *J. exp. Anal. Behav.*, 1961, *4*, 225-232.

Holz, W. C., & Azrin, N. H. A comparison of several procedures for eliminating behavior. *J. exp. Anal. Behav.*, 1963, *6*, 399-406.

Homme, L. E., deBaca, P. C., Devine, J. V., Steinhorst, R., & Rickert, E. J. Use of the Premack principle in controlling the behavior of nursery school children. *J. exp. Anal. Behav.*, 1963, *6*, 544.

Hovland, C. I., Janis, I. L., & Kelley, H. H. *Communication and persuasion*. New Haven: Yale Univer. Press, 1953.

Hull, C. L. *Hypnosis and suggestibility—an experimental approach*. New York: Appleton, 1933.

Hutt, M. L., & Gibby, R. G. *Patterns of abnormal behavior.* Boston: Allyn and Bacon, 1957.

Isaacs, W., Thomas, J., & Goldiamond, I. Application of operant conditioning to reinstate verbal behavior in psychotics. *J. speech hear. Disord.,* 1960, *25,* 8-12.

Iverson, M. A. Interpersonal comparability and verbal conditioning. Paper presented to Amer. Psychol. Assoc., St. Louis, August 1962.

Jack, Lois M. An experimental study of ascendant behavior in preschool children. *Univer. Ia. Stud. Child. Welf.,* 1934, *9,* 3-65.

Jackson, D. (Ed.) *The etiology of schizophrenia.* New York: Basic Books, 1960.

Jakubczak, L. F., & Walters, R. H. Suggestibility as dependency behavior. *J. abnorm. soc. Psychol.,* 1959, *59,* 102-107.

Janis, I. L. Personality correlates of susceptibility to persuasion. *J. Pers.,* 1954, *22,* 504-518.

Jersild, A. T., & Holmes, Frances B. Methods of overcoming children's fears. *J. Psychol.,* 1935, *1,* 75-104.

Jones, Mary C. The elimination of children's fears. *J. exp. Psychol.,* 1924, *7,* 382-390.

Kagan, J., & Lemkin, Judith. The child's differential perception of parental attributes. *J. abnorm. soc. Psychol.,* 1960, *61,* 440-447.

Kahn, M. A polygraph study of the catharsis of aggression. Unpublished doctoral dissertation, Harvard Univer., 1960.

Kanfer, F. H. The effect of partial reinforcement on acquisition and extinction of a class of verbal responses. *J. exp. Psychol.,* 1954, *48,* 424-432.

Kanfer, F. H. Verbal conditioning: reinforcement schedules and experimenter influence. *Psychol. Rep.,* 1958, *4,* 443-452.

Kanfer, F. H. Verbal rate, content, and adjustment ratings in experimentally structured interviews. *J. abnorm. soc. Psychol.,* 1959, *58,* 305-311.

Kanfer, F. H. Incentive value of generalized reinforcers. *Psychol. Rep.,* 1960, *7,* 531-538. (a)

Kanfer, F. H. Verbal rate, eyeblink, and content in structured psychiatric interviews. *J. abnorm. soc. Psychol.,* 1960, *61,* 341-347. (b)

Kanfer, F. H., Comments on learning in psychotherapy. *Psychol. Rep.,* 1961, *9,* 681-699.

Kanfer, F. H. Experimental analogues of psychotherapy. Paper presented to Amer. Psychol. Assoc., St. Louis, Sept. 1962.

Kanfer, F. H., Bass, B. M., & Guyett, I. Dyadic speech patterns, orientation and social reinforcement. *J. consult. Psychol.,* 1963, *27,* 199-205.

Kanfer, F. H., Bradley, Marcia M., & Marston, A. R. Self-reinforcement as a function of degree of learning. *Psychol. Rep.,* 1962, *10,* 885-886.

Kanfer, F. H., & Karas, Shirley C. Prior experimenter-subject interaction and verbal conditioning. *Psychol. Rep.,* 1959, *5,* 345-353.

Kanfer, F. H., & McBrearty, J. F. Verbal conditioning: discrimination and awareness. *J. Psychol.,* 1961, *52,* 115-124.

Kanfer, F. H., & McBrearty, J. F. Minimal social reinforcement and interview content. *J. clin. Psychol.,* 1962, *18,* 210-215.

Kanfer, F. H., & Marston, A. R. Verbal conditioning, ambiguity, and psychotherapy. *Psychol. Rep.,* 1961, *9,* 461-475.

Kanfer, F. H., & Marston, A. R. The effect of task-relevant information on verbal conditioning. *J. Psychol.,* 1962, *53,* 29-36. (a)

Kanfer, F. H., & Marston, A. R. The relationship between personality variables and verbal response characteristics. *J. clin. Psychol.,* 1962, *18,* 426-428. (b)

Kanfer, F. H., & Marston, A. R. Control of verbal behavior by multiple schedules. *Psychol. Rep.*, 1962, *10*, 703-710. (c)

Kanfer, F. H., & Marston, A. R. Determinants of self-reinforcement in human learning. *J. exp. Psychol.*, 1963, *66*, 245-254. (a)

Kanfer, F. H., & Marston, A. R. Human reinforcement: vicarious and direct. *J. exp. Psychol.*, 1963, *65*, 292-296. (b)

Kanfer, F. H., & Marston, A. R. Conditioning of self-reinforcing responses: an analogue to self-confidence training. *Psychol. Rep.*, 1963, *13*, 63-70. (c)

Kanfer, F. H., & Matarazzo, J. D. Secondary and generalized reinforcement in human learning. *J. exp. Psychol.*, 1959, *58*, 400-404.

Kanfer, F. H., Phillips, Jeanne S., Matarazzo, J. D., & Saslow, G. Experimental modification of interviewer content in standardized interviews. *J. consult. Psychol.*, 1960, *24*, 528-536.

Kantor, J. R. *Interbehavioral psychology.* (Rev. ed.) Bloomington, Ind.: Principia Press, 1959.

Kelleher, R. T., & Gollub, L. R. A review of positive conditioned reinforcement. *J. exp. Anal. Behav.*, 1962, *5*, 543-597.

Kelly, G. A. *The psychology of personal constructs.* Vol. II. *Clinical diagnosis and psychotherapy.* New York: Norton, 1955.

Kelman, H. C. Three processes of acceptance of social influence: compliance, identification, and internalization. *Amer. Psychologist*, 1956, *11*, 361. (Abstr.)

Kerr, Nancy, Meyerson, L., & Michael, J. A procedure for shaping vocalizations in a mute child. In L. P. Ullmann and L. Krasner (Eds.), *Case studies in behavior modification.* New York: Holt, Rinehart and Winston, 1965.

King, G. F., Armitage, S. G., & Tilton, J. R. A therapeutic approach to schizophrenics of extreme pathology: an operant-interpersonal method. *J. abnorm. soc. Psychol.*, 1960, *61*, 276-286.

Koenig, K. P. The manipulation of personality test scores by the technique of selective verbal reinforcement in a free verbal situation. Unpublished M.S. thesis, Univer. Wash., 1962.

Koenig, K. P. The experimental manipulation of anxiety self-report and related measures. Unpublished doctoral dissertation Univer. Wash., 1963.

Krasner, L. Personality differences between patients classified as psychosomatic and as nonpsychosomatic. *J. abnorm. soc. Psychol.*, 1953, *48*, 190-198.

Krasner, L. The use of generalized reinforcers in psychotherapy research. *Psychol. Rep.*, 1955, *1*, 19-25.

Krasner, L. Studies of the conditioning of verbal behavior. *Psychol. Bull.*, 1958, *55*, 148-170. (a)

Krasner, L. A technique for investigating the relationship between the behavior cues of the examiner and the verbal behavior of the patient. *J. consult. Psychol.*, 1958, *22*, 364-366. (b)

Krasner, L. Role taking research and psychotherapy. *VA Res. Rept.*, Palo Alto, Nov. 1959, No. 5.

Krasner, L. Behavior control and social responsibility. *Amer. Psychologist*, 1962, *17*, 199-204. (a)

Krasner, L. The therapist as a social reinforcement machine. In H. H. Strupp and L. Luborsky (Eds.), *Research in psychotherapy*, Vol. II. Wash., D. C.: Amer. Psychol. Assoc., 1962. Pp. 61-94. (b)

Krasner, L. Reinforcement, verbal behavior and psychotherapy. *Amer. J. Orthopsychiat.*, 1963, *33*, 601-613. (a)

Krasner, L. The behavioral scientist and social responsibility: no place to hide. In symposium on "Social responsibilities of the psychologist," annual meeting, Amer. Psychol. Assoc., Phila., 1963. (b)

Krasner, L. The therapist as a social reinforcer: man or machine. In symposium on "Social influence, counseling and psychotherapy," annual meeting, Amer. Psychol. Assoc., Phila., 1963. (c)

Krasner, L., Knowles, J. B., & Ullmann, L. P. The effect of verbal conditioning of attitudes on subsequent motor performance. Paper presented at annual meeting, Amer. Psychol. Assoc., Los Angeles, Sept. 1964.

Krasner, L., & Kornreich, M. Psychosomatic illness and projective tests: the Rorschach test. *J. proj. Tech.*, 1954, *18*, 355-367.

Krasner, L., & Ullmann, L. P. Variables in the verbal conditioning of schizophrenic subjects. *Amer. Psychologist*, 1958, *13*, 358. (Abstract)

Krasner, L., & Ullmann, L. P. Variables affecting report of awareness in verbal conditioning. *J. Psychol.*, 1963, *56*, 193-202.

Krasner, L., & Ullmann, L. P. *Behavior influence: the effect of social reinforcement on individual behavior.* New York: Holt, Rinehart and Winston (to be published in 1966).

Krasner, L., Ullmann, L. P., & Fisher, D. Changes in performance as related to verbal conditioning of attitudes toward the examiner. *Percept. Motor Skills*, 1964, *19*, 811-816.

Krasner, L., Ullmann, L. P., & Weiss, R. L. Studies in role perception. *J. gen. Psychol.*, 1964, *71*, 367-371.

Krasner, L., Ullmann, L. P., Weiss, R. L., & Collins, Beverly J. Responsibility to verbal conditioning as a function of three different examiners. *J. clin. Psychol.*, 1961, *17*, 411-415.

Krasner, L., Weiss, R. L., & Ullmann, L. P. Responsivity to verbal conditioning as a function of awareness. *Psychol. Rep.*, 1961, *8*, 523-538.

Krumboltz, J. D., & Thoresen, C. E. The effect of behavioral counseling in groups and individual settings on information-seeking behavior. *J. counsel. Psychol.*, 1964, *11*, 324-333.

Kushner, M. Desensitization of a post-traumatic phobia. In L. P. Ullmann and L. Krasner (Eds.), *Case studies in behavior modification.* New York: Holt, Rinehart and Winston, 1965. (a)

Kushner, M. The reduction of a long-standing fetish by means of aversive conditioning. In L. P. Ullmann and L. Krasner (Eds.), *Case studies in behavior modification.* New York: Holt, Rinehart and Winston, 1965. (b)

Landreth, Catherine. *Education of the young child.* New York: Wiley, 1942.

Lang, P. J. Behavior therapy with a case of nervous anorexia. In L. P. Ullmann and L. Krasner (Eds.), *Case studies in behavior modification.* New York: Holt, Rinehart and Winston, 1965.

Lang, P. J., & Lazovik, A. D. Experimental desensitization of a phobia. *J. abnorm. soc. Psychol.*, 1963, *66*, 519-525.

Larder, Diane L. Effect of aggressive story content on nonverbal play behavior. *Psychol. Rep.*, 1962, *11*, 14.

Lazarus, A. A. Group therapy of phobic disorders by systematic desensitization. *J. abnorm. soc. Psychol.*, 1961, *63*, 504-510.

Lazarus, A. A. The results of behaviour therapy in 126 cases of severe neurosis. *Behav. Res. Ther.*, 1963, *1*, 69-79.

Lazarus, A. A., & Abramovitz, A. The use of "emotive imagery" in the treatment of children's phobias. *J. ment. Sci.*, 1962, *108*, 191-195.

Lazarus, R. S., Deese, J., & Osler, Sonia F. The effects of psychological stress upon performance. *Psychol. Bull.*, 1952, *49*, 293-317.

Lefkowitz, M., Blake, R. R., & Mouton, Jane S. Status factors in pedestrian violation of traffic signals. *J. abnorm. soc. Psychol.*, 1955, *51*, 704-706.

Leiderman, P. H., & Shapiro, D. A physiological and behavioral approach to the study of group interaction. *Psychosom. Med.*, 1963, *25*, 146-157.

Lennard, H. L., & Bernstein, A. *The anatomy of psychotherapy: systems of communication and expectation.* New York: Columbia Univer. Press, 1960.

Lenneberg, E. H. Understanding language without ability to speak: a case report. *J. abnorm. soc. Psychol.*, 1962, *65*, 419-425.

Lerner, Gina. Reinforcement of aggression in children's doll play. Unpublished manuscript, Univer. Oreg., 1960.

Lesser, G. S., & Abelson, R. P. Personality correlates of persuasibility in children. In I. L. Janis and C. I. Hovland (Eds.), *Personality and persuasibility.* New Haven: Yale Univer. Press, 1959, pp. 187-206.

Levin, G., & Shapiro, D. The operant conditioning of conversation. *J. exp. Anal. Behav.*, 1962, *5*, 309-316.

Levin, G. R., & Simmons, J. J. Response to praise by emotionally disturbed boys. *Psychol. Rep.*, 1962, *11*, 10.

Lewis, D. J., & Duncan, C. P. Vicarious experience and partial reinforcement. *J. abnorm. soc. Psychol.*, 1958, *57*, 321-326.

Lifton, R. J. *Thought reform and the psychology of totalism: a study of "brainwashing" in China.* New York: Norton, 1961.

Lindquist, E. F. *Design and analysis of experiments in psychology and education.* Boston: Houghton Mifflin, 1956.

Lindsley, O. R. Studies in behavior therapy. Metropolitan State Hospital, Waltham, Mass. *Status Report III:* 1954.

Lindsley, O. R. Operant conditioning methods applied to research in chronic schizophrenia. *Psychiat. Res. Rep.*, 1956, 5, 140-153.

Lindsley, O. R. Experimental analysis of cooperation and competition. Paper presented to Eastern Psychol. Assoc., Phila., Apr. 1961.

Lindsley, O. R. Direct behavioral analysis of psychotherapy sessions by conjugately programmed closed-circuit television. Paper presented to annual meeting, Amer. Psychol. Assoc., St. Louis, Sept. 1962.

Lindsley, O. R. Direct measurement and functional definition of vocal hallucinatory symptoms. *J. nerv. ment. Dis.*, 1963, *136*, 293-297. (a)

Lindsley, O. R. Experimental analysis of social reinforcement: terms and methods. *Amer. J. Orthopsychiat.*, 1963, *33*, 624-633. (b)

Lindsley, O. R. Free-operant conditioning and psychotherapy. *Current psychiatric Therapies.* New York: Grune & Stratton, 1963. (c)

Lippitt, R. Polansky, N., & Rosen, S. The dynamics of power: a field study of social influence in groups of children. *Hum. Rel.*, 1952, *5*, 37-64.

Long, E. R., Hammack, J. T., May, F., & Campbell, B. J. Intermittent reinforcement of operant behavior in children. *J. exp. Anal. Behav.*, 1958, *1*, 315-339.

Lovaas, O. I. Effect of exposure to symbolic aggression on aggressive behavior. *Child Develpm.*, 1961, *32*, 37-44.

Lovaas, O. I., Freitag, G., Gold, Vivian J., & Kassorla, Irene C. Experimental studies in childhood schizophrenia: I Analysis of self-destructive behavior. *J. exp. child Psychol.*, in press.

Lovaas, O. I., Freitag, G., Kinder, M. I., Rubenstein, B. D., Schaeffer, B., & Simmons, J. Q. Experimental studies in childhood schizophrenia: II Establishment of social reinforcers. Paper presented to Western Psychol. Assoc., 1964.

Lovibond, S. H. The mechanism of conditioning treatment of enuresis. *Behav. Res. Ther.*, 1963, *1*, 17-21. (a)

Lovibond, S. H. Intermittent reinforment in behaviour therapy. *Behav. Res. Ther.*, 1963, *1*, 127-132. (b)

Luborsky, L. Psychotherapy. In P. R. Farnsworth and Q. McNemar (Eds.), *Annual review of psychology*. Palo Alto: Annual Reviews, Inc., 1959.

Luborsky, L., & Strupp, H. H. Research problems in psychotherapy: a three-year follow-up. In H. H. Strupp and L. Luborsky (Eds.), *Research in psychotherapy*. Vol. II. Washington, D. C.: Amer. Psychol. Assoc., 1962.

Luchins, A. S. *A functional approach to training in clinical psychology*. Springfield, Ill., Charles C. Thomas, 1959.

Lumsdaine, A. A., & Glaser, R. *Teaching machines and programmed learning*. Washington, D. C.: National Educational Assoc., 1960.

Lundin, R. W. *Personality: an experimental approach*. New York: Macmillan, 1961.

Maccoby, Eleanor E. Role-taking in childhood and its consequences for social learning. *Child Develpm.*, 1959, *30*, 239-252.

McDavid, J. Jr. Some relationships between social reinforcement and scholastic achievement. *J. consult. Psychol.*, 1959, *23*, 151-154.

McDavid, J. Jr. The incentive and reward value of social approach and disapproval. *Tech. Rep.*, ONR Contract 840 (22), 1962.

McGuigan, F. J. The experimenter: a neglected stimulus object. *Psychol. Bull.*, 1963, *60*, 421-428.

McNair, D. M. Reinforcement of verbal behavior. *J. exp. Psychol.*, 1957, *53*, 40-46.

Madsen, C. R. Jr. Positive reinforcement in the toilet training of a normal child: a case report. In L. P. Ullmann and L. Krasner (Eds.), *Case studies in behavior modification*. New York: Holt, Rinehart and Winston, 1965.

Makarenko, A. S. *Road to life*. London: Stanley Nott, 1936.

Maltzman, I. Thinking: from a behavioristic point of view. *Psychol. Rev.*, 1955, *62*, 275-286.

Maltzman, I., Simon, S., & Licht, L. Verbal conditioning of common and uncommon word associations. *Psychol. Rep.*, 1962, *10*, 363-369.

Marmor, J. Psychoanalytic therapy as an educational process. Paper presented at Acad. of Psychoanal., Chicago, May 1961. In J. H. Masserman (Ed.), *Psychoanalytic education*. New York: Grune & Stratton, 1962.

Marston, A. R., & Kanfer, F. H. Group size and number of vicarious reinforcements in verbal learning. *J. exp. Psychol.*, 1963, *65*, 593-596. (a)

Marston, A. R., & Kanfer, F. H. Human reinforcement: experimenter and subject controlled. *J. exp. Psychol.*, 1963, *66*, 91-94. (b)

Marston, A. R., Kanfer, F. H., & McBrearty, J. F. Stimulus discriminability in verbal conditioning. *J. Psychol.*, 1962, *53*, 143-153.

Masling, J. The effects of warm and cold interaction on the interpretation of a projective protocol. *J. proj. Tech.*, 1957, *21*, 377-383.

Masling, J. The influence of situational and interpersonal variables in projective testing. *Psychol. Bull.*, 1960, *57*, 65-85.

Matarazzo, J. D. Prescribed behavior therapy: suggestions from interview research. In A. J. Bachrach (Ed.), *Experimental foundations of clinical psychology*. New York: Basic Books, 1962, pp. 471-509.

Matarazzo, J. D. The interview. In B. B. Wolman (Ed.), *Handbook of clinical psychology*. New York: McGraw-Hill, 1965.

Matarazzo, J. D., Hess, H. F., & Saslow, G. Frequency and duration characteristics of speech and silence behavior during interviews. *J. clin. Psychol.*, 1962, *18*, 416-426.

Matarazzo, J. D., & Saslow, G. Differences in interview interaction behavior among normal and deviant groups. In I. A. Berg and B. M. Bass (Eds.),

*Conformity and deviation.* New York: Harper & Row, 1961, pp. 286-327.

Matarazzo, J. D., Saslow, G., & Guze, S. B. Stability of interaction patterns during interviews: a replication. *J. consult. Psychol.*, 1956, *20*, 267-274.

Matarazzo, J. D., Saslow, G., & Hare, A. P. Factor analysis of interview interaction behavior. *J. consult. Psychol.*, 1958, *22*, 419-429.

Matarazzo, J. D., Saslow, G., & Matarazzo, Ruth G. The Interaction Chronograph as an instrument for objective measurement of interaction patterns during interviews. *J. Psychol.*, 1956, *41*, 347-367.

Matarazzo, J. D., Saslow, G., & Pareis, E. N. Verbal conditioning of two response classes: some methodological considerations. *J. abnorm. soc. Psychol.*, 1960, *61*, 190-206.

Matarazzo, J. D., Saslow, G., Wiens, A. N., Weitman, M., & Allen, Bernadene V. Interviewer head-nodding and interviewee speech durations. *Psychotherapy*, 1964, *1*, 54-63.

Matarazzo, J. D., Weitman, M., & Saslow, G. Interview content and interviewee speech durations. *J. clin. Psychol.*, 1963, *19*, 463-472.

Matarazzo, J. D., Weitman, M., Saslow, G., & Wiens, A. N. Interviewer influence on durations of interviewee speech. *J. verb. Learn. verb. Behav.*, 1963, *1*, 451-458.

Matarazzo, J. D., Wiens, A. N., Saslow, G., Allen, Bernadene V., & Weitman, M. Interviewer "mm-hmm" and interviewee speech durations. *Psychotherapy*, 1964, *1*, 109-114.

Matarazzo, Ruth G., Matarazzo, J. D., Saslow, G., & Phillips, Jeanne S. Psychological test and organismic correlates of interview interaction patterns. *J. abnorm. soc. Psychol.*, 1958, *56*, 329-338.

May, R. R. Individual freedom and social values. In symposium on "Social responsibilities of the psychologist," annual meeting, Amer. Psychol. Assoc., Phila., August 1963.

Mertens, G. C. *The therapist's manual—a manual for assisting an alcoholic in his development of self-control.* Willmar, Minn.: Willmar State Hosp., 1964. (a)

Mertens, G. C. *The manual for the alcoholic.* Willmar, Minn.: Willmar State Hosp., 1964. (b)

Michael, J. Behavioral approaches to rehabilitation. Paper presented at Stanford Med. School, 1963.

Miller, G. A., Galanter, E., & Pribram, K. H. *Plans and the structure of behavior.* New York: Holt, Rinehart and Winston, 1960.

Miller, N., & Dollard, J. *Social learning and imitation.* New Haven: Yale Univer. Press, 1941.

Moore, O. K. *Autotelic responsive environments and exceptional children.* Hamden, Conn.: Responsive Environments Found., Inc., 1963.

Moore, R., & Goldiamond, I. Errorless establishment of visual discrimination using fading procedures. *J. exp. Anal. Behavior*, 1964, *7*, 269-272.

Mowrer, O. H. Identification: a link between learning theory and psychotherapy. In O. H. Mowrer, *Learning theory and personality dynamics.* New York: Ronald, 1950, pp. 69-94.

Mowrer, O. H. What is normal behavior? In L. A. Pennington and I. A. Berg (Eds.), *Introduction to clinical psychology.* New York: Ronald Press, 1954, pp. 58-88. (a)

Mowrer, O. H. The psychologist looks at language. *Amer. Psychologist*, 1954, *9*, 660-694. (b)

Mowrer, O. H. *Learning theory and the symbolic processes.* New York: Wiley, 1960.

Mowrer, O. H., & Mowrer, Willie M. Enuresis: a method for its study and treatment. *Amer. J. Orthopsychiat.*, 1938, *8*, 436-459.

Murray, E. J. A case study in a behavioral analysis of psychotherapy. *J. abnorm. soc. Psychol.*, 1954, *49*, 305-310.

Murray, E. J. A content-analysis method for studying psychotherapy. *Psychol. Monogr.*, 1956, *70*, (13, Whole No. 420).

Mussen, P., & Distler, L. Masculinity, identification, and father-son relationships. *J. abnorm. soc. Psychol.*, 1959, *59*, 350-356.

Narrol, H. G. Toward a life-like operant technology for alcoholic rehabilitation. Unpublished manuscript, Univer. Indiana Med. School, 1963.

Neale, D. H. Behaviour therapy and encopresis in children. *Behav. Res. Ther.*, 1963, *1*, 139-149.

Noblin, C. D., Timmons, E. O., & Reynard, Marian C. Psychoanalytic interpretations as verbal reinforcers: importance of interpretation content. *J. clin. Psychol.*, 1963, *19*, 479-481.

Nuthmann, Anne M. Conditioning of a response class on a personality test. *J. abnorm. soc. Psychol.*, 1957, *54*, 19-23.

Oakes, W. F. Effectiveness of signal light reinforcers given various meanings on participation in group discussion. *Psychol. Rep.*, 1962, *11*, 469-470. (a)

Oakes, W. F. Reinforcement of Bales' categories in group discussion. *Psychol. Rep.*, 1962, *11*, 427-435. (b)

Oakes, W. F., Droge, A. E., & August, Barbara. Reinforcement effects on participation in group discussion. *Psychol. Rep.*, 1960, *7*, 503-514.

Oakes, W. F. Droge, A. E., & August, Barbara. Reinforcement effects on conclusions reached in group discussion. *Psychol. Rep.*, 1961, *9*, 27-34.

Orlando, R., & Bijou, S. W. Single and multiple schedules of reinforcement in developmentally retarded children. *J. exp. Anal. Behav.*, 1960, *3*, 339-348.

Orlando, R., Bijou, S. W., Tyler, R. M., & Marshall, D. A. A laboratory for the experimental analysis of developmentally retarded children. *Psychol. Rep.*, 1960, *7*, 261-267.

Orne, M. T. The nature of hypnosis: artifact and essence. *J. abnorm. soc. Psychol.*, 1959, *58*, 277-299.

Orne, M. T. On the social psychology of the psychology experiment: with particular reference to demand characteristics and their implications. *Amer. Psychologist*, 1962, *17*, 776-783.

Orne, M. T., & Scheibe, K. E. The contribution of nondeprivation factors in the production of sensory deprivation effects: the psychology of the "panic button." *J. abnorm. soc. Psychol.*, 1964, *68*, 3-12.

Osgood, C. M. *Method and theory in experimental psychology.* New York: Oxford Univer. Press, 1956.

Page, Marjorie L. The modification of ascendant behavior in preschool children. *Univer. Ia. Stud. Child Welf.*, 1936, *9*, 3-65.

Pasamanick, B., Dinitz, S., & Lefton, M. Psychiatric orientation and its relation to diagnosis and treatment in a mental hospital. *Amer. J. Psychiat.*, 1959, *116*, 127-132.

Patterson, G. R. Fathers as reinforcing agents. Paper read at Western Psychol. Assoc., San Diego, April 1959.

Patterson, G. R. The reinforcement of delinquent behavior by the delinquent peer culture. Unpublished manuscript, Univer. Oreg., 1963. (a)

Patterson, G. R. Parents as dispensers of social disapproval. Unpublished manuscript, Univer. Oreg., 1963. (b)

Patterson, G. R. An empirical approach to the classification of disturbed children. *J. clin. Psychol.*, 1964, *20*, 326-337.

Patterson, G. R. A learning theory approach to the treatment of the school phobic child. In L. P. Ullmann and L. Krasner (Eds.), *Case studies in behavior modification.* New York: Holt, Rinehart and Winston, 1965. (a)

Patterson, G. R. An application of conditioning techniques to the control of a hyperactive child. In L. P. Ullmann and L. Krasner (Eds.), *Case studies in behavior modification.* New York: Holt, Rinehart and Winston, 1965. (b)

Patterson, G. R., & Anderson, D. Peers as social reinforcers. *Child Develpm.,* 1964, *35,* 951-960.

Patterson, G. R., Helper, M. E., & Wilcott, R. C. Anxiety and verbal conditioning in children. *Child Develpm.,* 1960, *31,* 101-108.

Patterson, G. R., & Hinsey, W. C. Investigations of some assumptions and characteristics of a procedure for instrumental conditioning in children. *J. exp. child Psychol.,* 1964, *1,* 111-122.

Patterson, G. R., & Littman, Isabelle. Methodological studies in imitation. Unpublished manuscript, Univer. Oreg., 1963.

Patterson, G. R., Littman, R. E., & Hinsey, W. C. Parents as social stimuli. Unpublished manuscript, Univer. Oreg., 1963.

Patterson, G. R., Littman, R. E., & Hinsey, W. C. Parental effectiveness as reinforcers in the laboratory and its relation to child rearing practices and child adjustment in the classroom. *J. Pers.,* 1964, *32,* 180-199.

Patterson, G. R., & Ludwig, M. Parents as reinforcing agents. Paper presented to Oreg. Psychol. Conv., 1961.

Patterson, G. R., Ludwig, M., & Sonoda, B. Reinforcement of aggression in children. Unpublished manuscript, Univer. Oreg., 1963.

Paul, G. L. Comparative psychotherapeutic effectiveness in the treatment of performance anxiety: stress condition results. Paper presented to Midwest Psychol. Assoc., St. Louis, May 1964.

Peterson, D. R., Becker, W. C., Shoemaker, D. J., Luria, Zella, & Hellmer, L. A. Child behavior problems and parental attitudes. *Child Develpm.,* 1961, *32,* 151-162.

Peterson, D. R., & London, P. A role for cognition in the behavioral treatment of a child's eliminative disturbance. In L. P. Ullmann and L. Krasner (Eds.), *Case studies in behavior modification.* New York: Holt, Rinehart and Winston, 1965.

Petrullo, L. Small group research. In A. J. Bachrach (Ed.), *Experimental foundations of clinical psychology.* New York: Basic Books, 1962.

Phillips, E. L. Parent-child psychotherapy: a follow-up study comparing two techniques. *J. Psychol.,* 1960, *49,* 195-202.

Phillips, Jeanne S., Matarazzo, Ruth G., Matarazzo, J. D., Saslow, G., & Kanfer, F. H. Relationships between descriptive content and interaction behavior in interviews. *J. consult. Psychol.,* 1961, *25,* 260-266.

Piaget, J. *The moral judgment of the child.* New York: Free Press, 1948.

Pierrol, R., & Sherman, G. *Barnabus, the Barnard rat demonstration.* New York: Barnard College, 1958.

Platonov, H. I. *The word as a physiological and therapeutic factor.* Moscow: Foreign Languages Publishing House, 1959.

Poindexter, W. R. Mental patients become employees. *Summaries of scientific Papers,* Paper No. 84, Amer. Psychiat. Assoc., Toronto, Canada, 1962.

Polya, G. *Induction and analogy in mathematics.* Princeton: Princeton Univer. Press, 1954.

Polya, G. *How to solve it.* (2nd ed.) New York: Doubleday, 1957.

Pope, B. Socio-economic contrasts in children's peer culture prestige values. *Genet. Psychol. Monogr.,* 1953, *48,* 157-220.

Portnoy, Stephanie, & Salzinger, K. The conditionability of different verbal response classes: positive, negative, and nonaffect statements. *J. gen. Psychol.*, 1964, 70, 311-323.

Prince, A. I. Relative prestige and the verbal conditioning of children. *Amer. Psychologist*, 1962, 17, 378. (Abstract)

Quay, H. The effect of verbal reinforcement on the recall of early memories. *J. abnorm. soc. Psychol.*, 1959, 59, 254-257.

Rachman, S. Spontaneous remission and latent learning. *Behav. Res. Ther.*, 1963, 1, 133-137.

Rafi, A. A. Learning theory and the treatment of tics. *J. psychosom. Res.*, 1962, 6, 71-76.

Raines, G. N., & Rohrer, J. H. The operational matrix of psychiatric practice: I. Consistency and variability in interview impressions of different psychiatrists. *Amer. J. Psychiat.*, 1955, 111, 721-733.

Raines, G. N., & Rohrer, J. H. The operational matrix of psychiatric practice: II. Variability in psychiatric impressions and the projection hypothesis. *Amer. J. Psychiat.*, 1960, 117, 133-139.

Raush, H. L., Sperber, Z., Rigler, D., Williams, J., Harway, N. I., Bordin, E. S., Dittmann, A. T., & Hays, W. L. A dimensional analysis of depth of interpretation. *J. consult. Psychol.* 1956, 20, 43-48.

Read, Katherine H. *The nursery school.* (2nd ed.) Philadelphia: Saunders, 1955.

Reece, M. M., & Whitman, R. N. Expressive movements, warmth, and verbal reinforcement. *J. abnorm. soc. Psychol.*, 1962, 64, 234-236.

Rheingold, Harriet L., Gewirtz, J. L., & Ross, Helen W. Social conditioning of vocalizations in the infant. *J. comp. physiol. Psychol.*, 1959, 52, 68-73.

Rickard, H. C., Dignam, P. J., & Horner, R. F. Verbal manipulation in a psychotherapeutic relationship. *J. clin. Psychol.*, 1960, 16, 364-367.

Rickard, H. C., & Dinoff, M. A follow-up note on "verbal manipulation in a psychotherapeutic relationship." *Psychol. Rep.*, 1962, 11, 506.

Rickard, H. C., & Dinoff, M. Shaping adaptive behavior in a therapeutic summer camp. In L. P. Ullmann and L. Krasner (Eds.), *Case studies in behavior modification.* New York: Holt, Rinehart and Winston, 1965.

Rickard, H. C., & Mundy, Martha B. Direct manipulation of stuttering behavior: an experimental-clinical approach. In L. P. Ullmann and L. Krasner (Eds.), *Case studies in behavior modification.* New York: Holt, Rinehart and Winston, 1965.

Riecken, H. W. A program for research on experiments in social psychology. Paper read at Behavioral Sciences Conf., Univer. New Mexico, 1958.

Riecken, H. W. Social psychology. In P. R. Farnsworth and Q. McNemar (Eds.), *Annual review of psychology.* Vol. 11. Palo Alto, Calif.: Annual Reviews, Inc., 1960.

Roff, M. A factorial study of the Fels parent behavior scales. *Child Develpm.*, 1949, 20, 29-45.

Rogers, C. R. *Counseling and psychotherapy.* Boston: Houghton Mifflin, 1942.

Rogers, C. R., & Dymond, Rosalind, F. (Eds.), *Psychotherapy and personality change.* Chicago: Univer. Chicago Press, 1954.

Rogers, J. M. Operant conditioning in a quasi-therapy setting. *J. abnorm. soc. Psychol.*, 1960, 60, 247-252.

Rosenberg, M. The association between self-esteem and anxiety. *Psychiat. res. Rep.*, 1962, 1, 135-152.

Rosenblith, Judy F. Learning by imitation in kindergarten children. *Child Develpm.*, 1959, 30, 69-80.

Rosenblith, Judy F. Imitative color choices in kindergarten children. *Child Develpm.*, 1961, *32*, 211-223.

Rosenthal, R. On the social psychology of the psychological experiment; with particular reference to experimenter bias. Paper presented to Amer. Psychol. Assoc., New York, Sept. 1961.

Rosenthal, R. The effects of experimenter bias in the performance of the albino rat. Unpublished manuscript, Univer. N. Dakota, 1962.

Rosenthal, R. On the social psychology of the psychological experiment: the experimenter's hypothesis as unintended determinant of experimental results. *Amer. Sci.*, 1963, *51*, 268-283.

Rosenthal, R., & Fode, K. L. Psychology of the scientist: V. Three experiments in experimenter bias. *Psychol. Rep.*, 1963, *12*, 491-511. (a)

Rosenthal, R., & Fode, K. L. The effect of experimenter bias on the performance of the albino rat. *Behav. Sci.*, 1963, *8*, 183-189. (b)

Rosenthal, R., Fode, K. L., Vikan-Kline, Linda, & Persinger, G. W. Verbal conditioning: mediator of experimenter expectancy effects. *Psychol. Rep.*, 1964, *14*, 71-74.

Rosenthal, R., & Halas, E. S. Experimenter effect in the study of invertebrate behavior. *Psychol. Rep.*, 1962, *11*, 251-256.

Rosenthal, R., & Lawson, R. A longitudinal study of the effects of experimenter bias on the operant learning of laboratory rats. *J. Psychiat. Res.*, 1964, *2*, 61-72.

Ross, Dorothea. The relationship between dependency, intentional learning, and incidental learning in preschool children. Unpublished doctoral dissertation, Stanford Univer., 1962.

Rotter, J. B. *Clinical psychology.* Englewood Cliffs, N. J.: Prentice-Hall, 1964.

Russell, P. D. Counselor anxiety in relation to clinical experience and hostile or friendly clients. Unpublished doctoral dissertation, Pennsylvania State Univ., 1961.

Russell, W. A., & Jenkins, J. J. *The complete Minnesota norms for responses to 100 words from the Kent-Rosanoff Word Association Test.* Tech. Rep. No. 11, Contract No. N8 ONR66216 between the Office of Naval Research and Univer. of Minn., 1954.

Salzberg, H. C. Manipulation of verbal behavior in a group psychotherapeutic setting. *Psychol. Rep.*, 1961, *9*, 183-186.

Salzinger, K. Experimental manipulation of verbal behavior: a review. *J. gen. Psychol.*, 1959, *61*, 65-94.

Salzinger, K. Some problems of response measurement in verbal behavior: the response unit and intraresponse relations. Paper presented to Conf. on Methods of Measurement of Change in Human Behavior, Montreal, Canada, 1962.

Salzinger, K., Feldman, R. S., & Portnoy, Stephanie. The effects of reinforcement on verbal and nonverbal responses. *J. gen. Psychol.*, 1964, *70*, 225-234.

Salzinger, K., & Pisoni, Stephanie. Reinforcement of affect responses of schizophrenics during the clinical interview. *J. abnorm. soc. Psychol.*, 1958, *57*, 84-90.

Salzinger, K., & Pisoni, Stephanie. Reinforcement of verbal affect responses of normal subjects during the interview. *J. abnorm. soc. Psychol.*, 1960, *60*, 127-130.

Salzinger, K., & Pisoni, Stephanie. Some parameters of the conditioning of verbal affect responses in schizophrenic subjects. *J. abnorm. soc. Psychol.*, 1961, *63*, 511-516.

Salzinger, K., Portnoy, Stephanie, & Feldman, R. S. The effect of order of approximation to the statistical structure of English on the emission of verbal responses. *J. exp. Psychol.*, 1962, *64*, 52-57.

Salzinger, K., Portnoy, Stephanie, & Feldman, R. S. Experimental manipulation of continuous speech in schizophrenic patients. *J. abnorm. soc. Psychol.*, 1964, *68*, 508-516.

Salzinger, K., Portnoy, Stephanie, Zlotogura, Phyllis, & Keisner, R. The effect of reinforcement on continuous speech and on plural nouns in grammatical context. *J. verb. Learning verb. Behav.*, 1963, *1*, 477-485.

Salzinger, K., & Waller, M. B. The operant control of vocalization in the dog. *J. exp. Anal. Behav.*, 1962, *5*, 383-389.

Salzinger, Suzanne, Salzinger, K., Portnoy, Stephanie, Eckman, Judith, Bacon, Pauline M., Deutsch, M., & Zubin, J. Operant conditioning of continuous speech in young children. *Child Develpm.*, 1962, *33*, 683-695.

Sapolsky, A. Effect of interpersonal relationships upon verbal conditioning. *J. abnorm. soc. Psychol.*, 1960, *60*, 241-246.

Sarason, I. G. Interrelationships among individual difference variables, behavior in psychotherapy, and verbal conditioning. *J. abnorm. soc. Psychol.*, 1958, *56*, 339-344. (a)

Sarason, I. G. Effects on verbal learning of anxiety, reassurance, and meaningfulness of material. *J. exp. Psychol.*, 1958, *56*, 472-477. (b)

Sarason, I. G. Intellectual and personality correlates of test anxiety. *J. abnorm. soc. Psychol.*, 1959, *59*, 272-275.

Sarason, I. G. Empirical findings and theoretical problems in the use of anxiety scales. *Psychol. Bull.*, 1960, *57*, 403-415.

Sarason, I. G. Individual differences, situational variables, and personality research. *J. abnorm. soc. Psychol.*, 1962, *65*, 376-380.

Sarason, I. G., & Campbell, J. M. Anxiety and the verbal conditioning of mildly hostile verbs. *J. consult. Psychol.*, 1962, *26*, 213-216.

Sarason, I. G., & Ganzer, V. J. Anxiety, reinforcement, and experimental instructions in a free verbalization situation. *J. abnorm. soc. Psychol.*, 1962, *65*, 300-307.

Sarason, I. G., & Ganzer, V. J. Effects of test anxiety and reinforcement history on verbal behavior. *J. abnorm. soc. Psychol.*, 1963, *67*, 513-519.

Sarason, I. G., & Harmatz, M. G. Test anxiety and experimental conditions. *J. pers. soc. Psychol.*, in press.

Sarason, I. G., & Minard, J. Interrelationships among subject, experimenter, and situational variables. *J. abnorm. soc. Psychol.*, 1963, *67*, 87-91.

Sarason, S. B. *The clinical interaction.* New York: Harper & Row, 1954.

Sarbin, T. R. The concept of role-taking. *Sociometry*, 1943, *6*, 273-285.

Sarbin, T. R. Contributions to role-taking theory. III: A preface to a psychological analysis of the self. *Psychol. Rev.*, 1952, *59*, 11-22.

Sarbin, T. R. Role theory. In G. Lindzey (Ed.), *Handbook of social psychology.* Cambridge: Addison-Wesley Press, 1954.

Sarbin, T. R. Physiological effects of hypnotic stimulation. In R. M. Dorcus (Ed.), *Hypnosis and its therapeutic applications.* New York: McGraw-Hill, 1956.

Sarbin, T. R. Contributions to role-taking theory: I. Hypnotic behavior. *Psychol. Rev.*, 1960, *67*, 255-270.

Sarbin, T. R. (Ed.), *Studies in behavior pathology.* New York: Holt, Rinehart and Winston, 1961.

Sarbin, T. R. Anxiety: the reification of a metaphor. Paper presented to Western Psychiat. Assoc., San Francisco, Dec. 1963.

Sarbin, T. R. Role-theoretical analysis of psychological change. In P. Worchel and D. Byrne (Eds.), *Personality change.* New York: Wiley, 1964.

Sarbin, T. R., & Andersen, M. L. Base-rate expectancies and perceptual alterations in hypnosis. *Brit. J. soc. clin. Psychol.,* 1963, *2,* 112-121.

Sarbin, T. R., & Chun, K. Role demands, stimulus types and perceptual defense. Unpublished manuscript, Univer. Calif., 1964.

Sarbin, T. R., & Hardyck, C. D. Conformance in role perception as a personality variable. *J. consult. Psychol.,* 1955, *19,* 109-111.

Sarbin, T. R., & Jones, D. S. An experimental analysis of role behavior. *J. abnorm. soc. Psychol.,* 1955, *51,* 236-241.

Sarbin, T. R., & Lim, D. T. Some evidence in support of the role-taking hypothesis in hypnosis. *Int. J. clin. exp. Hypnosis,* 1963, *11,* 98-103.

Sarbin, T. R., Taft, R., & Bailey, D. E. *Clinical inference and cognitive theory.* New York: Holt, Rinehart and Winston, 1960.

Saslow, G. On the concept of comprehensive medicine. *Bull. Menninger Clinic,* 1952, *16,* 57-65.

Saslow, G., & Chapple, E. D. A new life history form, with instructions for its use. *Appl. Anthropology,* 1945, *4,* 1-18.

Saslow, G., Matarazzo, J. D., & Guze, S. B. The stability of interaction chronograph patterns in psychiatric interviews. *J. consult. Psychol.,* 1955, *19,* 417-430.

Saslow, G., & Matarazzo, J. D. A technique for studying changes in interview behavior. In E. A. Rubinstein and M. B. Parloff (Eds.), *Research in psychotherapy.* Washington, D. C.: Amer. Psychol. Assoc., 1959, pp. 125-159.

Saslow, G., & Matarazzo, J. D. A psychiatric service in a general hospital: a setting for social learning. *Int. J. soc. Psychiat.,* 1962, *8,* 5-18.

Schachter, S. *The psychology of affiliation.* Stanford: Stanford Univer. Press, 1959.

Schaefer, E. S., & Bayley, Nancy. Consistency of maternal behavior from infancy to preadolescence. *J. abnorm. soc. Psychol.,* 1960, *61,* 1-6.

Schroeder, W. W. The effect of reinforcement counseling and model-reinforcement counseling on information-seeking behavior of high school students. Unpublished doctoral dissertation, Stanford Univer., 1964.

Schutz, W. C. *FIRO: a three-dimensional theory of interpersonal behavior.* New York: Holt, Rinehart and Winston, 1958.

Schwitzgebel, R., & Kolb, D. A. Inducing behaviour change in adolescent delinquents. *Behav. Res. Ther.,* 1964, *1,* 297-304.

Scott, W. A. Attitude change through reward of verbal behavior. *J. abnorm. soc. Psychol.,* 1957, *55,* 72-75.

Scott, W. A. Research definitions of mental health and mental illness. *Psychol. Bull.,* 1958, *55,* 29-45.

Sears, R. R., Maccoby, Eleanor E., & Levin, H. *Patterns of child rearing.* New York: Row Peterson, 1957.

Shapiro, A. K. A contribution to a history of the placebo effect. *Behav. Sci.,* 1960, *5,* 109-135.

Shapiro, D. The reinforcement of disagreement in a small group. *Behav. Res. Ther.,* 1963, *1,* 267-272.

Shapiro, D., & Morningstar, Mona. Some factors affecting disagreement in a small group. ONR Tech. Rep. 6, Contract NONR-1866 (43) Group Psychol. Branch, 1963.

Sheehan, J. G. The modification of stuttering through non-reinforcement. *J. abnorm. soc. Psychol.,* 1951, *46,* 51-63.

Sheffield, F. D. Theoretical considerations in the learning of complex sequential tasks from demonstration and practice. In A. A. Lumsdaine (Ed.), *Student responses in programmed instructions: a symposium.* Washington, D. C.: National Acad. of Sci.–National Res. Council, 1961, pp. 13-32.

Sheffield, F. D., & Maccoby, N. Summary and interpretation of research on organizational principles in constructing filmed demonstrations. In A. A. Lumsdaine (Ed.), *Student responses in programmed instruction: a symposium.* Washington, D. C.: National Acad. of Sci.–National Res. Council, 1961, pp. 117-131.

Shoben, E. J. Psychotherapy as a problem in learning theory. *Psychol. Bull.,* 1949, *46,* 366-392.

Shoben, E. J. The therapeutic object: men or machines? *J. counsel. Psychol.,* 1963, *10,* 264-268.

Shor, R. E., Orne, M. T., & O'Connell, D. Validation and cross-validation of a scale of self-reported personal experiences which predict hypnotizability. *J. Psychol.,* 1962, *53,* 55-75.

Sidman, M. *Tactics of scientific research.* New York: Basic Books, 1960.

Siegel, Alberta E. Film-mediated fantasy aggression and strength of aggressive drive. *Child Develpm.,* 1956, *27,* 365-378.

Singer, J. L. Delayed gratification and ego development: implications for clinical and experimental research. *J. consult. Psychol.,* 1955, *19,* 259-266.

Singer, R. D. Verbal conditioning and generalization of pro-democratic responses. *J. abnorm. soc. Psychol.,* 1961, *63,* 43-46.

Skinner, B. F. The generic nature of the concepts of stimulus and response. *J. genet. Psychol.,* 1935, *12,* 40-63.

Skinner, B. F. The verbal summator and a method for the study of latent speech. *J. Psychol.,* 1936, *2,* 71-107.

Skinner, B. F. *Behavior of organisms.* New York: Appleton, 1938.

Skinner, B. F. *Walden two.* New York: Macmillan, 1948.

Skinner, B. F. Are theories of learning necessary? *Psychol. Rev.,* 1950, *57,* 193-216.

Skinner, B. F. *Science and human behavior.* New York: Macmillan, 1953.

Skinner, B. F. *Verbal behavior.* New York: Appleton, 1957.

Skinner, B. F. *Cumulative record.* New York: Appleton, 1959.

Skinner, B. F. Operant behavior. *Amer. Psychologist,* 1963, *18,* 503-515.

Slack, C. W. Experimenter-subject psychotherapy: a new method of introducing intensive office treatment for unreachable cases. *Ment. Hyg. N. Y.,* 1960, *44,* 238-256.

Sommer, R., Witney, Gwynneth, & Osmond, H. Teaching common associations to schizophrenics. *J. abnorm. soc. Psychol.,* 1962, *65,* 58-61.

Spielberger, C. D. The role of awareness in verbal conditioning. In C. W. Eriksen (Ed.), *Behavior and awareness.* Durham, N. C.: Duke Univer. Press, 1962.

Staats, A. W. Learning theory and "opposite speech." *J. abnorm. soc. Psychol.,* 1957, *55,* 268-269. (a)

Staats, A. W. Verbal and instrumental response-hierarchies and their relationship to problem-solving. *Amer. J. Psychol.,* 1957, *70,* 442-446. (b)

Staats, A. W. Verbal habit-families, concepts, and the operant conditioning of word classes. *Psychol. Rev.,* 1961, *68,* 190-204.

Staats, A. W. *Human learning.* New York: Holt, Rinehart and Winston, 1964.

Staats, A. W., Finley, J. R., Minke, K. A., & Wolf, M. M. Reinforcement variables in the control of unit reading responses. *J. exp. Anal. Behav.,* 1964, *7,* 139-149.

Staats, A. W., Minke, K. A., Finley, J. R., Wolf, M. M., & Brooks, L. O. A reinforcer system and experimental procedure for the laboratory study of reading acquisition. *Child Develpm.*, 1964, *35*, 209-231.

Staats, A. W., & Staats, Carolyn K. Attitudes established by classical conditioning. *J. abnorm. soc. Psychol.*, 1958, *57*, 37-40.

Staats, A. W., & Staats, Carolyn K. Effect of number of trials on the language conditioning of meaning. *J. gen. Psychol.*, 1959, *61*, 211-223. (a)

Staats, A. W., & Staats, Carolyn K. Meaning and *m:* correlated but separate. *Psychol. Rev.*, 1959, *66*, 136-144. (b)

Staats, A. W., & Staats, Carolyn K. A comparison of the development of speech and reading behavior with implications for research. *Child Develpm.*, 1962, *33*, 831-846.

Staats, A. W., & Staats, Carolyn K. *Complex human behavior.* New York: Holt, Rinehart and Winston, 1963.

Staats, A. W., Staats, Carolyn K., & Crawford, H. L. First-order conditioning of meaning and the parallel conditioning of a GSR. *J. gen. Psychol.*, 1962, *67*, 159-167.

Staats, A. W., Staats, Carolyn K., Finley, J. R., & Heard, W. G. Independent manipulation of meaning and M. *J. gen. Psychol.*, 1963, *69*, 253-260.

Staats, A. W., Staats, Carolyn K., & Heard, W. G. Language conditioning of meaning to meaning using a semantic generalization paradigm. *J. exp. Psychol.*, 1959, *57*, 187-192.

Staats, A. W., Staats, Carolyn K., & Heard, W. G. Denotative meaning established by classical conditioning. *J. exp. Psychol.*, 1961, *61*, 300-303.

Staats, A. W., Staats, Carolyn K., Heard, W. G., & Finley, J. R. Operant conditioning of factor analytic personality traits. *J. gen. Psychol.*, 1962, *66*, 101-114.

Staats, A. W., Staats, Carolyn K., Heard, W. G., & Nims, L. P. Replication report: meaning established by classical conditioning. *J. exp. Psychol.*, 1959, *57*, 64.

Staats, A. W., Staats, Carolyn K., Schutz, R. E., & Wolf, M. M. The conditioning of textual responses using "extrinsic" reinforcers. *J. exp. Anal. Behav.*, 1962, *5*, 33-40.

Staats, Carolyn K., & Staats, A. W. Meaning established by classical conditioning. *J. exp. Psychol.*, 1957, *54*, 74-80.

Staats, Carolyn K., Staats, A. W., & Heard, W. G. Attitude development and ratio of reinforcement. *Sociometry*, 1960, *23*, 338-350.

Staples, F. R., & Walters, R. H. Anxiety, birth order, and susceptibility to social influence. *J. abnorm. soc. Psychol.*, 1961, *62*, 716-719.

Staples, F. R., Wilson, F. S., & Walters, R. H. Increasing the verbal responsiveness of chronic schizophrenics. Unpublished research, Ontario Hospital, New Toronto, and Univ. of Waterloo, 1963. (Cited in A. Bandura and R. H. Walters, *Social learning and personality development.* New York: Holt, Rinehart and Winston, 1963.)

Stevenson, H. W., & Cruse, D. B. The effectiveness of social reinforcement with normal and feeble-minded children. *J. Pers.*, 1961, *29*, 124-135.

Stevenson, H. W., & Fahel, Leila S. The effect of social reinforcement on the performance of institutionalized and noninstitutionalized normal and feeble-minded children. *J. Pers.*, 1961, *29*, 136-147.

Stevenson, I., & Wolpe, J. Recovery from sexual deviations through overcoming non-sexual neurotic responses. *Amer. J. Psychiat.*, 1960, *116*, 737-742.

Strupp, H. H. Psychotherapy. In P. R. Farnsworth, Olga McNemar, and

Q. McNemar (Eds.), *Annual review of psychology*. Vol. 13, Palo Alto, Calif.: Annual Reviews, Inc., 1962.

Sulzer, E. S. Behavior modification in adult psychiatric patients. In L. P. Ullmann and L. Krasner (Eds.), *Case studies in behavior modification*. New York: Holt, Rinehart and Winston, 1965.

Sutcliffe, J. P. "Credulous" and "sceptical" views of hypnotic phenomena. *Int. J. clin. exp. Hypn.*, 1960, 8, 73-101.

Sutcliffe, J. P. "Credulous" and "skeptical" views of hypnotic phenomena: experiments on esthesia, hallucination, and delusion. *J. abnorm. soc. Psychol.*, 1961, 62, 189-200.

Symons, R. T. Specific experimenter-subject personality variables pertinent to the influencing process in a verbal conditioning situation. Unpublished doctoral dissertation, Univer. Wash., 1964.

Szasz, T. S. The myth of mental illness. *Amer. Psychologist*, 1960, 15, 113-118.

Szasz, T. S. The uses of naming and the origin of the myth of mental illness. *Amer. Psychologist*, 1961, 16, 59-65. (a)

Szasz, T. S. *The myth of mental illness*. New York: Hoeber, 1961. (b)

Taffel, C. Anxiety and the conditioning of verbal behavior. *J. abnorm. soc. Psychol.*, 1955, 51, 496-501.

Tatz, S. Symbolic mediation in "learning without awareness." Paper presented to Eastern Psychol. Assoc., Atlantic City, March 1956.

Terrace, H. S. Discrimination learning with and without "errors." *J. exp. Anal. Behav.*, 1963, 6, 1-27.

Terrell, G., Jr., Durkin, Kathryn, & Wiesley, M. Social class and the nature of the incentive in discrimination learning. *J. abnorm. soc. Psychol.*, 1959, 59, 270-272.

Tomkins, S. J., & Messick, S. *Computer simulation of personality*. New York: Wiley, 1963.

Tuason, V. B., Guze, S. B., McClure, J., & Beguelin, J. A further study of some features of the interview with the Interaction Chronograph. *Amer. J. Psychiat.*, 1961, 118, 438-446.

Tuddenham, R. D. Studies in reputation: I. Sex and grade difference in school children's evaluation of their peers; II. The diagnosis of social maladjustment. *Psychol. Monogr.*, 1952, 66, (1, Whole No. 333).

Turing, A. M. Computing machinery and intelligence. *Mind*, 1950, 59, 433-460.

Ullmann, L. P. Productivity and the clinical use of TAT cards. *J. proj. Tech.*, 1957, 21, 399-403.

Ullmann, L. P. Clinical correlates of facilitation and inhibition of response to emotional stimuli. *J. proj. Tech.*, 1958, 22, 341-347.

Ullmann, L. P. Untestability of schizophrenics upon admission to psychiatric hospitals. *J. clin. Psychol.*, 1961, 17, 199-202.

Ullmann, L. P., Forsman, R. G., Kenny, J. W., McInnis, T. L. Jr., Unikel, I. P., & Zeisset, R. M. Selective reinforcement of schizophrenics' interview responses. *Behav. Res. Ther.*, in press.

Ullmann, L. P., & Giovannoni, Jeanne M. The development of a self-report measure of the process-reactive continuum. *J. nerv. ment. Dis.*, 1964, 138, 38-42.

Ullmann, L. P., & Krasner, L. (Eds.) *Case studies in behavior modification*. New York: Holt, Rinehart and Winston, 1965.

Ullmann, L. P., Krasner, L., & Collins, Beverly J. Modification of behavior through verbal conditioning: effects in group therapy. *J. abnorm. soc. Psychol.*, 1961, 62, 128-132.

Ullmann, L. P., Krasner, L., & Edinger, R. L. Verbal conditioning of common associations in long-term schizophrenic patients. *Behav. Res. Ther.*, 1964, 2, 15-18.

Ullmann, L. P., Krasner, L., & Ekman, P. Verbal conditioning of emotional words: effects on behavior in group therapy. *Res. Rep. of VA, Palo Alto,* No. 15, 1961.

Ullmann, L. P., Krasner, L., & Gelfand, Donna M. Changed content within a reinforced response class. *Psychol. Rep.*, 1963, *12*, 819-829.

Ullmann, L. P., Krasner, L., & Sherman, M. MMPI items associated with pleasantness of emotional words used in thematic story-telling. *Res. Rep. VA, Palo Alto,* No. 25, 1963. (a)

Ullmann, L. P., Krasner, L., & Sherman, M. The verbal conditioning of pleasant and unpleasant emotional words: further investigation of an effect of social reinforcement. Progress report, Grant M-6191, NIMH, Sept. 1963. (b)

Ullmann, L. P., Krasner, L., & Weiss, R. L. Personality correlates of students' and patients' response to reinforcement of emotional words in an interpersonal situation. Paper presented to Calif. State Psychol. Assoc., San Francisco, Dec. 1963.

Ullmann, L. P., & McFarland, R. L. Productivity as a variable in TAT protocols —a methodological study. *J. proj. Tech.*, 1957, *21*, 80-87.

Ullmann, L. P., Weiss, R. L., & Krasner, L. The effect of verbal conditioning of emotional words on recognition of threatening stimuli. *J. clin. Psychol.*, 1963, *19*, 182-183.

Underwood, H. W. The validity of hypnotically induced visual hallucinations. *J. abnorm. soc. Psychol.*, 1960, *61*, 39-46.

Verplanck, W. S. The control of the content of conversation: reinforcement of statements of opinion. *J. abnorm. soc. Psychol.*, 1955, *51*, 668-676.

Verplanck, W. S. Unaware of where's awareness: some verbal operants— notates, moments, and notants. In C. W. Eriksen (Ed.), *Behavior and awareness.* Durham, N. C.: Duke Univer. Press, 1962.

Walker, E. L., & Heyns, R. W. *An anatomy for conformity.* Englewood Cliffs, N. J.: Prentice-Hall, 1962.

Walters, R. H. Emotionality and discrimination learning of children. Unpublished manuscript, 1962.

Walters, R. H., Leat, Marion, & Mezei, L. Inhibition and disinhibition of responses through empathetic learning. *Canad. J. Psychol.*, 1963, *17*, 235-243.

Walters, R. H., Marshall, W. E., & Shooter, J. R. Anxiety, isolation, and susceptibility to social influence. *J. Pers.*, 1960, *28*, 518-529.

Walters, R. H., & Ray, E. Anxiety, social isolation, and reinforcer effectiveness. *J. Pers.*, 1960, *28*, 358-367.

Walters, R. H., & Thomas, E. L. Enhancement of punitiveness by visual and audiovisual displays. *Canad. J. Psychol.*, 1963, *17*, 244-255.

Walton, D., & Black, D. A. The application of learning theory to the treatment of stammering. *J. psychosom. Res.*, 1958, *3*, 170-179.

Warden, C. J., Fjeld, H. A., & Koch, A. M. Imitative behavior in the Cebus and rhesus monkeys. *J. genet. Psychol.*, 1940, *56*, 311-322.

Warden, C. J., & Jackson, T. A. Imitative behavior in the rhesus monkey. *J. genet. Psychol.*, 1935, *46*, 103-125.

Watson, J. B., & Rayner, Rosalie. Conditional emotional reactions. *J. exp. Psychol.*, 1920, *3*, 1-14.

Watson, R. I. The experimental tradition and clinical psychology. In A. J. Bachrach (Ed.), *Experimental foundations of clinical psychology.* New York: Basic Books, 1962.

Weiss, R. L., Ekman, P., Ullmann, L. P., & Krasner, L. The context of reinforcement in verbal conditioning. *J. clin. Psychol.*, 1965, *21*, 99-100.

Weiss, R. L., Krasner, L., & Ullmann, L. P. Responsivity to verbal conditioning as a function of emotional atmosphere and pattern of reinforcement. *Psychol. Rep.*, 1960, *6*, 415-426.

Weiss, R. L., Krasner, L., & Ullmann, L. P. Responsivity of psychiatric patients to verbal conditioning: "success" and "failure" conditions and pattern of reinforced trials. *Psychol. Rep.*, 1963, *12*, 423-426.

Weiss, R. L., Ullmann, L. P., & Krasner, L. On the relationship between hypnotizability and response to verbal operant conditioning. *Psychol. Rep.*, 1960, *6*, 59-60.

Weitzenhoffer, A. M., & Hilgard, E. R. *Stanford Hypnotic Susceptibility Scale, Forms A and B.* Palo Alto: Consult. Psychologists Press, 1959.

Wenar, C., & Coulter, Jane B. A reliability study of developmental histories. *Child Develpm.*, 1962, *33*, 453-462.

White, R. W. A preface to the theory of hypnotism. *J. abnorm. soc. Psychol.*, 1941, *36*, 477-505.

Whiting, J. W. M. Sorcery, sin and the superego. In M. R. Jones (Ed.), *Nebraska symposium on motivation: 1959.* Lincoln: Univer. Nebr. Press, 1959, pp. 174-195.

Whiting, J. W. M. Resource mediation and learning by identification. In I. Iscoe and H. W. Stevenson (Eds.), *Personality development in children.* Austin: Univer. Texas Press, 1960, pp. 112-126.

Williams, C. D. The elimination of tantrum behavior by extinction procedures. *J. abnorm. soc. Psychol.*, 1959, *59*, 269.

Williams, R. I. Verbal conditioning in psychotherapy. *Amer. Psychologist*, 1959, *14*, 388. (Abstract)

Wingate, M. E. Calling attention to stuttering. *J. speech hear. Res.*, 1959, *2*, 326-335.

Winkel, G. H. The effects of experimenter variables upon performance in a free verbalization setting. Unpublished manuscript, Univer. Wash., 1963.

Winkel, G. H., & Sarason, I. G. Subject, experimenter, and situational variables in research on anxiety. *J. abnorm. soc. Psychol.*, 1964, *68*, 601-608.

Wolf, M. M., Birnbrauer, J. S., Williams, T., & Lawler, Julia. A note on apparent extinction of the vomiting behavior of a retarded child. In L. P. Ullmann and L. Krasner (Eds.), *Case studies in behavior modification.* New York: Holt, Rinehart and Winston, 1965.

Wolf, M. M., Risley, T. R., & Mees, H. I. Application of operant conditioning procedures to the behaviour problems of an autistic child. *Behav. Res. Ther.*, 1964, *1*, 305-312.

Wolpe, J. Reciprocal inhibition as the main basis of psychotherapeutic effects. *AMA Arch. Neurol. Psychiat.*, 1954, *72*, 205-226.

Wolpe, J. Psychotherapy by reciprocal inhibition. Stanford: Stanford Univer. Press, 1958.

Wolpe, J. Isolation of a conditioning procedure as the crucial psychotherapeutic factor: a case study. *J. nerv. ment. Dis.*, 1962, *134*, 316-329.

Wright, J. D. Problem solving and search behavior under non-contingent rewards. Unpublished doctoral dissertation, Stanford Univer., 1960.

Yates, A. J. Symptoms and symptom substitution. *Psychol. Rev.*, 1958, *65*, 371-374.

Zigler, E. F., & de Labry, J. Concept-switching in middle-class, lower-class, and retarded children. *J. abnorm. soc. Psychol.*, 1962, *65*, 267-273.

Zigler, E. F., Hodgden, Laurel, & Stevenson, H. W. The effect of support and nonsupport on the performance of normal and feebleminded children. *J. Pers.*, 1958, *26*, 106-122.

Zigler, E. F., & Kanzer, P. The effectiveness of two classes of verbal reinforcers on the performance of middle- and lower-class children. *J. Pers.*, 1962, *30*, 157-163.

Zimmerman, Elaine H., & Zimmerman, J. The alteration of behavior in a special classroom situation. *J. exp. Anal. Behav.*, 1962, *5*, 59-60.

# Author Index

# Subject Index

Abnormal behavior, 6, 22, 48
Adolescence, 13, 20, 25
Aggression, 159–161, 170, 176, 310, 321–327, 329, 331
Alcoholism, 9, 23, 298, 335
Anxiety, 25, 111, 154, 176, 220–223, 231, 233–237, 239, 241, 335, 339–340
Assessment, 29, 34, 54, 57, 70, 211, 245, 285, 360–362
Attitude, 228–229, 302–303, 342
Attitude change, 2, 48, 213, 222, 224–226
Autistic children, 6–8, 47, 49, 57, 66, 91, 101, 103, 105
Awareness, 217–218, 220, 244–245, 253–255, 257

Behavior, aversive, 16, 18, 23, 156, 320
avoidance, 10, 13, 17, 23–25, 111, 148, 150–152, 155, 161
classification, 2, 26
control of, 14, 20–21, 24, 96
deficit, 23, 362
deviant, 2, 22, 59, 177, 326
disadvantageous, 285–288, 290, 361
functional analysis of, 9, 11–12, 22, 51, 56–58, 75, 106, 134
influence, 1–2, 7, 216–217, 219–220, 224, 227, 230, 233, 284, 295, 358–359, 363
maladaptive, 3–4, 6–7, 107, 212, 215, 362–363
modification, 1–5, 8, 52–53, 58, 106, 137, 148, 153–154, 156, 214, 245, 249, 252, 285–286, 289–290, 292, 310, 343, 357, 360–364
pathology, 6, 26, 51
shaping, 13, 68, 100, 109, 139, 142, 311–312, 314, 360
therapy, 54, 69, 83, 107, 179, 200, 214, 218, 310
verbal, 11–12, 27, 31, 51–52, 59, 82, 84, 87, 95, 102, 104, 108, 134–136, 142, 153, 155–156, 180, 212–213, 215–216, 219–220, 223, 227, 229,

238, 242, 245, 249–251, 270, 286, 311
vocal, 94–101
Behavioral engineering, 268
Brainwashing, 2, 213, 217, 303, 341

Child development, 7, 13, 45, 57, 63, 102–103, 310, 319
Child-parent relationships, 10, 15
Child-rearing practices, 14, 21, 58, 167
Children, conditioning of, 165–167, 177
cooperative behavior, 60–61, 160
disturbed behavior, 7, 49, 66, 70, 72, 79, 85, 159, 177
modeling research with, 2, 314–315, 322–327, 330, 332–333, 336–338, 359
nursery school, 7, 58, 62–63, 66, 321
reinforcement of, 56, 157, 162, 168, 170, 314–318
treatment of, 50, 54, 61–62, 64–65, 67–69, 74, 79, 175
Clinical applications, 1–4, 22, 24, 59, 61, 66, 218–220, 358–360, 364
Clinical Psychology, 1, 3, 30, 57, 79, 81, 156, 175, 179, 211, 232, 245–248, 283–284, 341, 358, 360
Clinicians, role of, 4, 5, 62, 177, 180, 182, 246–247
Computers, 2, 305–309
Concept formation, 58, 75–78, 360
Conditioning, 48, 127, 338
Conditioning, verbal, 2, 211–221, 224, 226–229, 231, 235–236, 239, 241, 244–245, 250–254, 256, 259, 285, 299, 341, 359
Counseling, 142, 146, 153
Creativity, 58

Delinquency, 13, 160–161
Deprivation, 10, 36, 51, 158, 361
Deprivation, sensory, 2, 29, 341
Depression, 9, 14, 24–26, 200, 298, 335–336